UCD WOMEN'S CENTER

Meeting the Challenge

D0219848

Meeting the Challenge

Innovative Feminist Pedagogies in Action

edited by
Maralee Mayberry
and
Ellen Cronan Rose

Routledge
New York and London

Published in 1999 by
Routledge
29 West 35th Street
New York, NY 10001

Published in Great Britain by
Routledge
11 New Fetter Lane
London EC4P 4EE

Annis Hopkins. "Women's Studies on Television? It's Time for Distance Learning."
  Copyright © 1996. From *National Women's Studies Association Journal* 8.2, pp.
  91–106. Reprinted with permission of Indiana University Press.
Maralee Mayberry. "Reproductive and Resistant Pedagogies: The Comparative Roles
  of Collaborative Learning and Feminist Pedagogy in Science Education." Copyright
  © 1998. From *Journal of Research in Science Teaching*, pp. 443–59. Reprinted with
  permission of John Wiley & Sons, Inc.
Maralee Mayberry and Margaret N. Rees. "Feminist Pedagogy, Interdisciplinary Praxis,
  and Science Education." Copyright © 1997. From *National Women's Studies Association
  Journal* 9.1, pp. 57–75. Reprinted with permission of Indiana University Press.
Ellen Cronan Rose. "This Class Meets in Cyberspace: Women's Studies via Distance
  Education." Reprinted by permission of the publisher from G.E. Cohee, et al. (Eds.),
  The "Feminist Teacher" Anthology: Pedagogies and Classroom Strategies (New
  York: Teachers College Press, © 1998 by Teachers College, Columbia University. All
  rights reserved), pp. 114–32.

Library of Congress Cataloging-in-Publication Data

Meeting the challenge: innovative feminist pedagogies in action / Maralee Mayberry
  & Ellen Cronan Rose, eds.
     p. cm.
  Includes bibliographical references and index.
  ISBN 0-415-92248-8 (hardbound). —ISBN 0-415-92249-6 (pbk.)
  1. Feminism and education. 2. Critical pedagogy. I. Mayberry, Maralee. II.
Rose, Ellen Cronan.
LC197.M44 1999
370.11'5—dc21   98-37302
                                                                                    CIP

CONTENTS

A SPECTRUM OF CLASSROOMS

FEMINIST PEDAGOGY AND THE COMMUNITY

INTRODUCTION

Maralee Mayberry and Ellen Cronan Rose

In 1990, Ernest Boyer issued a challenge to the professoriate. Proposing that we "move beyond the tired old 'teaching versus research' debate and give the familiar and honorable term 'scholarship' a broader, more capacious meaning, one that brings legitimacy to the full scope of academic work," Boyer suggested that "the work of the professoriate might be thought of as having four separate, yet overlapping functions: the scholarship of *discovery*; the scholarship of *integration*; the scholarship of *application*; and the scholarship of *teaching*" (16, emphasis in original).[1] It is now eight years since Boyer issued his challenge and universities are still struggling to implement new educational models that will produce the widespread and sweeping reforms Boyer envisioned. Indeed, the Boyer Commission on Educating Undergraduates in the Research University just recently entered the continuing debate about how best to rise to Boyer's earlier challenge in their report, *Reinventing Undergraduate Education: A Blueprint for America's Research Universities*. The report calls for the "radical reconstruction" (6) of undergraduate education to include the establishment of new institutional student-centered research environments or "synergistic system[s] in which faculty and students are learners and researchers, whose interactions make for a healthy and flourishing intellectual atmosphere" (11). The report's core pedagogical recommendations include inquiry-based learning, collaborative efforts, graduate-student teacher-apprentice programs, field internships, interdisciplinary courses, capstone experiences, and creative uses of new technology. While the report does not give any concrete examples of how the recommendations could be implemented,[2] its authors anticipate that the "recommendations urged in this report will be controversial; some administrators and faculty will protest that they are unreachable or impractical, or that the goals entertained can be achieved by minor adjustments of existing practice" yet the authors hope their recommendations will "stimulate new debate about the nature of undergraduate education in research universities that will produce widespread and sweeping reform" (1–2).

The Boyer Commission's report was released as we were completing the final editing for this anthology on feminist pedagogies in action and we were reminded painfully of feminist scholarship's marginalized position in the larger educational context. In the last twenty-five to thirty years feminist scholarship has created not only new knowledge but also new and innovative pedagogies that address the issues raised in the commission's report. Neither the professoriate nor the Boyer Commission has recognized this scholarship. Had the authors of *Reinventing Undergraduate Education* been aware of feminist scholarship, the report could have provided educators with specific examples of innovative learning environments where, in Boyer's own words, "teaching, at its best, means not only transmitting knowledge, but *transforming* and *extending* it as well."

The chapters in this anthology provide inspiring examples of the scholarship of teaching; some also illustrate the scholarship of integration and the scholarship of application; all represent that most rewarded of academic endeavors, the scholarship of discovery. The contributors to this volume can each be characterized as what Patricia Cross of the University of California, Berkeley has called a *"classroom researcher*—one who is involved in the evaluation of his or her own teaching and learning, even as it takes place" (cited in Boyer 61). Yet the essays collected in this volume were not generated to illustrate Boyer's expanded definition of scholarship. They represent the imaginative new pedagogical approaches that feminist educators have implemented in diverse institutional settings across the United States and internationally. The contributors attest to feminist scholars' commitment to creating educational processes in which, as Carolyn Shrewsbury states, "a community of learners is empowered to act responsibly toward one another and the subject matter and to apply that learning to social action" (8).

Our book is intended as a "practical" reader, demonstrating how feminist pedagogical techniques can be implemented in a wide assortment of institutional settings (liberal arts colleges and research universities, rural and urban colleges and universities, small and large institutions, diverse regions of the United States as well as Australia, Canada, and New Zealand) and disciplines (women's studies, English, history, sociology, the natural sciences, health sciences, and law). During the last decade much has been published on the topic of feminist pedagogy, whose diverse theoretical positions and conceptual assumptions have been well documented.[3] This scholarship provides an important and necessary understanding of feminist pedagogical discourses and poses questions for practitioners. This anthology builds upon this scholarship by providing readers with detailed examples of how feminist educators are putting into practice the theories and concepts formulated in the existing literature.

We conceive the anthology as a detailed and specific exploration of how feminist pedagogies are implemented in a variety of classroom, university, and community settings. Yet we are also aware that institutionalizing the types of imaginative new courses and pedagogical approaches the authors write about has often proved problematic, for in many ways they violate traditional academic norms. Many of the chapters in this anthology respond to these institutional challenges by also addressing a series of questions: How can feminist pedagogies and innovative course designs best respond to institutional resistance to change? How can progressive academics adapt our classroom practice and course content to accommodate fiscal, demographic, technological, and political challenges without sacrificing feminist learning goals? What kinds of innovative courses have feminist teachers designed? In what ways have they scandalized traditional academic structures and values? In what ways have feminist teachers creatively circumvented disciplinary and institutional barriers?

OVERVIEW OF CHAPTERS

The anthology begins by delineating the pedagogical frameworks that inform succeeding chapters. Feminist pedagogy has often been referred to as the "action arm" of feminist theory, and the course contents and teaching techniques described in this anthology illustrate both the commonalities across and the diversity within activist feminist approaches to education. The two chapters in the book's first section constitute a guide for understanding the epistemological, theoretical, and practical aspects of feminist pedagogy.

Maralee Mayberry makes epistemological and theoretical distinctions between collaborative learning and feminist pedagogy. She argues that understanding these distinctions is crucial if feminist educators are to challenge and ultimately transform existing relations of power, oppression, and domination. She illustrates this point with reference to science education, where the dominant approach to reform—collaborative learning—falls short of reaching the goals envisioned by feminist scholars of science: to transform both how students of science learn and the science curriculum that students are expected to learn. Several accounts of science education courses infused with feminist (as distinguished from merely collaborative) pedagogical goals provide pragmatic information for feminist educators in general and feminist science educators in particular, whose interests are to

implement pedagogical strategies designed to "resist" rather than "reproduce" dominant discourses.

Sandra Bell, Marina Morrow, and Evangelia Tastsoglou describe moments of student resistance to their efforts to implement critical feminist/
antiracist pedagogies in two women's studies and one sociology course at
two different universities in the Maritime region of Canada. They attribute
student resistance to (1) an educational system characterized by the
"banking model" of pedagogy Brazilian educator Paulo Freire critiques as
the context within which both they and their students were socialized;[4] (2)
students' partial understanding of feminist pedagogical practice, e.g., as
invoking the "authority of experience" to validate students' voices; and (3)
their own inexperience as feminist pedagogues. These moments of resistance are painfully familiar to feminist educators. The authors conclude
with specific suggestions for averting similar moments of student resistance in their own and others' classes.

Part two takes up the issue of institutional contexts. Higher education
faces many challenges at the moment (e.g., fiscal constraints, increasingly
diverse student populations, an ever more conservative political climate).
Given these barriers to enacting progressive change, how can feminist educators best implement innovative courses and programs? The authors in
this section describe ways in which they have successfully met institutional
challenges without sacrificing feminist learning goals.

Maryanne Dever acknowledges that recent changes in higher education associated with funding cutbacks and a consequent move toward a
corporatized, market-driven philosophy pose a seeming threat to feminist
pedagogical praxis, but she argues that feminist practitioners should instead regard these changes as an opportunity to reinvigorate feminist pedagogy at the level of both classroom practice and curriculum development.
Her chapter shows how we can achieve this goal in practical terms in our
own classrooms.

Jane A. Rinehart recognizes the possibility of co-optation but nonetheless believes that it is better for women's studies practitioners to be at the
table when institutional resources are distributed than to refuse all compromise. Indeed, she argues that aligning our goals as women's studies
administrators and faculty with institutional goals that are apparently in-
imical to feminist educational goals—e.g., reducing costs, providing "practical" education to students conceived of as "consumers"—may provide a
serendipitous if paradoxical opportunity to infuse feminist educational
content and praxis into the "mainstream" curriculum and to demonstrate
to students that a women's studies liberal arts education has practical

applications. Specifically, she discusses her experience with learning communities and internship programs and examines how they can achieve transformative goals.

Jodi Wetzel describes an assessment tool that has proved highly successful since it was instituted in 1992 within the Metropolitan State College of Denver's women's studies program. Unlike administratively mandated, quantitative, bureaucratically administered assessment instruments, the senior thesis requirement at Metropolitan State College links assessment directly to the women's studies program's skills and knowledge goals. Although students are not all equally sophisticated in critical thinking and writing skills, they do all demonstrate understanding of and commitment to multicultural, interdisciplinary women's studies scholarship. The chapter provides detailed information about how assessment tools were collaboratively developed (by faculty and students), their content, and the method of implementation.

Part three introduces the debate among feminist educators over one increasingly visible institutional component: technology. The four chapters in this section address both the problems and the potential of distance education and listserve technology for feminist educators. Each chapter, reflecting different experiences, raises provocative questions for feminist educators who are choosing or being directed to use new technologies in their courses.

Annis H. Hopkins gives an upbeat, indeed proselytizing, account of her experience of five years of teaching an introductory women's studies survey course via live cable TV to a studio audience at Arizona State University of sixty students plus approximately ninety students per semester who register to take the course at home, often in videotaped form, not to mention TV cable surfers who just happen to tune in. She presents the arguments in favor of using distance education technologies to teach women's studies courses (e.g., bringing the new scholarship on women to a wide population, dispelling [negative] myths about women's studies scholarship, enhancing community goodwill for women's studies and the university) and uses her experience to counter skepticism about the compatibility of these technologies with principles of feminist pedagogy. Specifically, she answers feminist objections to teaching women's studies in a lecture-only format that problematizes interaction among students and between students and instructors by attempting to demonstrate that these are obstacles that can be overcome.

Ellen Cronan Rose shares Annis Hopkins's commitment to teaching women's studies courses via distance education for philosophical and administrative reasons. But teaching a seminar in feminist theory to students at her own university and, via compressed video, to students at another university in the state taught her that if distance education technologies are not to raise "insuperable barriers to feminist pedagogy," certain precautions must be taken and certain conditions met: (1) it is vital to bridge the actual and psychological distance between students at the primary and remote sites; (2) e-mail can be an effective means of building that bridge if students are given adequate instruction in using the technology; (3) it is important to establish equivalent requirements and prerequisites for enrollment in the course by students at both primary and remote sites; and (4) the instructor must never allow technology to dictate her or his pedagogical practice.

Ellen's postscript describes her subsequent attempt to teach a distance education women's studies course. Believing she had learned from her first experience of teaching women's studies via distance education valuable lessons that would enable her to avoid feminist pedagogical pitfalls, Ellen offered an introductory women's studies course to students on campus and, via compressed video, to high school students at remote sites. Because it was a larger class than the seminar in feminist theory she had previously offered via distance education, she was faced with Hobson's choice: either lecture, which violated her pedagogical principles, or risk alienating students at the remote sites who felt (and were, effectively) excluded from full participation in the course. Until her university acquires and installs technology that will support her pedagogical goals, she has decided not to offer women's studies courses via distance education. This chapter also describes the type of technology she maintains feminist educators need in order to teach in a distance education format.

Kathy Boardman, Jon Alexander, Margaret Barber, and Pete Pinney discuss the dynamics of teacher-student interaction on a listserve devoted to gender issues, based on their experience of teaching eight composition courses at universities in Alaska, Colorado, and Nevada, whose students and teachers were linked through an electronic listserve. Using specific examples from listserve interactions, the authors address the connections between electronic discourse and a range of feminist pedagogical issues, especially the pedagogical implications of the decisions teachers make about the extent of their intervention into discussion on-line.

Part four demonstrates how the tenets of feminist pedagogy can be put into practice in a wide range of institutional and disciplinary settings. It builds upon the earlier topic of institutional contexts by providing clear snapshots of feminist classrooms and their participants' experiences.

Maralee Mayberry and Margaret N. Rees developed and taught an innovative, interdisciplinary course, Earth Systems: A Feminist Approach, which combined geological education, sociological inquiry, and feminist pedagogy and was offered for credit through the departments of geology, sociology, and women's studies. This inspirational story narrates their own and their students' struggles with and eventual success at overcoming institutional, disciplinary, and learned personal impediments to creating a process-oriented interdisciplinary learning environment that educated student-teachers and teacher-students as social-change agents. The course was premised on two interrelated observations that are central to feminist science scholarship: (1) that science and science education are "masculine"; and (2) that scientific inquiry and education fail to situate scientific knowledge in a social, political, and historical context. This chapter illuminates the pedagogical implications of these observations and describes how revisionary interdisciplinary science courses can be constructed and taught.

Cheyenne Bonnell dispels the feminist shibboleth that "the master's tools will never dismantle the master's house" (Audre Lorde). To make her point, she describes a required course (freshman [sic] composition) she uses to teach women's studies to a heterogeneous population of students early in their academic careers. Her approach is subversive: the phrase "women's studies" is never employed. On the assumption that eighteen year olds are mesmerized by sex, Cheyenne makes sex and gender the focus of the course, designing units on such topics as media images of gender, the origins of gendered behavior, gendered language, sex on campus, marriage, and homosexuality. She uses "active or experiential learning" techniques to forestall student resistance to being "force fed" information and reports widespread student satisfaction with the course. The chapter gives readers valuable practical tips about how to infuse feminist issues into "mainstream" required courses.

Sue Kuntz and Carey Kaplan ask the questions: "How can gender and women's studies thrive within the traditionally misogynist environment of a small Roman Catholic college? How, given limited resources and institutional pressure for reproduction of conventional knowledge, can instructors and students participate in authentically transformative feminist pedagogy?" Sue and Carey answer the first question with an account of how they established a gender and women's studies minor at Saint Michael's College in Colchester, Vermont, and offer their experience of teaching a large introductory course in gender studies, with visiting lecturers, small-group discussions, and a diverse, heterogeneous student population as an inspiring answer to the second question. Particularly moving are quotations from students' journals, recording their responses to the intellectual and personal challenges posed by the course content and pedagogy and the transformative effects of the course on them "as the 'general' became 'particular' and the 'particular' 'political,' causing changes in ways of seeing and being."

Diana L. Gustafson relates her experience in an unusual health course that involved "two parallel ways of knowing the body, health, illness, and healing—the knowing that is concretized in text and the knowing that is discoverable in our experiences as embodied beings." In this course, she studied Chinese medical practices through reading texts and by practicing an Asian breathing technique called *qi gong*. She says "implicating" her body in the course challenged the ways she, a registered nurse, had formerly understood the body, health, illness, and healing practices and demonstrates how this innovative pedagogy has implications for other (particularly women's studies) courses.

Prudence Ann Moylan has designed and implemented a version of a required two-semester sequence of western civilization courses that uses gender as a central category of analysis and employs feminist pedagogical principles. Her chapter addresses both the theoretical and practical challenges of transforming a core, required course in history that is based on a widely accepted canon of scholarship reproduced in multiple versions of standard textbooks by providing a step-by-step account of how the courses took shape, including how central questions were defined, themes organized, course materials selected, pedagogical strategies implemented, and student work assessed.

Wendy Ball closes this section by writing about how using feminist pedagogical theories and practices to teach law is extremely difficult given that the law is "essentially gendered, essentially a male domain." Specifically, she discusses her experiences teaching about "the law of sexual violation" in a required course entitled Crimes, highlighting the institutional barriers that present themselves to educators attempting to teach "sensitive" subjects and describing the specific strategies she employed to "step over the barriers." Of particular interest is her detailed description of setting up a "safe zone" to create a learning environment that allows for free and safe expression while simultaneously encouraging students to confront critically their preconceptions about topics such as rape, child and adult sexual abuse, sexual assault, abortion rights, domestic violence, and children's rights.

Part five, the book's concluding section, takes up the issue of how feminist programs within the university can serve the needs and problems of the larger community. The anthology's concluding chapter demonstrates how university, community, and feminist connections can be made through carefully designed courses that locate community-based projects within universities and focus their attention on transformational personal and societal changes.

Melissa Kesler Gilbert, Carol Holdt, and Kristin Christophersen describe their experience of teaching a community-based course titled Politics of Motherhood, in which an interdisciplinary team of students—working in conjunction with a county-based family-services organization and graduate-student mentors from English, sociology, and public health—developed a feminist research project to ascertain county and city officials' perceptions of the needs and problems of local families. The authors trace the self-reflexive work students were required to do in the course, the efforts both students and teachers put into creating a collaborative research team, and the discoveries students made about their own epistemological limitations. The article weaves together the instructors' personal narrative and students' journal reflections to produce a detailed account of how community projects located within academic institutions can help "to move students' knowledge of the inequities of society from inside the boundaries of our feminist classroom into a community where they lived, worked, and went to school."

EMERGENT AND INTERRELATED THEMES

As we stated earlier, the chapters in our book were not written to illustrate Boyer's expanded definition of scholarship to include, in addition to the scholarship of discovery ("pure" research), the scholarship of integration, application, and teaching; yet it will be clear to the reader that they do. Moreover, these contributions make concrete, practical suggestions about how to implement the kind of sweeping educational reforms called for in the report on *Reinvigorating Undergraduate Education* recently promulgated by the Boyer Commission on Educating Undergraduates in the Research University. Of the "ten ways to change undergraduate education" for the better outlined in that report, at least seven are illustrated by the practices described by our contributors: "Make research-based learning the standard" (Bonnell; Dever; Gilbert et al.; Mayberry and Rees; Moylan; Rinehart); "construct an inquiry-based freshman year" (Boardman et al.; Bonnell; Moylan; Rinehart); "remove barriers to interdisciplinary education" (Gilbert et al.; Mayberry and Rees; Rinehart); "link communication skills and course work" (Boardman et al.; Bonnell; Moylan); "use information technology creatively" (Boardman et al.; Hopkins); "culminate with a capstone experience" (Gilbert et al.; Wetzel); and "educate graduate students as apprentice teachers" (Moylan).

Readers of this book will note other themes that thread through several chapters: (1) the desirability of infusing feminist scholarship and pedagogy into the core curriculum (Bonnell; Moylan); (2) the importance of creating in the classroom a "safe space," especially when teaching sensitive topics (Ball; Bell et al.; Boardman et al.; Gustafson; Hopkins); (3) attempts to re-create the classroom-community link that characterized women's studies in the late 1960s, when early practitioners described it as the academic arm of the women's movement (Dever; Gilbert et al.; Rinehart; Wetzel); and (4) the benefits and costs of team teaching, both actual and "virtual" (Boardman et al.; Mayberry and Rees; Rinehart).

Sometimes essays actually seem to "talk to" each other. In section three, for example, the problems that kept distance education from "working" for Ellen Rose (her failure to get students to engage in constructive dialogue with each other, her reluctance to lecture in a feminist pedagogical environment) appear as opportunities, not problems, for Annis Hopkins and for Kathy Boardman and her colleagues. In her essay, Annis directly addresses the "but you can't employ feminist pedagogy in a large-class lecture format" caveat (as, in another section of the book, Carey Kaplan and Sue Kuntz implicitly demonstrate that you can), and Kathy, Margaret, Jon, and Pete's listserve experience suggests ways Ellen could have made e-mail work better, at least in the UNLV-UNR feminist theory course, where all students had access to the Internet.

In another example of essays "talking to" each other, Maralee Mayberry and Jane Rinehart differ in their representations of collaborative learning. Maralee compares collaborative learning negatively to feminist pedagogy, while Jane clearly considers collaborative learning one form of feminist pedagogy. In this example, because Maralee's chapter previously appeared as a journal article, Jane responds to Maralee's position in a lengthy footnote.

Even when essays do not so clearly talk to each other, the collection as a whole manifests the spirit of collaboration that, in our experience, characterizes feminist scholarly and pedagogical praxis. All contributors share a common goal: to empower our students to understand and ultimately transform the interlocking systems of oppression that deform contemporary life. We hope that readers of this book will engage with the authors in self-reflexive analysis of their own pedagogical practices and will gain from this meditative exchange of ideas and strategies that will enrich their classroom environments, stimulate their students, and address the pressing needs and problems of their communities.

A PERSONAL NOTE

Although editing this collection is our first formal scholarly collaboration, we are not strangers to feminist collaboration. We have worked together and with other colleagues to create and administer the women's studies program at the University of Nevada, Las Vegas. Both of us have team taught courses, though not yet with each other; and we have both written coauthored texts.[5] Ellen has even written about collaboration with another contributor to this book, Carey Kaplan—who, in this instance, writes with another colleague, Sue Kuntz. And, after a year spent corresponding with the contributors to this volume by mail and e-mail, discussing refinements and revisions of their and our ideas, we have expanded our circle of collaborators dramatically and beneficially. We conclude this introduction by thanking each other, our longtime collaborators Carey Kaplan and Peg Rees, and all the contributors to this volume, who generously shared their pedagogical expertise and enthusiasms with us, each other, and now you, the reader. This book, we believe, testifies to "the potential of collaborative work to contribute to a feminist transformation of the academy" (Cafferty and Clausen 82).

●　　●　　●

NOTES

1. According to Boyer, the scholarship of "discovery" asks, "What is to be known, what is yet to be found?" (19). By "integration," Boyer means "making connections across the disciplines, placing the specialties in larger context, illuminating data in revealing ways, often educating nonspecialists too" (18). Integrative scholars ask, "What do the findings *mean*? Is it possible to interpret what's been discovered in ways that provide a larger, more comprehensive understanding?" (19, emphasis in the original). The scholarship of "application" goes on to ask, "'How can knowledge be responsibly applied to consequential problems?' 'How can it be helpful to individuals as well as institutions?' And further, 'Can social problems *themselves* define an agenda for scholarly investigation?'" (21, emphasis in the original). Finally, the scholarship of teaching means that faculty, as scholars, are also learners. Accordmg to Boyer, "all too often, teachers transmit information that students are expected to memorize and then, perhaps, recall. While well-prepared lectures surely have a place, teaching, at its best, means not only transmitting knowledge, but *transforming* and *extending* it as well (24, emphasis in the original).

2. An omission noted by Barry Leshowitz of Arizona State University, who

lamented in a comment to the "join the debate" forum on the SUNY Stony Brook website, where the commission's report can be accessed, that "What is disappointing about the Boyer Report [is] that it offers almost no concrete suggestions about 'where to go from here.'" Leshowitz concludes his comment with a question: "Are there any concrete suggestions on how to begin?" We hope he will read this book.

3. See, for instance Gore; Luke and Gore; Luke; Stone; Weiner; Maher and Tetreault; and Middleton.

4. In the "banking model" of education, Freire says, "knowledge is a gift bestowed by those who consider themselves knowledgeable upon those whom they consider to know nothing." In this model, students are "containers" or "receptacles," to be "filled" by the teacher: "The more completely he fills the receptacles, the better a teacher he is. The more meekly the receptacles permit themselves to be filled, the better students they are" (58).

5. See Mayberry and Rees, reprinted in this volume; Mayberry et al.; Stockard and Mayberry; Kaplan and Rose 1988, 1989, 1990, 1993, and 1996.

WORKS CITED

Boyer Commission on Educating Undergraduate in the Research University. *Reinventing Undergraduate Education: A Blueprint for America's Research Universities*, 1998. Copies of the report are available free from Mary Leming, Office of the President, SUNY Stony Brook, Stony Brook, NY 11794. The report can also be accessed on a website (http://www.sunysb.edu/boyerreport).

Boyer, Ernest L. *Scholarship Reconsidered: Priorities of the Professoriate*. Princeton: Carnegie Foundation for the Advancement of Teaching, 1990.

Cafferty, Helen, and Jeannette Clausen. "'What's Feminist about It?' Reflections on Collaboration in Editing and Writing." *Common Ground: Feminist Collaboration in the Academy*. Ed. Elizabeth G. Peck and JoAnna Stephens Mink. Albany: State University of New York Press, 1998. 81–98.

Freire, Paulo. *Pedagogy of the Oppressed*. Trans. Myra Bergman Ramos. 1970. New York: Continuum, 1983.

Gore, Jennifer M. *The Struggle for Pedagogies: Critical and Feminist Discoveries as Regimes of Truth*. New York: Routledge, 1993.

Kaplan, Carey, and Ellen Cronan Rose. *The Canon and the Common Reader*. Knoxville: University of Tennessee Press, 1990.

_____. "On the Other Side of Silence." *Lesbian Friendships: For Ourselves and Each Other*. Ed. Jacqueline S. Weinstock and Esther D. Rothblum. New York: New York University Press, 1996. 107–16.

_____. "Strange Bedfellows: Feminist Collaboration." *Signs: Journal of Women in Culture and Society* 18.3 (1993): 547–59.

Kaplan, Carey, and Ellen Cronan Rose, eds. *Approaches to Teaching Lessing's* The

Golden Notebook. New York: Modern Language Association, 1989.

_____. *Doris Lessing: The Alchemy of Survival*. Athens: Ohio University Press, 1988.

Lorde, Audre. "The Master's Tools Will Never Dismantle the Master's House." *Sister Ousider*. Freedom, CA: Crossing Press, 1984. 10–13.

Luke, Carmen, ed. *Feminisms and the Pedagogies of Everyday Life*. Albany: State University of New York Press, 1990.

Luke, Carmen, and Jennifer M. Gore, eds. *Feminism and Critical Pedagogy*. New York: Routledge, 1992.

Maher, Frances, and Mary Kay Thompson Tetreault. *The Feminist Classroom: An Inside Look at How Professors and Students Are Transforming Higher Education for a Diverse Society*. New York: Basic Books, 1994.

Mayberry, Maralee, J. Gary Knowles, Brian Ray, and Stacey Marlow. *Home Schooling: Parents as Educators*. Newbury Park, CA: Corwin/Sage Press, 1995.

Mayberry, Maralee, and Margaret N. Rees. "Feminist Pedagogy, Interdisciplinary Praxis, and Science Education." *NWSA Journal* 9.1 (1997): 57–75.

Middleton, Sue. *Educating Feminists: Life Histories and Pedagogy*. New York: Teachers College Press, 1993.

Shrewsbury, Carolyn. "What Is Feminist Pedagogy?" *Women's Studies Quarterly* 21.3–4 (1993): 8–16.

Stockard, Jean, and Maralee Mayberry. *Effective Educational Environments*. Newbury Park, CA: Corwin/Sage Press, 1992.

Stone, Lynda, ed. *The Education Feminism Reader*. New York: Routledge, 1994.

Weiner, Gaby. *Feminisms in Education*. Buckingham, England: Open University Press, 1994.

Laying the Pedagogical Groundwork

REPRODUCTIVE AND RESISTANT PEDAGOGIES
The Comparative Roles of Collaborative Learning
and Feminist Pedagogy in Science Education

Maralee Mayberry

Why aren't women and minorities rushing into the science vac-
uum? I contend that an important reason is that the science curriculum itself and the dominant views of science as an a-historical
and hyper-rational system of thought makes the science classroom
an alien and hostile place for women and people of color. Students
often decide whether to pursue a particular line of study based on
a combination of intrinsic interest in the subject and something I
might call the "comfort zone." Baldly stated, the science classroom
is usually an uncomfortable place for women and people of color.
If we are to address the crisis in science personnel we must ask not
only about how we teach science but also about the subject matter
itself. (Fausto-Sterling 5)

The call for science-education reform has been fueled by the plethora
of recent reports suggesting that traditional science-education environments neither attract nor retain sufficient numbers of women or men of
color—the most underrepresented groups in the natural sciences (American Association of University Women; National Center for Education Statistics; National Science Board; National Science Foundation [NSF]). In
response, some science educators across the country are employing new
pedagogical approaches and curricular materials in hopes of developing
learning environments and course materials that are more inclusive of the
rich perspectives, learning styles, and cultural backgrounds of an increasingly diverse student population.

Much literature now focuses on how innovative classroom approaches
such as small-group collaboration, peer learning, investigation-oriented

laboratories, experiential and hands-on exercises, and curricula grounded
in real-life experiences can make science courses more attractive and inviting to all students (Kahle; National Research Council [NRC]; NSF; Rosser;
Roychoudhury and Roth). These approaches draw strongly from construc-
tivist theories of knowledge acquisition and place the learner's experience
"at the heart of the teaching-learning enterprise" (Roychoudhury, Tippins,
and Nichols 900). Those who advocate the reform of science education's
pedagogical practices, however, seldom address either the social or political consequences associated with the innovative pedagogical approaches
they champion. Thus, the socially reproductive or socially transformative
aspects of how we teach or what we teach remain invisible. I contend that
we must understand the social and political implications embedded within
our pedagogical approaches if we are to begin to develop a more democratic and liberatory science education. Without such an understanding, our
teaching strategies could work to sustain, rather than transform, the existing relations of power in science communities, and consequently maintain
specific values, beliefs, and behaviors that impede progress toward achieving a more equitable and just society in which the science community
would be far more diverse.

    This chapter addresses the implications and consequences of reproduc-
tive versus resistant or transformative pedagogies. It provides a critical
comparison of two pedagogical approaches to reforming the science classroom: collaborative learning and feminist pedagogy. The first section very
briefly traces the theoretical and epistemological development of these two
pedagogies. It illustrates that collaborative learning is rooted in an interpretive epistemology that circumvents any meaningful conversation about
the gender, race, or class nature of knowledge production, dissemination,
and utilization. In contrast, feminist pedagogy is linked to the theoretical
and practical concerns of feminist theory and works to uncover, understand, and transform gender, race, and class oppression and domination.
The second section discusses the social and political consequences of implementing either collaborative learning or feminist pedagogy in science
classrooms. Educators' full awareness of these consequences is critical because collaborative learning is a socially reproductive pedagogy that encourages students to gain proficiency in the dominant discourse of existing
science systems, whereas feminist pedagogy is a socially transformative
pedagogy that invites students to critically analyze existing science systems
and their relationship to social oppression and domination. Thus, choosing
a pedagogy is not an apolitical act. The final section of the article provides
some examples of what a feminist classroom might look like and concludes
with some thoughts about the practical barriers science educators may face

as they begin to construct feminist science classrooms. The vision of feminist educators, regardless of their discipline, is to implement a classroom pedagogy that challenges the dominant masculinist assumptions about knowledge and education, and ultimately challenges the oppressive power relations embedded in the wider society. To be successful, the movement for developing a more democratic science education for all and for building a more diverse science community will require a similar feminist vision and a more widespread awareness and implementation of feminist pedagogy.

SIMILAR TECHNIQUES, DIFFERENT VISIONS: A BRIEF OVERVIEW OF COLLABORATIVE LEARNING AND FEMINIST PEDAGOGY

Collaborative Learning: A "Conversation of Mankind"[1]

Collaborative learning applies, legitimizes, and establishes in college and university education practices that are in fact already familiar and well established in American educational, political, and social life. This familiarity accounts for the alacrity with which one form of collaborative learning, peer tutoring, has been adopted by American colleges and universities over the past twenty years. Other forms of collaborative learning will be educationally persuasive, pervasive, and effectual to the degree to which they are [. . .] appropriated or grafted on to existing practice. For educational change of the sort advocated here to achieve maximum effectiveness, the academic and professional disciplines, college and universities as a whole, and the general public must come to regard collaborative learning as analogous to, adaptable to, or in harmony with ways of doing things that they are already familiar with, find useful, and depend on. (Bruffee, *Collaborative*, 9–10)

The call to restructure science education dates back to the late 1960s when the academic preparation of U.S. students came under fire from business and scientific elites. During this period, a plethora of national "state of education" studies were sponsored to pinpoint why U.S. students appeared to be academically less prepared than their international counterparts (Coleman; Newcomb and Wilson). The common recommendation made was to replace the traditional, formal classroom environment with a new classroom culture that would involve students in a network of informal social relations and encourage them to engage in the construction of collaborative, or communal, knowledge. The reasoning behind this advice came from the era's new corporate management models that had been designed to increase worker productivity and, in turn, to ensure American business success. Across industries, top-down management styles were rapidly replaced by small problem-solving units composed of both workers and managers. American educators were slow to recognize how similar organizational arrangements, when introduced in school environments, could bolster students' math and science performance. Becker and Wells pointed out that the call to create collaborative classroom environments fell on deaf ears throughout the 1970s. Not until the mid-1980s, after years of relying on traditional approaches to educational reform (teaching basic skills and more standardized testing), did educators begin to acknowledge the research showing that students learn more when they actively participate in a network of informal social relations and work in collaborative learning settings (Astin; National Institute of Education).

Today, the business community (and funding sources such as the NSF) recognizes the need for a larger and more literate scientific workforce that, as a result of demographics, will have to be drawn from groups who have traditionally not pursued science education or science careers. Recent reports from the NSF and NRC signal that science educators, faced with a more diverse student population and the persistence of low science and math achievement, are envisioning collaborative learning environments as the new panacea of the science-education reform movement.

Collaborative learning approaches restructure the educational environment within which students learn. In collaborative settings, student learning is not designed to be an individual activity; rather, learning takes place as students work in small groups and collectively pose questions, define problems, gather data, interpret findings, and share their conclusions with other class members. Collaborative settings also encourage student groups to probe deeply into course assignments and to actively search for a breadth of information regarding the topic under study (Cohen, Lotan, and Leechor; Johnson and Johnson). Because the aim of collaborative learning is for students to construct and share knowledge, the collaborative classroom is built around the strategy of interdependence. Group activities and group reports are the common methods teachers use to organize the construction of knowledge (Cooper, Prescott, Cook, Smith, and Mueck; Kagan). Group work requires students to claim authority in and take responsibility for their participation in classroom activities. In turn, the teacher's role shifts from being a disseminator of information to being a facilitator of student groups, providing to students the resources necessary to ensure a group's success.

Research has noted that collaborative group work is an effective way to foster student achievement, promote positive attitudes toward school, and develop thinking skills (Blumenfeld, Marx, Soloway, and Krajcik).

Johnson and Johnson noted that collaborative methods of learning promote positive peer relationships and higher self-esteem among students.
Creating successful collaborative-learning environments may provide students with a positive learning experience. However, collaborative environments do not necessarily provide students with an adequate model of
critical thinking. That is, collaborative techniques restructure the environment within which students learn, but do not question *what* students learn
or why they should learn it. The reproductive epistemological and theoretical underpinnings of collaborative learning underscore this point.

Brown and Webb and Palincsar suggested that collaboration helps students understand the vocabularies, methodologies, and grammatical and
rhetorical structures, as well as the goals of knowledge, in any particular
discipline. Collaboration engages students in an ongoing conversation
about these aspects of disciplinary knowledge, and in turn trains students
who are capable of adapting to the "conventions of conversation" in educated communities. Similarly, Bruffee ("Collaborative Learning") viewed
collaborative learning as premised on the recognition that knowledge is a
social construction derived from unending conversation within a class, between groups in a class, and among community members. According to
Bruffee, the goal of collaborative learning is to "provide a social context in
which students can experience and practice the kinds of conversation valued by college teachers [. . .] the normal discourse of most academia, professional, and business communities"(642–43).

Although the work on collaborative educational methods does contain
some hints about the potential of collaborative learning strategies to open
knowledge communities to change, the explicit model assumes that knowledge production entails the learning, practicing, and mastering of the
discursive conventions embedded in existing knowledge communities, e.g.,
business, academic, government, and the professions. Furthermore, the
model implicitly assumes that members within and between knowledge
communities share similar knowledge interests. The race, class, and gender
aspects of how knowledge is produced and used are not addressed. As a result, collaborative learning settings create a social context in which students (apparently disembodied from their race, class, and gender) are to
learn, practice, master, and ultimately sustain the discursive conventions
of professional communities (also apparently devoid of race, class, or gender biases). And in the case of science education, a science that is disembodied from the doer of science. In this sense, collaborative techniques
reproduce existing forms of knowledge and provide students with the skills
and tools necessary to join established knowledge communities, rather
than to transform them.

Feminist Pedagogy: In Pursuit of Praxis

> Feminist theory [. . .] validates difference, challenges universal claims to truth, and seeks to create social transformation in a world of shifting and uncertain meanings. In education, these profound shifts are evident on two levels: first, at the level of practice, as excluded and formerly silenced groups challenge dominant approaches to learning and to definitions of knowledge; and second, at the level of theory, as modernist claims to universal truth are called into question. (Weiler 449–50)

Feminist education, Nancy Schniedewind reminded us, is "concerned with the content of what we teach—feminist scholarship—and the ways in which we teach—feminist pedagogy" (17). The form and content of educational practices are inextricably linked in the feminist classroom. Feminist pedagogy therefore embodies a concern for both what we teach and how we teach it.

The intellectual roots of feminist pedagogy lie in the lifelong work of Brazilian educator Paulo Freire. Freire's vision of education subverts public schooling's historical function of reproducing a class system where resources are shared unequally (Bowles and Gintis; Giroux). In Freire's model of education, students and teachers work collectively to interrogate traditional forms of knowledge and social ideologies, as well as one's own accepted beliefs and identities. The classroom serves as a center of participatory democracy where teachers and students alike engage in this dialogical experience, the aim of which is to challenge the structures of oppression, repression, and inequality.

The principles of feminist education and pedagogy are based on a Freirean pedagogy of liberation, although they expand and enrich Freire's model. Feminist pedagogy developed in the context of a growing number of women's studies programs nationwide, and it reflects the feminist political commitment to women's liberation (Weiler). It embraces the critical, oppositional, and activist stance of the Freirean model of education, yet expands Freire's pedagogical vision. In particular, the absence of the analytical concept of gender in Freire's pedagogy presents difficulties to feminists who are struggling to put their liberatory ideals into practice. Rowbotham pointed out that gender, in the texts of critical (Freirean) educators, is treated with "ominous politeness." O'Brien argued that the discourse of critical pedagogy pays attention to gender by either "commatizing" it or by making only occasional references to the most widely known and read feminist theorists and researchers (Kenway and Modra).

Feminist pedagogy rectifies this oversight by considering not only the class and race aspects of knowledge production and dissemination but also the gender aspects.

Feminist pedagogy invites students to critique the unequal social relations embedded in contemporary society and to ask why these circumstances exist and what one can do about them. To achieve these liberatory goals, feminist educators develop and use classroom process skills, many of which are used in collaborative learning environments. Informal relations among class members are built by initiating student-centered experiences such as group activities and group reports. Great care and skill go into developing a learning environment where students work together to design group activities that demonstrate an awareness of the race, class, and gender dynamics that permeate the larger society. Through dialogue and conversation, students and teachers negotiate a curriculum that articulates their needs and concerns. These classroom strategies are designed explicitly to empower students to apply their learning to social action and transformation, recognize their ability to act to create a more humane social order, and become effective voices of change within the broader social world (hooks; Romney, Tatum, and Jones; Schniedewind.

In some ways, collaborative and feminist approaches to education share similar interests. Both are concerned with the social context of learning, both apply similar pedagogical techniques to enhance informal classroom relationships where students construct knowledge interdependently through conversational process, and both construct a classroom culture where students feel safe participating in the learning process. However, contrary to the assumption that collaborative learning should train students to master knowledgeable discourses, the feminist classroom conversation and process of knowledge production are overtly political and aimed toward social and educational change (Kenway and Modra; Maher and Tetreault; Weiler). As Kathleen Weiler pointed out:

> The pedagogy of feminist teachers is based on certain assumptions about knowledge, power, and political action that can be traced beyond the academy to the political activism of the women's movement in the 1960s [. . .] feminist pedagogy continues to echo the struggles of its origins and to retain a vision of social activism. (456)

In essence, feminist pedagogy is based on the desire for social transformation. It explicitly seeks to dismantle the systems of oppression that collaborative learning leaves unquestioned.

COLLABORATIVE LEARNING AND FEMINIST PEDAGOGY IN SCIENCE EDUCATION: WOMEN IN SCIENCE OR A FEMINIST SCIENCE?

The discussion of gender issues in science has evolved in two directions. One line of thinking argues that science courses need to be developed that attract and retain women. This approach, women *in* science, encourages educators to redesign their courses to be more female friendly. Another line of thinking advocates the building of two-way streets between feminism and science. This approach argues that women's disinterest in modern Western sciences reflects sciences' disinterest in women and in their own social and historical context, as well as in the political and policy implications of scientific inquiry (Harding, "Forum" 50). The task facing science educators is to construct a new form of scientific knowledge, a feminist science, that accounts for the social context of modern Western science and becomes a resource for bettering the welfare of people around the globe (Harding, "Forum" 54). I suggest that these views are not necessarily incompatible and that each makes an important contribution to feminist projects within the sciences. There are important reasons to educate more women in sciences, and there are important reasons for feminists to take on a critical examination of the sciences and to train students in the study *of* science. Each view, however, has different pedagogical implications. To clarify some of these differences, I will sketch their central features and then turn to a more detailed discussion of what a feminist science education might look like. My discussion is not intended to minimize the importance of implementing female-friendly collaborative-classroom techniques, but rather to raise the issue (to science educators) of what feminism has to offer science education.

Making Science Friendly to Women

Data demonstrate that women (and minorities) are not fully represented in the sciences. Science, math, and engineering are three areas where the participation of women is the lowest in schools as well as in the workforce. In 1993, women earned only 15% of the doctorates in the physical sciences, mathematics, and engineering (Thurgood and Clarke). The NSF reported that in the science and engineering labor force, women with doctorates constituted only 4.6% of the physics workforce, 10.4% of the mathematics workforce, and 11.9% of the chemistry workforce. In addition, in 1993, women made up only "1 percent of working environmental engineers, 2 percent of mechanical engineers, 3 percent of electrical engineers, 4 percent of medical school department directors, and 6 out of close to 300 tenured professors in the country's top 10 mathematics departments" (Holloway 96).

Major institutes such as the NSF and the Sloan Foundation recognize the economic ramifications associated with the shrinking pool of qualified (read: white male) scientists in an increasingly diverse population and competitive, global, and technologically based economy. As a result, funding science-education programs designed to attract women and other underrepresented groups to careers in science, engineering, and technology is now a major priority.

Much literature documents the barriers to success that women traditionally confront in science courses. The earliest studies concentrated on ways to enable women to fit into the way science traditionally is taught (Kahle; Matyas and Malcolm; Skolnick, Langbort, and Day). The recommendations that were made centered on strengthening girls' cognitive skills (e.g., spatial visualization, numerical problem solving, logical reasoning), and affective skills (assertiveness, competitiveness, and goal-orientedness).

More recent scholarship suggests that only by changing the features of schools—the science curriculum and how science is taught—will significant changes in the participation of women in science occur (Tobias, *They're Not Dumb, Revitalizing*). Spear described the underrepresentation of women in science as a reflection of low teacher expectations about females' ability to do science. In schools where low teacher expectations persist, female students develop the feeling that they do not belong in science courses. Consequently, they are more likely to avoid additional science coursework and less likely to pursue science degrees and careers. Henderson; Manis, Thomas, Sloat, and Davis; Rosser; and Hollenshead, Soellner-Younce, and Wenzel examined the culture of competition that characterizes many science, math, and engineering classrooms. Their findings indicate that competitive classroom environments deter women from majoring in these disciplines. A competitive classroom culture appears to facilitate individual achievement for white men, but acts as a significant deterrent to women's achievement. Other studies suggest that the lack of curriculum images relevant to the daily lives of women (Kelly; Otto; Rosser; Trankina) and the androcentric bias of scientific knowledge and practice (Harding, *Whose Science?*; Keller, "How Gender"; Rosser; Tobias) are additional factors involved in women's attrition from science.

In light of these findings, the current reform efforts directed at developing a science curriculum and pedagogy that is capable of attracting women to science courses and careers—a female-friendly approach—share a common set of objectives: recognize female scientists, teach problem-solving skills from perspectives such as home economics and nursing, incorporate and validate women's experience in the curriculum and pedagogy, use less-competitive classroom models, provide cooperative and supportive learning environments, and rely more on interdisciplinary methods of teaching science. To achieve these objectives, some science-education reformers call on science educators to implement an assortment of collaborative-learning techniques in their classrooms: student-to-student exchange and collaboration, nonhierarchical teaching approaches, hands-on experiential learning, small-group learning and conversation, group reports, and student journaling.

Thus, within the context of those programs whose goal is to solely add women to science, implementing these collaborative learning techniques reproduces, rather than transforms, the existing system of science.

That is, the call to add women to science by implementing collaborative learning strategies fails to address the relationship between the persistent poverty of certain groups in society and the country's growing need for a scientific and technological workforce. Also absent is any critical analysis of science's relationship to the environmental crisis, technological advancement and unemployment, or the relationship between science, political power, and policy making. The implementation of collaborative learning strategies without a critical focus is explicitly linked to sustaining gender, race, and class inequalities.

It is likely that the current science-education reform movement may succeed in involving more women in some areas of scientific study. It is also likely that the popular pedagogical reforms will fail to articulate and analyze the role western science plays in sustaining systems of inequality, and thereby will serve to continue legitimating and perpetuating the existing social and scientific systems.

Remaking Science, Remaking Society

The recent feminist thinking about science and science education provides us with insight into how the existing system of science sustains social inequalities and, to a lesser extent, how classroom learning might be organized to be more inviting to women *and* to achieve transformative, rather than reproductive, goals. The question, "How can we make science more appealing to women?" is replaced with the question, "What is it about existing science cultures and methods of inquiry that excludes women?"

Given the reframing of this question, understanding the historical and social context of science (knowledge *about* science) is high on the feminist scholarly agenda. Feminist philosopher Helen Longino (76) reminded us that critical questions about science are missed when one considers how the sciences are inextricably related to the structures of power in modern and postmodern societies. Accordingly, feminist critics of science have examined the epistemology of Western science, the relation between social change and scientific change, the scientist's relationship to phenomena, and the effect of existing social distributions of power on scientific inquiry and implementation (Harding, *Science Question, Whose Science?*; Longino; Tuana). Feminist scholars have also critically examined traditional scientific inquiry on other grounds, including its tendency to privilege the masculine, reinforce existing power structures, and promote so-called objectivity while obscuring the interactional and interdependent relations among natural and social phenomena (Bleier; Harding, *Science Question, Whose Science?*; Keller, *A Feeling, Reflections*; Shulman). Underlying these issues is an educational concern: How can feminist scientists and educators incorporate a critical examination of science into courses in the natural sciences?

The pedagogical implications and practical applications embedded in the feminist critiques of science are just beginning to be developed, and examples of feminist science classrooms are limited. A review of recent educational grants awarded by the NSF's Program for Women and Girls reveals that from a total of forty-nine funded projects, only two explicitly addressed the concerns raised by feminist scholars of science. Forty-seven projects focused on designing pedagogical approaches and curriculum that would attract and retain women in traditional science communities. There have been, however, some recent works in this area that provide fruitful starting points for constructing a feminist science education that does not reproduce existing science systems, but rather challenges us to question our traditional understandings of scientific knowledge. This work illustrates how feminist pedagogy can be used to encourage students to look for the hidden assumptions of science and to question the underlying masculine biases of our culture regarding objectivity, truth, and the scientific enterprise.

A FEMINIST VISION OF TRANSFORMING SCIENCE EDUCATION

Clearly all of the emancipatory social movements—women's movements, antiracist and postcolonial movements around the globe, poor people's movements, gay and lesbian movements, the ecology movement, and others—intend to create sciences with

good consequences. They want sciences that are *for* them, not in-
different to or against them. (Harding, "Forum," 54)

A Theoretical Starting Point

Those involved in developing a feminist science education are beginning to
unravel the two seemingly conflicting pedagogical approaches to science education reform outlined above. Evelyn Hammonds, for instance, suggested
that women scientists whose interests lie in creating programs to increase
the participation of women in science seem to have little understanding of
the questions that feminist critics of science have attempted to address.
The point of contention, Hammonds argued, is located in the meaning of
gender. Hammond's research indicates that women science educators mis-
read feminist critics' "ideas about how gender is constructed within scientific discourses as statements *about* women scientists" (86). For these
women scientists, taking gender out of science means creating scientific
learning environments that bring more women into scientific practice.
    Without a clear understanding of the difference between the barriers to
women's participation in the sciences and the feminist critique of the *gendered* characteristics of scientific culture and scientific knowledge, the
pedagogical practices advocated by science educators will fail to have a
truly transformative effect on science education or the uses to which science is put. Without an emphasis on illuminating the race, class, and gender dimensions of scientific inquiry and science's relationship to political
processes and policy making, pedagogical techniques such as small-group
learning activities, making content relevant to diverse learning styles, and
legitimating experience as a valid form of knowledge may serve to entice
more women to study science but will not transform scientific inquiry.
Rather, these pedagogical techniques will serve the epistemological ends of
collaborative teaming: to reproduce existing knowledge that is in harmony
with the ways of doing that the general public are "already familiar with,
find useful, and depend upon" (Bruffee, *Collaborative* 9–10). Without a
feminist approach to scientific inquiry, it is likely that women scientists
will be socialized into the masculinist view of science and will remain unlikely to engage in transformative activities.
    In contrast, when the issues raised by feminist critics of science are ad-
dressed in classroom content and process, these pedagogical techniques
serve a different goal. They can help *all* students and teachers to develop a
critical analysis of the epistemology of Western science, its privileging of
the masculine, and its inability to reorient the relation of scientific inquiry
to social policy and social development (Clover). In short, transformative

potentials emerge in classrooms where the work of feminist critics of science is taken seriously and where establishing a set of values upon which the transformation of science can be grounded is the goal.

Some Practical Starting Points:
What a Feminist Science Classroom Might Look Like

Feminist approaches to science education can serve dual, although related and complementary, purposes. As feminist scientists begin to raise important questions about Western science (e.g., Who benefits and who does not from the uses to which science is put? What role does the historically specific context within which conventional science has developed and flourished play in constituting content, practice, and use in the natural sciences? What are the specific ideologies and values that are carried into scientific research? How has modern science sustained hegemonic structures and distributed benefits to some groups and cultures while ignoring or exploiting others?) and begin to create sciences that speak from the lives of women and other marginalized groups, not only will existing systems of science be challenged, but women's interest (as well as other marginalized groups' interests) in the sciences will rise (Harding). Consequently, not only will the face of the scientific community become more multicultural and gender, race, and class inclusive, but members of the community will be part of an enterprise that now encourages (rather than discourages) its members to become actively involved in asking new questions from fresh standpoints. New theories, methods of investigation, and practices will be created that fundamentally alter descriptions and explanations of the natural world and question who benefits from the uses to which science is put (Harding, "How the Women's").

One pedagogical approach that can be especially empowering to students of the hard or natural sciences is to demonstrate early on that the facts and concepts they are presented with are relative to a certain system of thought or worldview. That will empower students to gain an understanding of how all knowledge is constructed within a social context. Even the seemingly benign fields of math and physics can be understood and taught as contextualized disciplines. For instance, Bonnie Shulman's mathematics courses start from the assumption that the language of mathematics is neither culture fair nor culture free. Rather, she argued, value systems are encoded in the language of mathematics, and as teachers, "We have a responsibility to acknowledge that we are also teaching values when we teach mathematics." Further, Shulman argued that to present "mathematics as part of culture, it is necessary to specify whose culture and whose mathematics" (10). The specific pedagogical techniques she recommended are based on various feminist critiques of science, especially the works of Harding (*Whose Science?*) and Haraway:

> It is essential that we encourage our students to look for hidden as-sumptions and make them explicit. Most of them will have ab-sorbed the underlying biases of our culture about objectivity, truth, the scientific enterprise, and the nature of mathematics. We can start by helping them make their own ideas (however inchoate or ill formed) explicit and learn to question them. We must teach them to *expect* a standpoint in any scientific statement and in-clude it as part of their observations, as well as to look for it in oth-ers [. . .] in standard word problems, we can append questions that ask students to list what assumptions have been made [. . .] we need to emphasize that there are many valid alternative ap-proaches to the same problem, and even more important, there is often more than one single correct solution. [. . .] It is also impor-tant that we do not present mathematics as a fixed body of knowl-edge—complete, certain, and absolute [. . .] we owe it to our students to present this other image of mathematics, and to pro-vide them with experiences of the personal, intuitive, creative (and culturally dependent) process of doing mathematics, rather than merely reading the codified and axiomatic presentation that ap-pears in most recent textbooks. (11–12)

By illustrating how feminist critiques of science inform pedagogical prac-tices, Shulman provided us a way to think about how a contextualized sci-ence education might serve the political goal of challenging us to question (and replace) the scientific knowledge produced by the dominant cultural group in science—white males.

Karen Barad took these points a step further by demonstrating how the traditional approach to teaching quantum physics completely glosses over the fundamental meaning behind the theoretical framework. In a tra-ditional classroom, students are taught to use equations provided by quan-tum theory (because they work) but not to attempt to understand them, let alone allow their new knowledge to transform their views of science and nature. Barad described her own approach to teaching quantum mechan-ics within a framework she called "agential realism," which shares episte-mological and ontological concerns with feminist standpoint theories (Harding, *Whose Science?*; Haraway). Agential realism is inspired by the philosophical writings of Niels Bohr, who understood his own work in quantum theory as a rejection of the basic notion of duality in nature. Bohr argued that because there exists no clear-cut distinction between object and observer, scientific theories are necessarily "partial" and "located" types of knowledge. Barad wrote of teaching her quantum mechanics class: "Calculations are easier and more meaningful if students know what they are doing and why. A deep, new sense of relevance comes to the fore, since agential realism gives us a way to understand the role of human concepts in knowledge production" (67–68). Barad's use of agential realism, however, goes beyond making concepts relevant and science contextualized. Her work points us to a critique of modern science and an understanding of science's political nature:

> In fact, agential realism offers a way to interrogate not just classical notions of realism versus instrumentalism, objectivity versus subjectivity, absolutism versus relativism, or nature versus culture in science but also dualistic and fixed notions of race, class, gender, and sexuality in the realm of social dynamics. For example, according to agential realism, "gender," "race," "class," and "sexuality" refer to specific social dynamics, not to properties attributable to a particular person. These terms are historically, geographically, and politically situated. (69)

An interdisciplinary course, Earth Systems: A Feminist Approach, provides a starting point for constructing a feminist approach to geoscience education at the University of Nevada, Las Vegas (Mayberry and Rees). Founded on the vision of how social, scientific, and feminist inquiry and pedagogy can be drawn together to create a new atmosphere for science education, Earth Systems: A Feminist Approach infuses geological content with sociopolitical insights. For example, to demonstrate how the geological concepts of oil reservoirs and traps are tied to socioeconomic power relations, the students play a game. They are put in the role of independent petroleum companies with geologists and economists who need to make business decisions about where to purchase land and drill for oil. One student's journal entry contained the following comment:

> When we first started the game, I had a few unvoiced objections, [I wanted to ask] what about the environment, ecology, and social consequences of drilling for petroleum? However, these were quickly forgotten as the excitement mounted. Our team wanted to be the first to "strike gold." So we bought information about the land, searched for the best places to drill, bought land, and drilled.

We made a profit so we did it again. Soon we were up to $950,000,
we were rolling in money, and profits were soaring. Could we stop?
No! Did I have any reservation about continuing? No! We went
absolutely crazy with greed and power. We bought and drilled.
[. . .] I felt horrified at the greedy little capitalist I had become
(and so easily)! (Mayberry and Rees 65)

Thus, in an exercise designed to get students interested in learning about
sedimentary strata, faults, folds, and the difference between petroleum resources and reserves, students also gained a clearer understanding of the
social and economic forces (and consciousness) that shape our use of the
earth's natural resources.

Jill Schneiderman ("Curriculum") also wrote about the development
of a geology class that uses a feminist approach to understanding environmental degradation. The "interdisciplinary, interactive, writing intensive,
discussion-oriented course" developed and taught by Schneiderman required students to understand not only earth processes but also the
"global, multinational politics responsible" for environmental degradation
(48). Interdisciplinary materials (e.g., rocks, minerals, field trips, poetry,
literature, film, Native American folklore) are used throughout the course
to establish the relationships among science, feminism, and the environment. Schneiderman's goal for the course illustrates the *resistant* qualities
of feminist pedagogy:

As part of the project of revealing the effects of gender, race, class,
religion, and sexual orientation on the production, scope, and
structure of scientific knowledge, such curriculum transformation
offers hope. It promises ultimately to change the face of science
into a feminist science—one that not only provides women and
people of color with access to the power of science through greater
involvement in it, but into a science that has an agenda that reflects the needs of a global community. (49)

These poignant examples illustrate how feminists and scientists are beginning to breach their traditional knowledge boundaries to develop an
integrated feminist science education with the explicit goals of (a) constructing a contextualized science that exposes the cultural, social, and
political contexts within which science is produced and used; and (b) developing a critical consciousness empowered to apply scientific knowledge
to social action and social transformation. These projects move us closer to

creating sciences that respond to the needs of women and other marginalized groups—sciences in which these groups will have a vested interest.

Some Practical Concerns

Challenging the sanctity of science will not be an easy task. In the current educational climate, in which schools face increasingly conservative politics, it is unlikely that truly transformative models of science education will quickly appear. Many questions about the feasibility of implementing feminist pedagogies in schools and universities remain to be examined: How can feminist pedagogies best respond to fiscal constraints, increasingly diverse student populations, new technologies, and the conservative political climate? How can progressive academics adapt our classroom practice and course content to accommodate these challenges without sacrificing feminist learning goals? What kind of innovative courses can feminist teachers design and have administratively approved? In what ways can feminist teachers creatively circumvent disciplinary and institutional barriers as they implement courses that reflect feminist concerns? Feminist science educators will need to grapple with and write about these questions as they begin to construct feminist science classrooms. Further, as teachers develop their ability to integrate theory and practice, they will inevitably need to transform the curricular goals, course content, and daily teaching routines with which they are familiar. In so doing, feminist teachers may find themselves distanced from the traditional models of science teaching in which teachers rely on standardized approaches and course content. Tensions and conflicts over what constitutes scientific literacy and how national science standards will be met will inevitably emerge between feminist educators and the institutional settings within which they work.[2]

Pragmatically, feminist science educators may stand a better chance of gaining credibility and support if they appeal to the current emphasis on meeting the needs of an increasingly diverse student population through curricular and pedagogical reform (Roy and Schen). Peggy McIntosh's five-phase vision for curriculum transformation provides a door through which we can move science curriculum and pedagogy from female-friendly sciences (Phase III) to "sciences reconstructed to include us all" (Phase IV). (See Fausto-Sterling for a detailed description of how McIntosh's model can be applied to science education reform.) In this case, collaborative learning traditions may be used to help feminist science educators become institutionally positioned in a place where they will be more capable of moving toward more transformative and radical reforms.

The issues and concerns raised in this article are significant to the on-going development of feminist educators in all disciplines. Collaborative learning techniques may provide science educators with one avenue to move toward building a feminist science. However, the critical examination of science as a social institution, which is a hallmark of feminist peda-gogy's role in science education, cannot be ignored if we intend to trans-form science into a resource that is used to improve the welfare of all people around the globe. Without an appreciation of the reproductive impulse of collaborative learning and the resistant nature of feminist peda-gogy, I worry that science educators who are aligned with feminist con-cerns will find a safe and congenial home in the collaborative learning household. As we work to apply feminist theories, practices, and values in our classrooms, we should remember the words of Audre Lorde: "You can't dismantle the master's house by using the master's tools" (Lorde 112).

The preparation of this article was partly supported by the NSF under grant no. HRD-9555721.

●   ●   ●

NOTES

1. This section heading is taken from Bruffee's influential article, "Collabora-tive Learning and the 'Conversation of Mankind,'" which is commonly regarded as the classic statement on the epistemological foundations of collaborative learning.

2. During the last twenty-five to thirty years, feminist scholarship has created new knowledge and new epistemologies, as well as innovative pedagogies. The result has been a proliferation of imaginative new courses. However, little has been written that addressed the practical problems that feminist teachers face as they work toward institutionalizing courses that in many ways violate traditional academic norms.

WORKS CITED

American Association of University Women. *How Schools Shortchange Girls*. Washington, D.C.: American Association of University Women Educational Foundation, 1992.

Astin, A. W. *Achieving Educational Excellence*. San Francisco: Jossey-Bass, 1985.

Barad, K. "A Feminist Approach to Teaching Quantum Physics." *Teaching the Majority: Breaking the Gender Barrier in Science, Mathematics, and Engi-*

neering. Ed. S. Rosser. New York: Teachers College Press, 1995. 43–75.

Becker, H. S. "Studying Urban Schools." *Anthropology and Education Quarterly* 14 (1993): 99–108.

Bleier, R., ed. *Feminist Approaches to Science*. New York: Pergamon, 1986.

Blumenfeld, P. C., R. W. Marx, E. Soloway, and J. Krajcik. "Learning with Peers: From Small Group Cooperation to Collaborative Communities." *Educational Researcher* 25 (1996): 37–40.

Bowles, S., and H. Gintis. *Schooling in Capitalist America*. New York: Basic Books, 1976.

Brown, L. "The Advancement of Learning." *Educational Researcher* 23 (1995): 4–12.

Bruffee, K. "Collaborative Learning and the 'Conversation of Mankind.'" *College English* 46 (1994): 635–52.

———. *Collaborative Learning*. Baltimore: John Hopkins University Press, 1993.

Clover, D. "Gender Transformative Teaming and Environmental Action." *Gender and Education* 7 (1995): 243–58.

Cohen. E. G., R. A. Lotan, and C. Leechor, "Can Classrooms Learn?" *Sociology of Education* 62 (1989): 623–43.

Coleman, J. S. *Youth: Transition to Adulthood*. Report of the Panel on Youth of the President's Science Advisory Committee. Washington, D.C.: Office of Science and Technology, 1973.

Cooper, J., S. Prescott, L. Cook, L. Smith, and R. Mueck. *Cooperative Learning and College Instruction: Effective Use of Student Learning Teams*. Long Beach: California State University Foundation, 1990.

Fausto-Sterling, A. "Race, Gender and Science." *Transformations* 2 (1991): 4–12.

Freire, P. *Pedagogy of the Oppressed*. New York: Herder, 1972.

Giroux, H. *Theory and Resistance in Education*. South Hadley, MA: Bergin and Garvey, 1983.

Hammonds, E. "The Matter of Women in Science." Eds. J. Holland and M. Blair. *Debates and Issues in Feminist Research and Pedagogy* 70–89. Eds. J. Holland and M. Blair. Philadelphia: Open University, 1995.

Haraway, D. "Situated Knowledges: The Science Question in Feminism and the Privilege of Partial Perspective." *Feminist Studies* 14 (1988): 575–99.

Harding, S. "Forum: Feminism and Science." *National Women's Studies Association Journal* 5 (1993): 56–64.

———. *Whose Science? Whose Knowledge? Thinking from Women's Lives*. Ithaca: Cornell University Press, 1991.

———. "How the Women's Movement Benefits Science: Two Views." *Women's Studies International Forum* 12 (1989): 271–83.

———. *The Science Question in Feminism*. Ithaca: Cornell University Press, 1986.

Henderson, R. *Female Participation in Undergraduate Math, Science, and Engi-*

neering Majors. Organizational Features. Paper presented at the annual meeting of the Pacific Sociological Association, San Diego, CA. April 1993.

Hollenshead, C., P. Soellner-Younce, and S. Wenzel. "Women Graduate Students in Mathematics and Physics: Reflections on Success." *Journal of Women and Minorities in Science and Engineering* 1 (1994): 63–88.

Holloway, M. "A Lab of Her Own." *Scientific American* 269 (1993): 94–103.

hooks, b. *Teaching to Transgress.* New York: Routledge, 1994.

Johnson. D. W., and R. Johnson. "Cooperative, Competitive, and Individualistic Learning." *Journal of Research and Development in Education* 12 (1978): 3–15.

Kagan, S. *Cooperative Learning.* San Juan Capistrano, CA: Kagan Cooperative Learning, 1992.

Kahla, J. *Women in Science.* Philadelphia: Falmer Press, 1985.

_____. "Why Girls Don't Know." *What Research Says to Science Teachers.* Ed. M. B. Rowe. Washington, D.C.: National Science Teachers Association, 1990. 55–67.

Keller, E. F. *A Feeling for the Organism: The Life and Work of Barbara McClintock.* San Francisco: W. H. Freeman, 1985.

_____. *Reflections on Gender and Science.* New Haven: Yale University Press, 1988.

_____. "How Gender Matters, or, Why It's So Hard for Us to Count Past Two." *Inventing Women: Science, Technology and Gender.* Eds. G. Kirkup and L. Keller. Cambridge: Polity Press, 1992. 42–56.

Kelly, A. "The Construction of Masculine Science." *British Journal of Sociology of Education* 6 (1985): 133–54.

Kenway, J., and H. Modra. "Feminist Pedagogy and Emancipatory Possibilities." *Feminisms and Critical Pedagogy.* Eds. C. Luke and J. Gore. New York: Routledge, 1992. 138–66.

Longino, H. "Conflicts and Tensions in the Feminist Study of Gender and Science." *Debates and Issues in Feminist Research and Pedagogy.* Eds. J. Holland and M. Blair. Philadelphia: Open University, 1995. 70–89.

Lorde, A. *Sister Outsider.* New York: Crossing Press, 1984.

Maher, F. A., and M. T. Tetreault. *The Feminist Classroom.* New York: Basic Books, 1994.

Manis, J., N. Thomas, B. Sloat, and C. Davis. *An Analysis of Factors Affecting Choices in Majors in Science, Mathematics and Engineering at the University of Michigan.* University of Michigan, Ann Arbor: Center for Continuing Education of Women, 1989.

Matyas, M., and S. Malcolm. *Investing in Human Potential: Science and Engineering at the Crossroads.* Washington, D.C.: American Association for the Advancement of Science, 1991.

Mayberry, M., and M. Rees. "Feminist Pedagogy, Interdisciplinary Praxis, and Science Education." *NWSA Journal* 9 (1997): 57–75.

McIntosh, P. *Interactive Phases of Curricular Re-vision: A Feminist Perspective*. Wellesley, MA: Wellesley College Center for Research on Women, 1983.

National Center for Education Statistics. *NAEF 1992 Trends in Academic Progress*. Washington, D.C.: U.S. Department of Education, 1994.

National Institute of Education. *Investment in Learning: Realizing the Potential of American Higher Education (The Mortimer Report)*. Washington, D.C.: U.S. Department of Education, 1984.

National Research Council. *From Analysis to Action: Undergraduate Education in Science, Mathematics, Engineering, and Technology*. Washington, D.C.: Author, 1996.

National Science Board. *Science and Engineering Indicators—1993*. Washington, D.C.: U.S. Government Printing Office, 1993.

National Science Foundation. *Indicators of Science and Mathematics Education*. Washington, D.C.: Author, 1993.

National Science Foundation. *Women, Minorities, and Persons with Disabilities in Science and Engineering: 1994*. Washington. D.C.: Author, 1994.

National Science Foundation. *Shaping the Future: New Expectations for Undergraduate Education in Science, Mathematics, Engineering, and Technology*. Arlington, VA: Author, 1996.

Newcomb, T. M., and E. K. Wilson, eds. *College Peer Groups: Problems and Prospects for Research*. Chicago: Aldine Press, 1966.

O'Brien, M. "The Commatization of Women: Patriarchal Fetishism in the Sociology of Education." *Interchange* 15 (1984): 43–60.

Otto, P. "One Science, One Sex?" *School Science and Mathematics* 91 (1984): 367–73.

Romney, P., B. Tatum, and J. Jones. "Feminist Strategies for Teaching about Oppression: The Importance of Process." *Women's Studies Quarterly* XXI (1992): 95–110.

Rosser, Sue. *Female-friendly Science*. New York: Pergamon, 1990.

Rowbotham, S. "The Trouble with Patriarchy." *No Turning Back: Writing from the Women's Liberation Movement*. Ed. Feminist Anthology Collective. London: Women's Press, 1980. 72–79.

Roy, P., and M. Schen. "Feminist Pedagogy: Transforming the High School Classroom." *Women's Studies Quarterly* XXI (1993): 142–47.

Roychoudhury, A., and W. M. Roth. "Student Involvement in Learning: Collaboration in Science for Preservice Elementary Teachers." *Journal of Science Teacher Education* 3 (1992): 47–52.

Roychoudhury, A., D. Tippins, and S. Nichols. "Gender-inclusive Science Teaching: A Feminist-constructivist Approach." *Journal of Research in Science*

Teaching 32 (1995): 897–952.

Schneiderman, J. S. "What We Teach—Curriculum Transformation in the Earth Sciences: Women's Studies and Geology. *Alternative Pedagogies in Geological Sciences: A Workshop*. Eds. A. Bykerk-Kauffman, L. Savoy, and J. Schneiderman. Boston: Geological Society of America, 1993.

_____. "Curriculum Transformation in the Earth Sciences: Women's Studies and Geology." *Transformations* 5 (1994): 44–55.

Schniedewind. N. "Teaching Feminist Process in the 1990s." *Women's Studies Quarterly* XXL (1993): 17–30.

Shulman, B. "Implications of Feminist Critiques of Science for the Teaching of Mathematics and Science." *Journal of Women and Minorities in Science and Engineering* 1 (1994): 1–15.

Skolnick, J., C. Langbort, and L. Day. *How to Encourage Girls in Math and Science: Strategies for Parents and Educators*. Englewood Cliffs, NJ: Prentice Hall, 1982.

Spear, M. G. "Teachers' Views about the Importance of Science to Boys and Girls." *Science for Girls*. Ed. A. Kelly. Philadelphia: Open University Press, 1987.

Thurgood, D. H., and J. E. Clarke. *Summary Report 1993: Doctorate Recipients from United States Universities*. Washington, D.C.: National Academy Press, 1995.

Tobias, S. *They're Not Dumb; They're Different*. Tucson, AZ: Tucson Arizona Research Corporation, 1989.

_____. *Revitalizing Undergraduate Science: Why Some Things Work and Some Things Don't*. Tucson, AZ: Tucson Arizona Research Corporation, 1992.

Trankina, M. L. "Gender Differences in Attitudes Toward Science." *Psychological Reports* 73 (1993): 123–30.

Tuana, N., ed. *Feminism and Science*. Bloomington: Indiana University Press, 1989.

Webb, N. M., and A. S. Palincsar. "Group Processes in the Classroom." *Handbook of Educational Psychology*. Eds. D. C. Berliner and R. Calfee. New York: Macmillan, 1989. 841–73.

Weiler, K. "Freire and a Feminist Pedagogy of Difference. *Harvard Educational Review* 61 (1991): 449–74.

Wells, A. S. "Backers of School Change Turn Sociologists." *New York Times*, 4 Jan. 1989: 17.

2

TEACHING IN ENVIRONMENTS OF RESISTANCE
Toward a Critical, Feminist, and Antiracist Pedagogy

Sandra Bell, Marina Morrow, and Evangelia Tastsoglou[1]

INTRODUCTION

In contrast to traditional liberal curricula and pedagogies, critical, feminist, and antiracist pedagogies are designed to disrupt the canon of the academy in order to bring about social change. Such pedagogies highlight knowledge and ways of knowing that have traditionally been subjugated or invalidated, and they foster emancipatory aims. In particular, feminist and antiracist pedagogies place a high value on subjective experience as a route to understanding our lives and the lives of others and emphasize the legitimacy of knowledge that arises from socially marginalized positions. Critical pedagogy involves a similar idea. According to Henry Giroux, a "liberatory border pedagogy" involves a fundamental "decentering" of "dominant configurations of power and knowledge" (*Border Crossings* 246). Roger Simon adds that a "pedagogy of possibility" must include the ability to "interrogate both social forms and their possible transformations as to their compatibility with three additional basic principles: (1) securing human diversity, (2) securing compassionate justice, and (3) securing the renewal of life" (23).

Furthermore, a critical pedagogy requires that we help our students develop critical-thinking skills, partly by using material in the classroom that challenges the status quo and partly through teaching students to question and analyze. Ideally, critical-thinking skills should also be applied to feminist and antiracist course materials. It is through critical thinking that students actually shift from being passive receivers of knowledge to becoming engaged in a dynamic process of learning in which they are "actively transforming knowledges" (Mohanty 192). Critical-thinking skills also help students move from reflection to action, toward participating in emancipatory social change. As bell hooks puts it, "without the capacity to think critically about ourselves and our lives, none of us would be able to move forward, to change, to grow" (202).

Combining ideas from all three liberatory pedagogies and the political and social analyses that inform them, we think that a critical, feminist, and antiracist pedagogy ought to start from the experiences of marginalized groups. Second, such a pedagogy ought to aim at developing a collective, integrative analysis of oppression(s) to explore the interlocking, oppressive structures of race, ethnicity, class, gender, and sexuality. Third, such an analysis ought to be activist and geared especially to the development of a "multicentered politics" (Morrow) for social change. A critical pedagogy in particular calls for "a politics that reasserts the primacy of the social, incorporates multiple struggles, builds alliances, and recaptures the concept of solidarity" (Giroux, *Multiculturalism* 78).

Individually each of us has been inspired by the ideal learning environments described in the literature on critical, feminist, and antiracist pedagogies. Like many others in academe today, however, most of our own educational experiences, both as students and teachers, have been through what Paulo Freire refers to as the "banking system of education."[2] Although we have had some limited, direct exposure to progressive pedagogical practices in women's studies classrooms, we have not had extensive experience with alternative classrooms and, therefore, were ill prepared for the challenges of teaching "against the grain" (Simon) within traditional institutional structures. This chapter was generated out of our individual reflections and joint discussions about our diverse experiences with defining and implementing the values and principles of a critical, feminist, and antiracist pedagogy in our respective teaching environments.

In this chapter we subject certain difficult and ambiguous pedagogical "moments" in our classes to critical scrutiny and reflection. We do so with the belief that conscious attention to our own teaching practices is an important component of "engaged pedagogy" (hooks 13–22). We are also convinced that the method and the effect of our teaching are as important as the content of our curriculum. To this end, we believe that it is only through a self-reflexive process that we will come to better understand "what as a teacher one is effecting (and managing) on one's students, what way of being one's pedagogical practice is producing in them" (Yates 435). Further, through this process we are attempting to learn about ourselves and what lessons for improving our practices we can derive from students' reactions.

Following Elizabeth Ellsworth (3–23), we take the view that since the composition of each class is different, classroom political dynamics are a

priori "unknowable," and, therefore, a critical, feminist, and antiracist pedagogical practice has to be contextual. The chapter situates our specific
practices in the context of our respective classrooms and reflects on these
"moments" in order to identify the specific factors that undermined our attempts to implement progressive pedagogies. More specifically, we critically
take up student responses to our teaching as a way of better understanding
both the impact of our practices and their intersection with structural barriers. We conclude with a critical reflection about what we could have done
differently in our respective classrooms that might, in the future, make us
more mindful and effective in keeping abreast of the challenges arising
from the struggle toward implementing progressive pedagogical visions.

ENVIRONMENTS OF RESISTANCE

Despite the emancipatory aims of critical, feminist, and antiracist pedagogies, we have found that our students have not always welcomed practices
originating therein. Instead, they have often resorted to various resistance
strategies, ranging from refusal to comply with course requirements to
more subtle expressions that appear to undermine our pedagogical efforts.
The sources of these resistance strategies are multiple and integrally connected to students' own life histories, classroom dynamics, and, most important, to institutional and systemic factors. That is, both "structural
determinants" and "human agency" play a role in how forms of student
"resistance" are enacted (Giroux, "Theories of Reproduction" 283).

Critical pedagogy in its classic form emphasizes that instances of resistance reflect students' attempts to assert their own emerging political identities or simply to "reaffirm and validate their subjectivities as specifically
classed, raced, and gendered social actors" (Lewis 471) against the dominant educational discourse (Giroux, "Reproduction, Resistance, and Accommodation" 107–11). Alternatively, students whose practices and
perspectives are being challenged by critical discussions of power relations
may react with discomfort and hostility (Solomon 59). In other cases,
which are of most interest to us here, students may be expressing forms of
the dominant ideology (Lewis; Hoodfar) in which their practices are invested without necessarily being members of the dominant group. In these
instances, the teacher's tasks are to assist students toward understanding
ways in which their voices can be "inscribed with relations of oppression"
(Manicom 376), to refrain herself from claims of false consciousness, and
to guide students in their efforts to make sense of their multiple and often
contradictory roles as social actors in an unequal society. In Patti Lather's
terms, the task is to assist students in their struggle to make sense of "con-

tradictory information, radical contingency, and indeterminacies" (*Getting Smart* 119). Finally, some students may be resisting what they see as ideological impositions in the name of liberatory pedagogies (Lather, "Feminist Perspectives" 575–76). The challenge here is to refrain from imposing meaning on our students' experiences and lead them, instead, to understand how their experiences are shaped socially.

At the root of our own difficult pedagogical "moments" are some common characteristics that originate in institutions and structures rather than within individuals. This is not to deny the importance of our respective "educational life histories" (Middleton) or the individual agency of our students but rather to point to the particular distortions that occur when small-scale, localized efforts toward critical, feminist, and antiracist pedagogies are injected into the banking system of education. Despite challenges, this model of education still widely prevails. The authority-based banking system is hierarchical and fosters an uncritical acceptance and compartmentalization of knowledge. Based on a passive reception of "objective" knowledge, this system of education ultimately denies agency, the individual, subjective activity that forges connections and creatively reconstructs knowledge. The banking system of education is a product of a particular type of society (hierarchical, capitalist, patriarchal, and racist) and has recently been reinforced by right-wing backlash expressed in such ideas as John Fekete's "biopolitics," Christina Hoff Somers's attack on feminism, Daphne Patai and Noretta Koertge's internal critique of feminism and women's studies programs, and a general notion that feminism and antiracism have "gone too far."[3]

Two particular consequences of the banking system constitute structural obstacles (though of a different order) to the effective practice of critical, feminist, and antiracist pedagogy. First, this system mitigates against a historical and social analysis; and secondly, it blocks an integrative analysis. The former consequence de-historicizes and depoliticizes difference, the latter individualizes and fragments difference thereby making it irrelevant to any effort for social change. These consequences are particularly apparent when taking place within a liberal framework of equality and multiculturalism.

Multiculturalism as an ideology is based on a framework of liberal individualist philosophy that acknowledges the existence of cultural diversity and pledges a formal equality of cultures and races that can presumably freely express themselves. This ideology obscures inequities and the systemic privileging of certain social groups. Within this framework, difference and experience are defined in individual terms, rather than in historical and social terms. Individuals are supposed to "know" as members of particular groups and to speak "in the name" of such groups. The result of such assumptions is that all experiences are viewed as equally valid and therefore deserving of similar public (classroom) space. A particular form of identity politics[4] becomes operative and any critical perspective on experience becomes irrelevant or is viewed with suspicion as a relic of a conservative era. Dawn Currie points out that identity politics becomes problematic in the classroom when it leads to "epistemological relativism," when any or all efforts to assess truth claims are treated as invalid (353). In this form of identity politics, culture is depoliticized and de-historicized and group historical experiences are reduced to individual fragments, particular individual stories (Mohanty 190, 195). Identity politics and the authorization of individual experience can be empowering for those who have never had any public space to have their voices heard. However, this discourse is ultimately disempowering, because by individualizing experience it fragments people, does not address issues of historical domination and collective rights, and does not permit assessment of competing claims.

Despite our apparently different educational life histories and other course-related situational differences, all three of us were caught in the dilemma of this "liberal" classroom, torn between the students' demands to express experience and feelings freely and our apprehensions that the uncritical expression of experience would be detrimental to a broader understanding of oppression. On the one hand, we wished to acknowledge and validate individual experiences in the public space of the classroom, as a way of encouraging students to forge agency. On the other hand, we were each aware of the traps of liberal ideology (e.g., de-historization and fragmentation of difference), thus we struggled to bring our students to a critical, structural, and integrative understanding of issues.

CLASSROOMS IN ACTION: THE PEDAGOGICAL "MOMENTS"

Before we analyze our pedagogical dilemmas and our respective struggles to resolve them, we present a description of the "moments" that crystallize some of the difficult episodes in our three respective courses. These pedagogical moments were shaped by our differing individual personalities, educational life histories (Middleton), the social locations of class participants, classroom demographics that affected the psychosexual and social dynamics of the classroom, the institutional setting, and mandated practices of curriculum, evaluation, and attendance (Manicom 366). We argue that, despite such differences, the nature of the problems encountered in implementing a critical, feminist, and antiracist pedagogy and our efforts to resolve these problems were remarkably similar.

Two of the classes concerned were women's studies courses with an entirely female student population while the other, a sociology course, had
both male and female students. The students in all three classes were
mostly of Euro-Canadian, working-class background but with different
degrees of prior exposure to feminist and antiracist frameworks. As senior-
level seminars, the classes were similar in size and format but differed in
course content. One course,[5] a two-part requirement for completion of a
women's studies degree, was titled Feminist Methodology and Directed Research; the second course was Feminist Perspectives on Violence Against
Women; the third a senior undergraduate seminar, Gender, Ethnicity, and
Migration. Of the course instructors, all of whom are white women, one has
been raised and partly educated in a European country, another is third-
generation Euro-Canadian, raised and partly educated in the Canadian
Prairies, while the third is white Canadian, raised and educated in southwestern Ontario. Our universities are all located in the Maritime region.

The Battle of Meritocracy

The Gender, Ethnicity, and Migration seminar aimed at understanding the
connections between and among classism, racism, and sexism in the migration, settlement, and integration/ethnic formation processes in the context of Canadian capitalist state development. Starting from the lived
experiences of immigrant, ethnic, visible minority, and Aboriginal women
and men in those processes and within specific areas of social life, the
course investigated the social organization of such experiences by focusing
on the larger "relations of ruling" (Smith, *Everyday World* 3). Canadian
immigration and settlement policies and practices, multiculturalism and
race relations, Aboriginal policies, migrant workers, refugees, and the politics of language were some of the major issues addressed. Students were
evaluated on the basis of various assignments, the major one a community-
based project they did individually or with a partner, in the second semester. This project was especially designed to challenge stereotypes by
requiring students to work cooperatively with ethnic communities different
from their own. The class was a mixed-gender one, with the majority of
students being senior sociology majors, white, working class, from the
Maritime region. There was one Aboriginal male student in the class.

In this class, the working-class male students often challenged, with
some hostility, the foreign-accented female instructor,[6] whom they seemed
to perceive as the embodiment of their inability to secure career employment. Their resistance was intensified by the content of the course, for this
instructor, whom they viewed as the likely product of affirmative action,

was teaching them the very theory behind the policies they perceived as standing in the way of their social mobility. These students were quick to raise the issue of affirmative action[7] early in the course even before the instructor had introduced it. Their arguments against affirmative action usually ran as follows: (1) "quotas are a form of reverse discrimination" (the "two wrongs cannot make a right" argument); (2) "I understand that historically, women and minorities have encountered discrimination, but at this point in history things have been reversed and white males with superior qualifications cannot get a job" (the myth of equity having gone too far); (3) "the important thing in hiring should be who can do the job best, not who has historically been discriminated against" (the myth of meritocracy).[8]

The anger exhibited by these students may have been grounded in the historically high levels of unemployment and migration in Maritime working-class communities and in the fact that affirmative-action programs do not specifically address class inequities. However, male students' unwillingness to connect their own experiences with those of other oppressed groups resulted in their adoption of dominant discourses in which "group rights" and "equity" are outlandish notions in the individualistic ideology of the "free" market. From this point of view, people are supposed to be rewarded according to the effort they put into acquiring necessary skills and according to their native talent as proven through fair competition ("meritocracy"). In this instance of "naturalized" hegemonic discourse (Ellsworth 305) the students clearly identified certain aspects of their own experience as "reality" and saw the experience provided by any "other" as biased. The female students in the class did not take a different position and the only Aboriginal student was frequently absent from class.[9] For critical, feminist, and antiracist pedagogy, the educational dilemmas in this situation were (1) how to acknowledge the male students' "voices" without validating the racism and sexism inherent in their positions and, at the same time, empower the female and Aboriginal students; (2) how to do this without the instructor negating her own "voice" or censoring herself lest she be perceived as "biased"; and (3) how to get the male students to understand the experiences of "others" and understand differently their own experience.

The Fear of Knowing

The Violence Against Women course was designed specifically to examine feminist theory about violence against women. In particular, the course attempted to affirm the work of feminists who look integratively at different

forms of oppression (e.g., by gender, race, sexuality, and class) and demonstrate how feminist theories have enriched our understanding of the role
violence plays in women's subordination. The course also included a
discussion of the frameworks used by lawyers, police, mental health professionals, and academics in ways that reinforced psychological understandings of men's violence, rather than promoting structural and systemic
understandings. Students were evaluated on the basis of their ability to examine critically and integrate a number of sources of information—
personal experiences, feminist and antiracist theory and activism, and
psychological and sociological literature on violence against women. The
course was listed as a special-topics course with prerequisites: either other
women's studies courses or involvement in feminist activism. The course
therefore drew mostly mature students with already articulated commitments to feminism. Although not all of the students spoke personally about
their own histories, the majority had been raised in the Maritimes, had
working-class backgrounds, and, with one exception, were all white. The
one black student in the class was a visiting student from Kenya. Two
women in the course identified themselves as lesbian.

Because of the well-established popular and professional discourses on
violence against women that employ apolitical, individualistic frameworks,
it was difficult to keep students from adopting such frameworks in their
own discussions. The result was that initially, despite the instructor's efforts to get students to connect with their own experiences, they often
slipped into a "mental health" language that placed abused women apart
from themselves. In part, the students may have been resisting identifying
with experiences of oppression (i.e., violence and abuse) that accorded
them less agency in their lives rather than more (Lather, *Getting Smart*
143). Unwittingly, the instructor's own ambivalence about handling personal disclosure may have contributed to the students' reluctance to speak
from their own experience.

Ironically, once some students began to connect with and share their
own experiences, efforts on the part of the instructor to move the discussion toward understanding the structures that organize personal experience were met with resistance by some students, who claimed that the class
had moved to "a level of theoretical abstraction." This was crystallized
when one student became increasingly agitated during a discussion about
child sexual abuse. The student finally challenged the class by objecting to
the ways in which they talked about violence and abuse as though no one
present might have had these experiences. This student's comments helped
pave the way for other class members to discuss their experiences more
openly but it became increasingly difficult for the instructor to get students

to contextualize such experiences. Students in this case appeared to be re-sisting theory (Simon 79–100). The dilemma in this situation was how to help students integrate their concrete individual experiences—thus vali-dating student "voice"—with a theoretical understanding of the role of vi-olence in maintaining patriarchal structures.

Partial Knowing

Fostering an analysis of the structural nature of oppression also proved difficult in the Feminist Methodology and Directed Research seminar. In an effort to accommodate the interdisciplinary interests of the students, there were three instructors, from English, criminology, and sociology. With one exception, instructors and students were all white with working-class backgrounds. Most had been raised or educated in other parts of Canada. The one black student had been raised and educated in Nova Sco-tia. Another student identified herself as lesbian. This course was a re-quirement for the undergraduate degree in women's studies and was a vehicle for students to conduct their own research. The course was divided into two parts. In the first half of the course, students were required to develop proposals for a research project that would be carried out in the second half of the course. The research proposal was to be developed in stages, beginning with a literature review and discussion of their proposed research methodology. Students were to be evaluated on drafts of their proposals and on the final research paper. In the first half of the course, readings and class discussions centered on epistemological issues and examples of feminist research from various disciplines including history, literature, fine art, law, and sociology. Prominent feminists from the region made presentations on their work to the class.

In protest against what they perceived as the instructors' antifeminist practices, students refused to engage in the required literature review and would not adopt any structure in their research agenda. According to stu-dents, the instructors had been "co-opted by the patriarchal hierarchy of the academy" and course requirements were said to be antiwoman and antifeminist. The crucial pedagogical moments in this class arose through students arguing, "Why would we want to do a literature review or read other peoples' research? Aren't we supposed to write about our own expe-rience and about that which we know? Why would we want to 'bias' our work with someone else's thinking on the subject?" When the instructors suggested to a student interested in researching feminist theater that she talk to people involved in various aspects of the theater (including the au-dience) to see how their views compared to her own, she answered, "But why would I do that? I have been to feminist theater, and I know how it works." As in the Violence Against Women class, these students were practicing what they had (mis)learned in other feminist classrooms or in their nonacademic exposure to feminism. They were valuing their personal experiences exclusively, resisting attempts by the instructors to situate these experiences in a broader theoretical context.

UNDERSTANDING STUDENT RESISTANCE TO CRITICAL, FEMINIST, AND ANTIRACIST PEDAGOGY

What were the dilemmas specific to the pedagogical strategies that we each adopted in our classrooms? In the Violence Against Women course, the instructor attempted to assist students to see the historical importance of personal experience in shaping feminist theory on violence against women and encouraged students to relate to the course material through a personal lens. However, in resisting a focus that would ultimately play into the ways in which the issue of violence against women is being framed through professional discourses as an individual issue with an emphasis on personal healing, she also attempted to shift the emphasis away from the concrete experiences of the women in the classroom to a more "politicized" notion of experience (Mohanty 182). Further, in an attempt to move students beyond looking at their own experiences and toward integrating an analysis of class, race, and sexuality into their understanding of violence, she used work by a broad range of feminists in her course. As a result of these attempts, some of her students felt that their own experiences (sometimes only recently claimed) were being invalidated and that the discussion had become "too theoretically abstract."

In the Gender, Ethnicity, and Migration seminar, the instructor was caught in a similar dilemma. Willing to allow students the public space to name their experiences, she ended up in a situation where the white, working-class, Canadian-born, and primarily male students' experiences dominated the class and undermined her authority to facilitate the class or empower anybody else to participate. Concerned that the white male students' domination of the class precluded discussion of larger structures, she invoked her authority as the teacher to limit discussion and, in an effort to prevent further polarization and to deflect possible accusations of "bias," avoided any reference to her own personal experience. The result was a double negation, of both the students' agency and her own. Equally problematic in this course was the absence of any dissenting female "voices." Women's investments in man-made meanings may have been one cause of silence (Lewis 473–74). The women students may also not have felt safe to express dissenting views because of the obviously antagonistic atmosphere of the classroom.

In the Feminist Methodology and Research course, instructors were engaged in a highly polarized situation in which students insisted in talking exclusively from experience while instructors struggled to encourage students to contextualize their experiences theoretically and think critically. As a result, students and instructors reached an impasse and the possibility of raising questions about the social and historical construction of experience was greatly diminished. As in the previous two instances, the instructors were unable to get the students to use their concrete personal experiences as a springboard to launch into questions about the social construction of those experiences. Instructors here struggled with the contradictions inherent in valuing student experience while at the same time invoking authority (through assignment of grades) to convince students of the value of the tasks they were suggesting.

All three courses were marked by resistance against the instructor's efforts to initiate a structural and integrative analysis and foster critical thinking. Although course content, instructor's personality, and the particular dynamic of student-teacher interaction shaped the responses to each set of student-resistance strategies, the pedagogical challenges each faced were marked by similar characteristics attributable to the "liberal individualistic" philosophy of the contemporary Canadian multicultural classroom: (1) identity politics and essentialist arguments; and (2) a superficial acknowledgment or tolerance of difference with no consideration of how differences are socially produced.

For example, in the Feminist Methods and Research class, despite students' knowledge of feminist theory from other classes, they employed liberal essentialist arguments to insist that individual experiences are valid in and of themselves and do not need to be explored further. In the Violence Against Women class, some students initially had difficulty connecting the material to their own experiences, but once they did, they refused to contextualize their personal experience because they felt doing so devalued it. In the Gender, Ethnicity, and Migration course, white male students' fears of unemployment were fueled by liberal individualist ideology and resulted in the construction of liberal arguments to counter course material and silence others. Overall, in every class and regardless of our efforts, all three of us were left with the feeling that we were unsuccessful in helping students to shift from the center of their own experiences.

In all three classes, some students felt sufficiently empowered to resist the authority of the classroom in order to "center" their own experiences. While this form of empowerment could be viewed as testimony to the positive impact of liberatory pedagogies, it also raises a number of pedagogical dilemmas. Of concern are the extent to which student challenges impede a fuller understanding of how critical and analytical thinking can be used to understand oppression, the extent to which one considers a theoretical framework to be of importance in a feminist classroom,[10] and the possibility that students' refusal to examine views other than their own experience is caused by racism, classism, homophobia, or sexism.

Teaching against the grain in an educational model based on the banking system leads to almost predictable results: students have negative and even angry reactions in the little space provided to them to assert their subjectivities, sometimes for the first time. Instructors who, after all, have also come out of the same banking system of education, may take firm and even defensive attitudes toward what appears as students' abuse of rights, unfortunately serving further to negate student subjectivities and entrench adversarial positions. A particularly interesting distorted effect of the interaction of the banking system with a student-selected application of presumably feminist pedagogical principles took place in the Feminist Methods and Research course. In this instance, critical learning and the possibility of empowering agency were eschewed in the name of "political correctness" as defined by the students and as represented by one particular feminist discourse. Instructors' efforts to get students to theorize, generalize, and contextualize were misconstrued by students as a reimposition of the banking model, and they resisted.

In other instances, students who were accustomed to and accepted the banking system of education and had adopted an epistemologically passive role were often confused by challenges to authoritative scholars and by the multiple ways in which issues could be understood. This group of students preferred to be able to think in terms of "correct" or "right"[11] answers. On the other hand, when students were given the freedom to question knowledge, tensions arose over whose knowledge to value. In the Gender, Ethnicity, and Migration course, the "foreign" instructor's authority was structurally weakened by her difference and by systemic racism of which the students were unaware. Authority was also an issue in the Violence Against Women course but in this case suspicion was aroused by the instructor's youth and perceived lack of seniority. In all three courses, students liberally questioned the instructors' knowledge with what they reconstructed, in a hierarchical (sexist and racist) system, as "weaknesses": the instructors' gender, age, or foreign birth. In the context of no institutional support for alternative, critical teaching, every difference from the canon of the banking system of education can be and often is construed as weakness. Instructors' efforts to engage students as participants in the development of knowledge in the classroom provided evidence of these weaknesses. Thus, the adversarial roles of the banking system were re-created, albeit in a different dynamic.

TOWARD SITUATED RESPONSES TO SPECIFIC PEDAGOGICAL CHALLENGES

"I am striving to clarify the outlines of an educational practice based on the partial, situated, embodied (and therefore responsible) character of knowing and the hopeful ethos of a critical, responsive imagination" (Simon 11).

All three of us are familiar with liberatory pedagogies in theory and had given considerable thought to what we were trying to achieve in our respective classrooms. But we did not have much experience in actualizing these theories. All three of us have had similar educational experiences, predominantly through male-dominated, hierarchical, experience-leery curricula. As sociologists and feminists we are also familiar with structural analysis and have reflected on how our own experiences are connected with larger social structures. Each of us has taken slow and painful steps to forge our own agency, and we are still in the process of learning about ourselves and of naming and renaming our experiences. Our efforts, however, have been largely individual and/or outside the academy; we have had limited experience in witnessing a similar process unfold in the classroom. Herein lies our pedagogical dilemma: we define as our calling a critical, feminist, and antiracist pedagogy, teaching in a way that, except for the desire and the political commitment, we have had little formal preparation for. In our classrooms we grope toward an "unknown" (Ellsworth 321) with little support from our institutions and hardly any immediate rewards from our students.

"Unlearning" our own traditional educational training and coming to understand the theoretical and practical implications of reexamining knowledge using the tools developed through critical, feminist, and antiracist methods is clearly a lifelong learning process. To be effective this process must be nurtured, supported, and continually appraised and negotiated. To this end we attempt to resolve some of the dilemmas we have raised by suggesting specific responses that might have been adopted in each of the situations that arose in our respective classrooms.

The "Authorization of Experience"

Chandra Mohanty argues that "the authorization of experience" is a "crucial form of empowerment for students" (193). Indeed in each instance we described, validating students' experiences was a useful way of beginning.

However, to do this when we perceive a student's voice to have been marginalized based on their social location is clearly easier than when we are dealing with students whose "realities" we most wish to challenge (i.e., those of dominant social groups). For example in the Gender, Ethnicity, and Migration course validating the voices of challenging male students was complicated by the fact that affirming these voices might result in negating the instructor's and others' marginalized voices. In addition, authorizing only some students' experiences and not others can be problematic for the silencing effect it will have (Mohanty 193–94) and the antagonistic classroom dynamic it fosters. In this instance the instructor not only must use her authority as the teacher constructively to encourage as many voices as possible to speak but also to strive for relations in the classroom that allow for a critique of various positions. But her position is fraught with tension, as she uses her authority in order to deconstruct authority. To avoid the false accusation of "silencing free speech," she might have to define the range of debate from the beginning of the course by setting up "working assumptions" (Tatum 3–5) and "ground rules" for discussion (Cannon 129–33). An important working assumption would be the acknowledgment that we have all lived under racism and thus cannot be blamed for learning what we have been taught, but that we have a responsibility toward the future to identify, name, and interrupt the cycle of oppression (Tatum 4; Cannon 131). An equally important guideline for discussion in this instance would be that students speak from their own experience, rather than generalize their experience to others.

Authorizing experience in the case of the Violence Against Women course presented the dilemma of how to avoid the false dichotomy between personal experience and a structural and political understanding of experience. That is, how does the instructor guard against the classroom becoming simply a space of personal disclosure and support and resist a focus that would ultimately play into the ways in which violence against women is being framed as an individual, psychological issue. One possible solution is to acknowledge openly in the class the difficulty of the material and the need that the members may feel to share their experiences. In addition, efforts at formalizing an extracurricular support network—possibly as part of a team assignment—might have mitigated the effects of the instructor's attempts to work more comprehensively with theoretical issues. Requiring students to keep journals and encouraging an active integration of personal and theoretical material through student-teacher dialogue as part of this exercise can assist students in seeing the necessity of these connections. These approaches might have allowed students to work with the material on a personal level and at the same time take up the issues more critically, enabling them to contribute to theory building and more effective strategies for change. An open acknowledgment of the different reasons that women are taking the course as well as a clear message from the instructor about her own goals and concerns about the course might help to make varying expectations more explicit.

The use of experience as a pedagogical tool took a particularly interesting form in the Feminist Methods and Research class where students, partly as a result of their contact with other feminist classrooms, felt that knowledge based on their own experiences was the only legitimate way to understand the course material and meet course requirements. This development can be claimed as either a victory or a failure of the pedagogical practices in women's studies courses. Alternatively, it can also be seen as a necessary process through which individuals, whose voices have historically been marginalized, need to move.[12] If students need to pass through such a process, instructors must show respect and understanding for each student's development at any particular time. At the same time, the challenge must be offered continually to move beyond individual experience and undertake a critical analysis. In sum, it might be unrealistic to expect every student to make use of broader social and integrative analysis when they may still be struggling to identify and affirm their own life experiences.[13] A framework that highlights relational ways of knowing may help students better to understand the connections between subjective and "objective" knowledge and to see the usefulness of combining their experiences with contextual and analytical thinking (Currie 342). Here as well it would be helpful to establish working assumptions and discussion guidelines right from the beginning about respecting one another's individual process of change while at the same time outlining expectations for evidence of "progress" in each student's understanding of the issues by the end of the course (Tatum 21; Lather, *Getting Smart* 127). In addition, students could be asked to document and consciously observe their own process of change, by way of writing self-profiles at the beginning and end of the course.

The Social and Historical Construction of Experience

Showing students the important role that personal experience has had in shaping feminist and antiracist theory is essential. Further, creating an environment where students feel sufficiently "safe," affirmed, and nurtured to talk about their own experiences is crucial. However, getting students to "deconstruct" (Manicom 374) or "politicize" their experiences and move forward from there is a more difficult challenge. But, "unless [experience] is explicitly understood as historical, contingent, and the result of interpretation, it can coagulate into frozen, binary, psychologistic positions" (Mohanty 195). The absence of an historically situated perspective can reinforce notions of cultural pluralism or digress into what Giroux refers to as "the pedagogy of normative pluralism" (*Teachers as Intellectuals* 95), creating a classroom where differences are politely managed and a critical analysis of culture and experience is made impossible.

Different strategies may be necessary for different classroom situations and student knowledge bases. For example, students who have not been exposed to critical, feminist, and antiracist theories will need to participate in a process that will guide them in seeing that what they believe are objective truths have in fact been shaped by the historical domination of certain groups in society. Establishing a "working assumption" in the beginning that everybody in the class will actively pursue information and further understanding about his or her own group as well as of other groups (Cannon 132) might be a particularly fruitful strategy in this respect.

In discussions about affirmative action in the Gender, Ethnicity, and Migration course, for example, students could have been guided to see how traditional hiring practices and workplace environments have been designed with the skills and needs of a very particular (e.g., white, male) worker in mind. Discussions about the historical basis of this arrangement, as well as the contemporary impact on local communities, might also be useful in bringing students to understand the relevance as well as the problems of affirmative action. The goal here would also be to get working-class males to understand how allying themselves with people of color, immigrants, and women workers might transform work environments and create better work opportunities for them as well.

Students from marginalized positions who have come to reclaim their own knowledge and experiences must be encouraged to see these within a broader context and cautioned about the problems that ensue if their experiences are privileged exclusively. This becomes an issue especially in classroom situations, such as in the Feminist Methods and Research class, where students privilege the explanatory power of gender and personal experience. In these situations, students must be guided to see the danger of monolithic discourses whether those discourses arise from the margin or the center. The goal would be to help students see how an exclusive focus on their own experiences might lead them to replicate the very practices they thought their feminist politics were aimed at eradicating. Discussions of the importance of seeing more than one's own personal point of view could be enhanced through material that challenges the racism in some feminist theory or the lack of gender analysis in some forms of antiracist theory.

CHALLENGING NOTIONS OF WHAT "NORMATIVE" IS: "PIVOTING THE CENTER" AND FOSTERING A "CULTURE OF DISSENT"

Our objective was to assist students to "pivot the center, to center in another experience" (Bettina Aptheker cited in Brown 921). Elsa Barkley Brown suggests that confronting the normative (i.e., "pivoting the center") and bringing students to a point where they are able to move beyond their own notion of what is normative is not merely an intellectual process. She asks:

> How do our students overcome years of notions of what is normative? [. . .] I have come to understand that this is not merely an intellectual process. It is not merely a question of whether or not we have learned to analyze in particular kinds of ways or whether people are able to intellectualize about a variety of experiences. It is also about coming to believe in the possibility of a variety of experiences, a variety of ways of understanding the world, a variety of frameworks of operation, without imposing consciously or unconsciously a notion of the norm. (921)

A concrete way of getting students in each of our examples to see that there are a variety of ways of understanding a particular issue (i.e., of pivoting the center) is to draw upon differences as they are embodied in students in the classroom (hooks 84). To accomplish or achieve an effective, experiential understanding of "otherness," students must be provided with enough space for different individual voices to find expression in the classroom. This can be accomplished through the "power of self-generated knowledge" (Tatum 18). Arja Laitinen and Arto Tiihonen, for example, used a process of memoir writing and oral exchange in the classroom as a means of offering students an opportunity to transform the "subjective" into the "objective." Students in a seminar class were required to present their analyses of their own personal experiences, all on the same subject, and without interruption. Through this process, students studied their own experiences as well as those of others in the classroom.

This strategy might have been particularly useful in the Feminist Methods and Research class. It would be more difficult to accomplish in the Violence Against Women and the Gender, Ethnicity, and Migration courses. In those courses, students' experiences of racism or sexism and the contentious and difficult nature of some of the course material might have

caused some students to feel uncomfortable or intimidated about expressing their own views. We can only speculate here that establishing certain
guidelines for discussion at the beginning of the course (e.g., confidentiality, respect, listening, and speaking from one's own experience) might have
contributed to increasing the comfort and safety levels for some students in
these classrooms (Tatum 18).

It is necessary not only to open up a space for as many voices as possible to speak in our classes but also it is especially important to allow space
for dissenting ones, i.e., to foster "public cultures of dissent" (Mohanty
206–07). That is, our classrooms must foster an atmosphere in which students can and will question the master narratives that make up the official
curriculum so that they can come to understand the social construction of
otherness through processes of exclusion and discrimination. To achieve
this, it may be necessary to exercise teacher authority and interrupt relations and ideologies of domination in the classroom (Manicom 380–81). In
the case of the Gender, Ethnicity, and Migration course, the instructor
failed to interrupt power relations among students and, therefore, was unable to empower the female students to speak up. A good deal of energy
went into defensive strategies against what she perceived as racism directed toward her, as opposed to breaking the apparent power block and
forging alliances within the class that could lead to a "culture of dissent"
(Mohanty 193, 206, 207).

Awareness of How We Reproduce the "Master Narratives of Domination"
(Giroux, *Postmodernism, Feminism, and Cultural Politics* 253–55)

All of the above strategies require a critical awareness of how the processes
of exclusion and discrimination may be re-created and sustained in the
specific social and historical setting of the classroom through our unquestioned everyday practices, those of both students and instructors (Giroux,
"Postcolonial Ruptures" 34–36, "Postmodernism as Border Pedagogy"
247–55). Feminist and antiracist pedagogies can only arise out of specific
settings and contexts and can only be situated political practices
(Ellsworth 308). In other words, as teachers we must be continually aware
of the varieties of student-resistance strategies that we will encounter and
be prepared to respond to them in a constructive manner. The paradox of
our pedagogy is that we are also providing space for "master narratives" to
enter the classroom.

For students, an important part of the process of coming to see different viewpoints is realizing their own investment in "master narratives of
domination." For example, the working-class males who resisted notions

of affirmative action in the Gender, Ethnicity, and Migration course might have been made more aware of their personal investment in excluding certain groups from the workforce. Validating their fears about job loss while at the same time drawing on material that critically analyzes class relations might have been one way of addressing their resistance, which might have led to an understanding of how affirmative action might also be in their interest. In the Feminist Methods and Research class the students needed to see how their own investment in a particular feminist discourse (i.e., one that did not look integratively at all forms of oppression) might ultimately reproduce hierarchical relations and invalidate some women's voices. In this case the pedagogical objective would be to heighten students' awareness of the politics of knowledge. Toward this end, Patti Lather (*Getting Smart* 127–28) recommends a strategy that requires students to think about which knowledge claims they have opened up to and which ones they have resisted. Asking students to discuss, both in class and in journals, what they accept and reject, as well as their reasons why, entails a learning process for both students and instructor. Hearing from students why they have accepted or rejected particular knowledge claims could assist instructors to present these materials more effectively to future students.

Instructors' discussion of their role and position both as women and as teachers within a hierarchical and patriarchal institutional structure, where their interests lie both within such structure and against it, can illustrate to students how relations of domination are reproduced and encourage them to examine their own positions within these structures. Instructors must continually be conscious of our own power in the classroom and the ways in which this affects our interactions with students. As teachers, we must be able to talk about the historical processes of exclusion and discrimination and, at the same time, name and situate these processes as they are occurring contemporarily and in the classroom setting.[14] This task may be daunting indeed, when instructors' credibilities are questioned because of their ethnicity, age, gender, and the very fact that they have introduced progressive pedagogical practices in the classroom.

As we strive to unlearn our own traditional educational training and to develop critical feminist and antiracist pedagogical practices, we will be confronted with a series of challenges. The most significant of these is that we work within the very structure that we wish to challenge, hence we are confronted with a lack of institutional support for teaching practices that challenge authority.[15] This, coupled with other demands of academia (e.g., research, writing, publishing, administrative work, and competition for jobs in a time of increasing cutbacks), has an impact on our ability to work in an engaged way with our students or even to discuss the pedagogical

challenges that we face. Universities are, of course, inscribed with the relations of domination of the larger society, primarily sexism, classism,
racism, and heterosexism. By focusing on the banking system of education
and the challenges against pedagogical practices designed to undermine it,
we do not want to divert attention from other sources and forms of student
resistance. Despite the institutional and structural impediments, we wish
to "take human agency seriously" (Giroux, "Reproduction, Resistance and
Accommodation" 111) and, therefore, we believe that we must continue to
strive, individually and collectively, for more effective ways of working
progressively in our respective teaching environments. Our starting point
should be to view students' resistance as a positive factor; echoing Magda
Lewis's strategic advice, we should respond to resistance as an "active discourse of struggle derived from a complex set of meanings" in which student "practices are invested" (486).

●   ●   ●

NOTES

1. Authors' names have been listed in alphabetical order. This paper was
partly generated as a result of presentations each of us did at a conference entitled
"Knowing the Questions and the Questions of Knowing: Strategies for Feminist
Research, Pedagogy, and Knowledge in the 1990s" held in Halifax, Nova Scotia,
May 6–7, 1995 at Mount St. Vincent University. The authors would like to thank
Maureen McNeil and Roger Simon for their inspiration, encouragement, and help-
ful comments on earlier drafts of this paper.

2. The "banking system" refers to an educational system that is hierarchical
and based on relations of authority where students are the passive recipients of
"objective" knowledge as it is handed down by a knowledgeable authority, the
professor/teacher. It is a system where teachers memorize "objective/neutral" facts
and transfer these to students who repeat these same "facts" for evaluation. In
Freire's words, the banking system of education is "based on the depositing of 'reports' in the educatees" (*Pedagogy of the Oppressed* 149).

3. As we finalize this article, affirmative action is being dismantled in California. On some Canadian university campuses opposition to the practice of affirmative action in hiring teachers has been vociferous and given routine attention in
major newspapers. See, for example, Phil Resnick, "How UBC Is Embracing Reverse Discrimination," in *The Vancouver Sun* Sept. 21, 1996.

4. Historically, feminists' attention to identity helped to politicize areas like
sexuality, and identity politics were seen as central to the practice of radical, progressive politics. Distortions of this original intent, however, have sometimes re-

sulted in the move away from discussing institutional power to an apolitical, personal introspection.

5. This course was cotaught by three female instructors. While the pedagogical dilemmas of this course were discussed by all three instructors throughout its duration, the final analysis in this paper reflects the views of only one of the instructors. It is this person's educational life history and social location that are profiled in this paper.

6. There is evidence increasingly emerging in literature that such challenges are not exceptional, but rather the role in female- and/or minority-taught classes (Hoodfar; James; Mukherjee; Ng). The difficulty of working with white male students in particular has been noted by others, too (Sleeter 21).

7. They misconstrued it as preferential hiring and cited examples of what they perceived as white males being discriminated against in contemporary society.

8. See Evangelia Tastsoglou, forthcoming.

9. It is not clear why the female students were quiet, but Magda Lewis (482–84) offers some very convincing explanations about why female students may keep silent in mixed-gender classrooms. The Aboriginal student's frequent absence from class did not appear to be related to classroom dynamics but rather was the result of pressing personal problems.

10. Maher and Tetreault would insist that the women's studies classroom should not "speak theoretically" or "move beyond personal perspectives to a comparison of approaches in the abstract" or "divest discussions of experiential positional groundings." Other scholars, such as Sternhell, would disagree.

11. "Convergent thinking" forces the student to converge on the right answer, as opposed to learning by "divergent" production in which students are required "to produce their own answer" (J. P. Guilford, cited in Takata 253).

12. In suggesting that students may have to progress through different stages or go through a learning process, we do not wish to reinforce the notion that this process is linear or that it has a definite end point. Although critical, integrative analysis is the goal, the meaning of this is not fixed and is continually being learned and explored in each particular learning context.

13. In her discussion of traditional versus feminist students, Barbara Hillyer Davis suggests that instructors need to be sufficiently flexible to be able to validate and respond to all "levels" and "types" of student voice (92, 96–97).

14. For example, the absence, in particular, of Aboriginal, Black, and students of color in our classrooms is a continual reminder of systemic racism and its impact on access to education.

15. Extending Peta Tancred's dated analogy about the relationship between women's studies and the university, we may be the equivalent of "a state-funded communist cell, nonviolent and amicable, within Margaret Thatcher's [. . .] government" (Tancred 12).

WORKS CITED

Bannerji, Himani, Linda Carty, Kari Dehli, Susan Heald, and Kate McKenna. *Unsettling Relations: The University as a Site of Feminist Struggles*. Toronto: The Women's Press, 1991.

Briskin, Linda. *Feminist Pedagogy: Teaching and Learning Liberation*. Ottawa: Canadian Research Institute for the Advancement of Women, 1990.

Brown, Elsa Barkley. "African-American Women's Quilting." *Signs: Journal of Women in Culture and Society* 14.4 (1989): 921–29.

Calliste, Agnes, George Sefa Dei, and Jean Belkhir. "Canadian Perspectives on Anti-Racism: Intersection of Race, Gender and Class." *Race, Gender and Class* 2 (1995): 5–10.

Cannon, Lynn Weber. "Fostering Positive Race, Class, and Gender Dynamics in the Classroom." *Women's Studies Quarterly* 1–2 (1990): 126–34.

Currie, Dawn. "Subject-ivity in the Classroom: Feminism Meets Academe." *Canadian Journal of Education* 17.3 (1992): 341–63.

Davis, Barbara Hillyer. "Teaching the Feminist Minority." *Learning Our Way: Essays in Feminist Education*. Eds. Charlotte Bunch and Sandra Pollack. New York: The Crossing Press, 1983. 89–97.

Dei, George Sefa. "Integrative Anti-Racism: Intersection of Race, Class, and Gender." *Race, Gender and Class* 2.3 (1995): 11–30.

_____. "The Challenges of Anti-Racist Education in Canada." *Canadian Ethnic Studies* XXV.2 (1993): 36–51.

Ellsworth, Elizabeth. "Why Doesn't This Feel Empowering? Working Through the Repressive Myths of Critical Pedagogy." *Harvard Educational Review* 59.3 (1989): 297–324.

Fekete, John. *Moral Panic: Biopolitics Rising*. Montreal-Toronto: Robert Davis, 1994.

Freire, Paulo. *Pedagogy of the Oppressed*. New York: Herder and Herder, 1972.

_____. *Education for Critical Consciousness*. New York: Continuum, 1973.

Giroux, Henry A. *Multiculturalism and the Politics of Difference*. New York: Peter Lang, 1993.

_____. "Postcolonial Ruptures/Democratic Possibilities"; "Cultural Studies, Resisting Difference, and the Return of Critical Pedagogy"; and "Decentering the Canon: Refiguring Disciplinary and Pedagogical Boundaries." *Border Crossings*. New York: Routledge, 1992. 19–38, 161–79, 89–110.

_____. "Postmodernism as Border Pedagogy: Redefining the Boundaries of Race and Ethnicity." *Postmodernism, Feminism and Cultural Politics*. Ed. Henry Giroux. Albany: State University of New York Press, 1991. 217–56.

_____. *Teachers as Intellectuals: Toward a Critical Pedagogy of Learning*. South Hadley, MA: Bergin and Garvey, 1988.

_____. "Theories of Reproduction and Resistance in the New Sociology of Education." *Harvard Educational Review* 53 (1983): 282–93.

_____. "Reproduction, Resistance, and Accommodation in the Schooling Process." *Theory and Resistance in Education: A Pedagogy for the Opposition.* Ed. Henry Giroux. South Hadley, MA: Bergin and Garvey, 1983.

Giroux, Henry, and Peter McLaren. "Teacher Education and the Politics of Engagement: The Case for Democratic Schooling." *Harvard Educational Review* 5.3 (1986): 213–38.

Higginbotham, Elizabeth. "Designing an Inclusive Curriculum: Bringing All Women into the Core." *Women's Studies Quarterly* 1 and 2 (1990): 7–23.

Hoodfar, Homa. "Feminist Anthropology and Critical Pedagogy: The Anthropology of Classroom's Excluded Voices." *The Canadian Journal of Education* 17.3 (1992): 303–20.

hooks, bell. *Teaching to Transgress: Education as the Practice of Freedom.* New York: Routledge, 1994.

James, Carl E. "I've Never had a Black Teacher Before." *Talking About Difference.* Eds. Carl James and Adrienne Shadd. Toronto: Between the Lines, 1994. 125–47.

Lather, Patti. "Feminist Perspectives on Empowering Research Methodologies." *Women's Studies International Forum* 11.6 (1988): 569–81.

_____. *Getting Smart: Feminist Research and Pedagogy With/In the Postmodern.* New York: Routledge, 1991.

Laitinen, Arja, and Arto Tiihonen. "Narratives of Men's Experiences in Sport." *International Review for Sociology of Sport* 25.3 (1990): 185–200.

Lewis, Magda. "Interpreting Patriarchy: Politics, Resistance and Transformation in the Feminist Classroom." *Harvard Educational Review* 60.4 (1990): 467–88.

Maher, Frances, and Mary Kay Thompson Tetreault. *The Feminist Classroom: An Inside Look at How Professors and Students Are Transforming Higher Education for a Diverse Society.* New York: Basic Books, 1994.

Manicom, Ann. "Feminist Pedagogy: Transformations, Standpoints, and Politics." *Canadian Journal of Education* 17.3 (1992): 365–89.

Middleton, Sue. *Educating Feminists: Life Histories and Pedagogy.* New York: Teacher's College Press, 1993.

Mohanty, Chandra. "On Race and Voice: Challenges for Liberal Education in the 1990s." *Cultural Critique* 1989/90: 179–208.

Morrow, Marina. "Feminist Anti-Violence Activism: The Struggle Towards Multi-Centred Politics." Doctoral diss., Ontario Institute for Studies in Education of the University of Toronto, 1997.

Mukherjee, Arun. "The Race 'Consciousness' of a South Asian (Canadian of Course) Female Academic." *Talking about Difference.* Eds. Carl James and

Adrienne Shadd. Toronto: Between the Lines, 1994. 201–07.

Ng, Roxana. "Sexism and Racism in the University." *Canadian Woman Studies* 14.2 (1994): 41–46.

Patai, Daphne, and Noretta Koertge. *Professing Feminism: Cautionary Tales from Inside the Strange World of Women's Studies*. New York: Basic Books, 1994.

Simon, Roger. *Teaching Against the Grain: Texts for a Pedagogy of Possibility*. New York: Bergen and Garvey, 1992.

Sleeter, Christine E. "Introduction: Multicultural Education and Empowerment." *Empowerment Through Multicultural Education*. Ed. Christine Sleeter. Albany: State University of New York Press, 1991.1–23.

Smith, Dorothy. *The Everyday World as Problematic: A Feminist Sociology*. Toronto: University of Toronto Press, 1987.

_____. "An Analysis of Ideological Structures and How Women Are Excluded: Considerations for Academic Women. Women and Education." *A Canadian Perspective*. Calgary: Detselig Enterprises Limited, 1987. 241–64.

Solomon, R. Patrick. "Why to Teach from a Multicultural and Anti-Racist Perspective in Canada?" *Race, Gender and Class* 2.3 (1995): 49–66.

Somers, Christina Hoff. *Who Stole Feminism? How Women Have Betrayed Women*. New York: Simon and Schuster, 1994.

Sternhell, Carol. "The Proper Study of Womankind." *The Women's Review of Books* (Dec. 1994): 1–4.

Takata, Susan. "Who Is Empowering Whom? The Social Construction of Empowerment." *Empowerment Through Multicultural Education*. Ed. Christine Sleeter. Albany: State University of New York Press, 1991. 251–71.

Tancred, Peta. "Into the Third Decade of Canadian Women's Studies: A Glass Half-Empty or Half-Full?" *Women's Studies Quarterly* 3 and 4 (1994): 12–25.

Tastsoglou, Evangelia. "Mapping the Unknowable: The Stimulating Challenges and Bittersweet Rewards of Cultural, Political, and Pedagogical Border Crossings." *Anti-Racism and Critical Race, Gender, and Class Studies: A Canadian Reader*. Eds. Agnes Calliste and George Dei. Toronto: University of Toronto Press, forthcoming.

Tatum, Beverly Daniel. "Talking about Race, Learning about Racism: The Application of Racial Identity Development Theory in the Classroom." *Harvard Educational Review* 62.1 (1992): 1–24.

Yates, Lyn. "Feminist Pedagogy Meets Critical Pedagogy Meets Poststructuralism." *British Journal of Sociology of Education* 15.3 (1994): 429–37.

Transforming Institutional Obstacles into Opportunities

3

WRESTLING WITH THE DEVIL, OR
FROM PEDAGOGY TO PROFIT AND BACK AGAIN

Maryanne Dever

If, as Carolyn Shrewsbury has suggested, "feminist pedagogy begins with a vision of what education might be like but frequently is not" (8), what vision of the feminist classroom will practitioners take forward to the new century? Recent changes in the landscape of higher education have prompted me to tease out this question and to consider how feminist educators can respond creatively and effectively to a world of learning seemingly turned on its head by shifting institutional priorities, shrinking funding, and new technologies. Given the speed and drama of many of these changes, dedicated practitioners might be justified in questioning what space, if any, remains for feminist innovation or vision in institutions now dominated by the discourses of economic rationalism and the marketplace. But is the news all bad for feminist educators? Or can we locate in this moment an opportunity for the reinvigoration of our pedagogic practice and our programs? What follows are some speculative thoughts on how we might grapple with this level of upheaval, thoughts that essentially trace a double path. On the one hand I am keen to discover how, in the face of growing political and economic challenges to the principles and practice upon which they were based, we can preserve the valuable insights feminist practitioners have offered into the teaching and learning experience. After all, the case for continuing the quiet revolution we have started in our classrooms has seldom been stronger. At the same time, I'm curious to explore whether the same political and economic challenges we enumerate with such anxiety might actually provide a much needed occasion for us to rethink and perhaps even remake our understanding of feminist education, our roles as feminist educators, and our concept of a feminist classroom. In short, how might wrestling with the contradictions of the current educational environment help us in refurbishing our vision of a feminist education?

It is certainly true that many feminist assumptions about classroom practice and desirable models of teaching and learning aren't easily reconciled with the politics and priorities of the current educational environment where publicly funded institutions (and increasingly private ones) are pressured to accommodate more students invariably taught by fewer staff with shrinking resources (see Skeggs 475–79). Against a background of economic rationalism, burgeoning bureaucratization, and rapid corporatization, we have witnessed a redefinition of our universities' teaching goals away from earlier learning-based models toward conflicting and frequently counterproductive efficiency-based models. In my own university, this has meant subordinating concerns for what and how students learn to the crude economics of what each student is "worth" in relation to the budget of the teaching unit and to the cost of staffing a course. Thus we see increasing dependence upon mass lectures, reduced contact hours, and deteriorating staff-student ratios characterized as "streamlined servicing" by "good" departments and faculties. This paradigm shift presents quite particular difficulties for those feminist practitioners who would persist with nondominant teaching models. The immediate impact of these changes on a broad spectrum of feminist-inspired classroom practices is accurately attested to by bell hooks, who observes:

> even the best, most engaged classroom can fail under the weight of too many people. As I've become more and more committed to liberatory pedagogical practices, my classrooms have become just too large. So those practices are undermined by sheer numbers. [. . .] Overcrowded classrooms are like overcrowded buildings—the structures can collapse. (160)

But the problem is not simply that moving to bigger classes limits opportunities for innovation, although this is certainly a major problem. More damaging is the incursion of a marketplace mentality that equates those bigger classes with "better," more "efficient" teaching, thus encouraging "the belief that everything, including the relationship between teacher and learner, can be reduced to a set pattern [and an environment where] the idea that a course program could be modified by negotiation as it unfolds stands in stark contrast to the idea of a university as a corporation" (Terry 36). The same mentality fosters the assumption that one standard— preferably bulk delivery—pedagogic model fits all, sanctioning a return to the once denounced "banking model" of teaching (see Freire) where conservative notions of "knowledge transfer" consign our students to passivity, isolation, and competition in the classroom. There seems on the surface to be little room in this model of teaching and learning for the recognition of alternative pedagogic practices, let alone the valid educational and political reasons for using them. This new system is geared to highlighting and rewarding efficiency rather than innovation and to privileging an often ill-defined "product" over any sense of process. Rhetoric aside, in an environment such as this, "quality" assurance inevitably drifts toward a quantitative measure.

While these issues consume all practitioners who are committed to engaging critically with the nature of classroom transactions, they have particular resonances for those whose interests lie with feminist pedagogic practice. Indeed, the same pressures affecting the wider education system have also taken their toll in specific ways on the feminist classroom in recent years. Commentators note that commitment to curriculum transformation has generally remained high, resulting in widespread feminist-inspired change in the content of courses throughout the humanities and social sciences. But they suggest that involvement in innovative modes of teaching may actually have diminished in many institutions and that levels of classroom innovation now appear to rise and fall in inverse proportion to institutional pressures (see Lubelski 41; hooks 129). Various reasons for this trend have been explored. Lyndall Ryan, writing in the *Australian Universities' Review*, observes that the rise of women's studies and other feminist programs coincided with a dramatic and ongoing drop in university funding, arguing that as feminist programs fought to secure their positions in the face of successive rounds of funding cuts to the humanities and social sciences, individual practitioners may have been forced to compromise and to conform more closely to the prevailing classroom ethos in their institutions (3). It is also acknowledged that the heady early days of feminist activism in the academy where teachers frequently expressed their ambivalence toward the institutions that housed them through a subversion of the dominant pedagogic ethos were generally followed by a period of consolidation in which these same practitioners sought to legitimize the presence of feminist scholarship and women's studies within the academy. Wary of the fact that traditional teaching methods were privileged over their alternative ("Mickey Mouse") teaching methods, these practitioners may, in the interests of seeking all-important peer approval for their programs, have chosen to return, at least in part, to those more traditional methods.

In a similar vein, with increasing emphasis being placed upon teaching evaluations for promotion and tenure, individual staff members too may have been reluctant to persist with innovative teaching practices if confronted by students who might ultimately equate such innovations with diminished authority and competence. Added to this is the fact that many feminist programs have relied for long periods on the generous labors of committed staff teaching above their regular loads, understandably not a situation conducive to reflection, let alone innovation on the teaching front. Reviewing these same changes, Chris Ruggiero argues further that some of the changes may have been less conscious than others, speculating whether practitioners may not have simply internalized the values of a new, far less radical era, perhaps losing sight of feminist pedagogy's subversive possibilities. "Have we," she inquires, "as material reality has taken the ideological wind out of our sails, increasingly accommodated dominant values until they have reappeared within even the most alternative of programs?" (471). However we choose to interpret this trend, now is clearly an appropriate moment for feminist practitioners to reconsider how we make the challenge to the mainstream educational environment and its attendant values explicit through our teaching methods and how we promote an alternative vision of "what education might be like."

One of the original impulses for the introduction of women's studies and feminist programs was, as Janice Raymond has observed, the profound sense that "the teaching of the male academy ha[d] most often left its female learners with a passionless knowledge, devoid of any deep commitment to its content" (57–58). As our institutions continue to foster an increasingly homogenized and homogenizing teaching agenda elsewhere, a key defining feature of feminist courses in the coming years could well be our renewed commitment to alternative understandings of the contract between teachers and students and to the exploration of the gendered dimensions of knowledge and meaning-making in our classrooms. After all, a cornerstone of feminist pedagogic practice has long been the understanding that not all students are alike and that they do not all learn in the same ways. It is through the practical application of these insights with their attendant recognition of the politics of power and knowledge in the classroom that we can work to recover, retain, or reinforce that sense of the political and politicized context of learning that was once so central an element in our programs, but which may have been displaced or diluted in recent years. Examining the shifting conditions under which women today—both as teachers and as students—are required to undertake their intellectual work is also a crucial step in reidentifying wider institutional knowledge, patterns, and practice as political.

But how do we achieve this in practical terms in our own classrooms? How do we translate a series of desires and intentions into workable models of teaching and learning that fit our current environment? As we know, adopting and implementing feminist pedagogic principles need not mean delivering ourselves on political grounds into the most labor-intensive teaching options available. Despite murmurings to the contrary, innovative teaching has generally been about different work, not necessarily more work. But as the impact of both successive funding cutbacks and new market-oriented policies prompts us to scrutinize our classroom practice, how do we reconcile feminist learning outcomes with the realities of rising student numbers, new accountability structures, and the increasingly pressured lives of today's teachers and students? Although in many institutions new funding formulas eliminate the possibility of the small group teaching and coteaching practices so commonly advanced in feminist pedagogic literature, we need to continue to promote alternative models of learning that are flexible, participatory, and student-centered. There is also a growing awareness that these models of teaching and learning must contribute to empowering our students to negotiate the increasingly complex world beyond the classroom. At the same time, I believe teachers and students alike need to be liberated from the currently enshrined notion that students only "really" learn in a formal classroom setting in the physical presence of a teacher.

One answer may be to embrace so-called flexible, negotiated, or "open"[1] models of learning, models that transform (and critique) conventional classroom dynamics by offering students a more central and engaged role in classroom transactions. As Paine suggests, "open learning" promotes a more "student-centered" learning experience, "which allows the learner to choose how to learn, when to learn, where to learn, and what to learn as far as possible within the resource constraints of any education and training provision" (xi; see also Fraser and Deane). With its emphasis on students demonstrating greater independence and taking greater responsibility for their own learning, the open learning model appears a promising one for a variety of reasons. It encourages students to become active partners in an exchange of ideas, reshaping the contours of knowledge, power, and authority. As our students are also increasingly looking for ways to structure their learning around the multiple and often conflicting demands on their time both on and off campus, this format paves the way to more flexible, independent learning arrangements that are not so closely tied to fixed hours together in the seminar room or lecture theater. In replacing a passive learning environment with an active one where students are involved in decisions about their learning, this model of learning recalls Adrienne Rich's famous injunction to women students to "claim" their education rather than simply "receiving" it (231).

In my experience, Rich's directive has meant incorporating into my courses increased opportunities for negotiation, student choice, and self-regulation (see Ertmer and Newby). This might take the pattern, for example, of allowing students to decide on the form and format of their major assessment tasks, establishing for themselves how best to fulfill course requirements and learning outcomes. In my advanced-level course on feminist research methodology, for which students complete a major research project, information on basic project requirements (word-length equivalents and due date) is provided in week one; students have until week six to consult with me and to submit a formal research proposal in which they outline their project, the form it will take, members of the research team (if applicable), and their timetable for completion. In the past, students have successfully proposed exhibitions, oral histories, annotated resource guides to feminist archives, and websites as projects. Or, it could involve a radical departure from the regime of weekly classroom sessions. In recent years I have successfully incorporated regular "independent" or "reflective" learning weeks into courses: weeks in which students complete reading, research, and assessment exercises at their own pace in consultation with me, rather than attending a formal class. These can be placed at the conclusion of set topics to allow students to reflect upon and develop the ideas they have just encountered or, where students are required to tackle larger projects as in the research methodology course above, a block of three or four independent learning weeks with regular consultation sessions can be scheduled. Other productive alternatives to conventional classroom sessions might revolve around group devised projects, community-based internships, and programs of self-directed or mentored inquiry. For example, we are currently developing a special research internship in which advanced-level undergraduate students will undertake a monitored research project in and for a local women-centered organization, liaising with a member of our teaching staff but effectively undertaking all of the key work outside the classroom. Similarly, a number of our graduate students elect each year to undertake a course of self-directed inquiry where they work under supervision on a topic of personal interest, negotiating with their academic supervisor the parameters of their research and the form in which it will ultimately be presented. They maintain regular contact with their supervisor but attend no formal classes.

While many of these alternatives are easier to implement with smaller rather than larger numbers of students, it is possible with larger numbers to make greater use of work groups or teams that use reflective learning weeks to meet independently, share tasks, and attend consultation sessions as a group. Where I have used this option in recent courses, students have been surprised that in addition to the learning or assessment task at hand, they generally learned a good deal about one another, about team work, time management, and how to juggle their relative strengths and weaknesses in reading, writing, and researching. When these teams "clicked," members tended to develop a renewed commitment to and enthusiasm for the course through their ability to share and reflect upon the learning experience with a defined group within the larger class. More important, however, they (often unconsciously) reconfigured the conventional classroom dynamic by accepting that they could learn from one another and together as a group rather than relying solely on an instructor.

In each of the alternatives described here, the emphasis is upon dialogue and critical engagement with students, recognizing that they have something to offer or a knowledge base of their own from which to speak, and that "learning" and "class work" need no longer be synonymous with "class time." Obviously, the degree of independence expected of students should be commensurate with their particular stage of study, as beginning students may find it difficult to manage the same kinds or levels of independent work one might reasonably demand of their more advanced peers. Similarly, we need to be able to communicate effectively to students that these innovative approaches to teaching and learning, while offering them increased freedom, space, and choice in their study, should not be interpreted as being without structure or without a distinct set of commitments and responsibilities. The success of any innovative teaching program will depend on how well we are able to remake or revise our roles as both teachers and learners. Indeed, for these strategies to work we must be willing to transform our own roles from those of instructors responsible for holding a predetermined program of learning together to those of mentors and partners willing to take the risk of leaving many learning tasks and decisions in the hands of our students. And we must clarify the different set of expectations we have of those students with them from the outset. Arguably, it is only a short leap too from here to the types of mentored learning assumed by some of the new interactive educational software available for teaching on-line. By renewing debate on our campuses around issues of negotiated, independent, and mentored-learning models, feminist educators could provide an avenue to shine some much needed political and pedagogic light onto those otherwise technologically driven discussions of computer-facilitated teaching and learning. Indeed, feminist teachers committed to these particular learning models could make a significant contribution to campus discussion of both distance-education programs and innovative on-line courses by reminding our corporate administrators of just what is entailed in student-centered learning.

This pattern of negotiation and shared responsibility has the additional benefit of establishing an alternative collaborative-learning ethos that can stand in stark contrast to the traditional hierarchies and competitive individualism students encounter elsewhere in the educational system today. It promises a template for a different way of operating together in (and out) of the classroom, one that recognizes the value of student input and that focuses quite self-consciously on the issue of *how* we learn rather than simply *what* we learn. It is also a way of ensuring that what we offer in our classrooms is something more than "just another subject about women" (see Rowland 521). Not all of our students, however, will be familiar with the types of skills involved here, so it is important at the outset to spend time in class reflecting on students' existing expectations of the learning situation, how an alternative program of study might challenge those expectations, and how together we might transform the "contract" between teachers and students from the familiar fixed, hierarchical arrangement to a more reflexive and democratic one that balances individual with shared responsibilities, classroom support with student self-management. As Nancy Schniedewind points out, for such alternative teaching and learning strategies to succeed, we must foster "feminist process skills" in communication, organization, and interaction and remain sensitive to the fact that in the current environment "many students haven't had the opportunity to learn *how* to participate in a feminist classroom" (17). But when we take the time to foster these processes in our classes, we do so in the knowledge that students will be acquiring not only learning skills but also life skills.

But our students aren't—or shouldn't be—the only ones on a learning curve here. If we are to negotiate classroom and curriculum elements with our students, we need to do so from an informed base; that is, informed about those with whom we are negotiating. While the situation is changing, only a proportion of us currently teaching in women's studies and feminist programs have had the experience of studying in such programs as undergraduates, so we lack whatever insight that experiential knowledge might give into the situations of undergraduates currently enrolled in these programs. Building on this dilemma is the fact that our understandings of feminism, women's studies, and education in general are largely those of thirty- to fiftysomething academic practitioners and not those of the late-teenaged and twentysomething students we teach. Even in programs with large numbers of mature or returning students who are closer in age to their teachers, there is a strong likelihood that those students too have come to learning and to feminism by widely differing paths from those their teachers traveled. No matter how well we may feel we are doing now

in our teaching, we can only be helped by gaining a clearer picture of the
specific (and varied) expectations, needs, desires, ambitions, and anxieties
that bring young women into our classrooms today. Jean Fox O'Barr
framed this issue succinctly when she observed that "if connections are going to be made between what I am teaching and what students are learning, I have to learn much more about the students themselves" (266). Only
when we hear their voices will our students really begin to exist for us as
something more than ciphers or projections. Finding out more about our
"clientele" (as the corporate masters think of them) should be a crucial
step on the path to a fully negotiated classroom, a classroom that is based
upon acknowledged differences as well as acknowledged common ground.

Some may feel this question is best addressed class by class after the
fashion of informal focus-group discussions, in which the expectations and
attitudes of students and their teachers can be exchanged. Others may
wish to employ formal entry and exit surveys that promise analyzable data
to be shared and discussed among colleagues and provide for comparisons
over time or across different courses. For example, my colleagues and I are
currently implementing a three-campus pilot survey of enrolling women's
studies students to discover more about what draws students to our programs, what they hope to learn, and where they believe their studies will
take them. Whichever approach is adopted, the information garnered,
whether anecdotal or statistical, could go a long way toward determining
with what spectrum of expectations students now approach the feminist
classroom and how well those various expectations mesh with the existing
teaching and learning objectives in our programs. This is part of the reason
why for many years now I have begun all of my courses with a session in
which each student presents to the class her reasons for joining this particular course and what she herself would like to gain from taking part. After
all, it is one thing for me to establish a set of course objectives and outcomes and quite another to test those against the objectives and outcomes
the students have established for themselves. This usually means, however,
acknowledging that not all the students enrolled will necessarily begin and
end the course in the same place, that the paths of learning on which they
are embarking may take them in different directions, and that how they
approach and engage not only with the material in individual classes but
also with the broader politics of feminism may differ in dramatic and challenging ways. The task for us is to provide a pedagogic space where at least
some of those negotiations can take place. Tied to this is the fact that as local racial and cultural demographics continue to shift, as our classroom
populations include greater numbers of international students, and as our
universities implement further strategies for "internationalizing" our cam-

puses, acknowledging that we do not all come from the same place—literally as well as figuratively—will become an increasingly important element of our classroom practice. It will provide an avenue not only for analyzing the political, historical, and cultural contexts of teaching and learning in our individual institutions but also for exploring with our students new and more inclusive ways of knowing. Indeed, it is widely acknowledged that conventional classroom practices are more likely to meet productive challenges where students are truly diverse and bring with them differing assumptions about the educational process.

It is worth considering too whether our responses to the changing educational environment should go beyond issues of classroom dynamics to embrace important elements of course and curriculum development also. I have two reasons for suggesting this. First, in many areas funding cutbacks have prompted calls to justify, reduce, or rationalize course offerings and feminist programs have not been immune from these incursions. While such demands are never welcome in themselves, it is possible to find in them an avenue to open debate about the nature and direction of feminist study as we face the next century. Indeed, this might be an opportune moment to reexamine our programs of study, not in a piecemeal, reactionary way that seeks merely to accommodate successive rounds of external demands but in a systematic way that can assist us in producing coherent programs that fit the needs of a new generation of students. Could this then be a pertinent moment to consider whether there is or should be a common core curriculum for feminist study in our respective disciplinary or interdisciplinary areas? Are there specific knowledges (and accompanying skills) we feel it is important to explore with our students? If our program offerings must be "streamlined," which courses should be deemed central and which peripheral? Should all students undertaking feminist studies in whatever designated discipline be required, for example, to complete a course in the history of feminism, in contemporary feminist theory, or in feminist research methodology? The very exercise of accepting or rejecting such ideas can prompt us to articulate a range of often unacknowledged and unexamined judgments, values, investments, and priorities underpinning our programs in their current forms.[2] Maybe savage new political agendas can help us to explore our own sometimes less than transparent educational and political agendas, the famous "hidden curriculum" that often we would rather ignore.

My second reason for suggesting that we examine what we offer within the feminist classroom comes from a strong desire to reimagine how our curricula relate to the domain of the "vocational." Historically, our programs developed in concert with the wider women's movement, taking pride in the social accountability this relationship offered to academic feminism. But perhaps because these same programs did not emerge in direct response to employer demand for particular knowledge or training, we have seldom considered in detail how our teaching programs related to professional or vocational outcomes. Certainly successive strands of feminist critique by philosophers and social theorists provided us with the tools to dismantle the rigid polarization of theory and practice that characterized so many other academic projects. And yet, in the struggle to consolidate feminist scholarship as a genuinely "serious" academic enterprise, the balance in many programs has shifted over the years toward a more visible emphasis, for example, on the *studies* part of women's studies, with theoretical rigor often becoming the sole or superior marker of a program's legitimacy. There seems to be every reason for feminist practitioners to take the opportunity now to reexamine that emphasis and to reconfigure our relationship to the practical, the applied, and the vocational, challenging the conventional wisdom that feminist studies are necessarily nonvocational. After all, since feminist research and intervention have been instrumental in so many cultural shifts and policy transformations in the areas of rape laws, sexual harassment, citizenship, labor-market concerns, welfare, childcare, and so forth, why should we not seek to explore these and other applications more centrally in our curricula? Moreover, given that a significant proportion of our students do not progress to graduate study, should we not be attempting to integrate, exercise, and assess relevant skills (e.g., research techniques, policy analysis), as well as knowledge, in what we offer them? Should we not be making a greater effort to ensure that we offer our students appropriate skills to apply the knowledge they've acquired? Can we afford to continue to stress political competence over, or at the expense of, what we might term "social" competence in our curriculum development? Surely there are important practical, political, and pedagogic reasons why feminist practitioners should stress that the scope of their study does indeed extend to the vocational.

Such self-scrutiny might be useful too in helping us to meet that sometimes naive, sometimes pointed query as to what "use" feminist courses might be to our students and graduates. As Barbara Luebke and Mary Ellen Reilly remind us, "as funding continues to be cut, sometimes dramatically, among the most vulnerable programs are those perceived to be marginal, faddish, 'politically correct,' or peripheral to an institution's mission" (x). Conservative commentators have always been quick to cite women's studies and feminist programs as the definition par excellence of the "useless" and the "nonvocational." Overlooking for a moment the fact that both those terms usually beg definition in the contexts in which they

are used, I must admit to several, quite mixed responses to these labels. On
the one hand, I naturally would like to reject the idea that our work in the
feminist classroom has to satisfy someone else's unspecified notion of what
is "useful." While it is fair to say that today many areas within the humanities and social sciences are increasingly subject to this kind of scrutiny,
why should feminist work be singled out so consistently and so frequently
for the "utility test"? Why is it people who apparently have no trouble
imagining what you might "do" with linguistics or sociology, draw such a
blank with women's studies and feminism? After all, isn't the question really, what would you do *without* them? On the other hand, however, I find
there is a level on which this issue must be taken seriously by feminist
practitioners as I think there is much to be gained from taking up and exploring the implicit challenge offered by such offhand accusations. In the
face of the changes taking place both within higher education and outside
in the employment sector, I believe that there are cogent reasons why feminist practitioners can no longer afford to flinch before the question, "What
do you 'do' with feminist or women's studies?" First, when we as teachers
or course advisers are called upon to answer the question of what you "do"
with feminist-oriented studies, we can usually offer only the most general
of responses, frequently a list of occupations that we believe could or
should accommodate graduates with a demonstrated competence in feminist and gender issues. Whether, or to what extent, they actually do, often
remains a matter of conjecture. The bottom line is that we have seldom
gathered the type of information that would enable us to answer the question in a detailed and informed fashion, and I would strongly advocate that
feminist practitioners carry out the kind of graduate tracking and labor-
market research that will produce a clear and detailed picture of the paths
taken by our graduates.[3] Not only would such research be of assistance to
us in advising new generations of students on their career options but also
it could add vital strength to our hand when the financial masters and
their razor gangs come knocking on the door of so-called "useless" programs. Comparative international data would also enable us to construct
an extremely interesting snapshot of the differential social and cultural impact of our work across a variety of national domains. Moreover, by exploring in more detail how our students and graduates perceive their
studies in feminism relating to their future career goals and directions, we
may just find that they construct their feminist studies as vocational in
ways that we have never contemplated.

There are obviously considerable practical and political difficulties
associated with the dramatic changes we are currently witnessing in the
value systems and pedagogic paradigms of our universities. However, to

the extent that feminist practitioners have traditionally taken engagement with both the politics of knowledge production and the politics of pedagogy as central to their institutional mission, I would argue that we have a responsibility to respond directly and creatively to these changes, locating within them a range of opportunities for interrogating and ultimately reinvigorating both our programs and our pedagogic practice. Indeed, if we consider that feminist pedagogy has generally revolved around a broadly feminist response to the world of learning, the necessity for us to remain sensitive to the increasingly complex politics that shape that world is readily apparent. And posing creative challenges to those politics is the first step toward realizing our vision of what the world of learning might be like.

•   ■   ●

NOTES

1. "Open learning" as used here should not be confused with distance learning or off-campus study as exemplified in the British Open University model. As Paine's definition indicates, the term denotes a flexible learning experience in which individual students make key decisions about the process and pace of learning. See Lewis for further detail.

2. I am grateful to Julie McLeod of Deakin University for raising this point in discussion.

3. The most recent study of this kind is Luebke and Reilly. Together with two earlier studies from the National Institute of Education (Washington) by Reuben and Strauss, and Bose and Priest-Jones, it provides a useful methodological framework for undertaking research of this type. To date little comparative international data appear to be available.

WORKS CITED

Bose, Christine E., and Janet Priest-Jones. *The Relationship Between Women's Studies, Career Development, and Vocational Choice.* Washington, D.C.: National Institute of Education, 1980.

Ertmer, Peggy A., and Timothy J. Newby. "The Expert Learner: Strategic, Self-regulated, Reflective." *Instructional Science* 24 (1996): 1–24.

Fraser, Sharon, and Elizabeth Deane. "Why Open Learning?" *Australian Universities' Review* 40.1 (1997): 25–31.

Freire, Paulo. *Pedagogy of the Oppressed.* London: Macmillan, 1990.

hooks, bell. *Teaching to Transgress: Education as the Practice of Freedom.* New

York: Routledge, 1994.

Hughes, Kate Pritchard. *How Do You Know? An Overview of Writings on Feminist Pedagogy and Epistemology*. Melbourne: Victoria University of Technology, 1994.

Lewis, Roger. "The Progress of Open Learning." *Education and Training* 35.4 (1993): 3–8.

Lubelski, Cathy. "Teaching Methods in Women's Studies: Challenging the Mainstream." *Out of the Margins: Women's Studies in the Nineties*. Eds. Jane Aaron and Sylvia Walby. London: Falmer Press, 1991. 41–48.

Luebke, Barbara F., and Mary Ellen Reilly. *Women's Studies Graduates: The First Generation*. New York: Teacher's College Press, 1995.

O'Barr, Jean Fox. *Feminism in Action: Building Institutions and Community Through Women's Studies*. Chapel Hill: University of North Carolina Press, 1994.

Paine, Nigel, ed. *Open Learning in Transition: An Agenda for Action*. London: Kogan Page, 1989.

Raymond, Janice. "Women's Studies: A Knowledge of One's Own." *Gendered Subjects: The Dynamics of Feminist Teaching*. Eds. Margaret Culley and Catherine Portuges. Boston: Routledge & Kegan Paul, 1985. 49–63.

Reuben, Elaine, and Mary Jo Boehm Strauss. *Women's Studies Graduates*. Washington, D.C.: National Institute of Education, 1980.

Rich, Adrienne. *On Lies, Secrets and Silence*. New York: W. W. Norton, 1979.

Rowland, Robyn. "What Are the Key Questions Which Could Be Addressed in Women's Studies." *Women's Studies International Forum* 10.5 (1987): 519–24.

Ruggiero, Chris. "Teaching Women's Studies: The Repersonalization of Our Politics." *Women's Studies International Forum* 13.5 (1990): 469–75.

Ryan, Lyndall. "Women's Studies in Australian Higher Education: Introduction and Brief History." *Australian Universities' Review* 34.2 (1991): 2–7.

Schniedewind, Nancy. "Teaching Feminist Process in the 1990s." *Women's Studies Quarterly* 3–4 (1993): 17–30.

Shrewsbury, Carolyn. "What Is Feminist Pedagogy?" *Women's Studies Quarterly* 3–4 (1993): 8–16.

Skeggs, Beverley. "Women's Studies in Britain in the 1990s: Entitlement Cultures and Institutional Constraints." *Women's Studies International Forum* 18.4 (1995): 475–85.

Terry, Les. *Teaching for Justice in the Age of the Good Universities Guide*. Melbourne: Victoria University of Technology, 1995.

4

FEMINIST WOLVES IN SHEEP'S DISGUISE
Learning Communities and Internships

Jane A. Rinehart

INTRODUCTION

During the two-year-long process of designing, proposing, and gaining approval for the women's studies program at my university,[1] faculty members leading the effort met with many different university groups. One of these meetings, coming at the very end, was with the board of trustees. A few of us[2] were asked to have a discussion with the board before the vote on approval of the program would be taken. I was confident that the matter would not have gotten to this level without significant administrative support, and I felt optimistic about the outcome. Still, it was a difficult audience, despite the supportive presence of the wife of a past board president who had requested an invitation to the meeting as an observer.

We gave a short talk emphasizing points from the twenty-two-page proposal the board members had received a month earlier, followed by time for questions. I must have been more nervous than I admitted to myself at the time because I have no memory of this portion of the meeting except for one exchange. One of the board members, an engineer, said that he had been struck by the emphasis on "transformation" in our proposal. He said this did not make sense to him: What needed to be transformed? How would offering certain classes transform anything? What did transformation have to do with education? He presented himself as "a practical man" having difficulty with what seemed to be a grandiose goal, and, by his lights, an unnecessary one. Whoa!

This has become a defining moment for me because it captures my experience of the hazards in explaining women's studies to people who are not necessarily opposed to it, but skeptical about the claims made for this

kind of education. I cannot vouch for this particular person's general attitude toward feminism and women's studies because I do not know him.
However, his question seemed to arise from a conviction not that feminist
education is a bad idea but that it is not a revolutionary one, or should not
be thought about in those terms. For those of us faculty members who had
rethought our disciplines, reoriented our scholarly work and our teaching,
discovered new ways of relating to colleagues, and formulated big questions about the practices of our society and culture, women's studies definitely seemed to be a radical project with potential to change everything in
the university and society. It still does, and there are still folks like that
trustee who keep asking me to explain what I mean by that.

Having been put on this particular spot many times, it took me too
long to learn that sometimes it is better to leave out the radical impact
version of what we are doing in women's studies and focus instead on addressing practical concerns about how women's studies can make a positive difference in the "bottom line." This doesn't mean that I have given
up on the transformational quality of women's studies; actually, I have
more faith in it than ever because I have had direct experiences of that
kind of impact on students and colleagues since our program began in
1991. But I don't think that I have to emphasize this in all of the conversations I have with members of my university community. Sometimes, it
seems better to take a different tack and focus on women's studies as a
sound investment that brings the sort of immediate returns administrators
and trustees find impressive.

We live in hard times—hard for feminists, hard for educators, even
harder for feminist educators. The first blush has worn off women's studies,
and there are numerous critics of this educational project, both inside and
outside the university. Critics like Allan Bloom, Dinesh D'Souza, Wendy
Kaminer, Karen Lehrman, Daphne Patai and Noretta Koertge, Katie
Roiphe, and Christina Hoff Sommers have received a sympathetic hearing
for their charges that feminists have hijacked the academy, substituting
stale political ideology and groupthink for scholarship and abandoning the
classics for sensitivity training sessions. The opponents of feminist and
multicultural educational initiatives have been very adept at seizing the
higher ground and scoring points for their view of the terrain. Several
women's studies teachers have expressed frustration about how successful
this caricature has been; we hardly recognize ourselves and our universities
in these descriptions of feminist-dominated, anti-intellectual, rabidly
politicized campuses where students emote for academic credit and conservative white men (professors and administrators) fear (rightly) for the fu-

ture of western civilization (e.g., see hooks; Deats and Lenker; Rhode).

Apart from a particular animus toward women's studies and other efforts to open up the university curriculum to different questions and subjects, there are several other threats to many forms of educaional innovation. These include reduced funding, calls for basic education (no frills), students' and parents' narrow identification of what constitutes a "practical" education, and administrators' view of students and parents as consumers who should be "satisfied." Women's studies educators can make strong arguments for the necessity of including scholarship about gender and about women's lives and accomplishments in the curriculum, and we can show that this kind of education makes sound practical sense in our changing world. However, people who have a short list of practical subjects and a limited view of a college education as job training often dismiss these arguments. In addition, women's studies courses sometimes disturb students by calling into question cherished assumptions and habits. Although this is often affirmed as a goal of education, in practice many universities are fearful of offending students, parents, alumni, legislators, and benefactors whose financial support is vital.

At the same time, there are trends in the conversation about higher education that can be construed as favorable to the goals identified with women's studies. These general goals of today's universities include recruitment and retention of students and keeping costs down. Two educational innovations that serve these goals are the formation of learning communities and internship programs. In this kind of environment, characterized by both opposition to women's studies and some compatibility between the strengths of feminist education and the values espoused by university leaders, I think it is necessary for women's studies faculty and administrators to be nimble, shrewd, and creative. What do I mean by that? I think the project of bringing feminism into institutions of higher education is not an all-or-nothing venture. It is more like infiltration and subversion than overt attack. It is disingenuous for us to pretend that we do not want to be at the tables where decisions are made and budgets drawn up. Achieving results in those discussions is more likely when we are able to connect our goals with general ones to which many universities are already responsive. Of course, there are dangers of co-optation in this way of proceeding, but "everything is dangerous, which is not exactly the same as bad. If everything is dangerous, then we always have something to do" (Foucault 343).[3] I prefer to wrestle with these dangers when that is an option, rather than those associated with refusals to compromise on any matters.

Decisions about how to do women's studies are political.[4] Politics always involves choices that measure the distances between what we have, what we want, and what we can achieve. Different forms of politics calculate these distances differently. Some forms give up on the tensions the distances produce and settle on one piece of the territory; e.g., by becoming idealistic outsiders who always criticize but offer no alternatives for action short of revolutionary change; or by becoming cynics who deny that any change is possible and seek instead to make deals that protect immediate self-interests. A different option is to explore places where the three points overlap—where what we have makes possible some of what we want. This is, I believe, the choice manifested in the project of women's studies, although not perhaps the political position of everyone involved in women's studies. By establishing women's studies within the institutions of higher education, feminist teachers and scholars have opted for reformist practices, although perhaps holding on to revolutionary aspirations. Operating in this fashion does not have to mean giving up on our visions and best hopes, although it always contains the possibility of becoming accommodated to the status quo. Sometimes, it preserves and fosters our ideals because achieving a piece of what we desire and succeeding with that allows us to make a stronger argument for gaining more.

Developing this preference for practical wisdom has not come easily for me. When I first began teaching courses incorporating feminist critiques, I tended to regard any disguise as evidence of hypocrisy. I was determined to state my views fully and forcefully on all occasions. This did not mean I strove for confrontation or rudeness. I was careful of the feelings of others and pleasant in manner. But I was not strategic. I did not bring to my early work in women's studies a well-honed sense of the possibilities in each situation. I was more concerned with avoiding the temptation to please. I still honor that way of proceeding and recognize it as the best course some of the time. However, I am grateful to have learned from a valued colleague[5] another way of acting that takes into account likely openings for success.

I think women's studies can accomplish many of its goals by acting strategically to integrate its purposes with general university aims. In this essay, I will describe how learning communities and internships can serve the aims of women's studies education while also accommodating the "bottom line" thinking characteristic of many of the university's constituencies. These are practical innovations; that is, they are capable of being put to use.[6] They reflect a commitment to engagement and a willingness to struggle with the risks this entails. In the final section, I will return to general issues in the politics of doing women's studies as a framework for assessing the perils and promises of such practicality.

LEARNING COMMUNITIES

"Learning communities" is a broad term that covers various approaches to linking courses so that students gain a more integrated perspective on what they are learning, and faculty and students have more opportunities for enriching intellectual conversation (Gabelnick et al.; Graff 178–96). Such communities have positive effects on retention and satisfaction for faculty and students (Graff 185; McLaughlin 10, 18; Tinto and Love). They are also vehicles for faculty development. Learning communities are highly cost-effective, requiring little or no additional cost for significant result. There are five learning community models: Linked Courses (paired courses with individual instructors, but coordinated syllabi and assignments); Learning Clusters (three or four clustered courses with explicit connections developed by a faculty team); Freshman Interest Groups (three linked courses with a common first-year student cohort who also participate in some meetings with a peer advisor outside the classroom); Federated Learning Communities (three courses linked by an explicit theme, plus a seminar for credit led by a faculty member who acts as a "master learner"); and Coordinated Studies (the whole curriculum for a given semester or year is organized around interdisciplinary inquiry in team-taught programs).[7]

I have direct experience with the first model: a grant-funded pairing of two core-curriculum courses (philosophical ethics and studies in fiction) connected by an explicit focus on gender and feminist scholarship that was given during the spring 1993 semester. All students taking a degree in Gonzaga's College of Arts and Sciences are required to take a 200-level course in English literature (of which Studies in Fiction is one option) and a 300-level course in philosophical ethics. The courses composing Ethics and Fiction were listed under their department numbers and under women's studies, and a special flyer was distributed to students and faculty advisors explaining the learning community design and the focus on women's studies. Ethics and Fiction was optional; there were many other traditional alternatives for fulfilling the core requirements. This has both a positive and a negative side: the students enrolled in the course were highly motivated and interested in this kind of experience, and we missed the opportunity to persuade some skeptics of its value.

DESIGN OF ETHICS AND FICTION

I wrote the grant proposal for this project[8] and was involved throughout as a participant observer: as a resource teacher present in both classes, and as

a discussion partner for the two teachers outside of class. The grant sup-
plied funding for a small summer stipend to reimburse faculty for time
spent planning for the learning community and for producing materials for
a workshop to be given to interested faculty after the course was offered.
There was no provision for release time or adjunct replacement salaries because each of the linked courses was part of the teacher's regular teaching
load. The grant also committed the participating faculty to prepare a detailed report on the project for the Washington Center, and to discuss the
experience with its directors during their annual campus visit.

Ethics and Fiction was composed of a literature course that met three
times a week (Mondays, Wednesdays, and Fridays) and a philosophy
course that met two times (Tuesdays and Thursdays); the same twenty-two
students were enrolled in both of these courses. Each course had its own
teacher, but the syllabi, lectures, discussions, assignments, and journals
were coordinated. Decisions about all of these were shaped by a commitment to presenting feminist perspectives in the linked courses. This did not
mean that the students only read materials by feminist authors (they read
Hemingway, Faulkner, and Kant, for example), but that topics and questions central to feminist scholarship shaped how the readings were presented and interpreted. This learning community experiment was designed
to promote two founding goals of Gonzaga University's women's studies
program: to integrate the perspectives of feminist scholarship into the
university's core curriculum, and to foster interdisciplinary inquiry by students and faculty. Although the focus on any given class day was on readings drawn from either literature or philosophy, there was considerable
encouragement for movement back and forth across the boundary between
the disciplines in terms of assigned discussion questions and spontaneous
student responses.

The decision to connect the Ethics and Fiction design with charter
goals of the women's studies program at Gonzaga also meant that the
learning community was anchored in the university's mission statement.
The proposal to establish a women's studies program at Gonzaga University began with a rationale that drew explicitly on the university's identification with humanistic, Catholic, and Ignatian[9] educational traditions, and
the expression of these in the design of the university's requirements for
graduation (the core curriculum). This was a deliberate move to characterize women's studies as integral, rather than marginal, to the university's
general project. It also reveals our sense that arguing for a women's studies
requirement in the core would not have been successful at that time. Instead, the more practical course of action was to present women's studies
scholarship as a legitimate expression of the university's traditions and

ideals and to state that the program, in addition to offering a predominantly upper-division concentration in women's studies, would also develop optional courses within the required curriculum. Such core courses might be taken by many students without a declared interest in the field of women's studies, such as the majority of students who registered for Ethics and Fiction as a means of fulfilling their philosophy and literature requirements. The university's mission statement also commits to helping students integrate what they learn; explicit inquiry across disciplines is one strategy for assisting students in making connections among the questions, themes, and perspectives of various scholarly approaches. The program proposal claims this as a potential benefit of establishing women's studies, an avowedly interdisciplinary enterprise. Here too, then, Ethics and Fiction echoed the original vision of the women's studies program as located within the university's mission. Both echoes, the integration of women's studies into the core curriculum and an opportunity to practice interdisciplinary inquiry, were a self-conscious device to legitimate the learning community by associating it with the rationale of the women's studies program and of the university's mission.

The design of Ethics and Fiction also emphasized that collaborative learning strategies would be employed. After our women's studies program was launched in 1991, the faculty teaching in the program developed an explicit collective commitment to fostering collaborative learning. This pedagogical strategy was another connection between the two courses. "Collaborative learning" refers to a variety of classroom practices designed to foster shared inquiry and responsibility for a course. Students actively participate in figuring out course readings and formulating some agreements about their interpretation. Knowledge is not transmitted from the teacher to the students but accomplished through rigorous individual preparation for class, structured small-group conversations, and plenary sessions facilitated by the teacher in which the small groups give reports and the whole class works toward consensus (Bruffee). The collaborative learning approach and the learning community format are mutually reinforcing. Learning communities emphasize collaborative discussions among students and collaborative learning "locates knowledge in the community rather than in the individual" (Whipple 5). Matthews presents a cynical view of various efforts to give students greater responsibilities, placing collaborative learning within her discussion of cost-cutting measures on American campuses (180). This view does not fit either our aims or experience. Using collaborative learning methods in many women's studies classes and developing the Ethics and Fiction learning community have not saved money for our university in the sense of reducing salary allocations for teaching assistants (we do not have these in the College of Arts and Sciences). My point about the practicality of these innovations is based upon their limited cost and high payoffs in terms of faculty and student development.

Both the proposal to establish the women's studies program and documents developed within the first year of the program's existence explored the similarities and differences between collaborative learning and feminist pedagogy. Both are forms of active learning. Feminist pedagogy shares with collaborative learning models the conviction that classrooms should be places of activity where ideas are worked out together rather than passively received. Both the teacher and the students create what happens in the classroom. In addition to the commitments to shared responsibility and active engagement that it shares with collaborative learning methods, feminist pedagogy is a form of critical pedagogy committed to questioning social and cultural structures of privilege based on class, race, sexual orientation, and gender. Feminist pedagogy views gender as a topic of investigation, as a significant dimension of classroom relationships, as an influence on individuals' approaches to learning, and as a factor that has shaped the knowledge produced in various disciplines. Feminist pedagogy affirms that a rigorous pursuit of truth in the classroom necessitates an awareness of how gender constructs our texts and our conversations, and of how gender interacts with other differences that produce significant social inequalities. In the practice of feminist pedagogy, teachers and students assist each other in seeking knowledge about connecting this knowledge with their area of study and exploring how unjust structures might be changed.[10]

Ethics and Fiction was explicitly designed as collaborative and feminist, focused on an active classroom process of constructing understandings interdependently and on subject matter that criticized the assumptions and practices that produce and sustain social injustice. In both the literature and philosophy courses, the aim was not to reproduce the traditional forms of analysis and reflection but to show how these are transformed by attention to characters, experiences, and themes that usually have been excluded. When Alice Walker's Celie says, "I'm poor, I'm black, I may be ugly and can't cook, a voice say to everything listening, but I'm here" (214), she articulates the twofold aim of feminist pedagogy: to bring into speech the differences that make a difference and to challenge these. In retrospect, it is not surprising that the Ethics and Fiction students had their most powerful experience of collaborative transformational learning while working on *The Color Purple*, a novel about this same kind of learning.

Connecting collaborative and feminist pedagogies in the design of

Ethics and Fiction was, therefore, another instance of strategic thinking: associating our work with widely accepted methods in the academy, while also insisting on its distinctive commitment to liberatory goals. This kind of linkage resists the placement of feminist education as marginal and also refuses to sacrifice its ideals. Choosing subject matter that subverts dominant orderings of what is valuable and inviting students to examine this material collaboratively positions women's studies simultaneously both within and on the edge of current academic practices. It is the general argument of this essay that this is a productive location, although not an easy one. It is productive because it allows women's studies to gain resources, and uneasy because this acceptance must always be weighed against our commitments to challenging its terms.

EXECUTION OF ETHICS AND FICTION

Each of the teachers was present for all of the classes, and the resource teacher attended approximately two thirds of the time. On her nonteaching days, each teacher sat among the students, responded to lectures, and joined the small-group discussions; the resource teacher regularly participated in these ways. This was not part of the original plan, but emerged as an expression of the pleasures that accompanied this work. The classes were too good to miss and each of the faculty members enjoyed learning a different discipline. The decisions by the three faculty members to attend all or most of the classes taught in Ethics and Fiction made this learning community a hybrid form in that the faculty did function as team teachers, although the "extra course" (actually two extra courses for the resource faculty member) for each of them was an overload for which they did not receive a salary or release-time compensation.

This extra level of involvement would probably not be necessary if the learning community is offered in the future by the same two teachers, but it did seem important in its initial phase. It allowed the teachers to develop a much greater awareness of how the learning community was working and of what changes were needed than would have been possible otherwise. This suggests to us that a first-time experience of a linked-courses learning community may more closely emulate team teaching, at least in terms of the investment of time and energy of the participating teachers, than the distinctions in the definitions of these learning community models allows. Viewing the linked courses as individual courses that are part of the regular teaching load of each instructor is a single-edged sword. It allows the linked-course model to have strong appeal to administrators because it can be readily incorporated into existing structures and does not require extra expenditures in the form of release time or overload compensation. Administrators receive the dull side of the sword—no bleeding. At the same time, our experience indicates that simple linkage masks a considerably greater investment on the part of the faculty who may have to become a team in order to make the connections and build the community they intend. Faculty may, therefore, shed a considerable amount of blood due to encountering this sharp edge. I will return to this point later in relation to the topics of faculty satisfaction and institutional obstacles.

Since collaborative learning and feminist pedagogy are departures from the traditional structure of the classroom, two classes at the very beginning of Ethics and Fiction were spent discussing these approaches, focusing on a reading by Parker Palmer and on a summary of the "chilly climate" research by Roberta Hall and Bernice Sandler. The remainder of the first three weeks in each course was spent developing skills in working with materials from each of the two disciplines. In the fourth week, the philosophy class discussed an assigned short story in connection with the philosophical concept of autonomy. During this discussion, the students also introduced a story they had read previously for the literature class. These two moves initiated the process of making the connections between the two courses more explicit and, after mid-semester, the students and teachers made a major commitment to doing this.

The students' comments on the mid-semester evaluations expressed a strong desire for more opportunities to link the two courses explicitly, and the three teachers had a lengthy discussion of how to respond to this request. This resulted in an agreement to give priority to the interdisciplinary dimension. That commitment was expressed in several decisions: streamlining the syllabus by eliminating some of the planned readings, allowing more time for interdisciplinary writing and talking, including some review lectures that related key philosophical concepts to specific literary examples, and giving students greater responsibility for initiating and directing class discussions of the texts. The benefits of these decisions were demonstrated in the unit on friendship and moral development that linked Alice Walker's *The Color Purple* with various writings on virtue ethics and care ethics. During this unit, the students really emerged as active learners and that energy continued throughout the remainder of the semester. The dynamic of development in Ethics and Fiction corresponds closely to Jill Tarule's description of collaborative learning as a two-phase process:

> When collaborative classrooms work, the discourse usually moves through two phases: a first in which a "vocabulary" that may in-

clude specific disciplinary terms is established and always includes a more inchoate vocabulary of how conversation will proceed, and a second in which the learning becomes lodged in the discipline and the discourse. In the second phase, roles often shift dramatically for both the teacher and the student. (292)

STUDENT RESPONSES

Learning communities and collaborative learning methods empower students. Both take the position that learning can be an opportunity for discovering the value and efficacy of one's own resources and abilities. Such discovery is more likely to occur in courses based on practices of interdependence and shared responsibility, courses that require students to use their resources and talents rather than relying on the teacher to be the sole source of knowledge. One manifestation of this empowerment effect in Ethics and Fiction is that the students made suggestions for changes throughout the semester, rather than saving these for evaluations filled out during the final week of classes. At mid-semester, the students declared that they wanted more explicit and direct connections between the two courses. Initially, the teachers had employed an "echoes model"; that is, each course would echo themes from the other but identifying those echoes would be left to individuals and would be likely to happen mostly outside the classroom. In response to the students' request, the two teachers revised the syllabi and assignments to foster a more direct conversation about shared themes. Another example of empowerment is the students' decision to rearrange the desks into a circle in the literature class before the faculty arrived. The circle had been used previously in the philosophy class, and the students wanted to send a message that they preferred to face each other even during lecture classes.

Another aspect of student empowerment is the visibility students can attain by participating in a curricular alternative. Since almost all of the courses at Gonzaga University are not linked, clustered, or federated, Ethics and Fiction drew attention from students, faculty, and administrators. The students enrolled in this learning community were often asked about it. They were given many opportunities to explain what was different about this kind of experience and this encouraged them to think more about what they expected from their college courses. Four students from the course participated as speakers at the end of the semester workshop for faculty, an uncommon occurrence on my campus. At the workshop all four spoke about how the course had given them confidence that they took with them into a variety of situations. One cited an instance where she spoke up in another class to challenge her classmates about the way they related to the teacher.

The gain in confidence is directly related to the increased responsibilities students have within learning communities. Those responsibilities may seem burdensome at first, and it did take some time for all of the students in Ethics and Fiction to become comfortable with the expectations of conscientious preparation for all the classes and regular oral participation in discussions. The students who spoke at the workshop all mentioned having to acquire new habits for this learning community. These new habits included less complaining, and that is a significant alternative to a common construction of academia today as a place where disgruntled student "customers" encounter faculty members unwilling to regard their work as analogous to selling a product (Delucchi and Smith; Edmundson). In Ethics and Fiction the prevailing model was one of partners, rather than antagonists.

FACULTY RESPONSES

The faculty reactions included both elation and exhaustion. The choice to become one another's students proved to be very significant in shaping both responses. As I mentioned earlier, this level of commitment was not planned, but developed spontaneously. The teachers were committed to early attendance, and their continuing attendance grew out of the satisfactions provided by those classes at the beginning of the semester. This decision proved to have several different meanings: the teachers entered into small-group discussions as participants, rather than authorities or facilitators; observing the teachers as learners shifted standard notions of how power is distributed in a classroom for both students and teachers; and the teachers were able to act as resources for each other about how the groups were working. All of these were viewed as positive consequences that reinforced the teachers' decision to keep coming to the classes. On the other hand, I am certain that these pleasures would have been more fully appreciated if release time had been available, at least for the two instructors. Our grant provided for summer planning time, materials, and for workshop costs. In retrospect, we realize that we should have sought either external or internal funding to reduce the teaching loads. We did not anticipate that we would spend so much time in each other's classes. Based on our experience, we would now advise faculty doing something similar for the first time together to seek the support of release time from another responsibility.

I believe that the intensive practices of collaborative learning in the classroom fostered desires for more of this. Just as the students initiated study groups outside class, the faculty members were drawn to spend more time together experiencing the course and discussing it with each other. All of the faculty involved in Ethics and Fiction have said that the experience increased their awareness of how lonely they usually are in teaching. University teaching allows for considerable autonomy, but the price for that is a limited sense of connection to colleagues. Sustained conversations among department or program faculty can offset this to some degree, but participating in a teaching team does so more fully. Being part of a team means that there are other teachers with whom one can share decisions about syllabi, assignments, and evaluation.[11] The movement away from loneliness is also accompanied by fears. It can be unsettling to teach a class with colleagues in the room or to expose the decisions one makes about a course to questioning by peers.

Faculty development can happen within such a combination of comfort and risk. Linked courses like Ethics and Fiction draw their faculty participants away from habitual practices and toward greater self-consciousness about their assumptions. In our frequent conversations, as well as in the time we spent listening to and watching each other in the classroom, each of us realized that we could adopt different premises and behaviors. The two teachers had very different styles of interacting with the students, and those differences became more visible in the learning community context. This made it possible for each of them to recognize the strengths and weaknesses in their own approach, as well as to learn from another model. Learning to change some specific teaching behaviors, such as how to respond to student comments during lectures or how to write advice on student papers, is facilitated by the direct exposure to alternatives that teaching the same students in partnership with a colleague affords. University teachers do talk about such issues with colleagues, but rarely do we have the chance to observe different strategies in action with students we also have come to know well.

OBSTACLES

In my experience, institutionalized rewards make the biggest difference in fostering innovations in curriculum and teaching methods. Linked courses overcome one budgetary impediment to constructing learning communities in that each teacher may then carry the community as part of her or his regular teaching load. The linked course's learning community format does not incur the same institutional costs as assigning two teachers to one course, so it does not appear on budgets as an extra expense. When the linked courses are part of the core curriculum, their cost-effectiveness is enhanced further in that recruitment of students will generally not be a problem and the courses are part of departments' standard curricula. As long as the registration details can be facilitated by the university's system, there are no obvious structural obstacles that must be surmounted.

Nevertheless, faculty perception that the extra effort that goes into teaching in a learning community will not count significantly in decisions about tenure and promotion can be a serious problem. Faculty handbook criteria for promotion and tenure, as well as the weight assigned to each of these, can either hinder or enhance faculty participation. For example, faculty members at my institution have held many discussions about whether various efforts to innovate in the classroom should be considered a type of professional development, thereby acquiring some extra significance in evaluations of their productivity. These discussions seem to reflect many faculty members' anxieties about how to allocate their time. After all, it is possible to avoid such a major commitment to teaching in a new way, still receive positive evaluations of one's teaching performance, and use the time not spent meeting with colleagues and attending extra classes to do research and writing. Unless the institution sends a clear message that developing and sustaining learning communities will be rewarded, many faculty members may choose safer routes to tenure and/or promotion. Several faculty participants in the Ethics and Fiction workshop brought up this issue. Gerald Graff addresses it as a challenge to integrate research interests and teaching innovations, allowing research obligations to be enriched and fulfilled within experimental modes of teaching (177). Since the three teachers involved in Ethics and Fiction published an article based on this experience, we can be said to have taken Graff's challenge (Bona et al.).

Furthermore, collaborative effort itself raises difficult issues in academic evaluation, which is typically focused on individual achievement. The academic community often operates within a lone-wolf model, making collaborative practice problematic in terms of professional recognition and reward (Kaplan and Rose 558; Weber et al. 251). Several faculty participants in the Ethics and Fiction workshop raised questions about support and rewards for this kind of investment, and the teachers who participated in the learning community resonated with these concerns. The collaborative effort required for teaching in a learning community brings support, enhanced risk taking, creativity, and stimulation. However, it can also make it more difficult to represent one's work as worthy of significant recognition in tenure and promotion processes. This difficulty is compounded when collaborative work appears too pleasurable because having a good time is often regarded as evidence that one is not doing serious work. In learning communities the problems and the rewards are inextricably connected and a rough balance between them is useful. The problems keep the community on the edge, prevent too much coziness, foster critique, and require creativity. The rewards provide the reasons for staying on the edge and doing these difficult things.

Fears of lower ratings on the student evaluations constitute another obstacle to faculty participation in learning community experiments. Numerical evaluation of teachers by students is now a common practice in higher education, and these numbers are often influential in decisions regarding retention, tenure, promotion, awards, and merit pay. Many faculty are understandably nervous about jeopardizing their scores by undertaking a new form of teaching, especially one that makes high demands on students for preparedness, involvement in class discussions, and commitment to the often unfamiliar challenges of interdisciplinary inquiry. Paul Trout claims: "Almost every professional educator I have ever talked to about this topic acknowledges that the specter of being evaluated by students, and having these evaluations factored into performance rankings, negatively affect his or her morale and pedagogic practice" (35). Our experience in Ethics and Fiction did not confirm the fear that student evaluations would be lower. This may be explained by two features of this learning community: the students who enrolled were volunteers, and the students who remained in the course after the deadline for add/drop had already been given much information about the expectations and requirements. The students fit Trout's characterization of engaged students: "students who have shown themselves to be responsible learners by reading the books on time, by picking up and examining handouts, by talking in class, by meeting with the instructor outside of class, by being hungry for new experiences" (35). It is likely that learning communities in institutions where these are not required will attract such motivated students, and that this will decrease the possibility of resistance and subsequent negative evaluations of the teachers.

All of these obstacles related to institutionalized rewards are significant. Although we were able to minimize some of these in the ways discussed above (by using our experience as the basis for a publication and by generating extensive documentation of positive evaluations by students), we are also involved now in discussions about how our faculty handbook criteria for reappointment, tenure, and promotion might be changed to encompass innovations in teaching as an important component. The National Women's Studies Association has also recently announced that program administrators will be involved in discussions on this same topic: influencing the construction of standards by which faculty are assessed in order to reflect more fully the kinds of work many of us in women's studies are already doing.[12] It is impossible to measure the specific impact of Ethics and Fiction on the later promotions of two of the faculty involved, but it probably was a positive factor.

IMPLICATIONS

Ethics and Fiction was a highly visible innovation at Gonzaga University. Apart from an optional first-year course bloc (courses in composition, speech, and critical thinking), this was the only such effort to link courses. In addition, the explicit commitment to feminist perspectives and to collaborative learning further enhanced its uniqueness. The workshop for twenty faculty volunteers also contributed to making Ethics and Fiction a hot topic on our small campus. Response to this workshop was so positive that we offered it again in the fall for about twice that number of participants. The students enrolled in the learning community reported that they frequently talked about it with their friends, and many of them participated in a lively study group in the library lounge that drew attention during finals week. Taken together, all of this activity constituted a positive advertisement for the women's studies program on the campus. As with any advertisement, it is difficult to assess which of the many possible readings took precedence, but the feedback we received in terms of requests to do this again or to speak with colleagues who were interested in doing something similar was uniformly affirming.

In addition, Ethics and Fiction has elicited a favorable response from administrators at Gonzaga University. The dean of the College of Arts and Sciences has been especially supportive of efforts to innovate in the curriculum and in teaching. We documented the success of Ethics and Fiction, both in the final report sent to the source of seed-grant funding and in the women's studies program's annual report to the dean. We brought it up in conversations with administrators. We have used it to support our argument for increased funding for the program, with a positive result. Presently, it is being incorporated in a grant application for funds to support a collegewide teaching center that would promote the formation of similar learning communities and other innovations. Finally, all of the faculty members associated with Ethics and Fiction won the major award for faculty achievement during the three years immediately following the end of the learning community. The public presentations of the citations accompanying those awards recognized the excellence of the work done for Ethics and Fiction. The presence of these plaques in the program offices enhances the reputation of women's studies on our campus.

The best part of the success of Ethics and Fiction was that it indicated a path for bringing new vitality into the core curriculum, which can often seem, to both students and faculty, more burdensome than exciting. Learning communities turn courses into conversations. The point of this is "not to add more tasks to teaching, but to take advantage of the missed chances for dialogue that are already latent in what teachers do every day" (Graff 193). Worries about faculty burnout more properly belong to the traditional system of unrelated courses and duplicated efforts rather than to mechanisms that allow faculty members to work together. Teaching within a richer context of relationships with students and colleagues is a strategy for addressing problems of too much work and too little satisfaction.

Ethics and Fiction also gave our women's studies program access to the resources of a wider conversation about learning communities. The seed grant from the Washington Center placed us within a network extending beyond our campus. We had several contacts with the directors and staff of the center. A description of this learning community appeared in the center's publication, and we were invited to present our experience at the center's conference for educators. These connections provided resources, support, and challenges. They also allowed us to make stronger claims for the women's studies program within our institution because we could present our work as helping to strengthen our university's reputation for commitment to excellence in undergraduate education. We have followed the Ethics and Fiction project with several different efforts to promote faculty and curricular development, e.g., leading a series of faculty discussions about collaborative learning and faculty mentoring, actively participating in formulating a new approach to faculty evaluation, and advising colleagues working on revision of the criteria for tenure and promotion. What we learned in Ethics and Fiction provides both the motivation to get involved in these ways and the collaborative skills and perspectives to make that involvement more productive.

Ethics and Fiction has only been offered once. The most important reasons for this are the conflicts produced by sabbatical schedules and changing responsibilities for administration of the women's studies program. When we were engaged in this learning community, two of us were serving as codirectors for the program; subsequent sabbaticals shifted this to each of us as an individual director and now to the third member of the Ethics and Fiction team. I expect that the course will be on the schedule again within the next year or two, and I also think that two of us may draw on the experience to design a different two-course link in literature and sociology: we are also encouraging other faculty give this kind of teaching a try, and there are some prospects on the horizon.

INTERNSHIPS

Internship programs have been developed in many institutions as a response to student concerns about the practical benefits of an undergraduate degree, especially in a liberal arts discipline. From the beginning, women's studies programs have been indebted to the activism manifested in movements and organizations dedicated to changing the conditions of women's lives. In addition, women's studies has maintained an interest in connecting scholarly inquiry and teaching to the promotion of gender justice. Providing a place for students to practice this connection within their program of studies makes sense. In the case of Gonzaga University's women's studies program, that good sense was first expressed by students. During the third year of our program's existence, students requested that internships be offered. They expressed an interest in pursuing careers in organizations dedicated to women's concerns and wanted to get some hands-on experience in that kind of work. The students' timing was perfect in that their request coincided with growing encouragement by the administration to build internships into more academic programs. We read the initiative from the career resources center urging departments and programs to establish internships as an opportunity to increase the attractiveness of the women's studies program to students, and as an avenue for cultivating the founding vision of women's studies as a bridge between academics and community workers. In other words, we treated the university's promotion of internships as an opportunity to connect our program's vision with an emerging institutional priority and this worked.

GETTING STARTED

We began with some community listings of resources for women. We composed a form letter explaining our interest in placing interns and sent this to all of the women's programs, projects, agencies, and organizations on our general list. The letter contained a description of our women's studies program and a statement of our reasons for developing an internship option for students taking the women's studies concentration (twenty-one credits).[13] This introductory letter included a simple reply form on which the recipient could indicate interest in further contact. We then followed up on all the positive replies. When we had an agreement with a specific place, we sent them an information sheet.[14] The completed information forms served as the basis for the list headed Women's Studies Internships, which we used to advertise this option. The list contained descriptions of eight places where interns would be welcomed. These descriptions included a brief characterization of the organization's purpose, the type of work available for interns, and information about who to contact to arrange for an interview. We placed internships within our course listings, instructing students to contact one of the program directors for additional information before registering. During the initial interview, interested students were given the list, as well as a handout detailing the academic requirement: a lengthy paper examining their internship experiences in relation to their learning in women's studies courses and meeting with the faculty mentor every two to three weeks. Students were expected to make all the arrangements with the sites before adding the internship to their course schedule. We followed up with the organization contacts to ensure that there were no misunderstandings about the responsibilities, hours, and expected outcomes. Both the students and their supervisors were told that a verification of the hours worked and an evaluation of performance would be requested at the end of the semester.

REQUIREMENTS AND RATIONALE

We made the decision to offer the internships only to students already committed to taking the full twenty-one-credit concentration in women's studies, with a minimum of twelve credits already completed. This was not an easy choice. A good argument can be made for making the internships more widely available, perhaps as an option for students who have taken the required introductory course in women's studies and want some "real world" experience before deciding to take the concentration; or as a possibility for seniors who know that they will not be able to finish the concentration but who are considering future work on women's issues. We made the more restrictive choice because we wanted the internship to be a meeting place for ideas and experience. We judged that students who had already taken at least four courses in women's studies would have some ideas about women's situations and struggles that they could explore in a different way outside the classroom, in settings where the ideas are translated into policies and actions. These settings are also places where stories are told that many of our students had not yet heard or read. Stories can be a powerful antidote to the dangers of disengaged abstract thought. Many students may experience what they learn in women's studies courses as distant from their own lives. Some may use this distance as grounds for criticizing feminism, e.g., "I have never been discriminated against because I am a woman" or "I do not have any prejudice against women."[15] Even among those who are drawn to women's studies there is often a limited sense of the diversity, complexity, and richness of women's lives. Moving away from theories and toward stories is one of the benefits of immersion in praxis, and that immersion can bring us back to theorizing in a different form.

In *The Call of Stories*, Robert Coles explores the significance of stories in developing our moral character. He testifies to the enormous power of stories. The first chapter of this testimony is titled "Stories and Theories." The longest part of this chapter presents some of Coles's experiences as a resident in psychiatry, surely an experience akin to what we intended for our women's studies interns. The focus of Coles's story about this part of his life is the contrast between the two senior psychoanalysts who supervised his work. One of these doctors urged him to theorize about his cases, to find the correct categories and explanations for the behaviors he was recording. The other supervisor, called "Dr. Ludwig" in Coles's account, emphasized that patients tell stories through which they hope their doctors will understand "the truth of their lives" (7). Coles writes that this phrasing jolted him. He had been intent upon abstractions and now discerned a shift of direction that seemed vague and unpromising to him. Coles is candid about the pleasure he took in his meetings with the more theoretical supervisor: "I think, in retrospect, I got an intellectual fix from him" (8). Listening to this experienced psychiatrist made Coles feel less afraid, less beset by his inadequacies and self-doubts. Thus, Coles helps us to recognize the danger that we will be attracted to theories because they give us a false sense of security, an overconfident sense of knowing exactly who we are, what is real, and what we should do.

Dr. Ludwig kept nudging Coles to take a different route in becoming a psychiatrist: ask people to tell you their stories and pay careful attention when they do. Gradually, Coles recognized that he was being given a lesson, by this supervisor and by his patients, in openness and patience. Listening to stories, he reminds us, develops these qualities; it cultivates habits of mind that are respectful of the concrete and specific other and encourages us to notice the many things that categories cannot capture. Stories nurture careful attention to the particular and the claims it can make on us when we lower our analytical defenses.

Coles is careful to point out that neither he nor his former mentor regards theory as worthless. He is critical of how theory is often used as a device to force conclusions prematurely, to establish a framework for events that appear chaotic, to squeeze the mystery out of things and leave us with what we are pleased to call certainties and to display as our badge of membership in a community of experts. Coles's Dr. Ludwig, the celebrator of attentive listening to stories framed by patients, urged him to look up the meaning of the word "theory." Coles discovered that the Greek root of this word means "I behold." Theory, he comes to believe, should make us "eagle eyed." So theory has an important place, when its function is understood as enlarging observation, not replacing it. We do not have to choose between storytelling and theorizing, but rather see the great value of both and their close connection. Theories alert us to common themes and patterns, while stories remind us the importance of using theories carefully so as not to erase the complexities and contradictions expressed in narratives.

Coles is speaking about conditions for reflexive knowing. He describes these conditions as attainable within a practice of listening to stories. He contrasts this practice with a distorted form of theorizing in which a theorist is not beholding what is given to her or him, but instead imposing names, slicing and manipulating her or his experience of others so that it fits into the available file drawers. Coles imparts a sense of how disorienting it is to theorize in the ancient way—opening oneself up to whatever others may bring, allowing for surprise and mystery. Coles shows how theories may be held loosely and applied gingerly. Coles's stories about his residency make plain how distant many of the typical modes of theorizing are from this soft-voiced, tentative, exploratory, receptive mode. His telling of this story about his relationships with the two supervisors and with patients during his residency is a reflexive performance, a movement back into and through the sources of his own thinking. We read Coles reconstructing his intellectual commitments and values through his reflection on their roots in his experiences.

This is what we hoped to read in the internship papers we required and to hear in the conversations we held with interns every two to three weeks during the semester. We hoped that the internships would challenge students to practice reflexivity. Joanna de Groot and Mary Maynard have identified women's studies as having three projects: recuperating women as a necessary topic of research and teaching; reconstructing inquiry with new concepts, theories, and methods; and reflecting on its own approaches in light of continuing questions and criticisms, from both within and outside the field (2–4). We believed that internships would be especially useful as occasions for questioning perspectives, for fostering greater awareness of assumptions, and for encouraging self-criticism. We expected that internships would help students to hold their ideas more lightly, explore the limits of their views, and become more able to honor complexity.

The codirectors of the women's studies program took turns supervising this part of our curriculum, acting as the academic mentor who worked with both the student and the supervisor on the site. In the guidelines for the internship paper, we posed four questions that the paper should answer: What did you do in your internship? What did the internship mean to you? What connections did the internship have with your coursework in women's studies? (Here we asked for specific references to authors, texts, concepts, theories, and research findings.) What is your evaluation of your internship experience? We asked for papers of about eighteen to twenty-two pages, the length confirming the detail and depth of analysis we expected. Students were given these guidelines for the paper before registering for an internship, in the expectation that the questions would guide their reflections throughout the semester. We did not want the paper to seem to be an extra hurdle, tacked on at the end, but an incentive to think about the internship in certain ways throughout and then to come up with some summarizing reflections in writing. The final copy had to be accompanied by the record sheet signed by the supervisor. Before these final papers were submitted, the interns had many opportunities to discuss outlines and drafts with the faculty member mentoring their internship. Although we did not require the students to keep a journal of their internship experiences, we strongly suggested this and several did so. These records proved to be very useful resources both for the conferences during the semester and for the writing of their papers.

THE RUBBER MEETS THE ROAD

When we designed the internships and started offering them to students, I thought we had a good foundation. We had a good variety of sites, including programs for women in transition from prison, drug treatment, and/or abusive relationships, a sexual assault center, a shelter for homeless women and children, and an outreach program for single parents. We had confidence in the contact persons' understanding of our goals. We had a challenging writing assignment aimed at bringing together theory and practice, perspectives and experiences. We required regular contact between the interns and the mentors. We had limited the internships to students with a serious commitment to women's studies who had already completed several courses in this field. I did not expect any serious difficulties, and by some calculations there have not been any: no one has failed to complete an internship, received an unsatisfactory evaluation from a supervisor, or refused to meet with the mentor. Our interns thus far have been serious and dedicated. Nevertheless, some of the internships have worked better than others, and in trying to figure out why, I have come up with some pretty obvious reasons for these differences. I wish I had anticipated what now seems straightforward and simple. Instead, I have learned the hard way that it is easy to get caught up in the details of management—arranging the sites and supervisors, organizing the necessary forms, stipulating requirements—and neglect the human-resources side of internships.

I can identify three dimensions of internships that make a significant difference in their success. The first of these is the type of work to be assigned to the intern. Initially, we allowed the sites to define the tasks, asking only that these not be centered on routine clerical work. Some of our sites gave very general descriptions of their internships, e.g., "will attend ongoing programs," "will help out the director," or "research hours." Others stated specific areas in which interns might work (e.g., case advocacy and support, mentoring, curriculum development, program evaluation). We relied on the students to make these more concrete and specific in their initial visits to arrange the internships. This was not a reasonable expectation in some cases. Several students felt reluctant to "push" and preferred to leave the details up to their supervisors at the agency or organization. The consequence of this is that some waited several weeks to gain a specific job description, and one intern believed that she never achieved a clear sense of her duties and was often given small jobs that did not challenge or engage her. We might have intervened, but we were uncertain about how to do this because we had not included continuing monitoring and feedback in our original understanding with the sites. In the case of the student whose job assignments were unsatisfying, I did speak with the supervisor on the phone about this two or three times. Each time I was given assurances that things would change, but this did not happen. The student also tried without success. She eventually turned her attention to reading more about the kind of work her organization was doing and writing in her journal and paper about how this work might be conceptualized differently in terms of feminist theories. She made lemonade out of lemons. Since that experience, we have communicated more clearly with the site contact people about what kinds of work are not acceptable for an internship and about the necessity of an explicit job description before the end of the add/drop period. We have also stressed to the students contemplating an internship how important it is for them to have definite goals and to state these in their first visit to the organizations.

The second dimension that has a major impact on the quality of the internship experience is the degree of autonomy given to the intern. Here there is no fixed rule because the personalities of the interns and supervisors and the kind of tasks expected of the intern influence what amount works best. Let me explain what I mean with two examples. One of our interns worked in our city's peace and justice center. Her job was to organize the one-day conference on international women's issues planned for the middle of her semester and then to follow up with a design for acting on the conference's recommendations and evaluating its impact. She worked with the center's codirectors, but it became apparent quickly that they had many other more pressing demands on their time and that the intern was capable of managing on her own. She is assertive, organized, and hard-working. Her supervisors were able to let go and allow her considerable flexibility and independence. There was a considerable amount of mutual trust and respect. Her task allowed for creativity in that there was no fixed agenda in place when she started, only some general directions from the center's board and staff about their hopes for the conference and their intention that it foster some concrete plans for local actions on the issues. This internship was a success because there was such a good fit between the task and the individuals involved. The intern had a great deal of autonomy and this contributed to her sense that she gained a lot from the experience.

In the second example, however, too much autonomy was a problem. In that case, two interns were expected to design and carry out research on the impact of a women's drop-in center serving many different kinds of clients. The students were social-science majors with training in research methods and statistics. Everyone involved in this project was committed to it and worked hard, but the objectives and logistics of the research were not clear. The interns had difficulty figuring out what the center's staff wanted them to achieve, probably because there were some conflicting views about the purposes of the research and how to incorporate it into the already busy schedule of activities at the center. Perhaps everyone's expectations were too high about the quality of research that two undergraduates could accomplish during a four-month semester in a situation that was very much in flux. The students came to me frequently with their frustrations and anxieties: "Is this what they want us to do? Will this questionnaire design work? How can we be more assertive in getting clients to fill these out?" At the time, I could see that they had too little direction and that the center's staff were not able to supply direction because they were consumed with providing services, meeting immediate needs. The outcome was a study and a final paper that was not as thorough or as helpful as hoped. The lesson I learned is that research (and also direct client service) are types of internship work that require a considerable amount of definition and supervision. Although we met with the center's leadership team before the semester of the internship, this was not sufficient because we agreed to leave too many decisions in the hands of the interns.

The third critical dimension that contributes to the success of an internship is the understanding that students have about its rationale. I described above how influenced we were by Coles's understanding of reflexive practice as involving immersion in the particular and concrete, coupled with regular challenges to think about the experience in relation to broader theories and to reflect on assumptions. It should have been obvious that students might need to read and think about the value of different routes to understanding, but we did not assign them any readings at the beginning of their internships about the general topic of integrating community service into academic learning. The questions for their papers gave them the responsibility for constructing connections between their internship experiences and their coursework in women's studies, and we did not offer sufficient resources for accomplishing this. We made ourselves available for consultations about this, but this was not the same as putting the tools into their hands.

Now, it seems to me that a packet of materials that provide a basis for reflecting about community-service learning should be an essential ingredient for internships. On our campus, we now have an office that coordinates community-service learning and provides these kinds of resources. Another valuable resource is the recent book, *A Tradition That Has No Name: Nurturing the Development of People, Families, and Communities*, by Mary Field Belenky et al. This book explores the work of a variety of community projects and organizations dedicated to bringing excluded groups into voice and action. The last two chapters in this book, one on the philosophy and practice of developmental leadership and one on the conditions necessary for passing on its wisdom, seem especially pertinent aids to encouraging interns to think about the broader implications of their work. I intend to use these additional materials the next time I mentor an intern, and I have spoken to the current women's studies director about developing a packet for interns that will more clearly present its challenges and provide more resources for meeting them.

Overall, I would characterize internships as a challenge for all the partners—site supervisors, faculty mentors, and student interns. The main challenges for site supervisors are to formulate a clear understanding of the responsibilities of interns and their contributions to the organization, to make sure that these provide genuine learning experiences and are not simply "busy work," and to be open to making adjustments in response to the specific talents and interests of individual interns. Faculty mentors have to be careful to balance concern for the quality of the student's experience with respect for the student's and supervisor's responsibilities; this requires paying attention, providing resources for reflecting on the connections between the work and their academic study, offering regular opportunities for interns to meet with each other and the mentor, and avoiding the temptation to assume tasks that belong to the other partners in this project. For students, the biggest hurdle is overcoming too much reliance on the supervisor and/or the mentor and becoming the main actor in the internship; that is, students need to recognize that the outcome of their

internship is mainly up to them, that this experience is shaped by their investment and conscientious commitment. Just as many teachers have
learned the value of putting more explicit information about course objectives, expectations, and procedures on their syllabi, we have learned from
our early experiences with women's studies internships the value of clearer
thinking and communication about what they involve.

Despite some mistakes, I think it is accurate to say that women's studies internships have been a success thus far on my campus. The internship
during the fall 1997 semester is a positive example of this. The student
worked in our city's downtown drop-in center for women, which offers a
wide variety of services, including workshops, support groups, counseling,
and assistance with immediate needs for shelter, clothing, or access to
other community agencies. This is the same site where previously two of
our students had experienced the difficulties in attempting to carry out a
research project that I discussed earlier in this section. The more recent intern, a woman returning to formal education after several years as a full-
time wife and mother, formulated clear goals, worked with the site
supervisor to develop assignments that would draw on her abilities, and
made good use of what she had learned in women's studies courses in her
internship paper. She was both ready and eager for the chance to move beyond the classroom, and she was given the direction and support she
needed. She sought out an internship placement that fit her individual
goals of preparing for a future career in social services for women and children. She was very explicit about wanting to connect ideas with action and
excited about the specific kinds of work she was doing at the center. A few
years of experience have helped us to create better matches between student hopes, the program goals of women's studies, and the needs of outside
organizations. Institutionally, the internships can be considered successful
in that the university continues to encourage this kind of learning opportunity and the women's studies program is able to show that we have taken
this to heart. At the same time, internships are also an expression of the
heart of women's studies itself: the passion for knowledge that can help to
change the world for the better.

IS THE DISGUISE A TRAP?

What about the potential for wolves to become sheep? The question
points to a genuine possibility that in acting strategically to link women's
studies with popular innovations in higher education, the ideals of feminist
education may be diluted or lost. In choosing this metaphor for learning
communities and internships in women's studies, I want to claim that the

disguise does not impair the transformational goals of these teaching practices. Nevertheless, I acknowledge that the claim is not obvious and requires some additional discussion. Three influential women's studies thinkers and educators offer different ways of thinking about this potential for co-optation.

Marilyn Frye describes herself as uncertain about aligning herself with the curriculum integration and transformation projects often identified with women's studies programs. Her doubts about such efforts have to do with their accommodation to existing rules and structures within the academy. She favors, instead, a politics of knowledge and culture "that minimizes adversarial, coercive, and/or reformist engagement (struggle) with established institutions and disciplines and frees one's energy for maintaining, strengthening, and creating other knowledges" (792). Frye advocates "a politics of separation, creation, and autonomy" (793). Frye would have women's studies programs concentrate on cultivating their own gardens, rather than engaging in projects to carry feminist scholarship and pedagogies into the wider university.

Jean O'Barr's position is reformist, based on twenty-five years spent building a women's studies program by making strategic interventions in established practices. She has been a leader in developing discussion groups for students, giving workshops for faculty, raising funds from alumni, and creating coalitions with other groups on campus and in the community. It is impossible to think about what O'Barr has accomplished and not regard her as practical and change-oriented, as someone who works with university structures in order to alter them. This does not mean she is unconcerned about the perils for women's studies in becoming part of the mainstream: losing its critical edge and scattering its energies (281–83). She has made the decision to live within this tension, rather than electing the separation that Frye recommends. Neither O'Barr nor Frye is naive; neither would claim that their choices are guarantees of good outcomes. Both seem to have decided to do what best fits their talents and convictions.

Susan Bordo's characterization of feminist scholarship as "the Other" makes a different move. Bordo argues that feminist work is marginalized, even ghettoized, and that its distinctive contributions to contemporary theory are portrayed (incorrectly) either as derivative from works by philosophical masters (Derrida, Foucault, Rorty) or as limited to criticizing sexism or showing the significance of gender. Bordo urges feminist thinkers to work against these distortions. This work requires feminists to be concerned not only with inclusion but also with the cultural meaning of inclusion (209). Thus, Bordo shares Frye's view that inclusion may tame or minimize feminist critique. In Bordo's examples, various efforts by feminist

philosophers to mount a general critique of culture and intellectual traditions are revealed as often reduced to pleas that more attention be paid to
women and minorities or tacked on under the label of "special topics." The
"Othering" of feminism, then, takes more forms than simple attacks de-
monizing feminists as the enemies of reason and truth. It is also manifest in
actions that reduce feminism to a specialized domain covering a few specific topics and representing a narrow political and intellectual agenda.
Bordo takes the position that this is an untenable situation for feminist
scholars and activists. For Bordo, integration of feminist scholarship into
universities, in the sense of inclusion in the general conversation with full
rights to contest all definitions, limits, claims, and conclusions and to present alternatives, is necessary to avoid marginalization and trivialization.

This essay argues for an overall strategy in women's studies programs
that resembles O'Barr's practices and is authorized by Bordo's warning.
Taking advantage of structural openings that allow women's studies commitments to be seen as compatible with institutionalized goals, thus fur-
thering both the visibility and the integration of women's studies into the
university, is both possible and worthwhile. At the same time, it is important not to deny the tension that such actions may create between the
ideals of feminist education and the rule-following accommodations required of players in the current system. Frye's analysis is useful for encouraging remembrance of this danger. Learning communities using feminist
pedagogy and women's studies internships share the promises and perils of
the general project of building women's studies into institutions of higher
education; women's studies educators want both a place at the table and
the opportunity to criticize the guest list, place settings, decorations, eti-
quette, and menu. We are both eager and impertinent dinner partners.
Gonzaga University's women's studies program is now in its seventh year
of existence and does not show any signs of losing that impertinence. Actually, the accomplishments of each succeeding year seem to me to have
added to it in that they have raised our confidence about the value of what
we are doing and our ability to give strong evidence for that.

Learning communities and internships are intrinsically rewarding
activities. Both are opportunities to enact the values associated with
women's studies. In Ethics and Fiction we were able to integrate women's
studies scholarship with dynamic pedagogical approaches to produce a
compelling and rewarding learning experience for both faculty and students. The internships in women's studies connect theory and praxis; both
students and faculty mentors grow in their understanding of how research
and theories about women's lives can inform direct services to women. In
addition, our experience at Gonzaga University with the learning commu-

nity and internships has been characterized both by positive extrinsic gains for the women's studies program in visibility, credibility, and administrative support and by tensions related to faculty rewards for investment in these endeavors.

The tensions have been more prominent in the learning community project than in the internships, and there are structural explanations for this. Organizing and managing the internships have been part of the task of the women's studies administrators. Once the initial work of setting up the placements was finished, all that remained was to mentor the students who signed up for internships and maintain contact with the site supervisors about three times per semester. Only the program directors have served as mentors for the students, and each semester only a small number (under five) of students have elected to do an internship. So, even though internships are an extra for the director (not counted as part of the regular teaching load), they have not been particularly burdensome and could be considered part of the administrative responsibilities for which the director does receive a course reduction each year. Continuing to develop learning communities among women's studies faculty is more problematic for the reasons I mentioned earlier in this essay that have to do with extrinsic rewards for individual faculty participants. These problems can be addressed by working to change criteria for assessing faculty performance so that faculty investment in such innovations is regarded favorably and rewarded.

As women's studies administrators and teachers, we do not want to become sheep, but rather be wily wolves alert to opportunities for making our way across unfriendly territory. Linking courses promotes the crossing of disciplinary boundaries that has given so much energy and creativity to feminist scholarship, while at the same time it reduces the resistance that administrators may have to investing in faculty teamwork. If such linked-course learning communities gain strong student support, their success can be used as evidence that a small investment in developing similar communities is worthwhile. Likewise, administrators and departmental colleagues outside women's studies may not accept the activist orientation of women's studies, its desire to turn theories into actions to change cultures and societies. Placing this activism in the framework of internships reduces criticism of women's studies as insufficiently academic and overly politicized by associating it instead with practical preparation for life after graduation. Learning communities and internships can be hospitable locations for the innovative practices of women's studies.

●   ●   ●

NOTES

1. Our story is very similar to the one Sarah Fenstermaker tells about the establishment of undergraduate women's studies at the University of California, Santa Barbara in the late 1980s. In both places, the effort began when these conditions were in place: a critical mass of interested and qualified faculty, feminist courses already existing in many departments, senior influential faculty members willing to manage the proposal process and eventually direct the program. Fenstermaker says the UCSB faculty involved established their women's studies program for themselves: to create more hospitable conversations than are likely within male-defined departments, to be excited as teachers, to offer a rigorous program for students, and to gain enough campus support so that their efforts would be rewarded. Fenstermaker also notes that sometimes the good academic citizenship that women faculty are often known for (and sometimes criticized for) pays off; that is, when establishing women's studies programs, relationships developed through the previous service can mean there is a network of support to draw upon.

2. In this essay I will use plural pronouns more often than the singular "I" because women's studies at Gonzaga University has been a collaborative effort throughout its existence, starting with codirectors and continuing to have an active advisory board. Decisions have been made collectively, rather than individually. "I" marks my own actions and opinions.

3. Although I agree with Foucault on this point and share his commitment to resistance and activism, I am more optimistic than he seems to have been about outcomes.

4. Of course, this also means that women's studies programs will exhibit the variety produced by locations in different sorts of political conversations. Gonzaga University is a Catholic and Jesuit institution. Although it has five professional schools, business, education, engineering, law, and professional studies (nursing and organizational leadership), its primary focus is on undergraduate education and a liberal arts core curriculum. This essay will contain frequent references to the characteristics that identify Gonzaga, with the dual intention of making a general argument for why attending to such specifics is important in decision making and of showing the difference our differences make.

5. Eloise Buker was a member of Gonzaga University's faculty for ten years. She is now a professor of political science and director of the women's studies program at Denison University in Ohio.

6. The poet Marge Piercy has celebrated being of use. See "To Be of Use," especially these lines: "I love people who harness themselves / An ox to an empty cart, who pull like water buffalo, with massive patience / Who strain in the mud and the muck to move things forward, who do what has to be done, again and again."

7. I have drawn this list from an article by Jean MacGregor distributed by the Washington Center. She identifies four learning community models by grouping together the freshman interest group and the federated learning community forms.

8. Ethics and Fiction received a seed grant from the Washington Center for Improving the Quality of Undergraduate Education, located at Evergreen College in Olympia, Washington. The staff and programs of this center have played an important role in disseminating knowledge about a variety of educational innovations, as well as providing many different kinds of support for putting these into practice.

9. Gonzaga University's mission declares that the university is rooted in the liberal arts, the Catholic tradition, and the vision of St. Ignatius Loyola, the founder of the Jesuits. Our proposal placed particular emphasis upon the relevance of the Ignatian legacy because Ignatius called for education that integrates knowledge and values, emphasizes the active participation of students in learning, and aims to form people who will work for a more just society. The vision of Ignatius has been an important ingredient in our argument for the compatibility of women's studies with Gonzaga's traditions.

10. Maralee Mayberry discusses an important difference between collaborative learning and feminist pedagogy in science education in terms of the contrast between a "reproductive" and a "resistant" pedagogy. Mayberry argues persuasively that collaborative learning strategies do not produce an explicit critique of dominant discourses. In collaborative learning classrooms students may gain practice in using established perspectives, but not in identifying their silences, exclusions, and distortions: "Collaborative techniques reproduce existing forms of knowledge and provide students with the skills and tools necessary to join established knowledge communities, rather than to transform them" (4). Such transformation is an explicit goal of feminist pedagogy. In the concluding section of her article, Mayberry examines the achievement of this goal in light of practical concerns; that is, how can feminist educators gain credibility and institutional support and also maintain radical critique? I agree with Mayberry that women's studies is identified with both of these goals, becoming institutionalized and resisting co-optation, and that negotiating the contradictions between them is difficult and necessary.

11. Jane Tompkins has described her experience of team teaching in the same terms: "There is the joy of collaboration, the relief of shared responsibility, and the solace of knowing that one is not in this alone" (227).

12. NWSA's Faculty Roles and Rewards Project will be introduced at the 1998 NWSA conference and will continue throughout the 1998–99 academic year.

13. These are the reasons we stated in the letter: "Women's studies scholarship has always been associated with a practical commitment to changing women's lives for the better. Women's studies is the academic side of feminism and strives to be connected with its activist side. Both sides are committed to social justice through the elimination of social inequalities between men and women and among

women. In addition, many of the students who are taking women's studies courses have expressed an interest in pursuing careers in organizations that focus on women's concerns and/or offer expanded opportunities for women. These students realize that practical experience in such settings is vital for their preparation."

14. The information sheet requested the following: name of the organization, name of specific department or program in the organization, address, telephone number, name of contact person, brief statement of the organization's purpose and work, and possible opportunities for interns (specific tasks and responsibilities).

15. Deborah Rhode has recently argued that many Americans believe that the problem of gender inequality has been solved. In this view, the only ones who continued to talk about gender inequality are radical feminists who refuse to recognize the profound changes that have taken place. Further, Rhode points out many students believe that if there is some continuing inequality, it does not affect them personally (1–3). Patrice McDermott links this idea that the feminist agenda has already been accomplished to media representations of women's studies scholars and teachers as extremists who do not accept fairness and other mainstream values, characterize all women as victims and all men as oppressors, and are intolerant of dissent (669–71). These ideas can be interrogated and criticized in classrooms. Internships can complement this deconstructive project by putting students into contexts where they will be in direct contact with diverse experiences of inequality and with thoughtful activists engaged in seeking remedies for it. Such contact lowers the resistance based on dividing the world into a "safe private sphere inhabited by people like us" and a messy public one inhabited by "them."

WORKS CITED

Bloom, Allan. *The Closing of the American Mind: How Higher Education Has Failed Democracy and Impoverished the Souls of Today's Students*. New York: Simon and Schuster, 1987.

Belenky, Mary Field, Lynn A. Bond, and Jacqueline Weinstock. *A Tradition That Has No Name: Nurturing the Development of People, Families, and Communities*. New York: Basic Books, 1997.

Bona, Mary Jo, Jane A. Rinehart, and Rose Mary Volbrecht. "Show Me How to Do Like You: Co-Mentoring as Feminist Pedagogy." *Feminist Teacher* 9.3 (1995): 116–24.

Bordo, Susan. "The Feminist as Other." *Twilight Zones: The Hidden Life of Cultural Images from Plato to O. J.* Berkeley: University of California Press, 1997.

Bruffee, Kenneth A. *Collaborative Learning: Higher Education, Interdependence, and the Authority of Knowledge*. Baltimore: Johns Hopkins University Press, 1993.

Coles, Robert. *The Call of Stories: Teaching and the Moral Imagination*. Boston: Houghton Mifflin, 1989.

Deats, Sara Munson, and Lagretta Tallent Lenker. *Gender and Academe: Feminist Pedagogy and Politics*. Lanham, MD: Rowman and Littlefield, 1994.

de Groot, Joanna, and Mary Maynard. "Doing Things Differently: A Context for Women's Studies in the Next Decade." *Women's Studies in the 1990s: Doing Things Differently*. Eds. Joanna de Groot and Mary Maynard. New York: St. Martin's Press, 1993. 1–17.

Delucchi, Michael, and William L. Smith. "A Postmodern Explanation of Student Consumerism in Higher Education." *Teaching Sociology* 25 (1997): 322–27.

———. "Satisfied Customers Versus Pedagogic Responsibility: Further Thoughts on Student Consumerism." *Teaching Sociology* 25 (1997): 336–37.

D'Souza, Dinesh. *Illiberal Education: The Politics of Race and Sex on Campus*. New York: Free Press, 1991.

Edmundson, Mark. "On the Uses of a Liberal Education: As Lite Entertainment for Bored College Students." *Harper's* Sept. 1997: 39–49.

Fenstermaker, Sarah. "Telling Tales Out of School: Three Short Stories of a Feminist Sociologist." *Feminist Sociology: Life Histories of a Movement*. Eds. Barbara Laslett and Barrie Thorne. New Brunswick: Rutgers University Press, 1997. 209–28.

Foucault, Michel. "On the Genealogy of Ethics: An Overview of Work in Progress." *The Foucault Reader*. Ed. Paul Rabinow. New York: Pantheon Books, 1984. 340–72.

Frye, Marilyn. "Getting It Right." *Signs: Journal of Women in Culture and Society* 17 (1992): 781–93.

Gabelnick, Faith, Jean MacGregor, Roberta S. Matthews, and Barbara Leigh Smith. *Learning Communities: Creating Connections Among Students, Faculty, and Disciplines*. San Francisco: Jossey-Bass, 1990.

Graff, Gerald. *Beyond the Culture Wars: How Teaching the Conflicts Can Revitalize American Education*. New York: W. W. Norton, 1992.

Hall, Roberta M., and Bernice Sandler. *The Classroom Climate: A Chilly One for Women?* Washington, D.C.: Project on the Status and Education of Women, Association of American Colleges, 1982.

hooks, bell. *Teaching to Transgress: Education as the Practice of Freedom*. New York: Routledge, 1994.

Kaminer, Wendy. "Feminism's Identity Crisis." *Atlantic Monthly* Oct. 1993: 51–68.

Kaplan, Carey, and Ellen Cronan Rose. "Strange Bedfellows: Feminist Collaboration." *Signs: Journal of Women in Culture and Society* 18 (1993): 547–61.

Lehrman, Karen. "Off Course." *Mother Jones* Sept.–Oct. 1993: 45–68.

MacGregor, Jean. "Design and Implementation of Four Learning Community

Models." *Washington Center News* 3.1 (1988): 7–10.

Matthews, Anne. *Bright College Years: Inside the American Campus Today*. New York: Simon and Schuster, 1997.

Mayberry, Maralee. "Reproductive and Resistant Pedagogies: The Comparative Roles of Collaborative Learning and Feminist Pedagogy in Science Education." *Journal of Research in Science Teaching* 35 (1998): 443–59.

McDermott, Patrice. "On Cultural Authority: Women's Studies, Feminist Politics, and the Popular Press." *Signs: Journal of Women in Culture and Society* 20 (1995): 668–84.

McLaughlin, Tim. "Taking a Look at Learning Communities Nationally." *Washington Center News* 10.2 (1996): 6–21.

O'Barr, Jean Fox. *Feminism in Action: Building Institutions and Community Through Women's Studies*. Chapel Hill: University of North Carolina Press, 1994.

Palmer, Parker J. "Community, Conflict, and Ways of Knowing: Ways to Deepen Our Educational Agenda." *Change: The Magazine of Higher Learning* Sept.–Oct. 1987: 20–25.

Patai, Daphne, and Noretta Koertge. *Professing Feminism: Cautionary Tales from the Strange World of Women's Studies*. New York: Basic Books, 1994.

Piercy, Marge. "To Be of Use." *Circles in the Water*. New York: Alfred A. Knopf, 1982.

Rhode, Deborah. *Speaking of Sex: The Denial of Gender Inequality*. Cambridge: Harvard University Press, 1997.

Roiphe, Katie. *The Morning After: Sex, Fear, and Feminism on Campus*. Boston: Little, Brown, 1993.

Sommers, Christina Hoff. *Who Stole Feminism? How Women Have Betrayed Women*. New York: Simon and Schuster, 1994.

Tarule, Jill Mattuck. "Voices in Dialogue: Collaborative Ways of Knowing." *Knowledge, Difference and Power: Essays Inspired by* Women's Ways of Knowing. Eds. Nancy Goldberger, Jill Tarule, Blythe Clinchy, and Mary Field Belenky. New York: Basic Books, 1996. 274–304.

Tinto, Vincent, and Anne Goodsell Love. "Longitudinal Studies of Learning Communities at La Guardia Community College." University Park: National Center on Postsecondary Teaching, Learning, and Assessment, Feb. 1995.

Tompkins, Jane. *A Life in School: What the Teacher Learned*. Reading, MA: Addison-Wesley, 1996.

Trout, Paul. "Conflict in the College Classroom." *The Cresset: A Review of Literature, Arts, and Public Affairs* 60.7 (1997): 28–36.

Walker, Alice. *The Color Purple*. New York: Pocket Books, 1982.

Weber, Lynn, Elizabeth Higginbotham, and Bonnie Thornton Dill. "Sisterhood as Collaboration: Building the Center for Research on Women at the University of Memphis." *Feminist Sociology: Life Histories of a Movement*. Eds. Barbara Laslett and Barrie Thorne. New Brunswick: Rutgers University Press, 1997. 229–56.

Whipple, William R. "Collaborative Learning: Recognizing It When We See It. *American Association of Higher Education Bulletin* Oct. 1987: 3–5.

5

ASSESSMENT AND FEMINIST PEDAGOGY[1]

Jodi Wetzel

THE CALL FOR ACCOUNTABILITY AND FEMINIST EDUCATORS' RESPONSE

Since external pressure on higher education to be "accountable" emerged nationally in the 1980s, institutions and disciplines have been under fire from so-called "opinion leaders," highly visible "public intellectuals"—for example, during the Reagan and Bush administrations, William Bennett, Lynne Cheney, and Linda Chavez of the U.S. Civil Rights Commission and academics such as Thomas Sowell, Allen Bloom, and the National Association of Scholars.[2] Their influence, fomenting the backlash against multiculturalism and affirmative action, has prompted politicians at federal, state, and local levels to adopt an aggressive and intrusive stance regarding higher education, threatening both its traditional autonomy and intellectual viability. Their accusations—that postsecondary educational access to other than the children of economic, social, and political elites has led to grade inflation, dumbing down of the curriculum, and a disregard of the various traditional disciplinary canons—and their attempt to persuade the public, including employers and students' families, have resulted in broadbased accountability expectations intended in new ways to validate not only the competency of graduates but also, indeed, the competency of the professoriate.

Higher-education institutions now not only undergo the long-standing evaluation procedures of their own regional accreditation associations but also must increasingly meet the standards of a proliferation of disciplinary accreditation bodies and conduct departmental program reviews every five or six years. Individually, faculty now are routinely evaluated by students and peers; they confront the increasing escalation of tenure requirements and, most recently, the prospects of posttenure review, as well as annual evaluation for the purpose of awarding merit pay. The economics of "state-supported" higher-education institutions that are actually receiving fewer and fewer state dollars also dictate that new faculty are more and more frequently hired on time-limited, non-tenure-track appointments, or on a part-time basis. One might say that the current cultural climate is increasingly hostile to higher education, even anti-intellectual.

The profession has few choices. Activist state legislatures, commissions on higher education, and boards of regents/trustees rule, and they demand documentation of systematic degree progress and achievement. Institutions are now required to assess student competency upon admission in written and oral communication and in mathematics. This is perhaps the result of the practice of so-called "social passing," the promotion of K–12 students rather automatically to allow them to stay on track with their age peers even when they do not achieve the requisite academic goals. For higher education this and more new unfunded mandates have resulted in additional and complex bureaucratic structures necessitating reallocation of declining internal resources.

Another example of this intrusive external monitoring of higher education comes from the uncritical assumption of external agencies that students should be able routinely to complete a baccalaureate degree program in four years. That is not the case except for students who are children of the economic elites. This assumption ignores the fact that increasing access to higher education has changed the demographics in many schools. Women now constitute the majority of students and many of them are older, as are an increasing number of men, than the traditional higher-education cohort of eighteen to twenty-two year olds. Affirmative action has also brought many more students from communities of color and from nonelite economic backgrounds, the first generation in their families to aspire to higher education. These demographics mean students are more likely to have families and to need to be in the paid labor force in order to afford higher education at all. With multiple roles and increasing demands on their time, students are less and less able to attend classes full time for four consecutive years. Still, legislators and others hold higher education responsible and impose new advising requirements, again forcing additional accountability and more complex bureaucratic structures to document success in graduation rates after four years. Again, internal resource reallocation is necessary. Assessment of students prior to graduation is the third prominent feature of external intrusion into higher education. Also unfunded, it requires of every discipline a "capstone course" or "senior experience," which is designed to certify that students have mastered a certain body of knowledge and are thus prepared for employment. Such an expectation requires of faculty additional review and revision of curricula and, in many cases, the development of new courses and evaluation instruments that cumulatively measure student learning.

Academic administrators assert that if the profession does not assume responsibility for assessment, external agencies will, and academics will not like the results. National higher-education associations have given direction and a shared vocabulary to the task of assessment, but faculty may not take it seriously, department chairs and program directors may see it as just one more bureaucratic task, and students may see it as another threat to their being credentialed. Institutional responses may end up being merely quick and dirty quantitative measurement tools, fulfilling only the letter of the law—and that minimally—with a spirit of resistance growing from resentment of new limits on faculty autonomy and declining disciplinary credibility. Others, for example feminist educators, have reacted differently, employing qualitative measures to build real value into this externally imposed process and integrating the assessment of undergraduate student learning into the existing curriculum and structure of programs—without sacrificing the close ties among theoretical research-based knowledge, its critical review and application, and the activist social-change values that form the foundation of a women's studies education.

The use of portfolios as developmental and cumulative documentation of individual student intellectual growth and mastery is one response feminist educators have made to the demand for accountability. Portfolios need to include work from the introductory course level through the senior year, but that work need not only demonstrate critical reading, thinking, and writing skills. Nor should it only demonstrate the application of quantitative methods. It could include, for example, visual exhibitions; laboratory experiments; musical and theatrical compositions and performance; business applications (for example, the development and implementation of a diversity plan or a sexual harassment policy); the use of technology (for example, Web pages, or the creation and maintenance of student feminist interest lists, or electronic publications); the organization of nonprofit services designed to target a previously underserved female population; or new program development in already existing services; work in community fund-raisers and other giving programs designed to serve women and girls. As one assessment tool, portfolios provide the student with intellectual autonomy in making the choice of what to include. The process also enhances and expands the advising role of faculty meaningfully as they work with students on portfolio development—something that addresses a separate complaint of the external critics whose assumption is that faculty approach advising as necessary but a nuisance and therefore are uninformed and do not do the job well, causing students to take more than four years to graduate. The portfolio critique can be a community-building mechanism for all students and faculty in the program, a celebratory rite of passage where seniors exhibit and discuss their work with their student colleagues and faculty members. Written comments, questions, and recommendations from senior portfolio critiques can then be summarized to form the required assessment report, which in many states' institutions must deliver in summary form for all degree programs to their governing boards and/or commissions on higher education.

Another method of assessment is the senior thesis, which can also be developmental and cumulative since what it documents is both knowledge in designated content areas and methodological skills acquired over the time span of a student's entire undergraduate course of study. In addition, it demonstrates the quality of critical reading, writing, and analytical skills. Depending on the area of focus, it may also evidence qualitative or quantitative research skills. Finally, it exhibits technological skills in using and evaluating Web sources as well as printed and visual sources, and knowledge developed over the course of activist internships, paid employment, and community-service volunteer work.

THE MSCD WOMEN'S STUDIES ASSESSMENT PLAN

At Metropolitan State College of Denver (MSCD), a large urban, comprehensive, baccalaureate institution, without a football team, a Greek system, or residence halls, the Institute for Women's Studies and Services built assessment into its existing curriculum by using the already required senior seminar as its capstone course for purposes of assessment. We began the process in 1992 using the senior thesis as our assessment tool and refining our knowledge and skills goals annually to reflect curriculum development, the increasing use of technology, and what we learn from each year's assessment project itself. This "assessment of assessment" incorporates the ideas of students, administrators, faculty, alumnae, and community activists and other professionals who participate in the project. The entire process provides an opportunity for self-reflection, for review and continuing development of the women's studies curriculum, and for continuous analysis of what women's studies students need to know to lead satisfying lives as well as to be successful in graduate or professional school as well as in the paid labor force.

From employers of our students in both the public and private sectors who participate in the review process we understand that what students need to know includes: critical reading, writing, and thinking skills; computation skills; analytical and interpretive skills; technological skills; and research skills. They want new hires to know where and how to find answers to pertinent questions and how to make judgments and decisions that will achieve the desired results. Employers are willing and know how to train new hires for their particular work sites, but they are not equipped, nor do they want, to educate employees in these more general skills and capacities. For our own part, we also seek to educate students to make judgments and decisions that are consistent with their own identified values and needs, both professional and personal.

Our revised developmental core curriculum is formatted to work with students to meet individual needs. In addition to traditional on-campus daytime courses it includes correspondence, on-line, weekend, summer, and/or evening sections of all required courses:

WMS 1001	Introduction
WMS 2001	Research Methods
WMS 2010	Women of Color
WMS 3510	Feminist Theory
WMS 3980	Internship
WMS 4950	Senior Seminar

Students may select from five groups of courses to fulfill electives in the major or minor: (1) arts and humanities; (2) history; (3) multicultural studies; (4) psychology/biology; and (5) social sciences. Some courses—particularly those in the multicultural group—overlap categories. The Chicana/Latina studies course, for example, is in the arts and humanities, multicultural, and social science groups.

Since many transfer or reentry adult students make their first institutional contact through our women's services component for help with admission procedures and financial aid and scholarship information, we are able to identify early a number of potential majors and minors. Campus-wide workshops offered by women's services identify others. Traditional-aged students are most likely to identify an interest in women's studies in lower-division women's studies courses—for example, the introduction, the first-year seminar, U.S. women's history, or women of color. A close relationship with the college general-advising center has also proven helpful in instilling the "get advising early and often" principle, which speaks not only to the external demands for accountability but begins the important academic socialization process for students. In the spirit of a feminist pedagogy that holds information sharing in high value, women's studies distributes a description of the assessment project at the student's first contact point, explaining its procedures, purpose, and the expectations outlined in the skills and knowledge goals. Thus, students are not surprised when they enroll in the senior seminar with something that appears to be an add-on. Assessment becomes integral to the whole process of student intellectual growth.

The knowledge base they are expected to have acquired becomes not only more apparent and explicit but also their self-reflection—taking responsibility—and the opportunity to question the knowledge the faculty values—and to be heard—put students at the center of their own education. Student consciousness, the recognition of the deliberateness of the pedagogy itself, positions them at this point for the capstone senior seminar.

That knowledge base includes:

1. The main social, economic, political, technological, and psychological issues facing contemporary women in the United States;
2. The development, interdisciplinary nature, and methodological approaches of women's studies;
3. The major topics and approaches in the history of feminist thought;
4. The parallels and intersections between racism, sexism, heterosexism, and classism;
5. The history of women in a least one geographical area of the world;
6. Women's literary/artistic expression within a genre, time period, or theme.

Women's studies graduates also are expected to demonstrate:

1. Writing skills that show grammatical, organizational, and stylistic sophistication;
2. Identification of ideas and concepts about women in various disciplines and in gender-defining institutions and connections of those ideas thematically or topically;
3. Creation of a focused and coherent analytical research paper or essay based upon and sustained by evidence from both primary and secondary sources;
4. Analysis and interpretation of arguments and theories for internal consistency, bias, and underlying assumptions;
5. Assessment of library collections and other resources in the context of writing interpretive essays, critical analyses, and research papers;
6. Design and implementation of a research project that integrates

women's studies content and content from other disciplines within the student's course of study, and uses "fugitive" and ephemeral as well as traditional primary and secondary sources.

At the first contact, also, students are directed to initiate formal advising appointments designed to explore with them their options and choices within a women's studies degree program and answer the inevitable questions about professional positions in the field and/or the segue to graduate or professional school. (Future plans include a required one-credit workshop course that explores women's studies career options and directions.) When students make that first contact, they receive advising packets and are asked to review the contents, including the assessment plan, and to familiarize themselves with the degree programs and the support services provided by the institute prior to their first faculty visit. Once they have made the decision to pursue women's studies and have officially declared it their major, they may select their own faculty advisor if they know a particular faculty member with whom they want to work. If not, they are assigned an advisor. (Students may change advisors if they later develop a supportive relationship with a different faculty member.) Descriptions of the assessment project are again distributed in each required course, to provide a forum for additional student questions as they move through their degree programs in an orderly sequence governed by prerequisites.

Building on the already existing curriculum, the junior-level feminist-theory course has an intensive advising component. Academic records and student progress are reviewed in class as the initial project and the ensuing discussions generate useful suggestions regarding both making the most of core courses and merging electives with them seamlessly. The students generally all know each other from previous courses so the trust level among them is already high. Working with the knowledge and skills goals of the assessment project, they make their own assessments together of whether the faculty has taught them what they need to know thus far. The process is also self-reflective: with the foundation set in one-on-one advising in the first two years, they consider, as well, what they have given to and taken from their courses and how they are preparing themselves for graduation and subsequent choices. Some conclude they are less well prepared than others and a support system emerges allowing all of them to benefit from each others' strengths whether they need help with increasing their skills or peer advising on how to make the most of courses yet to be taken. Though, as in any group of students, there are always those who take their studies somewhat less seriously than they might, for the most part, students today are better prepared to be seniors than were the women's studies students who went through the curriculum before assessment was mandated.

While the senior seminar format first offers a common reading for analysis and interpretation, for example Elizabeth Minnich's *Transforming Knowledge* (1990), something that both synthesizes the basics and sets the tone of critical inquiry, its major focus is on the creation of the senior thesis. Each student's topic and methodological choices are individualized within a context that, while accounting for the shared knowledge of the core curriculum, is inclusive of the patterns emerging from a particular set of electives. Students orally outline their progress in the weekly meetings of the seminar, and their enthusiasm for the work is apparent in how eager they are to help each other in every stage of the process. Students struggling with focus, for example, are quite gratified to see their topics narrow as they outline their intentions and interact with other seminar members. As they do their research, they huddle with classmates over computers searching for key words that will generate appropriate Web sources; they gather in studios to assist at the birth of new art; they stand in line together at the interlibrary loan desk with expectations that the one perfect source of support for a central argument one student is helping another to develop is about to be delivered into their hands; they proudly bring real treasures to share with the seminar. As they do their own work they are at the same time on the lookout for things that might prove useful to others. They solve problems and surmount barriers together both in and outside of the seminar itself.

The last third of the semester focuses on students' oral presentations of the results of their research to the group. Encouraged to invite friends and loved ones to join in the discussion, they sometimes arrive not only with guests but also with an evening's repast to share. The broad range of topics, using a variety of methods, enhances everyone's learning because by then students know a considerable amount about each other's work and are able to speak knowledgeably during the ensuing discussions. Questions raised, suggestions made, problems solved, and points well taken all around allow time for revision, refinement of arguments, and development of more concrete support for particular positions. Accolades provide reinforcement. Students who select early presentation dates have several weeks for revision; those who determine they need more time before the oral, of course, have less. These judgments are at their discretion. Finally, the completed written thesis is ready to be delivered to the faculty.

Thesis topics vary widely, but most reflect the feminist value of melding activism and research. Some examples of senior theses from the last six years illustrate this.

Selected Senior Theses

"Open Politicizing of the Classroom: The Radical Teacher"

The author, now an English teacher in the Denver public schools, created this senior thesis using materials from her student teaching experience. Her research, starting from the premise of the "lack of female representation in the literature curriculum at all educational levels [. . .] focused on methods [. . .] to make [her] classroom more progressive and more centered in feminist pedagogy than it was on merely presenting the problems of lack of representation." Beginning from this base, she created a secondary education literary unit on the development of individuality and identity. Using fiction, poetry, music, and art, she had her eleventh-grade urban school students examine adolescent identity development. Her senior thesis included lesson plans providing overviews, specific learning objectives, and questions for study and discussion. She also provided reading lists and detailed class activities, homework assignments, and assessment tools.

"Looking from the Outside In: New Directions for Feminist Legal Theory"

Planning a career in the law when she wrote her thesis and currently enrolled in her last year at the University of Michigan School of Law, this student set out to explore ways in which "contemporary legal theory analyzes social oppression and [. . .] approaches strategies for social change [. . .] examining two forms of legal scholarship: feminist jurisprudence and outsider legal theory." The latter, primarily espoused by legal scholars who are women of color, critiques the essentialist nature of feminist legal theory and advocates "strategies for redirecting feminist jurisprudence in ways that are truly inclusive and radical." Outlining the critiques of both masculinist and feminist jurisprudence, the student creates a synthesis of outsider theory, or "multiple consciousness theory," and feminist theory that is truly subversive and that holds the promise of building "some powerful coalitions and activist strategies." Subsequently, she has tested her ideas empirically during a summer internship with a Palestinian human rights organization's women's rights project.

"Spinning Our Wheels: Enlisted Women during the Vietnam War"

Using a feminist perspective, this student revisited these women's experiences of sexual violence in the military when "sexual harassment" was not part of our shared vocabulary yet. The author discovered through a reunion she organized that many of these women found, as she herself had,

that writing poetry was cathartic in their recovery at a time when speaking
openly about their abuse was even more forbidden and dangerous than it
is today. Her position is that women were especially at once invisible and
devalued by both colleagues and superiors during the Vietnam War. In her
introduction she wrote:

> This paper is more to me than my senior thesis. [It] is only the be-
> ginning of my commitment to document the experiences of the
> thousands of women who wanted to do something constructive
> during an era fraught with destruction, corruption, and waste.
>
> I use the pronoun "we" throughout this work. I was a part of
> the enlisted troops during Vietnam; I share in the experiences, and
> I remember [. . .].

She is seeking a publisher for a collection of these women's poems.

"Feminism and Librarianship: Evolution or Revolution"

Written after an internship researching material for a women's history
monograph series for elementary school students and in government documents as a library assistant where she discovered for herself the difference
feminist librarians can make, this student's thesis examined the organization of a "feminist faction" in the American Library Association, its contribution to the visibility of women and women's issues among professionals
in the field, and the resulting benefit to library users in general as well as
feminist scholars in particular. She asserts that though changes have been
slow, the library profession has made far more progress than others. She
also affirms strongly that "in spite of the difficulties that the explosion of
feminist inspired knowledge has encountered elsewhere in [academe], li-
braries have been and remain among the staunchest and most productive
proponents of inclusion of feminist knowledge." This student went on to
complete a master's degree in library science at the University of Arizona
while working with Ruth Dickstein, a librarian well known in particular
for her work with the university's Southwest Institute for Research on
Women. Subsequently, this student was invited by Greenwood Press to
write an annotated bibliography of the work of feminist poet and novelist
Marge Piercy. It was published in 1997.

"The Dirtiest Little Secret: The Truth behind Genital Mutilation"

This thesis was written by a student who double-majored in women's
studies and art, requiring her to do two capstone courses. Her women's
studies senior thesis provided the material that gave historical and cultural

context to the art capstone, her senior exhibit, catalog, and labels. In graphic, highly stylized, colored pencil renderings of mutilated female genitals accompanied by written text detailing the actual experiences of young girls, she created horrific scenarios of a practice that is a human rights violation still common in many parts of the world. For thousands of years, at all levels of society, men have controlled women's bodies though clitoridectomy and female genital mutilation (FGM). "[P]erpetuated by the belief that it is tradition and [. . .] sustained through myths [that] are designed to justify and continue the mutilations . . . ," the practice, thought to have been eliminated in western cultures sometime ago, is again spreading due to shifts in patterns of human migration. In raising awareness, this student's intent was also to give voice to the women who have suffered by using their poetry with her own visual and prose elements in the exhibit. Since graduating she has joined two collectives, the Edge Gallery and Core, New Art Space, where she continues to exhibit her FGM work. Currently, she is president of the Colorado chapter of the Women's Caucus for Art.

"Sisters Are Doing It for Themselves: "'Zines and Feminism's Third Wave"

Also an artist, this student examined the phenomenon of "'zines," a shortened form of "fanzines," "a relatively new phenomenon, [. . .] similar in spirit to the underground press and poetry chapbooks of the 1960s." She reviewed a variety of 'zines, conducted an on-line survey of the publishers, created and distributed three 'zines of her own, and described, analyzed, and interpreted the network of young feminists—Gen X or 13th Geners—who were coming into their own voice, denying and decrying their mothers whom they labeled "corporate feminists," referring to the bureaucratic nature of national mainstream feminist organizations. "As a result of this 'zine 'revolution,' young women are able to network with each other like never before, and 'zines link together an entire sisterhood of third wave feminists with carefully xeroxed and stapled threads."

These two art students are also founding members of the Girlgoyles, a local feminist guerilla artists' group similar to the nationally known Guerilla Girls. A Girlgoyles's successful action on behalf of reproductive freedom was during Pope John Paul's 1993 visit to Denver. They widely distributed "pope-alactics"—individual communion wafers packed in plastic bags complete with instructions: "Hold carefully between the legs."

"Feminist Ethics in Psychology: A Call to Excellence"

Written by a student who faced an ethical dilemma regarding the behavior of a supervisor during her internship, the focus of this thesis is similar to that of "Looking From the Outside In: New Directions for Feminist

Legal Theory" described above. Early feminist psychological theories "overgeneralized white women's experience, making invisible the particular experiences of all other women." Describing a conscious attempt by feminist psychologists to build a multicultural discipline, the author noted the necessity of "conducting research in the multiple contexts of marginalized women to develop a sound database [. . .] and commit to including multi-cultural analyses in every forum [training, teaching, consulting, and therapy . . .]." Though the language differs, the intent is the same as that advocated in outsider/multiple consciousness legal theory. Now in the clinical psychology doctoral program at the University of Florida, this student continues work on ethical issues and is readying her writing for publication.

"Feminist Theory: A Multicultural Perspective"

This student, writing in 1992 and disappointed still in the lack of multiple perspectives in feminist thought, found the problems to be many: "exclusionary practices, academic elitism, inaccessibility to the field, and the acceptance of 'authoritative voices' in defining not only theory but also women's realities. These inequities [. . .] resulted in a severe limitation of 'what is theory' and 'who can define it.'" Her conclusion after a lengthy review of the literature was that "there is still much work to be done in this area if we are to arrive at an inclusive, multicultural, multifocal, interdisciplinary, feminist theory. [. . .] We must explore the question of what do identity politics, coalition politics, and interdependent, multicultural, multifocal, inclusive, interdisciplinary theory beget?" After graduation this student worked as a program office for the Latin American Research and Service Agency, then obtained a master's of Public Administration from the University of Minnesota's Herbert H. Humphrey Institute of Public Affairs, and is now employed as a policy analyst for the National Conference of State Legislators, in Washington, D.C.

"Reclaiming the Productive Power of Gossip"

This thesis asserts that "[W]omen's ambivalence about gossip is related to the fact that, historically, gossip has been associated with women, and while this association has sometimes been positive, primarily it has been extremely negative. Women, therefore, are understandably reluctant to embrace the word 'gossip' because of the negative stigma that it carries and because it has been and continues to be used to trivialize and insult them. [. . .] Women and gossipers are synonymous to many people, and this connection often reflects sexist judgments about the value and purpose of women's talk."

The author proudly acknowledges gossip as an avocation and, already published, seeks a career in writing about feminist issues, popular culture, and conservative politics.

"Black Women and Their Hair: The Silent Shame"

"The haunting reality is that Black women are bombarded by the media, white culture, and the Black community that Black hair in its natural state is unattractive and unacceptable. Black women [and girls] have been brainwashed to think that their hair is something to be ashamed of." The author, who sees this issue as central to the development of her own identity, weaves her experience as child into the thesis seamlessly, discussing the history and importance of hair in Africa, its obvious place as a symbol of shame in slavery, repeated and dangerous attempts later to make black women's hair conform to acceptable notions of white beauty, symbolic assertions of black identity and pride during and resulting from the Civil Rights Movement, and the increasing role of the beauty industry and the media throughout the twentieth century. She reclaims the history and beauty of Black women's hair in its natural state through a multimedia production including her written text, poetry, slides, material culture objects, and music. A recent graduate, she is a suburban high school English teacher.

Assessing Students's Achievement of Women's Studies Learning Objectives

One copy of each thesis is evaluated by the seminar professor as a significant factor in the student's course grade. Separately, copies are delivered to at least three others, and using the knowledge and skills goals as specific guides, they evaluate each thesis, not for a grade but for how well the assessment goals were met each year by seminar students—individually and collectively. This team of three evaluators varies in composition but every year includes representation from the core faculty and the extended women's studies faculty (cross-listing affiliates) as a given. The third evaluator is chosen from among a number of groups: the alumnae chapter of the women's studies honor society, Iota Iota Iota; leaders of women's organizations; community activists and service providers; internship supervisors; corporate professionals; small-business owners; and private nonprofit administrators. The nonfaculty category has a degree of overlap because some in these groups are also the employers of women's studies graduates. Using the reports of each evaluator, the seminar professor authors a summary that constitutes the annual assessment of how well the students have learned what faculty value and believe to be important to women's studies graduates.

During the six years since we began assessing our students' cumulative learning using the senior seminar as the capstone course and the senior thesis as the measurement tool, we have added one specific item to our knowledge and skills goals. The original eleven goals we outlined in 1992 have served well as determinants of student learning in both areas, but following the first two years' implementation, we added another goal to the skills component as it became more and more clear that the development of increasingly sophisticated written communication skills needed to be addressed explicitly, informing students well in advance of their enrollment in the capstone course of the prime importance of competency in this area. Not only was the need for this skill goal apparent from the course professor's judgment of the thesis in the early years but also it was a primary focus of the evaluation teams. Faculty paid particularly close attention to the high degree of importance noted by the external evaluators—the alumnae, advisory board members, and professionals in the community. That these colleagues represented dual constituencies—for example, alumnae who were legislators; advisory board members who were business owners and who employed our graduates; or professionals in the community who had been site supervisors of our students doing internships—made their judgments highly important, and they all noted a consistent unevenness in the sophistication of students' writing skills grammatically, organizationally, and stylistically. One early reviewer, the executive director of a large private nonprofit organization with extensive and successful grant-writing experience, noted "more and more complaints from business about [college and university] graduates' writing and communication [skills]." She added that were the theses she evaluated responses to RFPs, a few might get funding but others would not even make it out of a preliminary review because they were so poorly written.

Evaluators' judgments of the other knowledge and skills goals during those six years have pointed the way for curriculum and program development in other areas as well. Overall they believed most students wrote coherent and focused essays—some were assessed to be of graduate-school quality. They also determined that most had a clear understanding of feminist perspectives and competently used the analytical tools those perspectives supply. Most applied those tools using the insights of several disciplines to identify problems and propose solutions. Indeed, a major strength that eighteen reviewers noted during the six years was students' clear understanding of women's studies as interdisciplinary, their seeing single disciplines alone as inadequate in interpreting the myriad experiences of women's lives and history. Still, readers did identify places where individual theses could have been expanded to include the perspectives of

particular disciplines that were either not used at all or were used minimally. In 1995, for example, one reviewer wrote: "The weaker papers were
poorly written, unfocused and not analytical [. . .] fail[ing] to adequately
demonstrate knowledge of women's studies issues from a historical, developmental, cultural, and/or theoretical perspective." On the other hand,
readers also wrote that some students exhibited confidence as they took
risks topically, analytically, and stylistically. Of particular interest was that
students felt as free to examine critically the limits of feminist theoretical
constructs as they did to critique more traditional modes of thought.

Readers determined, too, that many students were well prepared to enter graduate or professional school, and almost 40% have, attending, for
example, the University of Michigan and the University of Denver law
schools, the Hubert H. Humphrey Institute of Public Affairs at the University of Minnesota, Bryn Mawr College, the University of Denver, and New
Mexico Highlands University Master of Social Work programs, and the
University of Arizona library school. Students are also doing or have completed postgraduate work in a variety of both liberal arts and professional
programs at Denver University, the University of Colorado at both Boulder
and Denver, Regis University, the Naropa Institute, the University of
Florida, and Rutgers University. In addition, many students have been
awarded significant—even full-ride—financial support packages.

Readers also concluded that most of the students demonstrated practical application or research and writing skills that would be useful in the
paid workforce. Several are teachers in Denver area public schools, and
many students upon graduation have taken positions in social-service
agencies or private nonprofits where both the knowledge and the skills
demonstrated in the senior thesis will be continuously useful in the development of grant proposals, public-policy initiatives, accountability reports,
and direct-client services.

The perspectives of their feminist education will help them to argue
convincingly for social, educational, and economic change that will improve the lives of women and children. Most students see clearly the differential impact of race, class, sexual identity, age, and disability as well as
gender in access to resources necessary to live a life not tainted by poverty,
ignorance, and deprivation. With skill, many of these students make the
interdisciplinary connections that will frame their critical-thinking skills
for social-change initiatives. Finally, evaluators noted, students also see
new ways of thinking that enrich the life of the mind.

The deans and the associate vice president for academic affairs/direc-
tor of program review and assessment annually receive the women's studies report as well as academic assessment reports from all other degree

programs and distribute copies to the college program review committee for discussion and analysis and, using their recommendations, may subsequently ask some programs to revise their goals, to refine methods, or to clarify how they report data in subsequent years. Though women's studies faculty have revised goals over time, it was done internally to meet additional needs identified in the program's curriculum. Indeed, in 1996 women's studies was commended by the associate vice president and asked to assist other programs upon request with further development of their assessment projects. Following on the work completed by the college program review committee, the associate vice president prepares the annual institutional assessment report and delivers it to the trustees who approve and forward it to the state commission on higher education. Though the commission's approval constitutes the official conclusion of this annual accountability process, it is not concluded for women's studies students and faculty. All copies of the theses are returned to students along with copies of the report itself. They are invited to discuss results and critiques of their own work with the seminar professor and members of the assessment team. Together all participants work to give concrete value to and make meaning from this process.

Results across six assessment cycles demonstrate in particular an increasing student currency in the field of women's studies through the evaluation and use of electronic resources and a serious commitment to the multicultural nature of best-practice feminist scholarship, which tries to account for all women's experiences. It is also apparent that externally imposed accountability practices do not diminish the promise of activist feminist learning and its implication for positive social change. Still, as the results also indicate, there remains a continuing unevenness in sophisticated critical thinking and writing skills, in analytical and interpretive ability, and in the ability to synthesize apparently disparate material. Self-reflection—of both students and faculty—and mastery in these areas are particularly important given the large percentage of our students who aspire to graduate- or professional-school education. That said, students overall do demonstrate an ability to examine issues from an interdisciplinary perspective, which places women at the center while at the same time acknowledging differences among women.

ASSESSING THE ASSESSMENT PROJECT

Since the assessment project began in academic year 1991–92, faculty and administrators have used its results to revise and further develop the curriculum, adding two courses to the core, Women of Color and Introduction to Research Methods. We have expanded the variety of internships; encouraged students, particularly those just entering the program, to avail themselves of support services such as the Writing Center and the informal tutoring offered by members of the women's studies honor society; improved the advising process; and created an opportunity—afternoon tea times—for students to gather informally at the institute to get to know each other better early on and to share ideas and resources. Beginning with the present assessment cycle, we have developed a more formal way for gathering student input into the actual process itself: a questionnaire that was distributed to senior seminar members for completion with the regular form for student evaluation of individual class instruction. Requesting self-reflection and critique as well as ideas about how faculty and staff might better help students, the questionnaire seeks narrative responses:

1. Considering the knowledge and skills goals of the women's studies and services assessment plan (attached), how have women's studies courses overall contributed to your learning?
2. How have women's studies and services faculty and staff in the aggregate contributed to your gaining the knowledge and learning the skills outlined in the assessment plan?
3. Which knowledge and skills goals are most important to you? Why?
4. Which ones do you think you have mastered? Why?
5. Which ones do you think you still need to work on? Why?
6. How could women's studies and services help you to master those goals in ways it does not do so currently?
7. Are there knowledge and/or skills goals you would add to the list? If not, why? If so, what would they be and why do you feel they are important to a women's studies education?
8. Are there other methods that might evaluate achievement of these goals better than the senior thesis? What would those be?

Results of the first-round administration of this student opinion survey are instructive. Illustrating the self-reflection faculty consciously sought to instill as a principle of feminist education, students candidly assessed their own strengths and those of the faculty and the women's studies curriculum. Though critical thinking was not listed specifically among the knowledge and skills goals of the assessment plan, all these students noted development of that skill as having been central to their learning. Their courses challenged them, as they were designed to, to reconsider ideas previously held. Students' courses of study not only raised their awareness and knowledge of women, broadening their understanding of themselves and the world, but also increased their self-esteem in the process. One student noted that "the program has surpassed its own expectations. The coursework I completed not only challenged me [. . .] but has informed me in all facets of being human. As education should change you wholly, I feel my years in women's studies [have] wholly changed me." Another wrote: "[W]omen's studies instructors have contributed to the very essence of my learning by teaching me to use in-depth analysis and [. . . to] critique [. . .] course material in other disciplines. In fact, it [sic] is such a basic core of women's studies curriculum that it is automatic for me to use these tools."

Students also noted that the institutes' administrators, faculty, *and* staff (including student staff) contributed significantly to their overall achievement of the assessment plan's goals. Their help, support, strength, skill, and patience were all noted. One student noted that the quality of the teaching in women's studies classes crystallized issues and gave her methods to move through and past problems. Another said that faculty were not only excellent but also made students want to learn; they pushed students to reach their own and current conclusions. They were "well informed, [. . .] extremely passionate, and enthusiastic about ideas. [. . .]"

The goals students found most important included knowledge of the history and development of feminist thought and the interdisciplinary nature and methodological approaches of women's studies. One noted that being interdisciplinary was women's studies greatest strength because it gave her undergraduate education more depth and a better, more holistic, picture of the world. Two students extolled the variety of courses, topics, and approaches to feminist thought. Most students rated as crucial critical and analytical thinking and writing skills and the ability to access and assess library resources using increasingly sophisticated electronic technology.

Though they felt their mastery of these goals had definitely increased, most also noted that that process of mastery is one of lifelong learning. Still their confidence in these areas had grown as had their consciousness of the processes of research and writing themselves. At the same time, several students felt their lower-division courses (in women's studies as well as general studies) did not adequately prepare them for the demands of more advanced work in the minor or major. One student felt this to be so important that she advocated forcing students in classes institution-wide to write from the beginning. Women's studies new lower-division Introductory Research Methods course should offer one focus for close attention to this point. Students also wanted more women's studies classes in general although they were not more specific in outlining the details, and one advocated that professors adopt a uniform grading standard. Still most felt that faculty were excellent in supporting their mastery of the goals and said that the program merely needed to continue focusing on individual student needs.

As to whether additional goals should supplement those presently in the assessment plan, most agreed they were already comprehensive. Some wanted oral communication and formal presentation skills added, especially since they have a particular focus in some required upper-division courses. They saw these skills as particularly important for maintaining civility in discourse when participants disagree. Others said activism, though part of many classes, should be an explicit component of the assessment plan since volunteerism was such an integral part of their lives. While the structured internship, historically a recommended elective, will also be a new core requirement, faculty in addition will explore formal service-learning opportunities in appropriate courses.

The survey's final question, regarding the effectiveness of the senior thesis as the capstone tool for assessing student learning, had only one student advocate a different measure: students doing oral presentations in all classes—some in small groups, others before the whole class. Everyone else thought the present method useful, even one who was loath to admit it. They believed it to be a good way to evaluate student achievement, one noting that it "gives students the freedom to utilize many of the tools learned throughout a women's studies education—I can't imagine a better way to evaluate/see these tools being applied." Another wrote, "The senior thesis along with the oral classroom presentations and the [written and oral] comments and suggestions of peers [as well as the professor's] is a very solid and comprehensive methodology of assessing the effectiveness of the program."

Though this project was externally imposed by an activist and conservative legislature, integrating it into the existing curriculum has given it the integrity it might otherwise not have had. It has also offered concrete opportunity for self-reflection by students, staff, and faculty, something that could have remained vague, nebulous, and unarticulated—though one would hope not, of course, given the foundations and purposes of feminist education.

•   •   •

NOTES

1. In addition to thanking the many students who have participated in our women's studies senior seminar since its inception and who have provided me with concrete examples from their theses and their assessment-plan evaluation question-

naires, I want specifically, to acknowledge the contribution of two of the institute's student staff members: Alicia Edwards for painstaking research through seminar archives and Teresa Harper for her meticulous assistance with the manuscript preparation. All of these students have enriched and continue to enrich my life.

2. Bennett, first appointed chair of the National Endowment of the Humanities and later to a cabinet position as secretary of education in the Reagan/Bush administrations, is the author of *To Reclaim a Legacy: A Report on the Humanities in Higher Education* (1984); Cheney followed Bennett at the humanities endowment; Chavez was a U.S. civil rights commissioner during the same Republican administrations; Sowell is a senior fellow at the Hoover Institution, Stanford University, and a nationally syndicated columnist; Bloom, now deceased, was on the faculty of the University of Chicago when he wrote *The Closing of the American Mind: How Higher Education Has Failed Democracy and Impoverished the Souls of Today's Students* (1986). The National Association of Scholars, founded in 1987 and with chapters of conservative academics across the country, has led the fight against the expansion of access to higher education, the creation of new disciplines, the new "outsider" scholarship, and has fomented the "canon wars," all under the umbrella charge of fighting "political correctness."

More scholarship with this perspective includes Charles Sykes's *Profscam: Professors and the Demise of Higher Education* (1988); Roger Kimball's *Tenured Radicals: How Politics Corrupted Our Higher Education* (1990); and Dinesh D'Souza's *Illiberal Education: The Politics of Race and Class on Campus* (1991).

For an outline of and broad perspective on the actual anti-intellectualism of these folks' work, see *To Reclaim a Legacy of Diversity: Analyzing the "Political Correctness" Debates in Higher Education* (1993), a report from the National Council for Research on Women.

WORKS CITED

Bennett, William. *To Reclaim a Legacy: A Report on the Humanities in Higher Education*. Washington, DC: National Endowment for the Humanities, 1984.

Bloom, Allan. *The Closing of the American Mind: How Higher Education Has Failed Democracy and Impoverished the Souls of Today's Students*. New York: Simon and Schuster, 1986.

D'Souza, Dinesh. *Illiberal Education: The Politics of Race and Sex on Campus*. New York: Free Press, 1991.

Kimball, Roger. *Tenured Radicals: How Politics Corrupted Our Higher Education*. New York: Harper and Row, 1990.

Minnich, Elizabeth Kamarck. *Transforming Knowledge*. Philadelphia: Temple University Press, 1990.

Schultz, Debra. *To Reclaim a Legacy of Diversity: Analyzing the Political Debates in Higher Education.* New York: National Council for Research on Women, 1993.

Sykes, Charles. *Profscam: Professors and the Demise of Higher Education.* Washington, DC: Regnery Gateway, 1990.

Technology: Pedagogical Enhancement or Impediment?

6

WOMEN'S STUDIES ON TELEVISION?
It's Time for Distance Learning

Annis H. Hopkins

Standing in line at Wendy's, my daughter nudges me in the ribs. "That guy keeps looking at us," she whispers.

"What guy?"

"That one over there. The one who looks like my grandpa."

Our food in hand, we head for an empty table in the corner. The elderly gentleman's eyes follow our progress, and as we near him, he raises his hand, tentatively, like a student unsure of his ground.

"Are you . . . aren't you . . . the lady who teaches on the TV?"

I stop. "I might be, yes; I *do*."

"You see there, Martha. I told you it was her." His head swivels. "I told her it was you. And this must be your daughter." Swivels again. "She talks about you all the time. Oh, don't worry. It's all good." Swivel. "It's her daughter, Martha. See, I told you." Back to me. "I've been watching your class for two years, and I just love it. Don't I Martha? Don't I tell you about it all the time? Don't I?"

It happens all the time—at Wendy's, at the grocery store, the mall, the bookstore. My students lovingly call our time together "The Annis Winfrey Show," and we have a cadre of faithful viewers who let me know they haven't gotten tired yet of hearing about "women in contemporary American society," even though they watch the "same old class" semester after semester. Some of them are channel surfers who've caught our curl, some have actually gone looking for "the educational channel," and some are even former students checking up on me, but they all come together on Tuesday and Thursday afternoons (or set their VCRs) to hear and see what the issue of the day will be.

Of course, there are registered students watching, too, about ninety each semester, most of them full-time workers who videotape "the show" and then invite me into their living rooms in the evening, or on Sunday afternoon, with husband, wife, kids, and neighbors buzzing through to comment and argue with what "that crazy lady is saying this time."

For the past five years, I've been teaching the only live-cablecast introductory women's studies survey course in my region, and in light of my research, perhaps the only course of its kind in the United States and Canada.

Why am I the only one? I have some ideas about the reasons. Equipment needs, lack of vision on the part of distance-learning departments, resistance to women's studies, and women's studies programs' own reluctance to participate may be obstacles that must be overcome. Concerns grounded in feminist pedagogy about conducting courses in a lecture format without direct interaction are valid but not insurmountable. In this essay I'm going to offer some strategies that have been working in my class, in the hope that more women's studies faculty will take the plunge. A course containing a balance of theory with personal narrative offered by the teacher, a selection of exciting guest speakers, and by the students themselves raises consciousness and leads students into analysis and skills that will permanently enhance their lives, whether they are in a traditional classroom or not.

DISTANCE-LEARNING METHODS AND PROGRAMS

Typically, distance-learning technology forms a part of a university's extended-education program.[1] Technologies such as cable television, public television, radio broadcast, satellite transmission, computer conferencing, audio- and videocassette, audio and audiographic conferencing, interactive audio and video, teleconferencing, and electronic mail

> serve adult students for whom distance is just one of several barriers to education, along with limited time, work and family commitments, and constrained financial resources. Distance education affords students greater control over where they study, and often, how long they take to complete a course. (*The Electronic University* xiii)

My students fit this national profile of students who can't get to campus. For example, nearly every semester, I have at least one brand-new mom who is homebound by health or by choice; I can't imagine a better way to start life than by having a budding feminist for a mom!

WOMEN'S STUDIES VIA DISTANCE LEARNING

Current Courses

Very few women's studies classes are currently being offered via distance learning.[2] The standard distance-learning guides list only four.[3] In May 1995, I posted a request for more information to the Internet via the Women's Studies List and the Distance Learning List sponsored by the Western Interstate Commission for Higher Education Telecommunications Cooperative. My e-mail respondents referred to electronic discussion groups, teleconferencing, Internet lists, video, and compressed-video courses rather than live courses like mine.

I received only two responses about current-video women's studies courses. Muriel Oaks, director, Extended University Services, reports that Washington State University offers "two video courses W St/Pol S 305, Gender and Politics (3 cr) and W St/Mgt 315, Women in Management (3 cr)."[4] Ellen Rose, women's studies, University of Nevada, Las Vegas, has "just completed the first-ever distance-education women's studies course in Nevada, a course in feminist theories, [which she taught . . .] via compressed video, to a small group of students [there] and another small group of students at University of Nevada, Reno." Evidently, while some of us are experimenting with the newer technologies, women's studies by distance learning is still in its infancy.

Obstacles to Distance Learning for Women's Studies

First, only about three hundred colleges and universities in the United States are now offering distance education; of these, fewer than one hundred have women's studies programs.[5] Thus it might not be possible to take women's studies immediately onto live TV everywhere, but most institutions do have the equipment to begin using video and audio technologies, even without the support of a formal distance-learning component. All it takes is a pioneer willing to be taped and to modify an existing course.

Second, most current distance-learning course work focuses on technology itself, rather than on meeting general-education requirements, especially where funding limits choices in the range of offerings to a particular audience. Many technology courses are offered primarily because local employers set up "universities" within their own systems. For example, here at Arizona State University Main in Tempe, far more distance courses are offered by the College of Engineering and Applied Sciences than by other colleges, and many of them go directly to major corporate centers, such as Motorola. However, distance learning pays for itself by expanding its services, and proposals are welcomed. Besides, heads of industry are finally beginning to notice that more of their workers are women. Might they not be interested in learning about contemporary American women, especially if their personnel could attend classes right in their employees' break room?

Third, women's studies continues to experience resistance on many campuses. Students still come into my classes fresh from the usual barrage of comments from friends who hear they're taking women's studies: "They're all a bunch of lesbians over there, you know." "Oh, when did you become a radical feminist?" "Why isn't there a men's studies class?" Wary administrators may not wish to have the college or university openly represented by what they identify as our theoretical stances. Televised courses are one of the most visible outreach vehicles available to a university, and cautious decision makers are careful to tailor the image portrayed to the expectations of those to whom they must answer, such as appropriations committees and alumni organizations. I think it is time for women's studies advocates to defuse such concerns by inviting administrators and politicians to visit our programs and classrooms, so that they may see exactly what goes on. Do we really gain anything by continuing to allow the popular media to define us in the minds of potential allies? Further, at ASU, the administration places a high priority on building links with the surrounding community; our president tells us this is a trend sweeping higher education. Women's studies programs can link with other units on campus in these efforts, increasing our visibility and making friends outside the academic realm. With or without distance learning these are connections women's studies programs need to be making.

WST 300: Women in Contemporary American Society

The purpose of Women in Contemporary American Society is to introduce junior-level general-studies students to the women's studies curriculum—specifically, to a feminist analysis of U.S. institutions in terms of the status and roles of women since World War II. I encourage students to conceptualize and experience social theory in ways that will lead them to become active participants in the task of challenging women's oppression, in other words, we work on consciousness raising that will lead to action.[6] On cable, I must also effectively introduce our curriculum to the unidentifiable audience tuning in on any given day; thus each segment must both conceptualize and concretize its own theoretical frameworks, being more or less self-contained while maintaining the integrity and flow of the course.

Teaching WST 300 on Television

WST 300 originates in a studio on ASU's Tempe campus, where sixty-two students attend two seventy-five-minute classes a week. The studio is a large lecture hall with a lectern in a pit at the bottom of tiers of immovable student tables and chairs. Viewers see the lecturer and students in the classroom, and students must use microphones on their desks so that the TV audience can hear them; this daily exercise keeps in-studio class members acutely aware of their "absent" classmates. A computer system makes the use of various graphics and other "presentation" programming possible, adding a colorful high-tech feel where appropriate. Pink and yellow graphs don't make women's income figures any less appalling, but they are more eye-catching than enlarged newspaper print.

There are three cameras positioned around the room, one directly in front of the lectern (for the speaker), one over the speaker's desk (for use as an overhead projector), and one in the right rear corner of the room to provide a wide shot of the entire classroom). The cameras are in fixed positions and are operated remotely from a tech room located behind a one-way window to the speaker's left. The technician can manipulate the cameras to provide close-ups of individual students when they are talking, so that we are all engaged by a full-face picture on the four monitors that show us the same picture home viewers are seeing.

While the setup may seem intimidating, teaching in this situation is not as different from teaching in the regular classroom as one might expect. There are no teleprompters and no stopwatches, although I do have to make that final point before the clock ticks and the camera is turned off. A novice might want to practice a few lectures on video before going on live, although it isn't really necessary. The essential ingredients are enthusiasm, a firm grasp of the material, and a willingness to take the risk.

To my continuing dismay, however, a format primarily based on lectures does work best in this setting, although some degree of general discussion is possible, provided one response is given at a time; the format accommodates only extremely brief small-group discussions. We have no choice but to forgo many of the teaching techniques and tools that have become a part of the feminist pedagogical array, including a low student-teacher ratio. Another difficulty is that here I cannot "wander," except with a very wide shot of the classroom; and students must remain seated. This structure is especially hard for me, since I prefer to roam around a classroom talking one-on-one with students.

Also, video clips that I might use in a regular classroom usually cannot be shown due to copyright restrictions and the limited availability and expense of broadcast-quality tape. It *is* possible to secure some permissions, if you start early enough and have the necessary funding.

Small-group discussion and in-class team projects are also problematic. For one thing, live television demands that "something" be happening at a focal point at all times, so extended "dead air space" is unacceptable. In a class whose material makes people want to talk, the broadcast medium's demand for "action" can be intimidating, even frustrating at times. To meet this challenge, we frequently have exercises in which all students quietly discuss the topic at hand in small groups, with a camera trained on only one pair or a triad, whose mike is activated. While the din in the background is distracting, cable students report positive reactions to being included in such "private" conversations between classmates. The conscious intention of the on-mike students to draw in and include the otherwise isolated viewer matters too.

A related difficulty concerns the fact that the cablecast is live; therefore anyone who speaks must be rather careful. Not only do FCC rules prohibit some language that might be appropriate in a nontelevised classroom but also speakers must be aware that everything they say is being cablecast and taped, without any possibility of editing.

On the positive side, live television encourages a level of preparation that might otherwise not occur. When I'm paying close attention to everything that comes out of my mouth, I tend to stick more closely to my outline and cover the material more completely than I do in some other situations. Even when I throw in personal anecdotes or get involved in a heated exchange with students, I take more care than I otherwise might, to everyone's benefit.

One last issue, the large class size, is familiar to all women's studies programs that provide "service courses" at a large university; the televised section is not significantly different from my usual class size. Even for those accustomed to small numbers, a class of 150 loses some of its negative impact when it is reframed and welcomed as an opportunity to reach more people with the messages and analyses of society so important to women's studies. After all, if what we want to do is change the world, what better place to start than in people's own living rooms?

ANSWERING PEDAGOGICAL OBJECTIONS TO DISTANCE LEARNING AS A TOOL FOR WOMEN'S STUDIES

Two significant objections to presenting a women's studies curriculum via live cable television still need to be addressed more fully: the resistance to a primarily lecture-only format and the lack of direct interactivity with students not in the classroom.

Lecture-Format Issues

The lecture as a teaching technique has been identified by some critics as part and parcel of the "traditional approach" to education that excluded both women and information about women from the learning process. Many feminist teachers have worked to eliminate the lecture as a primary teaching tool; in fact, at my university, lectures given by the instructor take up less than half the time in the average women's studies survey course. Frances Maher and Mary Tetreault observe that

> in traditional approaches, the scholarly expert, having distilled "the truth" from the best minds in the field, transmits it to students. Students learn either through lectures, or by engaging with the professor in a form of so-called "Socratic" dialogue, in which the professor elicits, through a series of probing questions, the right or appropriate answers to the problem posed. Learning is equated to understanding the material in the terms put forward by the scholarly authorities. (8)

When we resort to giving lectures, we may feel that we have somehow "gone back on" ourselves, but this need not be the case. To be successful in the distance-learning mode, lectures must and can be reconceptualized and restructured to eliminate the authoritarianism that gave rise to these critiques. As Maher and Tetreault point out, it is not the method so much as the motivation that matters. The aim of the pedagogy is key:

> Feminist and liberatory pedagogies aim to encourage the students, particularly women, working-class students, and members of underrepresented ethnic groups, to gain an education that would be relevant to their concerns, to create their own meanings, and to find their own voices in relation to the material. Just as the disciplines are evolving toward multifocal and constructivist forms of knowledge, based on the experiences and viewpoints of all groups in society and not just the most powerful, so does the enactment of these new epistemologies in the classroom draw upon the viewpoints and experiences of students and teachers in new ways. (9–10)

My cable course embraces most aspects of Maher and Tetreault's recommendations. My students regularly include reentry women and men, working-class students, and members of underrepresented ethnic groups who
might otherwise not be in college at all. The class also draws a large percentage of more "familiar" college students; this diversity contributes im-
measurably to the character of the learning environment.

In addition, the guest speakers who visit the class bring unique voices
that create a space in which nontraditional students can find their own
voices as well. When one of the first female underground miners in Kentucky spoke about sexual harassment and assault by male coworkers, for
example, at least five other reentry women in the studio shared similar
experiences they had had in the local fire department, at the airport, and
in construction work and thus helped to answer the questions of less-expe-
rienced students in ways I could never have done on my own. Cable students also reported both personal experiences and new understandings
that grew out of the theoretical discussions that surrounded the speakers'
presentations.

Our guests have included some quite remarkable speakers, such as
Gretchen Bataille[7] and Siera Russell,[8] sharing the past and present patterns of oppression experienced by Native American women in the United
States; two lesbian couples, explaining the effects of external and internalized homophobia; a sixty-five-year-old woman Mexican-American mayor;
and a Bosnian-American woman who had just spent a year in the camps
where Bosnian Muslim women, who have been raped by Serbian Christian
soldiers, come for assistance.

Guests' personal narratives help students to confront oppression as
real, not theoretical, as lived, not imagined. Examining the speakers' victo-
ries over oppression both highlights the oppression and discourages label-
ing the guests as victims. Survivors of oppression are inspiring role models
for all of us. In the context of the feminist theoretical framework, they
challenge students to look beyond preconceptions about the oppression of
women. As one of my distance-learning students wrote:

> I must admit that before I enrolled in this course, I believed that
> most of the discrimination against women was a thing of the past.
> However, I soon began to speak with my family and friends con-
> cerning this issue and found that many of them believed that men
> were fundamentally superior to women. As a result, they felt that
> women did not deserve equal treatment. I was dismayed that so
> many people I had known for years had these beliefs. [. . .] I now
> believe that an enormous amount of oppression continues to exist

in our society. [. . .] My first reaction was anger. I found it outra-
geous that so many people felt that I was in some way inferior to
males. I had several arguments with friends concerning this issue,
which only increased my anger. My second reaction was one of
fear. I found it extremely frightening that so many people considered women second-class citizens. My final and current reaction to
the acceptance of this information is one of action. I now feel that I
am able to offer more accurate advice to my friends when they are
in situations where oppression occurs. In addition, I can identify
oppression in my own life more easily and react accordingly. Although ignorance concerning the existence of oppression appears
to make life simpler, I feel very fortunate to have had the opportunity to learn of this oppression so that I can take further appropriate actions.[9]

This response from a cable student, who watched the course on tape,
shows that even without live participation, theoretical frameworks brought
to life by the experiences of real people change students' attitudes and inspire activism.

During these visits, we in the studio actively engage the guest lecturers.
When students see themselves playing a role in analysis, either actually or
vicariously, they see their opinions as critical to the dialogue. As a result of
such conversations, however brief, students learn not to blindly accept
everything people say, including everything their instructors say. I remind
them on an almost daily basis that their responsibility is to develop their
own social theory, to collect as many different perspectives as they can,
and then decide for themselves on an ongoing basis which are most likely
to get them what they want in their lives. Students often articulate these
learning processes quite clearly:

I completely accept the proposition that oppression must be challenged. [. . .] In order to obtain social justice, people must fight
oppressive structures. This course has taught me many ways to
combat oppression. People must acknowledge that oppression
exists. We must survive in spite of it. People need to educate
themselves and others about oppression. We must question authority even though our culture opposes it. We must learn to say
no to uncomfortable situations and refuse to participate in the
cycle of oppression. People need to set goals and meet them. This
is important because ending oppression begins small with individuals.

Thus I have found that lectures can be combined with brief discussions in ways completely consistent with feminist pedagogy to successfully present our material.

Interactivity Issues

Classroom interactivity has long been accepted as a positive characteristic by contemporary educators, including members of the collaborative-learning movement and those advocating feminist pedagogy. In *The Feminist Classroom* Maher and Tetreault point out that

> what has made feminist pedagogy unique [. . .] has been its atten-
> tion to the particular needs of women students and its grounding
> in feminist theory as the basis for its multidimensional and posi-
> tional view of the construction of classroom knowledge. As Maher
> puts it in one article, "we need an interactive pedagogy, a peda-
> gogy which integrates student contributions into the subject mat-
> ter, just as the subject matter integrates the new material on
> women."
>
> One mark of this pedagogy is that learning proceeds at least
> partly from the questions of the students themselves and/or from
> the everyday experiences of ordinary people. (9)

When, after five years in the regular women's studies classroom, I was initially invited to conduct a women's studies survey course via cable televi-
sion, I struggled with the problem of reduced interactivity. Some direct interaction with cable students *is* possible. Registered cable students may call a restricted-access telephone number during the cablecast to partici-
pate in discussion. Callers bring a fresh voice to the room and in-studio students perk up to listen, perhaps more carefully than to what goes on in the room. In-studio responses are most often welcoming and delighted, making the caller feel that she or he is a vital part of the class; students who cannot or choose not to call nevertheless report feeling welcomed into the discussion.

However, the majority of students taking the course on cable videotape the class for later viewing, because they work full-time or take other courses during the live cablecast. Thus our in-depth written communications serve as the primary link between classroom, teacher, and student. Cable students and teacher interact weekly through journaling (called learning evaluation), study questions that bring together readings and lectures, and formal essay assignments.

The amount of written work generated in this way is, quite frankly, mountainous. With a work-study student or TA available only for checking off graded assignments, I devote considerable time to reading and responding to student materials. I believe this commitment is necessary if my teaching is to remain consistent with my feminist ideology.

Lack of direct interactivity is a legitimate concern. However, studies on interactivity in distance-learning situations suggest that actual individual interactions with an instructor or with other students may not be as essential as sometimes thought. Shugiang Zhang and Catherine Fulford "examined relationships between student perceptions of classroom interaction and the actual amount of time allocated for interaction in a 10-session interactive television course with an enrollment of 260 students" (58). They found that "students' assessment of overall interactivity was found to be largely based upon their observation of peer participation rather than overt personal involvement" (58). In fact, they concluded that

> vicarious interaction—interaction that is observed but involves no direct and overt participation of the observing student—consistently contributes more to a person's assessment of overall interactivity than his or her own observable participation in interaction. [. . .] This provides an empirical basis for a claim that student perception of overall interactivity is shaped more by the participatory behaviors of the peers than by his or her own share of the action. (62)

Written comments from students in my televised course affirm these findings. Many report that they feel free to express opinions and to debate the material, even though they may never have actually participated live in such activity. In fact, some of the liveliest debates in the class develop on paper moving between cable students and me.

Students report that both the theoretical and the physical structures of the televised course are quite effective in overcoming issues of reduced interactivity and meeting the stated goals of women's studies. A portion of a student's answer to a final exam question serves as a representative response:

> The main reason why I accepted most of the material was the course structure. This is the first class that I have taken at ASU that requires you to look into your own self. [. . .] This class has enabled me to dig deep into my thoughts, to evaluate my own social theory, and to open my eyes to many problems that exist.

[. . . The structure] put the responsibility back onto the students to look at themselves and apply the material [. . .] to our own lives. This was accomplished in a number of ways. [. . .] Instead of placing emphasis on standardized tests, you place emphasis on hands-on learning. The weekly study questions and learning evaluations have required me to focus more on what I put into the class. The method of [. . .] lecture pulls in students to comment and participate. [. . .] Although I have not been in the classroom, but rather in the comfort of my own home, the message conveyed made me feel there. My wife has also learned from being there as I watch the tapes of your class. Yes, the class has liberated me.

These comments from a young man whom I have never met or spoken to are similar to those of many other students. A balance of theory and personal narrative draws students into the women's studies curriculum, even when they encounter it via television.

It must be noted as well, however, that there's more going on here than content. I know that my personality helps. Elsewhere in his essay, the student just quoted makes it clear that a large part of "the method of lecture" is my manner, my ease with the subject matter, and my consistent unflappability. It is true that neither teaching women's studies nor teaching on television is for the seriously faint of heart, but it's well worth the effort.

There are other benefits to learning about women's studies at home, especially on videotape, beyond the obvious advantage to the homebound or working student of class availability. Further research to find out which of these benefits are consistent, and whether they actually outweigh any disadvantages individual students may encounter is in order, but what I have already observed has convinced me of the positive impact of the course materials when students use videotaped class sessions.

One benefit is that whereas students taking women's studies in a normal classroom must take notes and experience their reactions to the material "as it goes by," students watching on video may stop the tape, rewind, listen again, and pick up details they missed the first time. This means that rather than "missing out," they actually get significantly more of the course material than students in the classroom. All students in this class are required to hand in notes covering each class session as evidence of "attendance." While there is great variation in the comprehensiveness of student note taking, it is possible to tell from a cursory examination which notes were taken on a single run through of the material—either in class or viewed live—and which were the result of a more reflective viewing of the taped broadcast. The physical distance entailed in the format actually provides more space for meaningful contemplation than can usually be afforded in-class students.

When a guest speaker presents highly emotional material, physical distance becomes crucial. For example, an incest survivor who regularly visits during the unit on violence against women provides such an intense experience that most "live" students take very few notes; they later wish they had, but the opportunity is gone. In contrast, students who view a taped version of the session usually submit detailed notes, often interspersed with personal comments; their learning-evaluation comments also reveal greater depth of analysis.

Again, whereas "live" students may be constrained in their reactions by the presence and perceived expectations of other students, most of whom they do not know well, students watching the class in the privacy of their own homes report they feel free to laugh, cry, express anger, shout, argue with the speaker, and discuss the material with family members or friends. At home there is no need for the false bravado that students often resort to in the classroom; at home, they are more able to "claim" their own reactions to the material. Powerful reactions show up more clearly in cable students' written work than in that of studio students. Like the young man quoted above, many students report important familial interactions that might not have happened had their entire experience of the class taken place in a regular classroom, especially not in front of three television cameras.

Writing assignments that are designed to create dialogue between me and the students provide another key form of interaction. Most text assignments are the subject of study questions that ask for both factual answers and personal responses. The study questions are graded closely for both content and presentation. In addition, each week students are asked to evaluate their learning; in these entries, students are to identify at least one area of disagreement with material they have encountered in the class, and one area of positive learning. They must explain how they intend to use something from the week's work to bring their lives more in line with what they would like them to be. In other words, they must address, in a journal-like form, the ways in which course information has affected their personal social theory.

Students undertake two independent projects: a written critical analysis of course-appropriate outside reading and an in-person investigation of a local agency that serves women, followed by an essay. Thus each student must do more than repeat theoretical information on a test in order to pass the course.

Women in Contemporary American Society ends with an essay-format final exam that asks students to examine their individual areas of acceptance and rejection of course material (using Patti Lather's model)[10] and to articulate their own social theories. The final exam is the only written assignment of the semester on which students do not receive some form of direct teacher response to their ideas.[11]

Through the exchange of written materials, especially those that offer personal opinion—mine as well as theirs—I become acquainted with many students as individuals; from their perspective, students routinely report that they feel well acquainted with me, since they are, after all, visiting with me in their own living rooms on a regular basis. My seemingly personal presence in their homes provides a level of bodily proximity and eye contact (however illusory) rarely available in any regular classroom. Such a "perception" of interaction, as described above, goes a long way toward making students feel a part of the class.

OTHER BENEFITS OF TEACHING WOMEN'S STUDIES ON TELEVISION

The resources and outreach provided by this class to the women's studies program, the university, and the community make it well worth the investment of energy and time required to offer women's studies on television.

Each class session is videotaped in our Video Resources Center, and copies remain available for student use for two weeks after each class. Thus it is possible to require "attendance"; students who miss class must go to the lab and make up the session within that time. The availability of classes on tape allows every student a kind of guaranteed continuity that cannot be achieved in a regular classroom. Further, I request a copy of each session for the women's studies program video collection (at women's studies' expense); the university retains copyright to the videos, but the women's studies program has permission to use them in its classes at our own discretion. Since the sessions are relatively self-contained, they can be used by other instructors in the event of an illness or other absence. Video also makes it possible for unusual or difficult-to-schedule guests—like a former state secretary of public instruction, one of the local founders of the Gray Panthers, or the head of the Governor's Office for Women—to be "reused" in other classes.

Finally, we now offer an Independent Study by Correspondence WST 300 package, which uses a set of the TV tapes, available to students anywhere the mail goes. This course is much like the ones offered at Washington State and the University of Nevada at Reno and Las Vegas.

Women's studies stands to benefit profoundly from having our classes on television. If our mission is to "change the world"—and I tell my students from the very first day that that is *my* goal—should we not consider seriously a medium that takes our message beyond the walls of our classrooms? Not only does a well-conducted course enhance the reputation of women's studies as a discipline by systematically refuting the objections put forth in the popular press, but it also makes people who might otherwise not know of its existence aware of women's studies. Whereas not everyone will come to the university to take our classes, nearly every home now has a television set. Televising courses breaks barriers of class and gender in uniquely powerful ways. Increasing our visibility allows people to see what we are really doing in our programs, replacing myth with firsthand experience. Offering our curriculum on television both brings us students and encourages feminist analysis in the lives of viewers we will never meet. Most important, it actually makes our curriculum available to the public in ways that make us more activists than simply the academic arm of the feminist movement.

The university benefits as well in terms of visibility and enhanced goodwill in the community. The contemporary, personal nature of our material appeals to a wide audience. We can help to represent the university as a thoughtful, caring, inviting place. Thus the program, the university, and the community benefit from the visibility of Women in Contemporary American Society on local television.

CONCLUSIONS

Making the case for using television and other distance-learning technologies in women's studies has brought me insights that will become a part of all my teaching in the future.[12] It would be good for all of us to examine "how we do things" regularly. We should ask ourselves, What is it that we wish to achieve in our courses, particularly in the large survey sections that serve the university by meeting general-studies requirements for graduation? What evidence do we have that our methods are effective? Although certain aspects of these questions deserve a great deal more research, my experience has revealed that it is possible to bridge even the actual physical distance between my podium and a student's living room. As one reentry woman student commented:

> This material has enriched my life and taught me to think in new and different ways. It has led me to be concerned with social justice for everyone. It has provided me with a chance to express my feelings and opinions about society and human nature. The information has taught me to be more open-minded. [. . .] It has also

inspired me to take action. I am very angry that society is full of oppressive structures. [. . .] We must take action.

Other students focus more on their personal growth:

This class [. . .] has taught me to think differently and to look at things from a different perspective. But what I have found most enlightening is a greater understanding of myself as an individual. This class came to me at a perfect time in my life. Because of this class, I now have a better sense of who I am what I am about, and what my goals are for the future.

I am convinced that a mix of feminist theory and personal narrative not only works to overcome the initial resistance of students and nonregistered viewers to the women's studies curriculum but also leads them to examine their lives as they have never done before. They learn that parts of their society are ugly, but they also learn that they can commit to not being ugly to each other. They learn that as caring, thinking human beings, they can contribute to the amelioration of the human condition.

I urge women's studies teachers, whatever their fears, to make our transformative curriculum available through distance learning. If framed appropriately, the material speaks for itself. It's time to move beyond the confines of our classrooms into the technology of the twenty-first century.

•　　•　　•

NOTES

1. Extended education includes evening and weekend classes both on and off campus, adult continuing-education programs, and correspondence study, as well as distance learning using technologies. While the 298 universities, colleges, community colleges, consortiums, public-broadcasting stations, and statewide telecommunications services listed in Oryx Press's 1994 *Guide to Distance Learning* by William Burgess offer a wide variety of course work, six subject areas predominate: accounting, business administration, computer science, engineering, nursing, and teacher education. Counted as one area, liberal arts forms a seventh category with myriad courses.

2. Written reports are scarce. A relevant article with an excellent Canadian-emphasis bibliography is "Tele-communication: Women's Studies through Distance Education" by Helen Lenskyj, who teaches at the Ontario Institute for Studies in Education and writes about Canadian efforts to reach women living in

remote areas. Lenskyj cites several other sources. One of my respondents, Janet Baldwin, a graduate student in Adult and Continuing Education at the University of Saskatchewan, is conducting research there, with a special interest in compressed video.

3. *The Electronic University* has none, and the *Oryx Guide* identifies these: Introduction to Women's Studies (University of Nevada, Reno—audio- and video-cassette); Northern Minnesota Women: Myths and Realities (University of Minnesota—audiocassette); and Women in Western Culture and Women in Judaism (University of Arizona—live broadcast). According to U of A Video Services, their two courses were taught only once, and the tapes were not retained.

4. "They include 15 video lessons, an extensive course guide with readings and lessons, and interaction via voice mail and/or e-mail with the instructor" (e-mail from Muriel Oaks).

5. This number was obtained by cross-referencing the distance-learning guidebooks with the National Women's Studies Association's 1990 directory; the overlap has likely increased somewhat with the proliferation of distance-learning technologies.

6. We define *social theory* as follows: a set of statements about how the world is, how it got to be that way, and how it ought to be changed, from a particular perspective, with a particular focus.

7. Gretchen Bataille's relevant texts include *American Indian Women: A Guide to Research* (1991), *American Indian Women: Telling Their Lives* (1984), and *Native American Women: A Biographical Dictionary* (1993).

8. Siera Russell is a Yavapai-Apache attorney working in the Indian Legal Program, College of Law, Arizona State University.

9. All of the anonymous student comments cited here are taken from written materials submitted by students in the spring 1995 cablecast WST 300 section.

10. In her chapter entitled "Staying Dumb? Student Resistance to Liberatory Curriculum," Lather explains that students either accept or reject oppositional information (information that is different from what they already accept as true, information that challenges their belief systems). She further describes acceptance as taking several possible directions: it can be burdensome, leading to hopelessness and fear, it can lead to anger, or it can be liberating, leading to action. For this final exam, students are asked to choose specific areas of "oppositional information" and place themselves in Lather's schema (127).

11. Paper exchanges are conducted in two ways. First, students who are on campus regularly may drop off and pick up assignments in the women's studies program office where the staff maintains a confidential file. Students who do not come to campus, perhaps a third of those registered via cable, mail assignments weekly. Mailing my responses back to them is the major expense the distance-learning format presents to the women's studies program.

12. Copies of my syllabus are available upon request at the following address: Annis H. Hopkins, SS 103, Arizona State University, Tempe, AZ 85287-1801, or via e-mail at ICAHH@asuvm.inre.asu.edu.

WORKS CITED

Burgess, William E. *The Oryx Guide to Distance Learning*. Phoenix: Oryx Press, 1994.

The Electronic University: A Guide to Distance Learning. Princeton: Peterson's Guides, 1993.

Lather, Patti. *Getting Smart: Feminist Research and Pedagogy with/in the Post-modern*. New York: Routledge, 1991.

Lenskyj, Helen. "Tele-communication: Women's Studies through Distance Education." *Resources for Feminist Research* 20 (1991): 11–12.

Maher, Frances, and Mary Kay Thompson Tetreault. *The Feminist Classroom: An Inside Look at How Professors and Students Are Transforming Higher Education for a Diverse Society*. New York: HarperCollins, 1994.

NWSA Directory of Women's Studies Programs, Women's Centers, and Women's Research Centers. College Park: University of Maryland University Press, 1990.

Zhang, Shuqiang, and Catherine P. Fulford. "Are Interaction Time and Psychological Interactivity the Same Thing in the Distance Learning Television Classroom?" *Educational Technology* (July–Aug. 1994): 58–64.

7

"THIS CLASS MEETS IN CYBERSPACE"
Women's Studies via Distance Education[1]

Ellen Cronan Rose

Educational theorists and policy makers alike are currently fascinated with a range of technologies called "distance education" because they see in these technologies possibilities for addressing a number of problems—from meeting the instructional needs of a demographically diverse student population (including many who work full-time or who live inconvenient distances from institutions of higher education) to pooling scarce resources in an increasingly stringent economy.[2] Women's studies administrators, faculty, and students are both eager to avail themselves of the benefits of distance education and wary of its possible pedagogical limitations. On the plus side, women's studies practitioners see in distance education a means of reaching out to homebound or rural women who would otherwise be unable to take courses. It also offers small programs with limited resources an opportunity to share faculty and courses with other similarly small programs with equally limited but different resources. But how congenial are these technologies to the kind of participatory, collaborative learning that is the hallmark of the feminist classroom? It was, in part, to answer that question that I agreed to offer my Feminist Theories course via distance education to students at the University of Nevada, Reno (UNR), as well as at my own institution, the University of Nevada, Las Vegas (UNLV). While my reflections on the experience of trying to teach a women's studies course in a distance-learning environment can make no more than a qualitative, experiential, and anecdotal contribution to the small but growing literature on women's studies and distance education, I believe they raise questions we need to ponder before unconditionally embracing these technologies.[3]

INSTITUTIONAL CONTEXT

Shortly after I arrived in Las Vegas in July 1993 as UNLV's first full-time director of women's studies, I learned about distance education and began to wonder whether it might help solve some of the problems facing UNLV's and UNR's women's studies programs, both young, small, and strapped for resources. Since 1992, UNLV has offered both an undergraduate major and minor in women's studies; UNR offers only an undergraduate minor. At both universities, most women's studies courses are departmental cross-listings. Developing a coherent interdisciplinary women's studies curriculum is difficult when so much depends on the willingness of faculty members from a range of disciplines to develop courses that meet criteria for cross-listing with women's studies and the cooperation of department chairs in scheduling these courses regularly. Consequently, there are gaps in both programs. It seemed evident to a number of us at both universities that we would all benefit from sharing our resources, perhaps making courses from each program available to students at both, through distance education. In fall 1994, the acting director of women's studies at UNR told me that Reno would not be offering their feminist theory course in the 1994–95 academic year and asked if I would be willing to allow UNR students to enroll, via distance education, in the feminist theory course I planned to teach spring semester. In her request, I recognized an opportunity to see how accommodating to feminist education distance education might prove to be.

FEMINIST EDUCATION HAPPENS

The proliferation of curriculum transformation projects across the country, designed to integrate the experience of women and other marginalized groups into the standard postsecondary curriculum, might suggest that feminist education happens when professors revise their syllabi in the light of feminist multicultural scholarship. Most women's studies practitioners, however, believe that how we teach is as important as what we teach. For many people, the word "pedagogy" signifies classroom techniques designed to transmit knowledge from teacher (and text) to students. Traditional pedagogies employ what Brazilian educator Paulo Freire calls "the 'banking' concept of education," in which "knowledge is a gift bestowed by those who consider themselves knowledgeable upon those whom they consider to know nothing."[4] In this model, students are "containers" or "receptacles," to be "filled" by the teacher: "The more completely he fills the receptacles, the better a teacher he is. The more meekly the receptacles permit themselves to be filled, the better students they are" (58).

By contrast, Freire developed what he called "problem-posing education," which "consists in acts of cognition, not transferrals of information":

> Through dialogue, the teacher-of-the-students and the students-
> of-the-teacher cease to exist and a new term emerges: teacher-stu-
> dent with students-teachers. The teacher is no longer merely the
> one who teaches, but one who is himself taught in dialogue with
> the students, who in turn while being taught also teach. They be-
> come jointly responsible for a process in which all grow. (67)

Despite Freire's (or his translator's) unredeemed use of the generic "he,"
many principles of feminist pedagogy are derived from his model of "problem-posing education."[5] Each member of the feminist classroom is a
learner and a potential teacher. Each brings something to contribute to the
collaborative construction of knowledge, and the knowledge collectively
produced exceeds, ideally, what any member—including the teacher—
knew when she entered the class. Members of a feminist classroom respect
each other and share responsibility for constructing knowledge.

But the egalitarianism of the women's studies classroom does not mean
that all statements made therein are equally validated. Rather, students
and teacher develop what Nancy Schniedewind identifies as "skills for
sharing feelings about difference and constructively confronting conflicts"
(27) as they acknowledge that they are "situated knowers," simultaneously privileged and handicapped by their class, race, gender, sexuality,
age, and ability.[6] The feminist classroom is a learning community in which
epistemological—and other—differences are acknowledged, respected, and
used to transform social relations in the classroom, to begin with, but ultimately in the world outside the academy.

REFLECTIONS OF A PIONEER

Would it be possible to create any community, much less a genuinely feminist learning community, within the technological parameters of distance
education? My initial anxieties occurred months before registration for
spring semester and were all related to an unknown, mysterious, and
rather frightening technology. At a workshop in October, sponsored by
UNR's Instructional Media Services, I was exposed for the first time to the
mission of the University and Community College System of Nevada's distance-education project ("to provide quality education outside the geographical area of the university" [Distance Education Workshop 2]) and

the array of technologies available to realize it. I was also given a thick handbook to guide me in preparing my course for "delivery" to Reno via compressed video. As the words "provide" and "delivery" should suggest, the educational philosophy animating distance education assumes a banking model pedagogy. The diagrams of classrooms specially equipped to "deliver" or "receive" distance-education classes show an instructor's podium at the front of the room facing rows of tables or individual desks for students. Students at both home and remote sites are provided with push-button microphones so that they can ask questions or participate in discussion, but both the layout of the room and the technology assume a lecture format for the class (*Distance Education Faculty Handbook* 18).

The notion that knowledge is a commodity that can be packaged and delivered is implicit in the handbook's injunction that the distance-education instructor prepare an "extended syllabus" which contains—in addition to the usual information (course objectives, required texts, topics to be covered, grading policy)—"for each class meeting: lesson objectives, lesson key ideas, lesson study activities, [and] lesson visual materials." The idea is to provide students with "a highly organized study guide" (*Creating Materials* 2) that will allow them—should they choose—to work on their own, at their own pace.

As it turned out, I was able fairly easily to subvert the technological imperative to lecture. Enrollment in the course was small enough that students at each site could cluster around a small table and thus be visible on the TV monitors as a group to students at the other site.[7] It was, I thought, a reasonable facsimile of the circular arrangement of chairs characteristic of many women's studies classrooms. (As it turned out, I was mistaken: what we had was less a circle than two rows of students, confronting each other over a 450-mile expanse.) I left the first class meeting hopeful that we could overcome technological barriers to effective communication and succeed in transforming the distance-education classroom into a feminist classroom. I had not reckoned on the lack of parity between UNR's and UNLV's women's studies programs, the material significance of the 450 miles that physically separated the two groups of students, and the impact on class dynamics of ancillary technologies such as the e-mail accounts I had set up for all class members. Above all, I had not anticipated the lingering and wide-ranging effects of the extended syllabus, a fourteen-page document detailing course objectives, required texts, course requirements, grade-distribution percentages, and a detailed calendar, not only designating readings for each class period but also providing three or four study questions for each reading.

SEPARATE AND UNEQUAL

When the acting director of women's studies at UNR asked if her students could enroll in my course, I did not make it sufficiently clear to her that WOM 301, Feminist Theories, was designed as the second in a three-course interdisciplinary sequence required of all women's studies majors and minors at UNLV, with WOM 101, Introduction to Women's Studies, or consent of the instructor, as its prerequisite. UNLV students who registered for WOM 301 had to demonstrate either that they had previously taken WOM 101 or that they had had a sufficient number of cross-listed courses to persuade me that they had a firm grasp of core women's studies concepts and some experience of feminist pedagogy. The analogous course at UNR–WS 450, Feminist Theory and Methods—is required of minors, but WS 101, Introduction to Women's Studies, is not required of students wishing to enroll in the theory course. UNR students registered for the course in Reno, without needing to seek my permission to do so. Only one had taken a women's studies course, Introduction to Women's Studies offered at one of the community colleges, and none identified herself as a women's studies minor. Beginning with registration, therefore, there was a lack of parity between students in Reno and Las Vegas.

It was further exacerbated because four of the five UNLV students who stayed the course were women's studies majors. They knew each other well. Not only had they taken one or more courses with each other, but, more important—at a university where women's studies is a small, relatively new, not widely understood or supported program—they formed with the other ten majors a tightly knit support group. They knew me, too. Two of the UNLV students had taken Introduction to Women's Studies with me, and as director of women's studies, I am academic advisor to all majors. By contrast, none of the UNR students had known each other prior to enrolling in this course, and I was an utter unknown to them all, as—of course—were the UNLV students.

The students were, from the beginning, keenly aware of these differences. On the first day of class, as I went over the syllabus with the students, I emphasized that this was not an introductory class. "You will have great difficulty in this course," I said, "if you have not had at least one women's studies class prior to this one." The UNLV majors chimed in, expressing their desire for at least one course where they would not be (as they are in most cross-listed courses) the "experts" in a room of novices. One of them, Pam, came right out and said, "I'm looking forward to a class where we don't have to define epistemology, pedagogy, hegemony, and paradigm—where we all know what those words mean and can move on to how particular thinkers understand them." When class ended, we in Las Vegas turned off our mike, but the Reno folks didn't, so we were inadvertent eavesdroppers on their postmortem. What we heard revealed that the UNR students were both envious of and daunted by what they read as a spirit of camaraderie and community among the UNLV students and between them and me, and they were intimidated by Pam's four words.

I now bitterly regret that I did not begin the second class by revealing to the Reno students that we in Las Vegas had overheard their comments after the first class had formally ended. Not only would such a confession have been ethically preferable to suppressing the truth (as I did, though not by conscious intention), but also it might have proved pedagogically useful as well, since it would undoubtedly have put the subject of perceived differences between the two groups of students on the immediate conversational agenda.

As it was, however, by the sixth class (we met twice a week, for seventy-five minutes at a time), a severe case of us versus them had set in. Not very subtly, the UNLV students were signalling their impatience with UNR students who seemed—to them—ignorant of what the UNLV students regarded as "fundamental" terms and concepts, such as essentialism, social constructionism, patriarchy, and sex-gender system. Understandably, the UNR students—including a very bright graduate student in English, who was concurrently taking a course in critical theory in which she was reading, among others, Foucault and Bakhtin—bridled at what they perceived as "the majors'" arrogance and condescension. It didn't help that the monitor in the Reno classroom was mounted high on the wall above the students. Literally, as well as figuratively, they had good reason to feel "talked down to."

It took only a few more weeks for an eruption to occur. Perhaps because the extended syllabus suggested to at least some of the students that I had privileged access to a body of "knowledge" that I could introduce them to, perhaps because some of the students had been convinced by "the majors" that they needed instruction, but more probably because I believed that my particular contribution to the collaborative construction of knowledge was my insistence that we begin discussion of any theorist or theoretical school by explicating the assigned text, I found myself "lecturing" (or at least *talking*) more than I had in ten years of teaching women's studies. And in class on Thursday, March 9, one of the UNLV majors called me on it. "I've taken a lot of feminist classes," Gayle said, "and this isn't one of them. In a feminist class, everyone shares information with and learns from each other. But Ellen is using the 'banking model of education' and lecturing—conveying information to empty vessels called students." Ashley, in Reno, said this didn't bother her because I was the teacher; I had constructed the syllabus, posed the study questions, and administered the midterm and she, for one, wanted to do well on the midterm.

Laura, in Reno, said that she had been bothered long before Gayle had at having knowledge "extended" to her, though it quickly became clear that she didn't think of me as the principal extender. Pam said, "The problem is that we don't all start from the same place." She used the analogy of a foot race, where those who were further ahead than others were waiting for them to catch up. For Laura, the problem was that "those who are 'ahead' are pushing those who are 'behind' to catch up. I don't mind Ellen being the coach and saying, 'Hey Laura, straighten out your legs or you'll never make it over the hurdle,' but I mind other students telling me what I 'should' know." "So what can we do," Pam asked, "to be less intimidating?" Laura, a graduate student in English, suggested starting with language. "In my research, I've learned about a 'feminine' speech pattern, marked by 'well, I don't know, but I just thought,' or 'it's just my opinion, but.' You guys [in Las Vegas] have done a fabulous job of overcoming this socialized speech pattern, but maybe in this class, you might adopt it again." By this time, we were out of time (the compressed video turned off, relentlessly, at the end of the allotted class time, leaving us frozen on TV), so there was general agreement that students should continue this discussion on e-mail during spring break.

If we had had more time, or if this had not been the last class before spring break, so that we could have resumed discussion in two days rather than two weeks, I hope we would have been able to analyze this exchange and detect what is now, in retrospect, glaringly apparent to me. Pam's disclaimer notwithstanding, the problem with this class *was* pedagogical. The three majors who had taken the greatest number of women's studies courses prior to enrolling in WOM 301—Gayle, Pam, and Joan Eve— viewed their comments in class as contributions to the collective construction of knowledge. The UNR students (and at least one UNLV student, as I later learned) heard the majors' remarks not as contributions to discussion among equals but as lectures to (perceived) inferiors. Some students felt intimidated by the majors; others felt, resentfully, that they were not being taken seriously as intellectual peers.

Earlier in the semester, I had flown to Reno to conduct a class from there, hoping thus to convey to the UNR students that they were as much my students as the majors—and I their teacher. We went out for dinner afterward, and by the end of the evening had at least begun to attach personalities as well as bodies to what had hitherto been small faces on a TV

monitor. But the students at both sites were still strangers, despite the sophisticated technologies that ostensibly enhanced communication between
them. During spring break, the inadequacy of technology to substitute for
face-to-face conversation became painfully evident.

THE E-MAIL WAR

At the beginning of the semester, I made arrangements with System Computing Services to open e-mail accounts for all students enrolled in WOM
301. Students had the option of communicating individually with me or
another member in the class or of posting a message to us all, using the
class "address book." I hoped that this would provide an additional forum
for discussion and, in the early weeks of the course, several students did in
fact use e-mail to continue discussing a topic raised in class. For Jaime, a
UNLV student who rarely spoke up in class, e-mail offered an opportunity
to express her ideas and engage in discussion with the one or two students
willing to join in.

    Yet, on balance, computer-mediated communication in this course did
not result in the "enhanced discussion" Sharon O'Hare and Arnie Kahn
describe in their account of using a computer bulletin board in their introductory women's studies course. Of the eight students in WOM 301, only
three regularly posted messages. Most did not have modems at home and
hence could gain access to e-mail only in campus computer labs, a problem for students who work from twenty to forty hours a week in the paid
labor force, as most UNLV and UNR students do. And at least three were
just plain terrified of the technology. So nothing like a "full discussion" of
various issues occurred.

    Furthermore, the very format of e-mail encourages altercation. Pine,
the mail server we use, allows you to respond to a posting by repeating it
and then interjecting comments. This encourages "you said/I say" discourse—the rhetoric of debate, not dialogue.

    This was particularly apparent during the semester break, when more
messages were posted to the class address book than at any other point
during the semester. This subject thread was initiated by Laura, responding to a suggestion made during the last class before break that students
use e-mail to continue the discussion of class dynamics that had been
abruptly terminated when we went "off air." Following up on her remark
in class that the UNLV students were "extending knowledge" to the UNR
students, Laura wrote, "I feel that my opinions do not carry the same
weight in class as that given to the opinions of others." Jaime replied that
she didn't think the Renoites's "perceptions/insights/questions [are] being

devalued nearly as much as you seem to feel they are, but I will not discredit your feelings [. . .]. We all need to be more sensitive to how what we say makes others feel." Then Gayle weighed in, expressing "total disagreement" with Laura's suggestion in class "that we start to talk in a more feminine tone of voice with phrases such as 'in my opinion,' 'could it be,' etc. To suggest that I take a step backward and start to speak in 'feminine' terms is to deny me the personal growth I have strived for during the past four years." Gayle went on, "Don't ask me to be different than what I am, for I have struggled long and hard to become what I am." Laura responded by repeating Gayle's message, intervening frequently to disagree or remonstrate. Gayle responded by repeating Laura's response, which—of course—itself contained Gayle's first posting. The length—and acrimony—of the postings expanded exponentially, as Laura responded to Gayle responding to Laura responding to Gayle, until finally Gayle gave up: "There is no way that I can now clarify what I was trying so hard to get across in my message. It is best that I drop it altogether." At this point, as spring break drew to a close, Jaime proposed a truce:

> I would like to "agree to disagree" with regard to communication styles. Some of us are more direct, others of us are not. This should not constitute a hindrance to class discussion. [. . .] We have a common goal, by virtue of having signed up for this class, of learning more about feminist theories. I suggest we study and discuss feminist theories. If anyone has a problem with something said in class, point it out, discuss it, and move on. Let's be Nike and "just do it."[8]

Because so few students participated in this discussion (although, as I later learned, a number of them had observed the escalating conflict between Laura and Gayle without intervening), it quickly "degenerated" into what looked, to Jaime at any rate, like "a very personal battle of wills." Personality conflicts arise in many classes, of course, including women's studies classes. But in my experience, when they are quite consciously addressed in the context of a general discussion of classroom politics, they provide an opportunity for students to learn valuable "feminist process skills," such as participatory decision making, problem solving, and conflict resolution (Schniedewind 21). Perhaps if we hadn't gone on spring break, the students in WOM 301 could have continued that Thursday night discussion in the next class, to good effect. One thing is certain. Voluntary participation in an e-mail discussion group proved to be an inadequate substitute for face-to-face interaction. And unfortunately, I will

never know whether or not the e-mail conflict between Laura and Gayle
would have been resolved once classes resumed after the break or whether
it would have poisoned the rest of the semester for all of us, because Gayle
came down with a severe case of pneumonia that confined her to bed for
the last six weeks of the semester.

LET'S BE NIKE AND "JUST DO IT"

Spring break lasted for two weeks because the two universities' calendars
are out of sync. During the first week, while UNLV was on break, the UNR
students met with Susan, their site facilitator, a graduate student in psychology who works part time at UNR's Women's Resource Center; the next
week, when the UNR students went on break, I met with the UNLV students. The assigned reading was bell hooks's *Feminist Theory: From Margin to Center*, and one chapter in particular seemed to students at both
sites to speak to the current crisis in WOM 301. In chapter 4, "Sisterhood:
Political Solidarity Between Women," hooks rejects the romantic (and
specifically white bourgeois) idea that "sisterhood" is the natural consequence of women's common oppression ("a false and corrupt platform dis-
guising and mystifying the true nature of women's varied and complex
social reality" 44). Rather, sisterhood is a sense of solidarity to be achieved
through hard work. "Women need to come together in situations where
there will be ideological disagreement," hooks insists, "and work to change
that interaction so communication occurs":

> This means that when women come together, rather than pretend
> union, we would acknowledge that we are divided and must de-
> velop strategies to overcome fears, prejudices, resentments, compet-
> itiveness, etc. [. . .] Expression of hostility as an end in itself is a
> useless activity, but when it is the catalyst pushing us on to greater
> clarity and understanding, it serves a meaningful function. (63)

Susan reported that the UNR students found hooks "very relevant to what
is going on with the class." One of them, in her reflection paper on the
hooks reading, said that it "explained much of the frustration our class has
been experiencing. [hooks's] definition of Sisterhood could be taken to
heart in our class with much benefit to all. Ellen, I do not think you could
have planned a more appropriate 'lesson' for us to ponder for our spring
break." And Jaime's motion to "move on" was based on her feeling that, in
the spirit of hooks's injunction to "actively struggle in a truly supportive
way to understand our differences" (64), "we have actively struggled to

determine what is 'wrong' with this class, we now understand our differences, and (hopefully) have taken steps toward changing 'misguided, distorted perspectives' that everyone has had regarding people's meaning, intentions, and styles of communication."[9]

Something else happened during spring break that had far-reaching pedagogical consequences in the second half of the semester. Memory, one of the Reno students, remarked that if some students didn't like that I was directing discussion, maybe the students were themselves partly to blame, because they had failed to assume responsibility for initiating and directing discussion. When Susan reported this comment to me, I finally knew how I wanted to begin our first post–spring-break class meeting. Combining the wisdom of Jaime and Memory, I would say that extensive conversations over the break had established that there were a variety of conversational styles in this class and perhaps some personality clashes, but that everyone seemed to agree that common ground existed in everyone's desire to study and discuss feminist theories. So let's get on with it, resolving to handle conflicts, as they might arise, on the spot, not on the Net. And I would ask for a volunteer to initiate discussion of the assigned text for each reading, relieving me of the obligation (and the temptation) to "lecture."

SO WHAT'S THEORY GOT TO DO WITH IT?

Class meetings in the second half of WOM 301 were remarkable for their cordiality and genuinely collaborative efforts to construct knowledge. The debacle of the last class before our consecutive spring breaks alerted everyone to the fact that *something* was going wrong. The sometimes acrimonious exchange on e-mail subsequent to that class, coupled with bell hooks's reflections on the necessity of working through conflict in order to achieve feminist solidarity, led to the students' expressed desire to make the class work. And when members of the class, rather than I, assumed responsibility for summarizing the assigned text and initiating discussion, the tyranny of the extended syllabus—with its preconstructed "study questions"—was overthrown. The last vestiges of "banking" education crumbled as the class moved—hesitantly at first, but with increasing confidence—toward dialogic, "problem-posing" knowledge construction.

I think it is also noteworthy that in the second half of the semester, we focused on postmodernist feminist theory and Black feminist thought. Bell hooks was the pivot, in more ways than one, between the first and second halves of the course. Earlier, in the context of discussing socialist feminism, students had read Nancy Hartsock's essay, "The Feminist Standpoint: Developing the Ground for a Specifically Feminist Historical Materialism."

To my surprise, almost none of the students understood the essay. Their reflection papers, as well as their comments in class, suggested that they found Hartsock's language impenetrable. When, however, they heard virtually the same ideas expressed in bell hooks's more accessible prose, it was as if they had for the first time encountered standpoint theory, and they found it very appealing.

Of course, as the students quickly realized, the prose of the postmodernist feminists they read after hooks was, if anything, more impenetrable and jargon-laden than Nancy Hartsock's.[10] And yet, some more willingly than others, they struggled through it, perhaps because the postmodernists' emphasis on pluralism, difference, and diversity, on partial vision and particular location, struck a resonant chord among students who had, so recently, experienced divisiveness and discord. I am only guessing here, since no one made a connection in class between what we were reading and the turbulence the class had encountered midway through the semester.

In many women's studies classrooms, as Frances A. Maher and Mary Kay Thompson Tetreault document in their ethnographic study of feminist classrooms in six colleges and universities across the nation, students learn about difference as they come to acknowledge their "situatedness" in particular social-class formations, ethnicities, racial and sexual identities. Our tiny class did not yield much diversity along those lines, so our discussion of white privilege, for instance, remained fairly abstract and academic. But, as was painfully evident by mid-semester, the class was teeming with differences—of temperament, intellectual style, prior experience in women's studies, exposure to theory in general and specific theories (e.g., psychoanalysis, Marxism) in particular. In the second half of the course, students began to use their diverse positions self-consciously and creatively to bridge the gaps that had divided them and to construct knowledge. A great deal of self-disclosure took place. One student confessed that she "just didn't understand a word of tonight's assignment [Donna Haraway's "A Manifesto for Cyborgs"] because that kind of language is really hard for me." Another student reported that the same text had taken over her dream life: "I dreamed of Haraway's cyborg last night, and guess who it was? Michael Jackson!" Alliances were formed across sites—between Laura and Joan Eve, for example, who discovered in postmodernist feminism a description of reality they recognized, as self-avowed members of Generation X (or the *13th Gen*, a book Laura introduced to Joan Eve). Ashley in Reno and Pam in Las Vegas, on the other hand, were extremely skeptical about postmodernism because they couldn't see that it led to any coherent political agenda.

Knowing "where they (each) were coming from," to reduce postmodernist positionality to colloquial cliché, the students could—and did—modulate the way they articulated their understandings of specific texts to speak to their classmates' anxieties. Postmodernists Laura and Joan Eve, for example, pointed out to Pam and Ashley the frequent advocacy by both postmodern feminists and feminists of color of a politics of "overlapping alliances" (Fraser and Nicholson 35), "conscious coalition" (Haraway 198), and shared "partial perspectives" (Collins 236). By the time we reached the last assigned reading, Maria Lugones's "Playfulness, 'World'-Travelling, and Loving Perception," even the skeptics had come to recognize the epistemological, ethical, and political value of the kind of speculative playfulness that so delighted Laura and Joan Eve.

By the end of the semester, the students had succeeded, albeit more by accident than design, in creating a feminist classroom, a learning community in which the acknowledgment and discussion of epistemological differences among its members resulted in transformed social relations. By highlighting differences between students in Las Vegas and Reno, distance education created problems for this class. It also—paradoxically—may have provided them pedagogical opportunities that would not have arisen had they been, as I know they would have preferred to be, in the same room.

(IN)CONCLUSIONS

At the end of the semester, the acting director of women's studies at UNR called me. "Well, how did it go?" she asked. "Would you do it again? Can and should we expand the number of women's studies courses we offer via distance education?" I said I'd let her know and set about finding the answers by writing this essay.

Yes, I would do it again—but differently; I learned much from the mistakes made this semester. And yes, I believe distance education is one way women's studies programs can collaborate to pool resources and serve our students better. The technologies involved need not raise insuperable barriers to feminist pedagogy. But they may, unless certain precautions are taken and certain conditions are met.

Here is what I learned. First, it is vital to bridge the (actual and psychological) distance between students at the primary and remote sites. I believe one reason the UNR students did not blame me for the breakdown in communications that happened mid-semester was because I had visited Reno and spent all evening working and socializing with them. Had the students had an opportunity to meet each other in the same fashion, I suspect the distrust and hostility that nearly destroyed the class would never have developed. As Jaime said, in an e-mail to the class toward the end of spring break:

> One last thing. Anyone who knows me will tell you I never pass up a chance to hang out and talk over some beers. If we were in the same city, this would have occurred, and I really think much of this [conflict] could have been worked out by simply getting to know each other better.

If possible, a meeting between students at both sites should be planned for the beginning of the semester. If travel money cannot be administratively budgeted (as my plane fare to Reno was), then students could be assessed a "lab fee." That's how important I think establishing real, face-to-face contact among class participants is.

Second, if I decide to set up a class e-mail account the next time I teach a distance-education course, I will do more than I did this time to make it an integral element of the course. The opportunity to extend discussion beyond the allotted 150 minutes a week is appealing, and, as the example of Jaime testifies, some students feel more comfortable expressing themselves in writing, having had time to reflect, than they do in class. Many students will also feel comfortable using this means of continuing discussion after class because they are accustomed to surfing the Net. But for others, the prospect of traveling on the information superhighway is as scary as flying to the moon. I did invite the manager of System Computing Center's user liaison office to class early in the semester to explain verifying, logging into, and using the class e-mail account, but I did not make special arrangements for hands-on workshops in both Reno and Las Vegas. Next time, I'll know better.

Third, if distance education is one component of a collaborative effort between two programs, such as the women's studies programs at UNLV and UNR, a set of equivalent requirements and prerequisites for enrollment needs to be established. While I believe that some of the tension that marred the first half of our semester was the result of distance and the limitations of technology ("Not being able to see the body language of the other group is a big problem," more than one student complained), it is at least equally true that the UNLV majors *were* frustrated to discover that their counterparts in Reno did not have the same grounding as they in core women's studies concepts, even if they later came to realize that that didn't mean the UNR students weren't as "smart" as they were, or as capable of sustaining lively, provocative discussion.

Finally, and most important of all, never again will I let awe of technology dictate my pedagogical practice. I was so terrified of this unknown technology that I slavishly followed the advice of "the experts," in this case, the professional staff of UNR's Instructional Media Services. "The 'extended syllabus' is integral to the distance-education course," they said (*Distance Education Faculty Handbook* 7), so I dutifully created one, not stopping to reflect that its mere existence contradicted everything I believed—and would tell the students—about the social and incremental construction of knowledge. To identify the objectives and key ideas for each class period over a fifteen-week semester and prepare study questions for the last assigned text before I'd even met the students obliged me to "construct knowledge" and made a mockery of my remarks to the students on the first day of class, my avowal that the course would be conducted according to the principles of feminist pedagogy, in which knowledge is socially constructed in the classroom. Of course, as Maralee Mayberry and Margaret Rees remind us, any course syllabus sends a message to students that knowledge can be "organized, prearranged, and transmitted from the professor to the student" (8–9). But syllabi can be altered and, in fact, rewritten in consultation with the students once the semester gets under way, as has repeatedly happened in courses I have taught. Some syllabi, however, may look less alterable, more cast in stone, than others.

In short, as I look back over the semester, I believe that the impediments to feminist pedagogy we stumbled up against in WOM 301 could have been removed, had we anticipated them. What I have attempted to provide, with the aid of students' retrospective reflections, is a map of one cyberclassroom so that others can see the hazards before crossing the electronic frontier.

* * *

NOTES

1. For the title, and much else in this article, I am indebted to Jaime Phillips. She, Laura Akers, Pam Gallina, Joan Eve Trimble, and Susan Trentham generously shared with me their written reflections on this cyberclass.

2. *The Electronic University* lists ninety colleges and universities in forty-eight states and five in Canada that offer courses and/or degrees via distance education.

3. For discussion of other experiments in teaching women's studies via distance education, see Burge and Lenskyj; Carl, Keough, and Bourque; Lenskyj; Moran; and Rutherford and Grana.

4. In what follows, I borrow freely from Kaplan and Rose, as shared with and

modified by Mayberry and Rees.

5. There is by now an extensive literature in feminist pedagogy. See Shrewsbury's 1993 bibliography. For a feminist critique of Freire, see Weiler.

6. "Situated knowers" is an allusion to Donna Haraway's influential essay, "Situated Knowledges: *The Science Question in Feminism* and the Privilege of Partial Perspective." The theoretical basis of feminist pedagogy is, I believe, feminist standpoint theory.

7. Eight students enrolled from UNR, seven from UNLV. By the end of the semester, there remained three students in Reno and five in Las Vegas.

8. Reflecting on the class afterward, Jaime felt "a little ashamed of my impatience with the 'disruption' in the class." She came to realize that, in a class "embracing feminist pedagogy, it was *very* important that some students felt unheard."

9. Thanks to Maralee Mayberry for pointing out to me that the students' ruminations on bell hooks illustrate the pedagogically contradictory nature of distance education. The anger and divisiveness that erupted midway through the semester was certainly exacerbated, if not solely caused, by the students' physical separation from each other—an inherent characteristic of distance education. But without having experienced this episode of confusion, frustration, and pain, the students might not so readily have understood the significance and relevance of hooks's insights about the necessity to work through conflict, rather than deny it, in order to achieve feminist solidarity.

10. In Linda Nicholson's anthology, *Feminism/Postmodernism*, they read essays by Nicholson and Nancy Fraser, Jade Flax, and Donna Haraway.

WORKS CITED

Burge, Elizabeth, and Helen Lenskyj. "Women Studying in Distance Education: Issues and Principles." *Journal of Distance Education* 5.1 (spring 1990): 20–37.

Carl, Diana R., Erin M. Keough, and Lorraine Y. Bourque. "Atlantic Canada Perspectives." *Toward New Horizons for Women in Distance Education: International Perspectives*. Ed Karlene Faith. London and New York: Routledge, 1988.

Collins, Patricia Hill. *Black Feminist Thought*. New York: Routledge, 1990.

Creating Materials for Distance Education Courses: Extended Syllabus Format Guide. Reno: University of Nevada, Instructional Media Services, 1993.

Distance Education Faculty Handbook. Reno: University of Nevada, Instructional Media Services. 1993.

Distance Education Workshop. University of Nevada, Reno, Instructional Media Services. 28 Oct. 1994.

The Electronic University: A Guide to Distance Learning. Princeton: Peterson's Guides, 1993.

Flax, Jane. "Postmodernism and Gender Relations in Feminist Theory." *Feminism/Postmodernism.* Ed. Linda J. Nicholson. New York: Routledge, 1989.

Fraser, Nancy, and Linda J. Nicholson. "Social Criticism without Philosophy: An Encounter between Feminism and Postmodernism." *Feminism/Postmodernism.* Ed. Linda J. Nicholson. New York: Routledge, 1989.

Freire, Paulo. *Pedagogy of the Oppressed.* Trans. Myra Bergman Ramos. 1970. New York: Continuum, 1983.

Haraway, Donna. "A Manifesto for Cyborgs." *Feminism/Postmodernism.* Ed. Linda J. Nicholson. New York: Routledge, 1989.

———. "Situated Knowledges: *The Science Question in Feminism* and the Privilege of Partial Perspective." *Feminist Studies* 14.3 (1988): 575–99.

Hartsock, Nancy. "The Feminist Standpoint: Developing the Ground for a Specifically Feminist Historical Materialism." *Feminism and Methodology.* Ed. Sandra Harding. Bloomington: Indiana University Press, 1987.

hooks, bell. *Feminist Theory: From Margin to Center.* Boston: South End Press, 1984.

Howe, Neil, and Bill Strauss. *13th Gen: Abort, Retry, Ignore, Fail?* New York: Vintage, 1993.

Kaplan, Carey, and Ellen Cronan Rose. *The Canon and the Common Reader.* Knoxville: University of Kentucky Press, 1990.

Lenskyj, Helen. "Tele-Communication: Women's Studies Through Distance Education." *Resources for Feminist Research* 20.1/2 (1991): 11–12.

Lugones, Maria. "Playfulness, 'World'-Traveling, and Loving Perception." *Lesbian Philosophies and Cultures.* Ed. Jeffner Allen. Albany: State University of New York University Press, 1990. 159–80.

Maher, Frances, and Mary Kay Thompson Tetreault. *The Feminist Classroom.* New York: Basic Books, 1994.

Mayberry, Maralee, and Margaret Rees. "Feminist Pedagogy, Interdisciplinary Praxis, and Science Education." *National Women's Studies Association Journal* 9.1 (1997): 57–75.

Moran, Louise. "Inter-Institutional Collaboration: The Case of the Australian Inter-University Women's Studies Major." *Journal of Distance Education* 5.2 (fall 1990): 32–48.

Nicholson, Linda J., ed. *Feminism/Postmodernism.* New York: Routledge, 1989.

O'Hare, Sharon L., and Arnold S. Kahn. "A Computer Bulletin Board in Women's Studies Courses." *Transformations: The New Jersey Project Journal* 5 (1994): 64–73.

Rutherford, LeAne H., and Sheryl Grana. "Fully Activating Interactive TV: Creating a Blended Family." *T.H.E. Journal* (Oct. 1994): 86–90.

Schniedewind, Nancy. "Teaching Feminist Process in the 1990s." *Women's Studies Quarterly* 21.3/4 (1993): 17–30.

Shrewshury, Carolyn M. "Feminist Pedagogy: An Updated Bibliography." *Women's Studies Quarterly* 21.3/4 (1993): 148–60.

Weiler, Kathleen. "Freire and a Feminist Pedagogy of Difference." *Harvard Educational Review* 61.4 (1991): 449–74.

8

FURTHER ADVENTURES OF A WOMEN'S STUDIES CYBERSPACE CADET

Ellen Cronan Rose

In fall 1994, I agreed to allow students at the University of Nevada, Reno (UNR) to enroll, via distance-education technology, in a feminist theory course I planned to offer students at the University of Nevada, Las Vegas (UNLV) in spring 1995. I did so, in large part, to find out whether distance-education technologies would allow for the kind of participatory, collaborative learning that characterizes the women's studies classroom, and I reported my (largely negative) findings in an article published in *Feminist Teacher* in winter 1995.[1] Since my article was published, I have received many requests from other women's studies instructors and program administrators to participate in discussions about how to adapt the technologies associated with distance education to achieve pedagogical goals defined by women's studies practitioners rather than to adapt women's studies instruction in response to administrative demands for cost containment. (As I noted in my article, educational administrators are increasingly attracted to technologies associated with distance education—e.g., cable television, compressed video, computer bulletin boards, websites—not only because they see them as a way of serving an increasingly diverse student population but also, perhaps even more compellingly, because they believe these technologies will enable them to cut costs.) Attendance was high at a workshop entitled Virtual Women's Studies: New Ideas in Electronic Education, which Candace Collins of Arizona State University (ASU) and I facilitated at a women's studies program administrators' conference sponsored in February 1997 by ASU's women's studies program, and there were six "technology" sessions at the 1997 annual National Women's Studies Association (NWSA) conference in St. Louis, including Women's Studies in Cyberspace, in which again I joined Candace and Annis H. Hopkins, also from ASU, in sharing with conferees our experience of using distance-education technologies to teach women's studies. Once again I found myself interjecting a discordant note into my colleagues' generally rhapsodic celebration of the potential of distance-education technologies for feminist education.[2]

I hadn't intended to sound negative when Annis asked, in fall 1996, if I'd join her and Candace in talking about women's studies and distance-education technologies at the 1997 NWSA conference. Indeed, I expected by then to have some positive experiences of my own to add to theirs, based on a second foray into pedagogical cyberspace. It happened thusly.

In summer 1995, almost immediately after I finished my less than happy but very instructive experiment in teaching feminist theory via distance education to some students at UNR, the Nevada legislature enacted a bill that made a second experiment in teaching women's studies via distance education possible if not inevitable. Senate Bill 204 set aside money to link high schools in the state to the university and community-college system by expanding access to the Internet and installing compressed video units at selected sites. UNLV responded eagerly to the legislature's invitation to submit a proposal for SB 204 funds, seeing this as a way of enhancing and improving the university's established practice of providing academic course work to residents throughout southern Nevada. For some years, qualified high school juniors and seniors had been permitted to enroll in freshman 100-level UNLV courses for credit, in effect beginning college while still in high school. Interactive compressed-video systems and increased access to the Internet would enable high school students who lived too far from UNLV to commute to participate in this early studies program, expanding and diversifying the curriculum for talented students in small, rural high schools.

While UNLV administrators envisaged enriching these students' educational opportunities by offering them courses in science, foreign languages, English composition, and mathematics, I saw in SB 204 a chance to introduce them to the new scholarship on women. Accordingly, when UNLV was granted funding under the legislation, I submitted a proposal to teach WOM 101, Gender, Race, and Class, to high school students in southern Nevada, confident that I had learned enough from teaching WOM 301, Feminist Theories, via distance education to avoid the problems that had vexed that course. Unfortunately, much of what I learned from that experience was inapplicable in this case. I had new lessons to learn.

Unlike WOM 301, WOM 101 satisfies a general-education requirement, so I was not entirely surprised to discover thirty-two students awaiting me when I entered the room on the first day of class in January 1997. Five of them were students from two Las Vegas high schools near the campus; in addition, there were two students at Eldorado High School in far-away northeast Las Vegas and one in a high school classroom in Pahrump, a small town seventy miles west of Las Vegas, linked to the UNLV class-room by compressed video. My challenge would be to incorporate these farflung students into what I hoped would become a learning community in the UNLV classroom. I thought of setting up a buddy system, asking for volunteers from the UNLV class to act as big sister/big brother to each of the students at the remote sites, making it their business to see that Valerie, Peter, and Doris[3] were routinely asked their opinion and invited into the conversation, knowing that I would have enough to do orchestrating dis-cussion among the students at UNLV.

I was right. Unlike WOM 301, Feminist Theories, a required course for women's studies majors and minors that is elected only by students predis-posed toward and somewhat knowledgeable about women's studies, this course had an extraordinarily diverse population. There were confirmed feminists, hostile free-market capitalists, first-year students and seniors, a range of majors from criminal justice to English, and (probably because the title of the course, which used to be Introduction to Women's Studies, is now Gender, Race, and Class) a better racial/ethnic mix than one finds in most UNLV classrooms. In fact, it was the most ethnically diverse class I have taught at any institution. After the usual and anticipated drops dur-ing the first two weeks of the semester, I was left with nineteen students in the UNLV classroom. There were two students whose parents' first lan-guage was Italian, one whose parents had immigrated from Yugoslavia, one who was bilingual in English and Hindi, one African American, one Native American, one Chicano (the only man in the course), one native Hawaiian, and one Jew, who claimed that as an ethnic identity. There were, as well, quite a few students who came from economically disadvan-taged backgrounds. Ultimately, students learned mutual respect as they traded stories and learned from each other what it felt to be "marked" racially, ethnically, or economically "other" than the white, male, middle-class norm. But along the way, the dynamics of the class were so intense and passionate that we more often than not forgot the students at the re-mote sites. In the midst of a heated discussion of Marilyn Frye's superb es-say on oppression,[4] for example, one of the UNLV students nudged me and whispered, "I think Valerie wants to say something." It was a good thing Shelley had her eye on the monitor, because I was so busy attempting to maintain civility between left-leaning Sally and well-dressed capitalist Linda that I had totally forgotten Valerie in Pahrump.

By mid-semester, of the eight high school students who had enrolled in the course, only three remained: Terry and Heather at UNLV and Valerie in Pahrump. The others piled up massive unexcused absences, didn't turn in assignments (or turned in substandard work), and seemed just generally nonplussed by a course that expected them to participate actively in the construction of knowledge. Terry, Heather, and Valerie stayed the course, but they didn't benefit equally from their perseverance.

Heather and Terry, who drove to UNLV twice a week after school to take WOM 101, loved the course and did well because they actively participated in discussion and engaged fully in the group presentations that concluded the semester's work. Valerie, on the other hand, wrote me a bitter letter at the end of the semester, saying that she had "never felt welcome" in the class. As Shelley's active intervention on her behalf attests, there was no animus against her. But she never was a real member of the class. The problem was technological.

When I taught my first distance-education women's studies course, there were five students in Las Vegas and four in Reno, and we could sit opposite each other, as it were, trading comments back and forth from one TV monitor to another (that course had its problems, as elaborated in the previous chapter, "This Class Meets in Cyberspace," but they weren't technological). This time, there was a lively group of students in Las Vegas who, during the course of the semester, got to know each other through conversational exchange. And out there in cyberspace, seventy miles away in Pahrump, all alone, was poor Valerie, who more often than not could not hear that exchange, much less participate in it.

Early in the semester the UNLV distance-education instructors[5] had a video conference with site facilitators at the half dozen or so remote sites, and my two facilitators both complained that their students (Valerie in Pahrump, Peter and Doris at Eldorado) couldn't follow the discussion because they couldn't hear it. As I have said, I had nineteen students at UNLV, seated in the usual women's studies circle of chairs. The particular distance-education technology we use at UNLV allows for only two microphones, which I placed in the middle of the circle, as I had placed them on the table around which the five UNLV students sat in WOM 301. But a circle whose radius is fifteen feet is a lot bigger than a five-foot-long table: when Shelley at one point in the circle responded to a comment by Carol at another location in the room, we at UNLV could hear her but her voice wasn't picked up by the mikes in the middle of the room. Only when I broke the class up into small groups for discussion, one of which sat in front of the TV monitor with a mike in its midst, could Valerie and Doris and Peter at the high schools hear and participate in the discussion.[6] The quick technological fix would have been to have me appropriate one mike and lecture, as did the instructors of the other SB 204 courses (in art history, astronomy, environmental science, finite mathematics, introductory psychology, and Russian), but lecturing is not the preferred modus operandi of most women's studies instructors. It is certainly not mine.

Valerie's journal, faxed to me at three-week intervals, was punctuated by complaints about her exclusion from the active construction of knowledge that was going on in Las Vegas ("I could not hear the discussion today"; "Today was the first time I could hear the discussion"; "Today's discussion was hard to hear so I don't have much to say"; "Professor Rose started the class with an exercise. Due to a communication problem I was unable to hear or participate. Five minutes into the discussion we were disconnected"; "Today we discussed the definition of ideology. I did not hear the discussion"; "Missing much of the discussion in the past I was not clear on what exactly was expected of us in the term paper"). In her end-of-semester letter, Valerie accused me and the UNLV students of intentionally excluding her from participation in WOM 101, but her journal told another story of the failures of the technological link-up.

I concluded "This Class Meets in Cyberspace" by listing four things I learned from teaching WOM 301, Feminist Theories, via distance education: (1) that it is vital to bridge the actual and psychological distance between students at the primary and remote sites; (2) that e-mail can be an effective means of building that bridge if students are given adequate instruction in using the technology; (3) that it is important to establish equivalent requirements and prerequisites for enrollment in the course by students at both primary and remote sites; and (4) that I must never allow technology to dictate my pedagogical practice.

Why did I not use what I learned to make a success of this second exercise in teaching women's studies via distance education? In fact, I did put into practice two of the four lessons WOM 301 taught me, lessons three and four. Because WOM 101 is an introductory course that satisfies a general-education requirement, the students were all tyros, those at UNLV no less so than Valerie in Pahrump. And I certainly refused to alter my feminist pedagogy even when it became evident that the technology could not support it. Ironically, I learned that lesson so well that it proved impossible put into effect the first lesson I learned from teaching WOM 301, that it was vital to bridge the actual and psychological gap between Valerie and the students assembled in the UNLV classroom. A class e-mail account might have helped, giving Valerie a chance for virtual if not actual interaction with her remote classmates. But although UNLV's Distance Education Policy Committee recognized, early in its discussion of the implications of SB 204, that "Internet access is essential for public school students taking interactive video classes,"[7] Pahrump High School had no access to the

Internet. Would it have helped Valerie feel more a part of the class, less excluded, had I packed the UNLV students (and Terry and Heather) into a
college van and driven to Pahrump for a Saturday picnic? Why didn't I at
least do what I had done in 1995 and teach at least one class from the remote site? Was it because two years ago there had been almost equal numbers of students at the primary and remote sites, making it seem worth the
effort to fly to Reno to meet the students and teach at least one class from
there, whereas I didn't feel compelled to make a similar effort for just one
student? Was it because I took teaching students at UNR more seriously
than teaching rural high school students because I saw that exercise in distance education as part of a larger project of coordinating the women's
studies programs at Nevada's two universities, a prelude to establishing a
statewide women's studies consortium? Whatever the reason, in retrospect
I'm sorry I didn't drive to Pahrump, either on my own or with a group of
the UNLV students, because I think such a gesture might have gone a long
way toward assuring Valerie that we wanted to involve her in the class.

But such a well-meaning and welcoming gesture would not, in itself,
have made Valerie part of the learning community that formed, over the
course of the semester, in the UNLV classroom. I feel bad about Valerie.
There she was, a seventeen-year-old high school junior, all alone in a classroom in a small town in southwestern Nevada, trying on her own to make
sense of the text (which her journal showed she couldn't do) because she
couldn't hear or participate in class discussion, where difficult concepts
were clarified. I wrote lengthy comments on each journal entry, trying in
effect to conduct a correspondence course, but Valerie's subsequent journal
entries indicated that she hadn't understood them.

On the basis of this experience, I have decided not to continue offering
WOM 101 to high school students via distance education. The problem is
not with high school students; the two who came to UNLV and participated in the course did well. The problems were strictly technological and
might not arise at other institutions, since UNLV's distance-education co-
ordinator assures me that there are other, more discussion-friendly technologies on the market. But the distance-education technology we have,
with its fixed camera and two microphones, is designed to "deliver"
knowledge to essentially passive "consumers." I was able to circumvent the
constraints of this technology when teaching WOM 301 because there were
so few students at both sites that everyone had equal access to the camera
and microphones.[8] But, as I have noted, with the two microphones on the
floor in the middle of a circle of nineteen students, it was impossible to
project the discussion to students at the remote sites or include them in it.
Had this been, as the other SB 204 courses were, a traditional lecture

course, Valerie would not have been at a disadvantage vis à vis the students at UNLV: they would all have gotten the same canned wisdom from me. But I do not want students passively absorbing women's studies concepts as if they are mathematical theorems. Despite an eminently lucid discussion of the distinction between "essentialism" and "social constructionism" in the text and my elaboration of the distinction, with further examples drawn from history and cultural anthropology, it took fifteen weeks and repeated attempts by virtually everyone in the class to come up with their own examples before the students in WOM 101 felt comfortable using those concepts. More important, learning in a women's studies classroom is not simply a matter of understanding and being able to deploy concepts, theories, and data. As I wrote in "This Class Meets in Cyberspace," the women's studies classroom is, ideally, "a learning community in which epistemological—and other—differences are acknowledged, respected, and used to transform social relations, in the classroom to begin with but ultimately in the world outside the academy" (183).

As I have said, this class was the most diverse collection of (differently) situated knowers I have ever been blessed with. There were abrasive moments. I remember a particularly incendiary discussion, in which left-leaning Sally, capitalist-entrepreneur Linda, and Amanda, the only African American in class, nearly came to blows over the subject of welfare mothers. The class ended at 3:45, and I later learned that the three of them had continued the debate, at a nearby Starbucks, until 7:30. Yet before the semester ended, Linda had become best friends with Sally and Amanda and collaborated with her newfound friends in preparing a superb group presentation on bell hooks's *Feminist Theory: From Margin to Center*. Linda introduced the presentation by thanking me for having assigned a group project: "We learned much more than what is in the book; we learned how to work together as a group and how much more we could learn from working together than working on our own."

From all of this initially frictional but ultimately transformative interaction (and learning) Valerie was excluded. But so, I believe, would be students taking a lecture version of WOM 101 or any women's studies course. If UNLV invests in distance-education technology that allows for genuine interchange between students on campus and those at remote sites, I will try again to offer women's studies courses to students in Pahrump, Tonapah, Laughlin, or other sites remote from Las Vegas. (At a minimum, we need additional microphones in the UNLV classroom, to enable students at remote sites to hear and participate in discussion.) Nevada is a large, sparsely populated state, served by two universities and five community colleges. There are women (and men) in small mining or ranching communities who cannot reasonably travel to a campus but who would benefit, as obviously did Linda, from a potentially life-transformative encounter with women's studies curriculum and pedagogy. Surely, on the cusp of the second millennium, we can invent (or install) technologies that offer them that possibility.

●   ●   ●

NOTES

1. Ellen Cronan Rose. See previous chapter in this collection.

2. Notes from Candace's and my workshop at the February program administrators' conference as well as information from her, Annis's, and my NWSA presentation (including a shorter version of this essay) can be found on ASU's women's studies website: <http://www.asu.edu/clas/womens_studies/virtual.htm>. See also Annis H. Hopkins. "Women's Studies on Television? It's Time for Learning." *NWSA Journal* 8.2 (summer 1996): 91–106.

3. Since I wrote "This Class Meets in Cyberspace" with the consent and assistance of students in WOM 301, I used their real names in the essay. I did not ask permission of the WOM 101 students to write this essay, so I refer to them pseudonymously.

4. I am referring, of course, to the by-now-classic essay, "Oppression," originally published in Frye's *The Politics of Reality: Essays in Feminist Theory* (Freedom, CA: Crossing Press, 1983). My students read it in the text I used for WOM 101, Karen E. Rosenblum and Toni-Michelle C. Travis, eds. *The Meaning of Difference: American Constructions of Race, Sex and Gender, Social Class, and Sexual Orientation.* New York: McGraw-Hill, 1996.

5. Under SB 204, high school students in southern Nevada could enroll, via distance education, in seven first-year (100-level) UNLV courses ranging from art history to women's studies.

6. I said earlier that five of the original eight high school students dropped the course because of absenteeism or failure to turn in assignments. That was certainly the case with three of the five students who drove to UNLV to take the course, but I now wonder whether Peter and Doris may have dropped out because they felt they couldn't take part in the class at all.

7. Undated memo from the chair of UNLV's Distance Education Policy Committee to the acting assistant vice president for academic affairs.

8. Small classes and seminars are viewed as a hard-to-defend luxury at a time when higher-education administrators are responding to fiscal constraints by increasing class enrollments and faculty workloads. I succeeded once in persuading the administration to waive the fifteen-student minimum enrollment by arguing

that it was a *good thing* to collaborate with our sister (and often rival) university, but I see no reason to hope that distance-education courses in the future will be exempt from demonstrating the required minimum enrollment.

9

TEACHER INVOLVEMENT AND TRANSFORMATIVE POWER ON A GENDER ISSUES DISCUSSION LIST

Kathleen A. Boardman, Jonathan Alexander,
Margaret M. Barber, and Peter Pinney

The use of networked discussions in college classes is still in its experimental stages, with teachers and students on many campuses trying to work out practical, rhetorical, and conceptual issues. Clearly, we want our educational goals to guide the use of technology, rather than the other way around; nevertheless, it appears that classroom technologies and pedagogical objectives have a dialectical, mutually transformative relationship. Teachers' relationships to students as well as students' relationships to teachers and each other all are profoundly affected in networked on-site and on-line classes.

Transformations of pedagogical roles and relationships have long been of interest to theorists of feminist pedagogy, like Jennifer Gore, who "emphasize the power relations which operate through the fundamental and specific relation of teacher and student" (xiv). Hoping to challenge patriarchal values and structures, we find that hierarchies only reassert themselves when we fail to address issues of power and authority. An instructor who speaks explicitly and persuasively toward a feminist agenda may still be reproducing traditional patterns of power, for institutional authority is represented in her position as teacher. At the same time, teachers who decenter their classrooms, promoting new forms of collaboration and urging the participation of many voices, need to remain aware of the potential coerciveness of the majority. In "Feminism and Composition," Susan Jarratt says, "Even when teachers announce the desire to create a particular climate, they can't neutralize by fiat the social positions already occupied by

their students" (113). The challenge, then, is to find ways to use such social positioning to increase the range of voices participating in discussion,
querying dominant views and trying out other perspectives.

This challenge is even greater when the classroom's circle of chairs is
augmented or replaced by a circle of computers. The potential for increased student-student interaction in electronic discussion complicates
teacher-student dynamics, which in turn affect other interchanges among
students. In on-line discussion, because everyone has the floor all the time,
no one can rely on traditional assumptions about teacher management and
evaluation of class discussion. Thus it is important that feminist educators
study how instructors might position themselves in their own classes' networked discussions. The increasing numbers of teachers trying discussion
lists for the first time should carefully consider the ways that teachers
might shape, model, and learn from the discourse. In this essay, we offer
our stories of our own collaboration with each other and with our students
on an e-mail gender issues discussion list. We hope that our experiences
with electronic discussions of gender and sexuality will suggest possibilities, prompt further thinking, and spark greater exploration of the e-mail
list's potential for developing innovative feminist pedagogy.

Studies of computer-assisted composition courses have asserted that
the teacher's customary classroom authority and involvement are necessarily reduced in electronic discourse, and that this is ultimately for the better.
Marilyn Cooper and Cynthia Selfe observed as early as 1990 the potential
that computer-mediated communication (CMC) offers for overturning
"the traditional hegemony of the teacher-student relationship" (850).
They found networked discussions to be "capable of making student-
teacher and student-student exchanges more egalitarian, reducing the
dominance of the teacher and the role of accommodation behavior in discussion and increasing the importance of the students' discourses"
(851–52). Other recent studies praise the potential of networked discussions for achieving equal voice not only for students in the classroom but
also for traditionally excluded groups in society: they have demonstrated
ways to use on-line discussions to address issues of racism and heterosexism (e.g., see Alexander; Bennett and Walsh).

All this sounds like good news to feminist educators looking for ways
to subvert patriarchal hierarchies and open up new possibilities for students. Yet other researchers have observed that these results do not *necessarily* flow from CMC. In her study of research findings from several
disciplines, Pamela Takeyoshi summarizes—and then problematizes—typical assumptions about the dynamics of CMC: that it "uninhibits users and
depersonalizes communication," alters the "structure and hierarchy of

groups," and "polarizes groups in decision making" (28–31). She warns that despite claims made about CMC, "Unless we adopt the computer network as a part of a larger focus and effort to create a safe discourse space, we are not doing anything new for our marginalized students. [. . .] The computer will not magically alter the relationships of gender, power, class, and race that so strongly and pervasively underlie classroom practices" (33). Indeed, Cooper and Selfe have also concluded that networked environments, not automatically, but only *when they are shaped by the correct theoretical perspectives* can encourage attempts to reconstruct and rethink existing social structures and visions" [emphasis added]. Their own vision remains hopeful if cautious:

> If we can't eliminate the effect of racism, sexism, and classism in our traditional classrooms because of social inertia, we may be able to set aside smaller electronic spaces in which such problems can find expression and be debated. And in these reduced-risk spaces, students can discover or evolve among themselves different patterns of power and linguistic exchange to facilitate these discussions, patterns which may run directly counter to those that have become habitual in our classrooms. (867)

Although we share Selfe and Cooper's hopefulness, we do not join them in assuming that electronic space is necessarily "reduced-risk" space for all students: though not physically dangerous, electronic discussion is not always distanced or depersonalized; it may challenge students' sense of identity and make them feel vulnerable. Recognizing the need to make a *safe space* for students to try out different points of view on such issues as domestic violence and rape, we also see that this same experimentation and diverse expression require *risk*. Some statements from some social positions may intimidate, alienate, or silence others; yet the same statements may provoke into speech (and voice) those who would otherwise be silent. While we agree with Selfe, Cooper, and others that there is much that students can "evolve among themselves" in the way of linguistic patterns and power relations, we believe instructors, too, should share in this discourse. We argue that shaping the networked environment in accordance with specific theoretical perspectives, in our case feminist ones, is only the beginning. After that, as we will show, what the teacher does or neglects to do both on- and off-line can significantly affect the degree to which experience in that environment may be transformative or empowering for students.

Recognizing that computer-mediated communication has the potential to perpetuate as well as challenge marginalization, we wish to examine the dynamics of teacher involvement in one form of networked discourse—the asynchronous discussion on e-mail.[1] In a field where collaboration of students, but not usually of teachers, has been explored and promoted, we hope to discover and highlight practices that respond to its risks while improving its potential to empower students in ways that may not be available in the traditional classroom. Hence we raise these questions: How might instructors interact with students—and perhaps with each other—in a networked environment, in this case on an e-mail discussion list, in a way consistent with feminist values? How might teachers constructively use face-to-face interaction with students to improve on-line interaction, and vice versa? What new models of collaborative teaching, teacher-student collaboration, and student interaction do computer networks make possible? And how might these models be applied in practice to facilitate reflective, even transformative dialogue on gender issues?

Sybille Gruber and Susan Claire Warshauer provide valuable analysis of some of these issues and suggest several roles for the instructor. Gruber examines the risks that on-line discussion of divisive issues, including gender issues, will increase tensions in face-to-face contact (e.g., classroom discussions and student-teacher conferences). But Warshauer discusses ways that face-to-face discussions are a vital part of responsible pedagogy in the networked classroom (110). That is, instead of using the electronic discussion simply as a sidelight or substitute for certain classroom activities, the instructor tries to have the electronic and in-class discussions reflect upon each other. Warshauer paraphrases a private communication from Locke Carter, who identifies four kinds of teacher involvement in INTERCHANGE discussions: "passive," "participatory," "intervening," and "dominating."[2] Warshauer adds a fifth category, "outside response," to include what a teacher might do face-to-face with a class or student to influence the dynamics of on-line activity. These five categories might also be applied to e-mail discussion lists, for those of us who use e-mail in the context of a classroom setting.

We do not believe an instructor—particularly in a course focused on gender issues—should set up and then ignore a class discussion list. Although a "passive" response may sometimes be appropriate, teacher "absence" is not an option for us because if students begin to make statements that may hurt or silence others (by using, for example, derogatory language about members of various groups), we want at least to have the option of addressing their use of language at that point. At the same time, instructor "domination" of a discussion clearly negates the list's potential for student negotiation and experimentation. Thus, we have been especially interested in how "participatory," "intervening," and "outside-response roles" might be articulated with feminist practice on a discussion list limited to gender issues. Given the peculiar qualities of electronic discourse, what potential does a networked discussion have to change students' minds on these issues, to what extent should instructors attempt to shape or model the discourse, and how might instructors have to change their own ideas about how discourse—and especially argument—ought to proceed?

The four of us became interested in the dynamics of teacher-student interaction in electronic discourse when our classes began participating in a gender-issues listserve. During 1996–97, at the University of Alaska (UAF), the University of Southern Colorado (USC), and the University of Nevada, Reno (UNR), we taught eight Composition II "theme" classes focused on gender issues, sharing some of the same readings and assignments. Each semester's classes were linked through a listserve, GE-L (Gender List), where students and faculty could make comments, ask questions, and respond to each other's posts. All but one of the classes were taught in a computer classroom, and the instructors ranged in on-line experience from novice to veteran. Due to other course assignments, Kathy and her classes were able to participate only one semester, but she continued during the remaining time as a list observer.

On all three campuses, our students are mostly in their first year of college and in the process of taking general-education courses. They tend to be evenly divided between male and female, to range in age from seventeen to forty, and to represent several ethnicities and a wide spectrum of majors. Each of our communities is relatively isolated geographically, and except for a few international students and out-of-staters, our students tend to commute from the surrounding areas. Thus, our first-year composition courses provide some of them with their first exposure to academic discussion, as well as to feminist perspectives and diversity issues in general. In 1996–97, our on-line discussions touched on a variety of topics: gender discrimination on the job, women's roles in the armed forces, parenting and child-custody issues, sexual harassment, and many others. The most persistent and most heated discussions were about issues related to sexual orientation.

The roots of this on-line experience reached back four years earlier, when, in response to Colorado's Amendment Two, which limited gay rights, Margaret introduced gender issues as the central topic of her first-year composition class. In spring 1994, at the University of Alaska in Fairbanks, Pete established a discussion list, the GE-L, so that students on the two campuses could converse about gender issues. After several semesters of correspondence between Pete's and Margaret's classes, Margaret approached Jonathan, a colleague at the University of Southern Colorado with special a interest in queer theory, to join the GE-L as a guest and to offer a second section of Gender Issues 102 the next semester. Upon meeting Kathy at a national conference session on feminist issues, Margaret suggested that she also join in coordinating English 102 courses during fall 1996. Three of us used a common textbook (Anna Katsavos and Elizabeth Wheeler's anthology *Complements*), and all four assigned David Mamet's play *Oleanna*. Students in all classes met three hours each week, learning research procedures, writing on gender-related topics, engaging in face-to-face discussions, hearing guest speakers, and participating in written networked discussions. Students at USC held class in a computer lab and were allowed class time to participate on the GE-L. (This was important as it was the only computer access some economically disadvantaged students had available.) Students at UNR used computers outside class time. At UAF, students went to the computer lab during class time one day a week; on the other day, they met face to face without computer-assisted instruction.

Students introduced themselves as soon as they got on-line and on the list. As the semester progressed, they asked questions (to start discussion threads), replied to questions or issues, requested help with their essays and research projects. Instructors joined in, too, with a few questions and a few responses: some of us were more participatory at this point, some more passive. Generally, we tried to blend in with the students' discourse; for example, when students began narrating personal experiences to help explain why they believed as they did, some instructors did the same. At some points in the semester, such as after all classes had read *Oleanna*, a time limit was placed on the asynchronous discussion ("post your comments about *Oleanna* before Friday") in order to focus and intensify the exchange. This was one kind of interventionist response: instructors were clearly managing the *Oleanna* discussion through the time limit, but students could still have posted later because the list was unmoderated.

Students' writing in composition classes is subject to varying degrees of privacy—from journals seen only by the teacher, to essays read by several students before a final draft was turned in, to networked discussions on INTERCHANGE limited to members of one class. Posting to the GE-L is often the most public writing that students do. They are aware that their words are read by an audience that includes approximately eighty to one hundred students in comparable courses at other universities. On an unmoderated list like ours, a teacher has less direct control over the course of the discussion than when all participants occupy the same physical space. Anyone can send a post at any time; no one has to wait to be called upon by the teacher. For students, then, the list seems an extremely *open* space, an invitation to challenge, risk, and even conflict. At the same time, because so few of our students had experience with electronic discussion and with gender as a topic, it was from the beginning a priority with us to promote (if we could not ensure) the electronic environment as a reasonably *safe* discourse space.

Writing on the e-list also tends to be less formal than that in structured writing assignments, and students can post as much or as little as they like. We did not require a certain number of posts, although those of us in computer classrooms did give students some class time to read and write to the list. Because of the ease of posting and quantity of text they produced, often with a high degree of engagement, students could communicate with less inhibition than they normally do in the classroom. The increased opportunity for students to participate, to take time to compose messages, to address issues, while it offers additional practice in writing, testing ideas, and sharing research, also offers more opportunity to reveal prejudices and to make unconsidered remarks than would be possible during class time. Although the option technically exists to remove a student from the list for disruptive behavior, we never felt the need to do so. Our intervention—when it did occur—took other forms, such as challenging certain language and assertions, attempting to introduce new discussion threads, sending electronic messages to individual students off-list, and talking to students face to face. The three stories that follow help to illustrate the complexity of teacher-involvement issues.

TIMOTHY: SELF-DISCOVERY WITHOUT TEACHER INTERVENTION

Timothy participated on the list frequently, sparring with a few of the students, but always with a respectful tone. Pete, Timothy's instructor, had no indication that any sort of transformation was occurring in Timothy's perspective until the last week of the semester, when the class evaluated their experience on the list and discussed how it had shaped their thinking. Timothy mentioned that he could not tell a person's gender by the e-mail account address displayed on the screen. When Pete asked him if this had had some impact on his correspondence on the list, Timothy made a remarkable admission: he had been astonished to find that some of the students he had corresponded with were women. Not that having women on the listserve was unusual in any way, but Timothy suddenly realized how his face-to-face discussions with women were different from his discussions with women on the list. When replying to a GE-L question or comment, Timothy said, he gave no thought to the gender of the person to whom he was responding. Later, after realizing that his correspondent was a woman, he often was surprised at the depth of conversation that had taken place.

Reflecting on his experience, Timothy confessed that he had always discounted women in face-to-face encounters, but on the listserve, he treated each posting with a sincere attempt to understand each person's point of view, regardless of gender. Further deliberating on his actions, he had come to realize that he would not like his own daughter to be subjected to the biases he had held toward women. The particular format and dynamics of the list had allowed the correspondents' gender, for a time, to become invisible for Timothy—at the same time that the subject matter (gender) became more visible to him than ever before. Eventually he came to reflect on the tensions between that gender "invisibility" and visibility. The listserve's exercise in anonymity had brought Timothy to a point where he was consciously reviewing his speech patterns and actions around his daughter to avoid instilling in her a sense of inferiority that she might later have to overcome. All this came about without any instructor intervention on the list: we might say that, as far as Timothy was concerned, Pete's role was completely passive. Yet Pete had also subtly intervened when he personally invited Timothy to do the reflection that allowed him to articulate a change of attitude toward gender.

JANE: THE RISKS OF DECENTERING

The story of Jane's participation on the list, however, suggests that neither instructor passivity nor instructor intervention is unproblematic. Many feminist teachers, on the theoretical level, disavow allegiance to hierarchical models but also in practice feel dissatisfied with scenarios that result from decentering the learning environment. This is not necessarily disingenuous or hypocritical: our own sense of authority to speak has often been hard-won, and the results that emerge from a decentered environment—classroom or listserve—are sometimes unpleasant. Jane's story vividly illustrates some implications of the decentering inherent in a listserve: one participant can suddenly turn the discussion into channels that are potentially threatening or embarrassing to some list members.

Jane was not a class member but an "invited guest." Noticing that most students had not entered into classroom discussion of issues related to sexual orientation, Margaret first asked Jonathan to participate on the GE-L as a contributor who could bring a slightly new perspective to the on-line discussion. As the only openly queer male faculty member at USC, he had often been asked to comment on, if not represent, les-bi-gay concerns and issues. For the GE-L list, his role would be to introduce the voice of a gay man into the mix, thus making the discussion less abstract and more personal. Striving for gender balance, Pete decided to invite Jane, a lesbian, to participate, believing that Jane's presence on the list would help open up opportunities for students to respond authentically to issues of sexuality without instructor intervention. Pete's role, as he saw it, was to lurk in the background and guide the experience through invited guests like Jane— taking a passive but still managerial role.

This strategy turned out to be explosive. Jane volunteered to reply to inquiries about her sexuality; her responses were open and even blunt. In response to one question, she described graphically her sadomasochistic expression of herself, adding a signature file of a home page should people want to know more. Even Pete was taken aback by the nature of the response, and a flood of postings created so much activity that he began to wonder if he should rethink having Jane on the listserve as a guest. A flurry of e-mail flew among the instructors. Part of our concern arose out of the upsetting of our initial assumptions—and our agenda for introducing les-bi-gay voices onto the list. Essentially, we had assumed that both Jane and Jonathan would provide a uniform gay voice that would be respectable, modest, and sedate—a voice that would know its place, as it were, and allay the very real fears that many homophobic heterosexuals have about alternative sexualities; put another way, the instructors had hoped that the homosexual participants would downplay the *sexual* and emphasize the *homo*, or the ways homosexuals are just like everybody else. We also assumed—incorrectly, as it turned out—that a strong emphasis on the details of sexual activity, like Jane's, would be hazardous to our students' development of tolerance for difference, as well as to their open discussion of sexuality.

The first response we thought of was authoritarian: we would remove Jane from the list. The idea of silencing her, however, was repulsive to our feminist pedagogical aims, and it was a good object lesson for us to discover how quickly we in authority were ready to move to silence as a method of control. Besides, since we had not established many ground rules for the discussion (e.g., what topics would and would not be allowed), we didn't feel empowered to take this route. At the other extreme, a passive approach also seemed inappropriate. The next option we considered was engaging Jane in a discussion of sadomasochism and attempting to bring such discussion back around to concerns with gender issues. Knowing that sadomasochism had occupied a challenging position vis-à-vis much feminist theory and activism, we decided to try to model for our students one kind of academic engagement with volatile, personal gender issues. We could demonstrate that we intellectuals were fully willing to think critically about the personal, and thus stand by our feminist deconstruction of the division between the personal and the political, the private and the public. Margaret took the lead:

> I admit I don't know much at all about SM theory or the subculture. I do gather, however, that SMers, whether they like to believe it or not, represent only a small fraction of people of whatever sexual orientation. [. . .] Many feminists, including lesbians, are embarrassed by their vocality and disagree with them on numerous points. [However,] there is an important distinction between the SM practice you describe and much feminist philosophy on violence. Feminists oppose the use or threat of any degree of violence to maintain a relationship of domination/subordination between men and women. You are not suggesting that at all, if I understand you correctly. In writing all this, I think I've clarified something for myself. I've probably confused everybody else—but "writing is thinking," *n'est ce pas?*

Margaret thus attempted to redirect the discussion by commenting on the uneasy relationship between feminism and sadomasochism while simultaneously modeling a process of rational thinking about difficult concepts. Concerned that this intervention would be too oblique to affect the conversation, Margaret followed immediately with a more forceful attempt to get the discussion "back on track": "This thread began as an 'aside' to the issue of whether women should be allowed/required to engage in military combat. I hope we can get back to that issue now to help all the people who are writing papers on the subject," she wrote.

Margaret's tactic worked for awhile, and discussion continued about various paper topics until someone asked Jane directly about her personal life. "Can you tell me a little about yourself?" the student wrote. "Are you in a relationship now and was it hard for you to state that you are a lesbian, like with your family and so on?" Jane's response was personal, intimate, and detailed. Worried about how the students on the list would respond to Jane's self-disclosures, Jonathan sent a private post to Margaret:

> [Jane] is going to scare the s_____ out of a lot of people—and that's a shame because I don't want her to be censored—yet she may ultimately be counterproductive for your classes. I'm not sure.

> You definitely need to think about her most recent postings and
> how they might affect your classes.

Margaret replied to her colleagues, "I'm not at present inclined to censor
her, but do you think she needs to know that this is an academic research
discussion list, not DYKENET? I just don't want the whole tone of the list
to disintegrate to the point that rational discussion isn't happening any
more. We can see what happens—but if a flame war doesn't erupt now, it
never will."

Our posts reveal that we were concerned about losing control of the
freewheeling discussion we ourselves had promoted. Further, we felt that
we were failing our less obvious agenda: the celebration of diversity, particularly vis-à-vis sexual orientation and feminism. We articulated these
concerns by privileging the academic and rational over self disclosure, personal detail, and the possibility of "flaming" (personal attacks or obviously
irrational statements of belief or opinion). Part of our worry may be attributed to our own internalized homophobia and squeamishness about sexual
practices; but all of us were concerned about handling delicate subject
matter in the most intelligent and objective fashion.

We had been trying to conduct—and at times enforce—a rational discussion via a medium that does not always encourage rational discourse.
Specifically, the disembodied discourse of listserves and e-mail in general
removes one's responses from an arena in which extraverbal cues, such as
body language and facial expression, shape and condition how we address
and reply to our interlocutors. At the same time, the speed and spontaneity
of the responses preclude carefully constructed written argument. Thus,
many participants say things on a listserve that they would never say in
public and write in ways that are sometimes surprising. We had to ask ourselves whether we really wanted this kind of openness in our classes. It was
beginning to dawn on us that we—not just our students—were reflecting
on difficult issues, and changing our minds. This is just one example of
how in a pedagogy emphasizing the collective construction of knowledge,
teachers often learn as much or more than their students do.

In the meantime, as the postings became more heated and caustic, Pete
began to recognize an opportunity for critical thinking. He posed the question to his own class: Should this guest be banned from the list? His question underscored the advantage of bringing listserve material back to
discussion by the classroom community, making students' involvement
relevant and meaningful. The discussion that ensued fit well with the argument paper Pete had assigned for that week, and the class had brainstorming sessions on the merits and pitfalls of banning someone from the list

who had remained true to herself, even though she was fully cognizant that her posts could offend some. After discussing all the merits of the case, the entire class (including three self-identified religious fundamentalists) agreed that Jane should stay.

Ultimately, the instructors decided, too, that we would not censor Jane or remove her from the list. We based our decision on a reunderstanding of the nature of listserve discourse and on a willingness to risk difficult subjects in the interest of opening up dialogue where none had previously existed. Jane's discussion opened a wide variety of subtopics, which were germane to our course's theme; some students engaged issues of feminism and violence, while others tackled the relationship between sexual orientation and politics—subjects directly stemming from Jane's comments.

Some teachers may object that we risked too much by not enforcing a strict code of speech or subject matter; that we failed to create a safe space in which students and guests—especially the nonstraights among them—could safely discuss sexual orientation issues without fear of attack, even if only verbally. But the world is not a safe place for most nonheterosexuals, and while we advocate the creation of such places, we also advocate giving les-bi-gays the voice to defend themselves and state their opinions and beliefs; sometimes, though, this occurs only if the individual les-bi-gay student is confronted with antigay views.[3] Opening up the interplay between these views is risky but also responsible in a course that stresses rhetoric and provides a language for talking about arguments.

As we put into practice the nonhierarchical teaching strategies feminists have been talking about for some time, new pedagogical opportunities arose. Students and teachers could meditate on the connection between silence and power. All of us could think about the use and value of decentralizing authority as a method of opening up possibilities for new voices, new connections, and new meanings to complicate and enrich the agendas and lives of those willing to participate in challenging discussions. Having metadiscussions about the listserve was as important as having the listserve in the first place. Ultimately, we had to revise our initial assumptions about discourse on listserves; we had believed that the listserve would provide a way to write out rational and academic discourses about delicate subjects, when, in fact, it opened up possibilities of engaging and creating alternate discourses, which challenged our assumptions about both list and classroom discussion. So, while the discussion list may not always serve as an alternative nonagonistic approach to argument and persuasion, it has potential as a powerful, if provocative, tool to encourage debate and further thought.

LENNIE AND LAURA: ON-LINE AND ON-SITE

The listserve exchanges between two students, Lennie and Laura, also raised questions about how the teacher's on-line role might be integrated with personal contact with students—both in and out of the classroom. Lennie's attempts to silence Laura, who flamed him because she had been hurt by his comments stereotyping gays, led during the semester to her developing an articulate written voice. That same semester, Lennie learned to think, before speaking or writing, about the ways words might affect an audience. For both of them, the list had transformative power. But without teacher involvement, both on and off the list, these students might have been silenced. Individual meetings with the two students, along with on-list advice for constructive argument and nonconfrontational discussion, were part of this intervention. Despite the advantages of risk and openness, the creation of a safe learning space—in class or in extensions of the class environment—also remains important; this kind of safety is certainly not guaranteed by the virtual environment.

The conflict between Lennie and Laura began three weeks into the semester. Students had introduced themselves to the list and posted tentative research topics, asking for feedback to help them refine their topics, identify useful sources, and collect various perspectives on the issues they had chosen to study. In the midst of a busy discussion of other gender-related topics, Heidi, one of Jonathan's students, posed the question, "Are women more accepting of lesbians than men?" Several posts followed on the subject before Pete asked for clarification of terms, questioning Heidi's essentialized notions of masculinity. Jonathan, Heidi's teacher, sat out the discussion, but Margaret entered with some comments and a personal experience that called Heidi's assumptions into question. For Heidi, Margaret was just another voice on the list; she didn't even know that Margaret *was* a teacher. Heidi finally announced her revised thesis: "There is no proof that men and women feel threatened by homosexuals because of their sex. [. . .] That only ignorance, culture, and other influences are the factors of people's attitudes toward homosexuality."

Using various teachers' responses (since few students seemed prepared to help her), Heidi had refined her question and worked out a provisional answer. Thus, the thread begun by Heidi had modeled the process, early in the semester, of questioning generalizations, defining terms, and identifying problems in logic. At this point, several students, including Laura, joined the discussion, elaborating on causes of homophobia, offering their own experiences, and agreeing that people tend to generalize about gays. Laura reported on the antilesbian comments she had heard at work. More students joined the discussion and the tone was cordial. At that point, homophobia as a topic of investigation was in the open, a subject of analysis, but with students sharing personal experiences without regard to personal sexual orientation. The teachers withdrew from active participation in this thread.

Soon, however, Laura wrote to Margaret off-list, asking to participate anonymously in order to conceal her gender and ethnic identity. (Laura was Jonathan's student, but she nevertheless initiated contact with Margaret. This may have been because Margaret was a woman, or because Margaret was a member of the Multicultural Council on campus. At any rate, Laura considered Margaret as much a teacher of her course as Jonathan, her classroom instructor.) Margaret sympathized with her request, but one purpose of having students write on the GE-L was to allow them to experience writing for an audience, publishing their words, and being accountable for what they said. While Margaret was considering Laura's request and asking her colleagues' opinions, Lennie started a flame war.

Lennie remarked on the list that gay men "talk funny." This began an energetic discussion that revealed how strongly Lennie and others were influenced by the representation of gay males on TV talk shows. Pete decided to question Lennie's assertions that speech patterns could easily mark a man's sexual orientation. Lennie became defensive and began to rail at anyone who challenged his comments. In this case, ironically, since one expectation of the list was that it would empower students, a teacher was empowered to speak directly to a student whom he might not have confronted in his own classroom. Pete also accomplished what Margaret preferred not to do publicly because she wanted to preserve her rapport with her own student and avoid silencing him. When she saw Lennie in class, he remarked, "I think everyone is mad at me." She assured him that she was glad he was attempting to engage in discussion on the list, but reminded him that the readership was diverse and could very easily include a number of people who would find his remarks hurtful or offensive. This surprised him. Margaret advised him to reread what he had written before posting his remarks to the list.

In the meantime, Laura dropped by Margaret's office to meet her in person, declaring that Lennie's disparaging remarks had changed her mind about her own request for anonymity. Now Laura did not want anyone to be able to speak without taking responsibility for their comments. Along with several other women, Laura began to speak strongly on the list in opposition to Lennie. After one of Laura's posts, Lennie responded, "Shut up!" When she retorted, the instructors feared a lengthy flame war that might turn students away from the list for good and even cause continuing hard feelings.

When Lennie, unused to having his sexist and homophobic remarks opposed or even questioned, slowed his barrage of posts, we were also concerned that he had been silenced. The purpose of the GE-L, after all, was to encourage practice in writing and critical thinking for all our students, and his disengagement would have signaled defeat of our purpose for him. Pete, too, wondered if he had been wrong in confronting Lennie. He tried to engage him off-list, so that he would not be subject to public scrutiny, but Lennie did not respond. Later when Lennie ventured onto the list again, he was somewhat subdued and cautious, with disclaimers at nearly every posting. He made the same remarks he had made before, but now he qualified them with comments like, "WELL YOU ASKED ME WHAT I THOUGHT SO THERE," and, "Well, I'M SORRY if I offended anyone, but that's a little bit of my opinion on the matter."

Although Lennie experienced Pete and others on the list as adversaries, he sought out Margaret in person for moral support. To her he revealed his regret for what he had said, and his desire to apologize to anyone he had hurt. Since he was a member of an ethnic minority himself, he told Margaret, he was well aware of how destructive stereotyping could be, but he had been unaware that he was doing the same thing to other groups. When Lennie told her he was afraid to apologize to the list, Margaret encouraged him to consider what it would mean to model good list behavior to others. After a few days, on the list, he said he regretted telling Laura to shut up, and added that he was sorry about grouping gay people, "although there could have been a lot worse written." His final disclaimer was a bit defensive: "Everything I've written is just MY opinion. We obviously all have one on everything so don't get upset. You know [at this institution] they have a way of helping you form your opinions." The response from other students was generally reassuring. For example, Kris (another invited guest), while still disagreeing with Lennie, offered, "I participate on this list because it helps me think critically about issues that are important [. . .] and articulating these types of arguments is the best way to answer hard questions."

Like Timothy, Lennie discovered through his interactions on the list that he was biased—something he had been unaware of. Using the list involved him in a process of self-discovery. It gave him his first exposure to a voice that directly challenged his thinking in specific ways, his first exposure to an articulate person who was openly lesbian and the discovery that he was capable of the same kind of stereotypical thinking he had formerly attributed only to others. Although not pressured to do so, Lennie decided to apologize to anyone who was gay who might be reading. Several students told him in class and on the list that they admired his courage in apologizing. Margaret remarked that he seemed to be learning an important lesson in how one's words can affect other people when one writes for an audience beyond the classroom. Although Margaret's face-to-face responses had been crucial for Lennie, he had also learned something from his list participation that Margaret alone could not have taught him.

Whereas Lennie eventually became quieter and more thoughtful on the list, Laura's posts increased in frequency and length. She found a voice, realized she was not alone, and told Margaret privately that until she saw women reinforcing each other on the list, she had been shy. At semester's end she wrote a letter thanking Margaret for encouraging her to speak out. This seems to have begun a process of empowerment for Laura, as she entered and won first place in the annual women's poetry contest with a piece entitled "I Am a Woman," declared a minor in women's studies, and a year later read a paper at a student conference analyzing her triple identity as a woman, a Chicana, and a lesbian. Apparently, the GE-L had offered her new options for student-teacher dynamics and a unique opportunity to expand discussions begun in class. The GE-L also provided Lennie and Laura and the other participants an opportunity to make and learn from mistakes in a relatively safe environment where all participants, including the teachers, were understood to be learners.

An electronic discussion list has the potential to extend and transform the dynamics of classroom interaction. It allows for easy access of invited guests. And, by networking several classes through a listserve, as we did, instructors can easily enlarge their "class" and increase the likelihood of diversity among participants. A listserve that links several classes or campuses also allows teachers to teach each other's students. We generally found it more constructive to question and challenge each other's students rather than our own, thus circumventing students' fears that their grades would be affected if they disagreed with their teacher. This collaboration among instructors also means that if one wants a particular feminist pedagogy employed consistently, one should choose teacher collaborators carefully. Participation in written discussion allows teachers to support, observe, and critique each other's practice. We instructors sent scores of messages to each other off-list, asking for advice and requesting other perspectives on what we had done on-line. Further, the list allows teachers flexibility to use differing degrees of directness in speaking with their own and others' students; they may use this latitude to model nonconfrontational discussion and argument in ways not available in a traditional classroom. Finally, the "oral" quality, particularly the ease of fluency on a computer, as well as the presence of a reading audience to whom the novice writer may be unaccustomed, increases the likelihood that someone will make comments or references that offend—even hurt—some list members of whose presence the writer was unaware. This is why we suggest that the list's potential as a de-centered, nonhierarchical medium be balanced with instructor involvement in a variety of roles.

The list transforms academic discourse in ways that are also difficult to predict. While teaching academic and rational discourse may be the goal of our writing classes, we should not overlook the ways in which irrational and nonacademic discourse can be used to teach what is appropriate and inappropriate in academic writing. Because lists are far more chatty and conversational than rhetorically formal, they may be used to brainstorm ideas and open up new directions for discussion—directions that a more formal rhetorical discussion might dismiss as irrelevant or digressive. List discourse powerfully twists, turns, and makes connections—for better or worse—that could not have been anticipated in our original agendas. Because all these variables are desirable as well as problematic, we would not want to use a class discussion list except as an integral element of a face-to-face classroom course—with reading, class discussion, and personal contact with students.

For many of our students, the GE-L has been their first experience of intense discussions of difficult issues that have not ended with shouting, anger, physical abuse, or condemnation. The interactions we have described are only a small fraction of what has transpired on the list—several hundreds, even thousands, of messages per semester. Many discussions proceed with little teacher intervention, except occasionally to provide information, but teachers nevertheless need to be prepared to intervene at any time, and in various ways. How potentially explosive situations are handled early in the semester can determine the nature of the experience for the entire group, so teachers must be ready to deal with them as soon as they occur.

A note written by a student, Dennis Hawley, after the end of the semester, captures the interplay of "safe space" and risk in what turned out to be a transformative experience for him:

The listserve made me feel more comfortable in talking about the issues at hand. I was talking to a person yet everyone [. . .] was reading (paying attention) my words. [. . .] I learned I can talk of my experiences and have for the most part confidence that some people (straight) developed a better understanding of the style of life I choose to live, while I better understood theirs. [. . .] I am more "out" due to the listserve and I know others may not like what I say and some will be cruel but many will hear and of those some will listen.

Mindful of Selfe's admonition that without (and even with) careful structuring, the electronic space may simply offer another environment in which existing hegemonies of the larger society are reproduced, we continue to search for ways to structure this new environment. It's important to use reflective practice to avoid self-deception. For example, instead of simply assuming that a story like Timothy's is a purely positive tale of self-development and enlightenment, we have to entertain the possibility that it might only be another example of a person conforming to the will of the group and the preferences of the teacher. Upon reflection, why do we think we're *not* simply reproducing hegemonic structures in our list activities? Surprise! Comments about surprise, about the unexpected, enter into all the examples we have provided in this essay. Timothy was surprised that some of the people with whom he enjoyed conversing on the list were women. Jane surprised all the instructors with her descriptions of her sexual practices. Lennie surprised Pete with the vehemence of his reaction to Pete's criticism. Laura surprised Margaret and herself with her change from shyness to outspokenness. Surprise suggests to us that at least in some cases social positions are being questioned and hegemonies disrupted. Class discussion lists, at this point in their development, are good catalysts for surprise.

Although we acknowledge that the potential for damage is present in list discussions of gender and identity, we believe that the electronic environment, especially when it can be carefully designed and enlarged beyond the immediate classroom, offers enough potential for positive, transforming experiences to offset most risks. It should be clear from our examples that we differed somewhat on how much risk we were comfortable with, how much we wanted our students to be challenged, how much teacher talk we thought appropriate, how much safe space we wished to ensure. Some teachers are more interventionist, some more participatory; others prefer to deal with issues off-list in order to avoid the possibility of dominating the on-line conversation. Our styles and experience differ, but we agree that a gender list needs to be managed with care. Thus, the model we favor is a multiclass, multi-instructor list with minimal but consistent ground rules. (The GE-L ground rules were that students had to use their real names, and their posts were to be limited to gender issues only.) The variety of teacher (and student) styles of involvement, along with the consistency of the ground rules, allow for both open space and safe space.

In 1993, Gail Hawisher and Charles Moran speculated that "five years from now we might regard e-mail as an invasive technology that has given us writing teachers additional invisible work" (637). Without doubt, making e-mail integral to course work adds to a teacher's workload. Maintaining e-mail discussion lists for several different classes can create such sheer volume that it may be difficult to maintain the kind of teacher involvement we recommend. Thus, we caution teachers who wish to attempt such a project for such sensitive topics as gender to focus on only one or two such lists; it is also helpful to coordinate with colleagues in other classrooms or on other campuses so that the work of attending to the lists may be shared. Because of experiences like those we have narrated, we support integrating this use of CMC (the gender list) into regular classes; using such projects in courses taught strictly on-line would not offer the teacher the option of face-to-face contact with students. This could result in increasing risk for already marginalized students, even though teachers could deal with some situations via personal e-mail. Keeping a variety of options open for teacher response is worth the extra work.

Generally, we feel that the GE-List has positively influenced our teaching. One must be willing to devote effort and hours of engagement to a project that can be avoided by simply remaining within the traditional classroom environment. But if we do not teach ourselves to function in an electronic environment in new ways, to use the tools technology increasingly provides us, proceeding carefully, taking educated risks, we may miss out on opportunities to engage students in genuinely transformative experience—one reason we entered teaching in the first place.

•   •   •

NOTES

1. In an asynchronous discussion, participants may introduce questions or make responses at any time. The "thread" of the discussion proceeds—with messages added as they are received—even though several hours or even days may elapse between some postings. For example, on an e-mail discussion list, a student in Colorado may post a question about homosexual marriage at 8 A.M. Mountain Standard Time. The first answer or comment on that question may come from a Nevada student at 10 A.M., Pacific Standard Time, when the Colorado student is no longer on-line. The next time he logs on, he will be able to read all the discussion his question has generated so far, and then add his own comments. In contrast, a synchronous (or real-time) discussion, such as a chat room on the Internet or in a Daedalus INTERCHANGE session on a Local Area Network, requires partici-

pants to be on-line and present at the time the discussion is occurring. A person who leaves the chat room for a few hours may not pick up the discussion where she left off.

The GE-L was an e-mail discussion list (or listserve) that Pete established at the University of Alaska in Fairbanks specifically as a forum for written discussion by members of the Gender Issues classes at the three universities. At the start of every semester, every student and instructor in these classes joined, or was subscribed to, the GE-L, thus becoming a list member. For the duration of the semester, any list member could send a message to the GE-L that would in turn be posted to every other member's e-mail account. Members could then read and respond to each other's messages whenever they checked their e-mail inboxes. They could choose to respond to the entire list or just to the individual member.

Many colleges and universities have Majordomo or other resources that will allow an instructor to set up an e-mail list for an individual class or for several linked classes. The list may be limited or opened to membership from outside the class, at the discretion of the list owner. The list owner usually posts a welcome message that is sent automatically to each new member, stating the purpose and policies of the list. Although Pete was list owner for GE-L, he did not moderate the discussion; that is, every message a list member posted went directly to all other list members without being read first or censored in any way. Comparatively small lists are often unmoderated; well-known international lists like WMST-L (Women's Studies List), with memberships in the thousands, are often moderated.

2. Dynamics of networked discussions differ greatly, and most studies do not cover all of them. E-mail, as we have seen, is asynchronous and requires use of the Internet, so geographical location of participants is irrelevant. MOOs are synchronous and also use the Internet. Wide Area Networks (WANs) also allow for synchronous discussion. Synchronous written discussions can also take place among students in a classroom on a Local Area Network (LAN) with software such as the INTERCHANGE feature of the Daedalus Integrated Writing Environment. INTERCHANGE allows users to send messages from individual computer stations to a common document.

Most of the scholarship we cite on the dynamics of networked discussions, including studies from a feminist perspective, has concerned networked discussions using INTERCHANGE. For example, Romano; Regan; Castner; Rickly; and Warshauer have studied synchronous discussions, which, unlike e-mail discussions, do not offer the flexibility of involving students from outside a given classroom. Also, they occur in a limited time frame, which would restrict the teacher's involvement. Still, these authors have raised important questions and concerns that can apply to asynchronous e-mail discussions.

3. More aware, now, that a similar dynamic might operate for other marginalized groups, we would at least have to consider offering the same opportunity for

them to risk and speak out, rather than rushing to provide protection and attempting to manage the discourse. Still, our own identities and group memberships would inevitably play a part in our decisions: we teachers represent a diversity of genders and sexual orientations, but not racial diversity.

WORKS CITED

Alexander, Jonathan. "Out of the Closet and Into the Network: Sexual Orientation and the Computerized Classroom." *Computers and Composition* 14.2 (1997): 207–16.

Alexander, Jonathan, Margaret M. Barber, Kathleen Boardman, and Peter Pinney. "Welcome to the GE-L: A Return from the Margins—Reexamining the Role of the Teacher in E-talk of Gender and Sexual Orientation. Panel presentation at the Computers and Writing Conference, Honolulu, HI. 6 June 1997.

Bennett, Michael, and Kathleen Walsh. "Desperately Seeking Diversity: Going On-line to Achieve a Racially Balanced Classroom." *Computers and Composition* 14.2 (1997): 217–28.

Castner, Joanna. "The Clash of Social Categories: Egalitarianism in Networked Writing Classrooms?" *Computers and Composition* 14.2 (1997): 257–68.

Cooper, Marilyn M., and Cynthia S. Selfe. "Computer Conferences and Learning: Authority, Resistance, and Internally Persuasive Discourse." *College English* 52 (1990): 847–69.

Gore, Jennifer M. *The Struggle for Pedagogies: Critical and Feminist Discourses as Regimes of Truth*. New York: Routledge, 1993.

Gruber, Sibylle. "Why We Contribute: Students, Instructors, and Pedagogies in the Computer-mediated Writing Classroom." *Computers and Composition* 12.1 (1995): 61–78.

Hawisher, Gail E., and Charles Moran. "Electronic Mail and the Writing Instructor." *College English* 55.6 (Oct. 1993): 627–43.

Hawley, Dennis. Personal e-mail communication. 2 March 1998. Used with permission.

Jarrett, Susan C. "Feminism and Composition: The Case for Conflict." *Contending with Words: Composition and Rhetoric in a Postmodern Age*. Eds. Patricia Harkin and John Schilb. New York: MLA, 1991. 105–23.

Katsavos, Anna, and Elizabeth Wheeler. *Complements*. New York: McGraw-Hill, 1995.

Mamet, David. *Oleanna*. New York: Vintage, 1993.

Regan, Alison. "Type Normal Like the Rest of Us: Writing, Power, and Homophobia in the Networked Composition Classroom." *Computers and Composition* 10.4 (1993): 11–23.

Rickly, Rebecca J. "Exploring the Dimensions of Discourse: A Multi-Modal Analysis of Electronic and Oral Discussions in Developmental English." Doctoral dissertation, Ball State University, 1995.

Romano, Susan. "The Egalitarianism Narrative: Whose Story? Which Yardstick?" *Computers and Composition* 10.3 (1993): 5–28.

Selfe, Cynthia S. "Technology in the English Classroom: Computers through the Lens of Feminist Theory." *Computers and Community: Teaching Composition in the Twenty-first Century*. Ed. Carolyn Handa. Portsmouth, NH: Boynton/Cook, 1990.

Takeyoshi, Pamela. "Building New Networks from the Old: Women's Experience with Electronic Communications." *Computers and Composition* 11.1 (1994): 21–35.

Taylor, Todd. "The Persistence of Difference in Networked Classrooms: Non-negotiable Difference and the African-American Student Body." *Computers and Composition* 14.2 (1997): 169–78.

Warshauer, Susan Claire. "Rethinking Teacher Authority to Counteract Homophobic Prejudice in the Networked Classroom: A Model of Teacher Response and Overview of Classroom Methods." *Computers and Composition* 12.1 (1995): 97–111.

A Spectrum of Classrooms

10

FEMINIST PEDAGOGY, INTERDISCIPLINARY PRAXIS, AND SCIENCE EDUCATION

Maralee Mayberry and Margaret N. Rees

INTRODUCTION

As a theoretical and methodological practice, feminist pedagogy embraces a commitment to incorporating the voices and experiences of marginalized students into the academic discourse as well as educating all students for social justice and social change (Kenway and Modra; Maher; Rosser; Shrewsbury). At its core, feminist pedagogy is a commitment not only to the development of cooperative, multicultural, and interdisciplinary knowledge that makes learning inviting and meaningful to a diverse population but also to the development of a critical consciousness empowered to apply learning to social action and social transformation.

Although the theory and practice of feminist pedagogy is an increasingly familiar concept to women's studies educators around the country, few science educators have yet to acknowledge its potential to transform the traditional conceptualizations of scientific thought that fail to investigate the role of culture in the production, dissemination, and utilization of scientific knowledge (Bleir; Harding, "Forum"; Shulman).

This chapter focuses on our vision of how social, scientific, and feminist inquiry and teaching can be drawn together to create a new vision of science education. What follows reflects our experience as two feminist educators teaching a unique interdisciplinary course, Earth Systems: A Feminist Approach. Earth Systems infuses geological education with the insights of sociological inquiry and feminist pedagogy and was offered in spring 1995 for credit through the departments of geology, sociology, and women's studies at the University of Nevada, Las Vegas. Seventeen white undergraduate students (fourteen females and three males), ranging from sophomore to senior level, enrolled for and completed the course. Twelve students were social science or humanities majors; three students were women's studies majors; two students were natural science majors. In addition, we granted permission to one female graduate student from the environmental studies program to enroll in the course. She received graduate credit for developing and implementing a session on "ecofeminism." It is also important to note that Earth Systems was developed and team-taught by a geologist and a sociologist, while most science education programs at the high school and college level remain under the direction of scientific experts and science education research teams who rarely, if ever, include academicians from either the social sciences or humanities.

Our methodological approach is experiential. We weave our experiences as well as the experiences of our students—male and female, natural and social science majors—into all aspects of our account. Personal experiences, therefore, provide the lens through which our discussion is refracted. We analyzed the written narratives of eight students collected from journal accounts compiled throughout the semester. We also conducted oral interviews with six students who volunteered to discuss the impact of the course on their knowledge of the relationship between earth processes and society as well as their commitment to social and environmental change. Finally, to provide an account of our experiences we draw on journals that we, the instructors, kept throughout the course and subsequent works that we produced about the course.

RATIONALE FOR TEACHING EARTH SYSTEMS: A FEMINIST APPROACH

Earth Systems: A Feminist Approach emerged from our awareness of recent feminist scholarship that presents a challenge to traditional Western scientific scholarship and science education (see the works of Harding; Rosser; Fausto-Sterling; Rosser and Kelly). Our approach to the development of the course was informed by the two interrelated issues that are central to this scholarship: (1) the "masculinity" of science and science education, which has contributed to the attrition of women, men of color, and people from working-class backgrounds from science courses and careers, and (2) the failure of scientific inquiry and education to situate scientific knowledge in a social, political, and historical context.

Numerous pedagogical implications for the transformation of the teaching and curricula in science education are embedded in these issues. As an increasing number of studies clearly suggest, elements of science education that need reform include the culture of competition that characterizes many science classrooms (Henderson; Hollenshead et al.; Manis, Seymour and Hewitt; Tobias); the lack of curriculum images that reflect diverse cultural and gender experiences and are relevant to the daily lives of students (Otto; Trankina; Kelly); and low teacher expectations about the ability of women and men of color to successfully participate in scientific inquiry (Hollenshead et al.; Spear). Furthermore, programs across the nation, such as Miami University's Project Discovery, the University of Michigan's Women in Science program, and Sue Rosser's University of South Carolina System Model Project for the Transformation of Science and Math Teaching to Reach Women in Varied Campus Settings, illustrate, to varying degrees, some ways in which science classrooms and science curricula can be redesigned to empower marginalized students, acknowledge different ways of knowing, and provide a safer environment within which students' experiences and concerns will become central to the learning process. While changing particular curricular content and pedagogical techniques may increase the diversity within the pool of scientists, it will not necessarily alter the theoretical, philosophical, and political perspectives upon which science is based—a concern central in recent scholarship on feminism and science.

The work of feminists on science challenges western scientific epistemology's inability to situate scientific knowledge in its historical, social, and political context. According to this view, what is wrong with Western science is that the social causes of scientific belief and behavior are neither exposed nor discussed in science domains. Sandra Harding and others have drawn attention to how the purportedly objective and value-free nature of science not only obscures the historical and social context of science but in fact may hide an androcentric bias (Bleier; Fausto-Sterling, "Women and Science"; Keller; Rosser; Shulman). The politically regressive consequences that follow from this position are clear: the scientific establishment's insistence on the "purity" of science supports the claim that scientific findings improve human welfare, and it protects the establishment from claims that scientific research could be used to work against the welfare of certain social groups (Harding, "Forum" 53–54)

In addition, an awareness of how scientific knowledge is socially constructed is considered an important beginning for the development of the competencies that enable disempowered groups to become critically resistant readers and writers of their social, cultural, and educational environments. The pedagogical challenge for feminists is to create a feminist science that acknowledges and critically addresses the social study of science and the associated power relations embedded in the scientific community as well as the manner in which science is traditionally taught. To this end, the creation of a contextualized science in science education not only will begin to speak to the interests of women and men of color but will challenge us all to examine the role science plays in shaping definitions of knowledge, power relations, and social inequalities and to recognize our capacity to act within the world. As Sandra Harding stresses, "It seems to me that for nonscientists, the failure of the sciences to show that they are *for* us and have always been committed to and reasonably successful at increasing human welfare—to show science in historical context in that sense—goes a long way toward explaining why not only many women but also the majority of men in the U.S. are scientifically illiterate" ("Forum" 49).

In order to address these concerns, the primary goals of Earth Systems: A Feminist Approach were twofold. First, we wanted to create a cooperative, noncompetitive learning environment where all student voices could be heard and where the collaborative production of geological knowledge was linked to daily lives through the lens of sociology and feminist theory. Second, we wanted to develop a curriculum that would strengthen the ability of students (including those marginalized from previous science education) to play an active role in transformative learning and environmental, social, and political action.

"DOING" GEOLOGY, SOCIOLOGY, AND FEMINIST PEDAGOGY: REFLECTIONS FROM THE FIELD

Our course was based on the principles of feminist pedagogy. Feminist pedagogy is not, as implied in the conventional view of pedagogy, merely a teaching method that transmits the content of knowledge but a pedagogy that signifies what Frances Maher and Mary Kay Thompson Tetreault call "the entire process of creating knowledge, involving the innumerable ways in which students, teachers, and academic disciplines interact and redefine each other in the classroom, the educational institution, and the larger society" (57). Thus the foundation of the course was built on the collaborative production of knowledge about the interrelatedness of earth and social systems in an environment that would demystify "doing sociology" and "doing geology."

We found that a combination of institutional requirements, such as course outlines and grades, and a lack of models and materials designed to develop cooperative, multicultural, and interdisciplinary knowledge often impeded our attempts to implement these goals. Many moments throughout the course, however, convince us that the blending of our pedagogical and intellectual commitments was successful. Although we cannot provide definitive ways to overcome institutional barriers to the implementation of feminist pedagogy or to bridge the gap between the social and natural sciences, our experiences offer some starting points.

Un(enclosed) Knowledge

A central organizing tool in traditional educational settings is the course syllabus, but it becomes a problematic tool when feminist pedagogy is implemented as the primary principle around which the classroom is structured. For example, professors at many universities are required to submit their course syllabus to their department chairperson before the beginning of each semester, and, at most universities, the course syllabus becomes the contract between student and professor, detailing the professor's expectations and requirements. Learning and knowledge, therefore, are organized, prearranged, and transmitted from the professor to the student. Paulo Freire refers to this approach as the "banking" method of education, in which "knowledge is a gift bestowed by those who consider themselves knowledgeable upon those whom they consider to know nothing." In this model, students are anonymous, interchangeable "containers" or "receptacles," to be "filled" by the teacher (58). In opposition to the "banking" method, women's studies practitioners have developed the practice of feminist pedagogy (Weiler). Sitting in a circle underscores, visually and kinesthetically, the decentralization of authority in the women's studies classroom. So does the fact that everyone in the room has a name and a voice. Each member of the classroom is a learner and a potential teacher. Each member brings something to contribute to the collaborative construction of knowledge, and the knowledge they collectively produce should, ideally, exceed what any member thought they knew when they arrived. Obviously, a preplanned course syllabus, specifying each week's class content, and a traditionally organized classroom limits the implementation of this process.

Committed to feminist pedagogy, we started our course with a vaguely structured syllabus that would allow for collectively developing course content and direction throughout the semester with the students. The syllabus did, however, specify the course goals, provide a set of guidelines for how classroom discussions and negotiations would be implemented, and stipulate a set of criteria for grading. In addition, it listed the dates of each class period but did not provide topics or readings.

As instructors, we immediately recognized our discomfort with beginning the course without a detailed outline. What would we do each class period? How could we guarantee that the course would cover the "necessary" information? Most unnerving, how could we assure our preparedness each class, given our other academic responsibilities, if we had to think through each class period on a week-to-week basis? We commonly felt that this was the "scariest classroom endeavor" that we had ever undertaken.

As we began to feel comfortable about our decisions regarding the syllabus and the unstructured nature of the course, class began. We discussed the syllabus with the students and emphasized that they would collectively help build the curriculum and could participate in reconstructing the grading criteria. The students quickly made us aware of their discomfort, which was not unlike our own. In the first week's journal entries, we discovered their fear about not being provided with a "banking" model of education:

> What outline? This makes me very nervous. We haven't even closed the date for the field trip, I would prefer things to be more set. I haven't been unsyllabled [sic] since high school. It makes prioritizing assignment times difficult. I'm used to structuring my week relative to my work load. This makes me think of *Zen and the Art of Motorcycle Maintenance*: A thing is either good or not good and we don't need an enforced system of letters to tell us what is what. On the other hand, life without letters could be difficult. I'm used to comparing myself to the class averages and I'm truly frightened of flying blind.
>
> There is one thing I find disturbing—grading. Most institutions require grading and therefore teachers of feminist pedagogy must grade. Why should one participant in a class receive a higher grade then [sic] another for a journal entry?

At the outset, some students were also unsure about the "transformed" classroom setting. In particular, the natural science majors expressed great discomfort about sitting in a circle and opening all inquiry to discussion. After class the first evening, a geology major confided to Peg (Margaret) that to sit in a circle and verbally participate in class discussions felt uncomfortable and foreign because she had been so well schooled in traditional science classrooms. Because of her discomfort, she was unsure whether or not she could continue in the class. In contrast, the social science and humanities majors in the course were quite familiar with this arrangement. Upon hearing about the discomfort that some students felt about the classroom organization, a women's studies major commented, "I wouldn't know what to do if I walked into a classroom and the chairs were not in a circle or if there wasn't a lot of discussion!" In time, however, we all became more comfortable with the classroom environment and the emphasis on "process" learning. Students soon started to provide us with a wealth of ideas about topics that they desired to explore. In response, we designed class periods to incorporate their interests and concerns. The strong classroom emphasis on experiential, collaborative, and self-directed learning, however, presented us with a web of other challenges.

(Un)connected Knowledge

Providing to students, and ourselves, the experience of a process-oriented learning environment was only one of the hurdles that we faced in our attempt to infuse the classroom with a feminist pedagogy and collaboratively constructed knowledge. Early in the course, we recognized that achieving the goal of constructing a truly interdisciplinary course was hindered by our own academic backgrounds. The following example illustrates this problem: Peg, trained as a geologist, *knew* the importance of understanding plate tectonics, the hydrologic cycle, the rock cycle, the composition of the earth, and geological hazards and processes. For students to become scientifically and environmentally literate, she maintained that these concepts should be discussed. Maralee, trained as a sociologist and women's studies scholar, *knew* that any solid interdisciplinary knowledge would need to include discussions about epistemology, feminist critiques of science, policy formation processes, and the relationship of race, class, gender, and power to scientific and environmental inquiry. She adamantly stated, "the students *must* understand the concepts of epistemology, ideology, hegemony, and standpoint before the end of the semester." During the first few weeks of the course, each of us was determined to center class discussions on many of the concepts that make up our introductory classes. As we struggled with allotting time for each of the various discussions that *must* occur, our joke became, "two-two-two introductory classes in one."

Students, however, did not find this humorous. They found jumping between discussions of feminist critiques of science and sessions devoted to earth processes quite unnerving. For example, after several weeks of discussing feminist critiques of science, we wanted to illustrate how a variety of perspectives could be employed to examine a scientific concept. We decided to discuss the concept of "plate tectonics" by exploring the numerous ways in which this theory is presented at the introductory level and then trying to understand the relationship between the history and development of plate tectonics and our everyday lives and culture. We had expected students to be fascinated by the idea that scientific knowledge can have a subjective, cultural, and historical component. What we discovered, however, was their hunger for more "scientific" inquiry. A female social science major commented in a journal entry:

If the continents never sink and they keep pushing against each other and erosion keeps happening, do the continents get smaller? Or is there enough volcanism to prevent this? Do new continents ever form? Have their shapes changed much? This subject fascinates me. Are there any classes on this that I could take as a non-science major?

Another student, a male biology major, obviously tiring of our attempts to always look at science within a social context, wrote this about the plate tectonics session:

This was the best class session yet. Hopefully, this will continue. It is very relieving to finally get into earth systems, which I thought was to be the mainstay of the class rather than feminism. I thought it is from a feminist approach we are to learn the earth systems, not to learn the feminist approach itself. If I solely wanted to learn the feminism, I would have enrolled in women's studies 101, not this class.

As feminist educators, we were thrilled by the fascination with science expressed by our female student who, we later learned, had shied away from science courses since her early high school years. We were less pleased by the reaction of our male science major. Why had the approach failed to be of interest to him? What could spur his desire to learn how feminist critiques of science could be a new approach to evaluating, understanding, and conducting science? It wasn't until the last two weeks of the course that we would begin to be able to answer these and other questions. In the meantime, we were slowly becoming aware of how difficult it is to develop integrated knowledge.

Our inability to create interdisciplinary knowledge continued to haunt us. At one point, the students agreed to spend two weeks researching the relationship between concentrations of nonrenewable natural resources and political economies. They were to find literature that addressed why a particular resource (e.g., diamonds or copper ore) was concentrated in one part of the world (e.g., South Africa or South America) *and* the relationship between the presence of that resource and the country's political organization (e.g., apartheid or revolutions). After the two-week period, one student reflected the sentiment of many others by commenting:

I found more than 300 entries in the library [relating to the mineral I wanted to study], some even in English, but none made any sense. I knew that science was not an easy subject, but I get the feeling I'm reading a foreign language. In another section of the library, I found that the De Beers people [an international family cartel] are known as the syndicate and insulated themselves into the financial fabric of a recalcitrant Australian government. They then threatened to disrupt the Australian economy if they [the syndicate] were not allowed to control newly discovered diamond mines. I understand some of what is being said, but I can't put it into words I understand or integrate what I am reading. This is an impossible task.

Furthermore, the resource librarian called us on the telephone during this stage of the course to convey her dismay at the graying of her hair as she worked with many of the students individually trying to help them locate the resources necessary for the successful completion of the project.

Solving the problem of "integrating knowledge" became a class goal. Students listened for and worked intently toward the moment that knowledge about earth and social processes would feel integrated.

Connected Knowledge

It was not until the last several weeks of the course that we began collectively to feel the integration of knowledge. On one occasion, we were engaged in an oil-exploration game intended to demonstrate the geological concepts of oil reservoirs and traps. The game was designed to get students interested in learning about sedimentary strata, faults, folds, and the difference between petroleum resources and reserves by having them play the role of an independent petroleum company with geologists and economists who needed to make business decisions about where to purchase land and drill for petroleum exploration. What our students gained, however, was a new understanding of capitalist consciousness. The game resulted not only in an increased knowledge about where petroleum may be trapped but also in a clearer understanding of the social and economic forces that shape our utilization of the earth's natural resources. The students identified the relationship between natural resources and economic imperatives, as evidenced by these journal entries:

When we first started the game, I had a few unvoiced objections, [I wanted to ask,] what about the environment, ecology, and social consequences of drilling for petroleum? However, these were quickly forgotten as the excitement mounted. Our team wanted to be the first to "strike gold." So we bought information about the land, searched for the best places to drill, bought land, and drilled. We made a profit so we did it again. Soon we were up to $950,000, we were rolling in money and profits were soaring. Could we stop? No! Did I have any reservation about continuing? No. We went absolutely crazy with greed and power. We bought and drilled and bought and drilled. [. . .] I felt horrified at the greedy little capitalist I had become (and so easily)!

My desire to finish first and make a profit clouded my thinking. Never once did I think about the flora or fauna on top of the earth, only what was underneath. I looked at risk factors in terms of dollars only, and never once thought of human penalties.

Perhaps one of our most successful efforts at integrating fields of knowledge occurred during a weekend excursion into Death Valley to see and experience many of the geological processes and features discussed in class. Sedimentary deposits, limestone, sandstone, and basalt, in the words of one student, "are easier to understand when they're tangible." We also encouraged the students (and ourselves) to pay attention to the group's social dynamics, hoping to develop a sense of comaraderie between individuals. The weekend experience, although trying because of seventy-two hours of strong winds, rain, and snow, effectively connected knowledge and process. The connectedness was experienced by many students as an "active" learning process. This journal entry reflects the comments made by many of the students:

The field trip to Death Valley was a great application of feminist pedagogy. It incorporated much of what we have learned in class into an understanding of geological processes with a societal and personal perspective. To be able to reach out and touch rocks that are 1.6 billion years old means so much more than hearing that rocks of such a great age exist. Physical involvement [with the earth] alone, however, doesn't guarantee a more holistic approach. The questions and comments and the camaraderie of the group was certainly a crucial part of the learning process That process would not have had such impact if it had been presented in the same dry, sterile method so common to the usual scientific field trip.

During the second day of the field trip, we entered Mosaic Canyon and observed faulted, brecciated, and polished limestone that is beautifully displayed in the steep-sided, narrow, curving passage into and through the mountains. We stopped to consider how the history of a fault (and its future) cannot be captured by observing a limited rock section. Suddenly, and spontaneously, the students began to discuss the unforeseen environmental problems that could result from the spatially limited geological study being conducted at the proposed Yucca Mountain Nuclear Repository site, which is located a hundred miles north of Las Vegas: a site marked by numerous active and inactive faults. To the onlooking tourists, students discussing the geological research at Yucca Mountain may have seemed disassociated from the geological story told by the rocks in Mosaic Canyon. To our group, however, the limited history of deposition, faulting, fracturing, and fluid flow that was recorded in the Mosaic Canyon outcrop constituted a warning. The important questions became apparent to us all: What geological questions were scientists at Yucca Mountain addressing? What geological evidence was being overlooked on account of the limited area within which geological observations were taking place? Should other questions be asked? Can geological questions truly be evaluated through "site assessment" or should more regional investigations be required? Who was being allowed (funded) to study the geology of Yucca Mountain? Do the questions asked, investigations conducted, and conclusions formed vary with funding agents? What are the potential human consequences? Have scientists not already destroyed the sacred land of the Western Shoshone by building roads, drilling wells, and digging tunnels for scientific inquiry to justify the disposal of human waste? Geological processes, the construction of scientific knowledge, power, influence, and human consequences all emerged as important topics of discussion while we observed the faults and fractured limestone of Mosaic Canyon.

After observing how our discussion had moved from the effects of local faulting to a critique of the geological studies being conducted at Yucca Mountain, one student commented:

> The field trip from heaven and hell. We are integrating a world view with a world we are only beginning to know. The discussion in Mosaic Canyon had the quality of synthesis that we search for when we reach out to read a book, touch a leaf, quench a thirst, or to hold the hand of another.

This is just one of many stories to emerge from our attempt to develop a truly interdisciplinary course, and teach it from a feminist perspective.

(De)constructing Knowledge

Developing interdisciplinary knowledge requires a collaborative effort and a commitment to process learning. Moreover, this process forces both students and teachers to engage in a continuous effort to invent new knowledge.

The significance of process-based learning became clear to us after a frustrating small-group exercise aimed at demonstrating the various types of information scientists need for determining the epicenter and focus of an earthquake. During this exercise many of the social science and humanities majors, who were mostly women, had difficulty working through a series of arithmetic and algebra problems, using ruler and compass, and plotting to scale on a map. The angst built to such a level that the exercise manuals were literally being pushed to the corner of their desks and shoved into backpacks—pushed away and out of sight, where they could not intimidate. One student lost all interest in scientific inquiry during this agonizing session:

> The inner workings of how an earthquake occurs and how its epi-center is calculated seem understandable. However, once I tried to do it, with the compass and equation in hand, I was dumbstruck. For the life of me I couldn't grasp what was seemingly an easy task. Is it really so important to know where the epicenter of an earthquake is?

We felt that the level of math anxiety and student disengagement with the project, which surfaced during the session, needed to be addressed. The following week we decided to place our central focus on this issue and "do math anxiety." Maralee, recognizing her own difficulty with the project, walked the students through the various mental images and thinking processes that she herself had had to use in an attempt to solve the mathematical equations. The presentation forced her to discuss her fear of confronting a problem that could not be contextualized or historicized and made her carefully prepare a step-by-step description of how a "mathematically challenged" mind might go about thinking through the problem. This strategy, we hoped, would allow students to see that fears and anxieties brought on by confronting math are neither unusual nor limited to the "uneducated." Furthermore, we hoped that the strategy would expose students to a multitude of ways to perform mathematical procedures.

The results were striking: the students fearful of math were now fully engaged in the problem-solving process; other students began to offer their classmates a variety of approaches to solving the equation, thereby helping us all develop a better appreciation for the multitude of ways that "scientific" procedures can be conducted; and Maralee learned that even she could "teach math." In addition, the experience underscored the importance of a classroom environment in which all members of the class care about each other's learning as well as their own.

In relation to this exercise, we also wanted to develop a sense of the social and political aspects of earthquakes in order to address the question "Is it really so important to know where the epicenter of an earthquake is?" We assembled a set of readings to demonstrate the human and social dimensions of earthquakes and illustrate the importance of distinguishing between natural occurrences and natural "disasters." The discussion that ensued allowed each of us to begin to understand the relationship between scientific knowledge, social policy, and social inequality. Throughout these sessions the language of sociology was spoken. For instance, the concept of "disaster" was revealed to be a socially constructed concept, one that varies historically, culturally, and regionally. We called into question the "naturalness" of disasters by discussing which segments of the population are most vulnerable to natural disasters and observed that such events overwhelmingly kill poor people in poor countries. The discussion illuminated how scientific language often obscures the social, political, and human consequences of scientific knowledge and provided us a new way to think about the social context of science. When students (and ourselves) posed questions about how scientific findings play out in everyday life, the distance between the natural and social sciences shrank.

By the end of the unit, we had discussed the science of earthquakes and how scientists locate and evaluate earthquakes, as well as how social policies regarding earthquake occurrences are formed. We discovered that an earthquake's impact on human life is interrelated with a variety of social policies and social conditions. Scientific procedures and findings were now joined with the question of who benefits from "science" and who doesn't. Reflecting on her newly acquired knowledge about where earthquakes are likely to occur, how scientists study them, and the social and political implications of earthquakes, one student wrote:

Almost like a puzzle where the scene is at first confusing and obscure, then suddenly becomes clear and obvious when completed. The discussion and reading led me to put together bits and pieces of information that I already had into a complete picture. I said "of course" when I finally recognized that, although we can do little

about natural "occurrences," we can do a lot about how humans
are impacted by them, and the social inequities of how different
groups are affected by natural phenomena.

IMPLICATIONS FOR SOCIAL TRANSFORMATION: FOSTERING PRAXIS

At its core, feminist pedagogy is a commitment not only to interdisciplinary knowledge and process learning but also to the development of a critical consciousness empowered to apply knowledge to social action and
social transformation. Nancy Schniedewind suggests that a fundamental
component of feminist pedagogy is "learning a process for applying theory
to practice, attempting to change a concrete situation based on that learning, and re-creating theory based on that activity" (25). Without this component, commonly known as praxis, feminist pedagogy merely becomes, in
the words of Jane Kenway and Helen Modra, "wishful thinking" (156).

Five months after the course had ended, we wanted to better understand the impact Earth Systems: A Feminist Approach had had on the students', and our own, social and political awareness. Had the class affected
day-to-day understandings of either the earth or society? Did the class
have an impact on a student's intellectual and personal life? Had the content and pedagogy of the class inspired new attitudes about environmental
and social change?

Kristin Kampschroeder, a sociology graduate student working as a research assistant in the Department of Geoscience, interviewed six students
from our class, asking them to discuss these questions. When students discussed their understanding of the interrelatedness of earth systems and social systems, some expressed concern over the role natural resources play
in the development of foreign policy:

> Anytime I hear about national policy or military policy (like in
> Rwanda), I am always wondering what is it that our country wants
> to export from the other country. What do they have that we want?
> I'm not as naive.
>
> I think the most important thing that I gained was a new in-
> sight into how geology and sociology are interrelated and how so-
> cial policies don't naturally evolve from things that we are taught
> to think of as beyond human control, such as mineral deposits.

A number of students also expressed a new awareness of the social context
within which scientific "knowledge" is produced:

I have a greater interest in the structure of scientific knowledge and how it has shaped our culture and political policies.

Most important to me was the idea that science is not objective. That was a new concept for me at the time.

The course greatly changed my perception of society. I was always earth-centered and it certainly helped me refine my feelings of frustration with environmental issues; particularly in regard to how capitalism and science shape our environmental policy.

For other students the course reinforced previously held beliefs and, for some, helped them better articulate their environmental and social attitudes:

Because I have a major that is interdisciplinary, women's studies, before the class I was always looking for things that were interrelated. The class was solid proof that everything is interrelated, even geology and sociology. Since being a women's studies major, I have become more active in my community. The Earth Systems class is definitely a part of my continued involvement, since it was a class in my major field.

I had a lot of knowledge about the earth and U.S. society before taking this class. What the class did was to clarify what I knew and also to give me the facts and figures to back up my general knowledge and intuition.

Everything in your life, any bit of learning has some effect. The course reinforced my feminist feelings and gave me more confidence in them. I now have fewer doubts about what I want to do, where I want to go, and what I want to accomplish.

For many students the awareness of earth processes and social systems impacted their daily activities. By engaging in individual activism, most students felt they could be effective agents of social change in everyday life:

I have stopped dying my hair! I wear cotton clothes now. It's not a good thing but I still get my nails done, you cannot make me stop. You don't know how much guilt [the class] made me feel. I cannot do anything in my house. I cannot throw away styrofoam containers, I cannot open my refrigerator without realizing the effect it is having on the ozone layer. When I take my one bag of garbage out a week, for both me and my husband, which I don't think is all

that much, I feel guilty because it is in a Hefty bag that probably
will way outlive me. I live differently. I don't leave the water running when I brush my teeth. I don't take bubble baths as often.
Okay, once in awhile I do. I deserve them, it's a right. I put in
desert landscaping in my backyard. I mean this class had a profound effect on me, preppy USA.

I quit shaving my legs while the water was running in the
shower. That was my big thing.

When I found out that the water table is diminished to the
point it is, now every time I turn on the faucets I look over my
shoulder.

Statements such as these suggest just how quickly students respond to
new ideas about the interrelatedness of earth and social processes.
Nonetheless, as we mentioned above, the emancipatory potential of feminist pedagogy is often subsumed in feminist classrooms by what Kenway
and Modra refer to as the "over-valorization of consciousness-raising"
(156). While consciousness-raising—or awareness that the personal is political—is certainly a mission of feminist educators, consciousness itself is
not readily transformed into a plan for social action or social change. The
potential of feminist classroom dynamics to succeed in raising consciousness and fail in engaging people to act collectively upon the world was
clearly demonstrated by a number of the students enrolled in Earth Systems: A Feminist Approach. Several students did articulate a plan of action, however, and expressed a commitment to becoming politically
involved in groups and organizations dedicated to environmental and social transformation. It is not surprising that these students had previously
been community activists for whom confronting the particular environmental and social issues examined during the course became one more
challenge. One student, a former local chapter president of NOW, expressed a new interest in becoming involved in environmental issues:

I think I would like to become more involved in environmental
change than I have been in the past. I have always stayed away
from environmental issues, not really understanding them. My political involvement in the past revolved around women's rights,
and I think that this class showed me a lot of things interrelated to
women's rights and clarified to me that relationship.

Another student, a self-defined environmental activist, commented upon
her new interest in women's issues:

I branched out my memberships in groups. I have always been an environmentalist and belonged to a lot of environmental groups. However, I recently joined NOW. Although I don't have time to really do a lot of things, my interests are a little broader now and I now make donations to environmental and women's organizations and help out on a local level in whatever ways I can.

One woman saw new challenges ahead:

So now I have another cause to which to commit my efforts. Not only will I be a crusader for environmental awareness, but I will also try to show people how the same misguided value system, and the controlling interests that helped create that value system, has led to not only environmental degradation but are destructive to the cultures and the lives of people around the world.

We noted earlier that feminist pedagogy premises the student as student-teacher and the teacher as teacher-student. We have thus asked ourselves the same questions we asked our students: Did the class affect our understanding of the earth and social systems? Did the class have an impact on our intellectual and personal lives? Did the class inspire us to act upon the world? As with many of our students, the movement we are making toward transformative knowledge and transformative social change is largely built upon our particular life situations. Peg currently teaches a moderately large section of Introductory Physical Geology, and she now weaves feminist pedagogy into this much more traditional classroom. As part of this change, she is committed to making the curriculum more environmentally oriented and more oriented toward the students' lives on a local and global level. In addition, Peg is a guest lecturer in Maralee's sociology classes, where she presents a deeply moving portrayal of her own experiences as a woman trained as a scientist, a scientist who is now questioning many of the assumptions upon which her academic and personal development are based. Peg describes her transition as, "scary, but once you start to question who you are and what you know, you can never go back." Maralee is now fascinated by exploring new ways of implementing feminist pedagogy in all her courses. More important, perhaps, is her new understanding of how sociology and the natural sciences can inform one another. She is developing sections on science in both her introductory sociology and women's studies courses. She is also giving seminars to geoscientists on the ways one can build bridges between feminism and science. Furthermore, her sabbatical leave is dedicated to further exploring the intersections of knowledge. Most recently, Maralee and Peg have received funding from the National Science Foundation to launch a three-year educational project, the Social Study of Geology.

Clearly, fostering praxis is a complicated and difficult task. However, we believe that any attempts to integrate social and scientific knowledge promote a better understanding of the ways in which knowledge can begin to be transformative.

CONCLUSION

We, as feminists, as well as many others, believe that the creation of a contextualized science education together with feminist pedagogy will speak to the interests of many people and will challenge us all to examine the role science plays in shaping definitions of knowledge, power relations, and social inequalities. Our experiences developing and participating in the teaching of Earth Systems: A Feminist Approach demonstrated that the gap between the social and natural sciences can be narrowed. Furthermore, our effort to implement feminist pedagogy in an interdisciplinary "science" classroom strengthened the ability of all students (and ourselves) in the class to play an active role in transformative learning and environmental, social, and political action. As we have pointed out throughout this paper, science education may be the pivotal arena in which theory and practice can become powerful agents of social change.

From our perspective, the course Earth Systems: A Feminist Approach and courses like it are important additions to the academy, providing new educational opportunities for faculty and students, illustrating the need for institutional change, and stimulating debate. We think that institutional changes must include supporting team-teaching for faculty education, funding interdisciplinary resource development, and rewarding curriculum reform. From the perspective of women's studies, our course provided to students an educational experience that reflected the fundamental tenets of feminist education: it was interdisciplinary, it emphasized social transformation, and it allowed students to play a central part in the construction of their education. Furthermore, it illustrated why it may be important to integrate natural science concepts into the traditional women's studies curriculum. From the perspective of conventional science, however, there may be some question regarding whether it was a "science course," regarding the degree to which students were prepared to enter the next level geology course, and regarding the need for the course in the curriculum. We are convinced that Earth Systems is a science course that prepares students to bring new perspectives to other science courses and provides an important educational component for all of us who live in a technologically advanced society.

Judging from the students' written work and journal entries, it is clear that their understanding of geological concepts and social processes had increased to widely varying degrees by the end of the semester. The social science and humanities majors demonstrated only a modestly increased understanding of geological concepts, but they had developed a much more complex understanding about how capitalist and hegemonic processes shape scientific inquiry and the uses to which science is put. The natural science students, by contrast, had developed at least an elementary understanding of how social systems shape scientific enterprises and had begun to recognize the importance of discussing scientific concepts in a historical and social context. We believe these changes are important. It remains unclear, however, to what degree this class inspired students to pursue other geology, sociology, or women's studies courses.

These considerations and questions bring us to suggest several broad areas for improvement within the academy and within our course. We believe that the significance of "doing science" and "doing social life" becomes clearest when course content and discussion continually illuminate the connections between everyday happenings and science and provide students the opportunity to construct connections between science and day-to-day experiences. Thus the primary point to consider is how educational activities, readings, and exercises can be developed and implemented to demonstrate, across disciplines, why the learning of scientific, sociological, and feminist concepts is important.

We have identified a number of specific areas for improvement for our course that may be applicable to other courses on the social study of science as well as to many other courses across the curriculum. First, a variety of well-planned field trips to sites within the local Las Vegas community must be designed to expose students to the connections between their everyday life and natural science processes. Outings of this kind may be more useful than one culminating field trip. Second, a broad range of interdisciplinary projects and experiential, hands-on labs need to be developed that require the active engagement of students and instructors at every step. The projects and labs would aim to help participants construct scientific and sociological understandings from their own observations and experiences. Third, numerous collaborative group projects that bring science and nonscience majors together, allowing them to be both teachers and learners, must be developed to create the space for a dialogue

to begin between diverse types of knowledge. Finally, new interdisciplinary
literature (especially from the environmental sciences, women's studies,
and the humanities) combined with the knowledge base of earth scientists
could be used to highlight the relationship between technology and geological or natural science processes and our everyday lives (especially those of
indigenous peoples and women).

Our discovery of new ways to develop a relational and interdisciplinary
science pedagogy and curriculum is an important first step in motivating
students to broaden their social and scientific knowledge. We hope, also,
that curricular changes like the ones we implemented may begin to allevi-
ate the fears and misconceptions many conventional scientists have about
interdisciplinary projects of this nature. These changes, combined with a
growing awareness that science education needs to reach a more diverse
audience in order to improve science literacy and to diversify the pool of
scientists, may foster the building of "two-way streets" (Fausto-Sterling)
between social, feminist, and scientific inquiry.

The authors would like to thank the *NWSA Journal* reviewers and Ellen Cronan Rose for their helpful comments on an earlier version of this manuscript.
The final preparation of this manuscript was, at least in part, supported by
the National Science Foundation under grant no. HRD-9555721.

•   •   •

WORKS CITED

Bleier, Ruth, ed. *Feminist Approaches to Science*. New York: Teachers College
     Press, 1991.
Fausto-Sterling, Anne. "Building Two-Way Streets." *National Women's Studies As-
     sociation Journal* 4.3 (1992): 5–15.
_____. *Myths of Gender: Biological Theories about Women and Men*. New York:
     Basic Books, 1985.
_____. "Women and Science." *Women's Studies International Quarterly* 13
     (1981): 30–32.
Freire, Paulo. *Pedagogy of the Oppressed*. Trans. Myra Bergman Ramos. 1970.
     New York: Continuum, 1983.
Harding, Sandra. "Forum: Feminism and Science." *National Women's Studies As-
     sociation Journal* 5.1 (1993) 49–55.
_____. *Whose Science? Whose Knowledge? Thinking from Women's Lives*. Ithaca:
     Cornell University Press, 1991.
Henderson, Rebecca. *Female Participation in Undergraduate Math, Science, and*

Engineering Majors: Organizational Features. Paper presented at the annual meeting of the Pacific Sociological Association, San Diego, CA, 1993.

Hollenshead, Carol, et al. "Women Graduate Students in Mathematics and Physics: Reflections on Success." *Journal of Women and Minorities in Science and Engineering* 1.1 (1994): 63–88.

Keller, Evelyn Fox. *Reflections on Science and Gender*. New Haven: Yale University Press, 1985.

Kelly, A. "The Construction of Masculine Science." *British Journal of Sociology of Education* 6 (1985): 133–54.

Kenway, Jane, and Helen Modra. "Feminist Pedagogy and Emancipatory Possibilities." *Feminisms and Critical Pedagogy*. Eds. C. Luke and J. Gore. New York: Routledge, 1992. 138–66.

Maher, F. A., and M. K. T. Tetreault. *The Feminist Classroom*. New York: Basic Books, 1994.

Maher, Frinde. "Toward a Richer Theory of Feminist Pedagogy: A Comparison of 'Liberation' and 'Gender' Models for Teaching and Learning." *Journal of Education* 169.3 (1987): 91–100.

Manis, J. M., et al. *An Analysis of Factors Affecting Choices in Majors in Science, Mathematics, and Engineering at the University of Michigan*. Ann Arbor: University of Michigan Center for Continuing Education of Women, 1989.

Otto, P. "One Science, One Sex?" *School Science and Mathematics* 91.8 (1991): 367–73.

Rosser, Sue. *Female-friendly Science*. New York: Pergamon Press, 1990.

Rosser, Sue, and B. Kelly. "From Hostile Exclusion to Friendly Inclusion: University of South Carolina System Model Project for the Transformation of Science and Math Teaching to Reach Women in Varied Campus Settings." *Journal of Women and Minorities in Science and Engineering* 1.1 (1994): 29–44.

Schniedewind, Nancy. "Teaching Feminist Process in the 1990s." *Women's Studies Quarterly* 21.3–4 (1993): 17–30.

Seymour, N. M., and E. Hewitt. *Factors Contributing to High Attrition Rates among Science, Mathematics, and Engineering Undergraduate Majors*. Report to the Alfred P. Sloan Foundation, 1991.

Shrewsbury, Carolyn. "What Is Feminist Pedagogy?" *Women's Studies Quarterly* 21.3–4 (1993): 8–16.

Shulman, Bonnie. "Implications of Feminist Critiques of Science for the Teaching of Mathematics and Science." *Journal of Women and Minorities in Science and Engineering* 1.1 (1994): 1–15.

Spear, M. G. "Teachers' Views about the Importance of Science to Boys and Girls." *Science for Girls*. Ed. A. Kelly. Philadelphia: Open University Press, 1984.

Tobias, Sheila. *They're Not Dumb; They're Different*. Tucson: Tucson Arizona Research Corp., 1990.

Trankina, M. L. "Gender Differences in Attitudes toward Science." *Psychological Reports* 73 (1993): 123–30.

Weiler, Kathleen. "Freire and a Feminist Pedagogy of Difference." *Harvard Educational Review* 61.4 (1991): 449–74.

11

FreshMAN COMPOSITION
Blueprint for Subversion

Cheyenne Marilyn Bonnell

Audre Lorde warned us about trying to dismantle the master's house with his own tools, but many times in higher education the only tools you have to work with *are* the master's tools. For example, in every college or university across this wide land of ours is a composition course for first-year students—to the chagrin of many feminists, it is often called FreshMAN Composition. The master's tools—and his name. But although it may bear the master's name, the course is the perfect candidate for feminist subversion. If, for instance, the course were feminist in content, then it would be the only required feminist course in many curricula. Can this be done?

Surprisingly enough, several elements are in place to help make freshman composition into a women's studies course. One is the concept of academic freedom: instructor's generally, even in first-year composition classes, have the right to choose the content, the research topics, and the literature to be studied, for example. Second is the permeation of feminist issues into all aspects of life. Studying women's issues is as simple as reading a newspaper: women in politics, in the media, in occupations, in the military, in sports, and so on. Popular culture has, to some degree, normalized gender issues, so when they surface on a syllabus there is less of a feeling that the instructor is importing exotic material. The third aspect that facilitates focusing on women is that any course that seems to focus even-handedly on gender issues really focuses to a large extent on women. This is a holdover from Victorian times when women were considered "the sex." If you study gender relations, you are studying new aspects of the topic, the aspects that now include women.

Those of us who have taught women's studies often bemoan the fact that juniors and seniors who elect the class take it too late in their college careers. Being subversive, we want access to students early in their college careers, when changes can still be acted upon; we want access to a broad variety of students, especially those who were not interested in women's studies—even those who were "allergic" to feminism. How to do this? The paternalistic, hierarchic system already in place can actually work for us, providing us with the beaming faces of first-year students in a required course called FreshMAN Composition.

INTRODUCING FEMINIST FRESHMAN COMPOSITION: CONSCIOUSNESS-RAISING

First, lessen the "red flags" that can heighten resistance. For instance, the words "women's studies" are anathema; this course is "composition." The students expect to be taught to write, and so they should be. But the choice of the topic of gender can automatically be of interest to eighteen year olds pulsing with hormones and finally provided with the freedom to unleash them. However, it is important to note that young people, both women and men, despite years of being exposed to sexual issues, are still young people. The life experience of a traditional composition student is limited in many respects. For instance, these young women are experiencing the most egalitarian span in their lives. They *do* receive the same pay as the young man pushing burgers across the same counter, and issues of child care, child support, promotion and tenure, and insurance coverage seem infinitely distant, the previous generation's problems and not theirs. In addition, young men, many of whom equate women's liberation with women's sexuality, also feel that feminist issues were solved years ago. So although they may be interested in sexual issues, it may be only on their terms.

What is called for is consciousness-raising. In order to lessen the resistance to gender issues in class, it is important that the awareness exercises target both women and men, allowing both men and women to discover something about themselves as well as the opposite sex. Below are three activities that generate a great deal of classroom discussion and are good icebreakers for the beginning of the semester.

One exercise that students enjoy is a "fishbowl" activity, which encourages students to listen, to learn more about the other sex, and to seek an understanding of the differences between men and women. This activity starts with either the women or the men (coin toss?) forming a circle; they are the fish. The group of the opposite sex forms a circle outside that circle of fish—a fishbowl. People in the inner circle—the fish—discuss the following prompts while the people on the outside of the circle *listen without commenting* (verbally or nonverbally). Discussion follows after both groups have been the fish:

1. Profile of the perfect mate—the perfect mate should be . . .
2. Being in love makes me feel . . .
3. The reason I want to share my life with someone is so that I can . . .
4. I know the relationship is over when . . .
5. I feel resentful when I'm in a relationship when . . .
6. [For the women's group] A woman's deepest fear is . . .
   [For the men's group] A man's deepest fear is . . .
7. [For the women's group] What really ticks a guy off is when . . .
   [For the men's group] What really ticks a gal off is when . . .

The next activity helps students examine the similarities and differences between the emotional needs of women and men. On a sheet are listed twelve basic needs: encouragement, caring, approval, understanding, admiration, respect, validation, acceptance, appreciation, devotion, trust, and reassurance. Out of this list, students must choose six that are their own primary emotional needs. When students have chosen their six primary needs, they meet with others of their sex and tally the responses of the group, finally coming up with the six primary needs of people of their sex. A discussion ensues as to the marked differences that usually typify the needs of men and women and the role of socialization. Finally, a short writing exercise asks both women and men to imagine a world in which they could have all these needs met.

The last activity is useful to examine and clarify values that are often hidden behind and defended as rational choices. This hypothetical situation is distributed to class members:

In the year 2250 a planet in another solar system has been found which can support human life. By this time there is little land and few resources left on Earth, so we are desperate to colonize this new planet named Virago. Because the cost of sending people on this mission is so prohibitive, only one space shuttle can be sent this century; therefore, these colonizers are responsible for founding and populating this new Viragon society. The space shuttle, packed with food, supplies, instruments, and other necessities, will hold only six individuals. Pick six of the following people to send on this mission:

| religious leader | chef | nurse |
| astronaut | political leader | geologist |

engineer	writer	electronic technician
farmer	plant geneticist	physicist
professor	doctor	entertainer
child	meteorologist	teacher
nutritionist	secretary	mechanic

Once everyone has made their six choices, make a list of how many votes each individual gets; the top six vote-getters would be sent to Virago. Once the list is made, it is time to unpack the gendered aspect of the choices. Were, for instance, students thinking of the sex of the individuals when they were making their choices? Did individuals in predominantly female professions (nurse, teacher, nutritionist, secretary) get chosen? Why or why not? What do the choices say about whom we value more in our society? Why do we value them? In this hypothetical scenario, what are women valued for? What are men valued for? Ethnicity can be factored in as well. This exercise often comes as a big surprise to women students, who discover that they, too, have packed their space shuttle with men because men are often seen as more competent and because they still have a monopoly on many prestigious professions.

But the trick to conducting FreshMAN composition is not just about consciousness-raising. Because most students do not get to choose this class, even more pains must be taken to lessen resistance. Make sure that you provide ample choices of subtopics for both women and men in order to avoid the ever-present complaint that feminism is being "forced down their throats." Also, instead of lecturing—and thus becoming the sitting-duck personification of the dreaded "f" word—about the evils of the patriarchy to card-carrying members and their prospective spouses, use the technique of active, experiential, or discovery learning. For instance, for the final paper students have to use the "lens" of gender to explore any topic of their choice. Some train it on sports, Greek organizations, the workplace, medicine; regardless of what topic they choose, they will discover a study that points out inequalities. But, because a feminist stance is a skeptical one, students are not permitted passive acceptance of what the researchers say; they have to replicate the study. When women's studies is coupled with this sort of experiential education, students prove it to themselves and no longer feel that they are being force-fed information from some flaming feminist. For the women students, who are still in some ways experiencing the most egalitarian period of their lives, the course acts as a springboard to bigger, more probing questions about socialization: Why, for instance, are they in the nursing program instead of the premed program or interested in being a school counselor instead of a clinical psychologist? For the men, it may be their first exposure to feminism, and some even find it a pleasant experience, too.

Another trick to lessening resistance is to admit that it will arise and prepare the students for it. I devote one class period to role-playing resistant situations and another to a writing exercise concerning the role-playing. After members of the class pair off, I distribute the role-playing scenarios to partners. I encourage them not just to blandly read the scripts but to act the role using gestures, body language, and facial expression to get in touch with what their character is feeling and thinking. After each scenario is acted out, the students analyze the strategies of resistance used by the resistant responder.

Table 1 below provides examples of scenarios involving resistance that can easily be acted out:

TABLE 1

SCENARIO	RESISTANCE RESPONSE
Life at [fill in name of your institution] is a gendered experience. What I mean by that is it's different for men and women students. There's the added dimension if you are a woman. For example, a woman student may think twice before planning to stay at the library late into the night. After all, she'll have to walk home alone. Maybe to get to her dorm she has to walk past places where women have been raped.	A friend of mine told me recently that one night on the way home from the library he was stopped by a drunk who wanted to fight.
Women between the ages of eighteen and twenty-four are America's most sexually vulnerable population. A nationwide survey of colleges reveals that one in eight women will be sexually assaulted while in college.	It's probably only the ones who "ask for it," ya know. It doesn't happen if you are with a guy you know, or if you are in a house with lots of people around. It hasn't happened to *anyone* I know.
Sexual harassment is a means of ensuring that women will not feel at ease, that they will remember their role as sexual beings available to men. It reminds them that they are not equal citizens participating in public life. By seeming harmless, it encourages men who would never commit a violent crime against a strange woman to engage in minor transgressions against her right to move freely. Its symbolic nature is its most important attribute.	Women love it. Relax why don't you! Don't make a big deal out of nothing.

Readers should recognize that each scenario represents a feminist perspective followed by a statement characterized by a resistant stance. The resistant statements, which are meant to diminish, contradict, nullify, or negate the feminist stance, are effective for teaching students how to identify fallacious logic in their writing. Many of these responses are hasty generalizations, a conclusion based on insufficient evidence, inadequate, and/or unrepresentative evidence. These responses often overgeneralize, trying to disarm by supplying one personal "fact" or experience of their own in order to totally discredit the feminist perspective. Some disguise their thinly veiled hostility by trivializing or poking fun rather than addressing the real issue. Some responses even stereotype people or resort to ad hominem tactics, attacking the person or name calling, in an attempt to disqualify the argument. Other responses appeal to emotion rather than reason. These statements are often put forth by people who are currently benefiting from the status quo and/or from people who have been so socialized by our misogynistic society that they cannot absorb new notions. By addressing them early in the semester, and by addressing them objectively in a lesson that teaches the valuable writing skill of identifying fallacies in arguments, you can often spare the class some of the resistant strategies.

NUTS & BOLTS OF THE COURSE:
COMBINING WOMEN'S STUDIES WITH COMPOSITION

Media images of gender is the first writing unit. To prepare the students for looking at media images, we acknowledge that both men and women are influenced by media representation. First, each class member makes a collage from magazine images which expresses what women "are" or what men "are." Each student talks about the images on their poster and sums up the roles that the media says are available to women and men—and what roles are missing. Then, to raise students' consciousness and to tie media images into self image, they fill out a worksheet that asks them to complete each of these stems:

Since I am a women [or man] I am:
  required to _____
  allowed to _____
  forbidden to _____

Then they picture themselves as the opposite sex and fill in these stems:

If I were a man [woman]:
    I could_____
    I could not _____
    Why? _____

Discussion focuses on how we learn these messages, and how these messages get reinforced. The students begin to see that the media is one of the prime reinforcers of stereotypical messages. Another experiential part of the unit involves a content analysis of a college publication—most school newspapers work nicely. Students are put in groups and each group is asked to analyze the publication and report on one of these topics:

How many pictures of women and of men are featured?
What are women and men doing in these pictures?
What kinds of articles/topics are associated with women?
What kinds of articles/topics are associated with men?

Naturally, students will discover that there are, in general, radically more pictures of men than women, even in publications at undergraduate institutions where women may outnumber men, and that both pictures and stories portray women as helpers of men, objects of male desire, in peripheral positions. Men are given prominent positions, are associated with "important" topics, are seen as instrumental subjects, not passive objects. A showing of Jean Kilbourne's video *Still Killing Us Softly* (available from Cambridge Documentary Films) is appropriate in this unit to help students put all this information in perspective and to help them see the far-reaching influences that the media have on our identity formation as women and men. This unit culminates in a student essay: "How Does the Media Shape Our Perceptions of Men and/or Women?"

Domestic abuse is the subject of the second writing unit. Since most of our students are planning on marital bliss, this unit, cleverly disguised as an analysis of literature, works well as a reality rub. In addition to helping students learn to use the logic of definition to construct an argument and to cite and document a literary work, it teaches them about power relations in marriage. To raise their consciousness, students are paired off by sex and given a gender-role negotiation sheet (When there are uneven amounts of men and women and same-sex couples have to be used, I explain that not all relationships are heterosexual. Some people are attracted to people of the same sex and most of us will have same-sex roommates or companions at some point in our lives.) Basically, this lengthy gender-role negotiation sheet asks them to say who, in a three-person family unit (two adults and a child), should take care of a variety of household roles from balancing the checkbook to bringing back the VCR tapes, from buying diapers and arranging for a sitter to watering the house plants and sending the drapes to be cleaned. Students are amazed to find out that women's tasks are the tasks no one else wants to do but have to be done repeatedly and with very little recognition or reinforcement. In addition, lively discussions generally follow when we explore the areas that prompted the most argument in their imaginary partnerships.

The literary work for the domestic abuse writing unit is Susan Glaspell's play *Trifles*, which students read aloud in class; as a supplement, they read the short story, "A Jury of Her Peers," that Glaspell wrote from the play. I give a little background information on this "recovered" piece of literature, that it was generated by a real domestic abuse court case Glaspell covered as a reporter for the *Des Moines Daily News* in 1901. In Glaspell's versions, Mr. Wright is strangled with a rope while in bed. In real life, Mrs. Hossack's husband was murdered with an ax in bed; Mrs. Hossack was convicted but the conviction was overturned and the retrial resulted in a hung jury. In Glaspell's fictionalization and dramatization, women neighbors know that Mrs. Wright has murdered her husband but become her de facto judge and jury, hiding and withholding incriminating evidence from the officers of the law. After each student brings in information on domestic violence garnered from the Internet and/or the Women's Center on campus, I show them how to construct a definition paper. Simply put, this is a paper that defines John Wright's behavior as domestic abuse by citing the various symptoms of domestic abuse, such as physical abuse, verbal and/or emotional abuse, sexual abuse, destruction of property or pets, and economic abuse, and then proving that these symptoms are present in the Wright's relationship. When I later show the video of the short story "Jury of Her Peers," students begin to see only too clearly that Minnie Wright was a victim of domestic abuse. Using the criteria and ample quotations from the text (now you can teach Modern Language Association [MLA] documentation, too), students write a paper on the topic of domestic abuse in Glaspell's *Trifles*. This unit not only teaches research, MLA documentation, and argument skills, it gives a real-life lesson on power and abuse in relationships.

The third writing unit is on gender inequities. However, lecturing on this subject—or even just selecting readings—makes students feel as if the instructor is imposing her epistemology on them or "stacking the deck" in such a way that only the feminist side of the issue is shown. Remembering that this is the generation who cut their teeth on Rush Limbaugh's view of feminists as "femi-Nazis," incorporating experiential learning into this writing unit becomes even more important. This means that students must not only read about gender but must conduct an experiment as well. In addition, the research paper uses a social sciences format for the written report: abstract, introduction, method (sample and instrument), results (both narrative and graphic), discussion, and the American Psychological Association style of documentation.

Students can research any topic that interests them, as long as they look at it through the lens of gender. I urge them to think of topics in their prospective majors. For instance, education majors might consider how gender might affect education. Premed students can explore gender and medicine. Welders might examine how gender has repercussions in the workplace. While scheduling the gender inequalities unit early in the semester may prompt students to ask, "Which topics have gender as a factor," scheduling it late in the semester allows students time to look at a range of subtopics: the issue then becomes "Which of the numerous topics which have gender as a factor shall I chose to research?"

I begin with the premise that we can use gender to look at any topic or subject—at anything, in fact. To illustrate this, I have eight student volunteers, four women and four men, leave the room. Then I tell the remaining students what will happen: I will ask each student subject to sit in a chair in the front of the classroom for one minute. I prepare the student observers to look for kinesics: bodily movements such as eye contact, facial expression, posture, movements, and gestures. After observing each subject, the observers are then able to make some of their own generalizations based on gender: women hold their legs together or cross them at the knees and keep their arms close to their bodies, for instance, while men tend to hold arms and legs from five to fifteen degrees from their bodies and cross their legs at the ankles or tap their feet; women use fewer gestures and may even put their hands in their laps; women smile more, men stare. They then can look up studies that corroborate these findings.

Another demonstration takes as its model Susan Pollak and Carol Gilligan's study of "Images of Violence in Thematic Apperception Test Stories." In class, I give each student a picture of a man and a woman positioned in "affiliation": in this case, a picture of a man and a woman sitting together on the beach looking out at the water. I then instruct the students to "finish the story," to write a paragraph about what happens next, share the paragraphs in mixed-sex groups, then come up with a generalization about what people wrote. Because of the water in the picture, at least one male student's story will evolve into a *Jaws* scenario. Women, who are less threatened by affiliation between women and men, usually write kinder, gentler story end-ings which include long-term relationships rather than sharks. Although I then distribute a copy of Pollak and Gilligan's research, an important aspect is that the students discovered the gender differences themselves.

But the discovery method doesn't just end with the students' articulation of gender differences in these two situations; they then have to replicate a study done in a field in which they are interested. It doesn't matter what they pick. Couch potatoes can do "gender and television." Fraternity brothers and sorority sisters can do "gender and Greek organizations." Jocks can do "gender and sports." As soon as they use "gender" as a search term, the bulk of the research will cover gender differences between men and women—and the bulk of the research will be done in the feminist vein. And if they found it using their favorite research tool, the Web, there is no way in which they can feel that the instructor stacked the deck—not with 453,729 "hits" on the subject. If students utilize the Internet, this exercise is especially good for teaching evaluation skills of Internet material, especially those Websites that have an agenda (see http://www.rice.edu/Fondren/Netguides/strategies.html for a checklist to help students evaluate Internet sources). After students have located some sort of valid study, then they have to replicate it, on a much smaller scale naturally, by doing the observation, writing sample, questionnaire, content analysis, and so on, that was done in the original study. Even though their samples may be considerably smaller than those in the scholarly prototypes, students' results generally point to gender inequity in whatever topic they researched.

The important thing in this whole process is that the students come to an understanding of the inequities in the media, in the classroom, in athletics, in anything they chose—and do not feel "set up" or forced to agree with anything without their own epistemological input. In other words, they aren't required to take the instructor's word for it or the word of any other authority figure. They chose their own experiment, and they got the results themselves. Even if they got different results than the studies they were replicating, that's fine; part of the discussion portion of the paper involves a thoughtful discussion of why the results varied. But the crucial thing is that students use their own experience as a gauge of validity as well as learn to be skeptical of any received knowledge.

COMPOSITION WITH CLOUT—STUDENT ACTIVISM

The assignments in composition class are designed to enlighten all students, women and men. However, in my composition classes I stop short of what I call an "activism" assignment, whereas in my women's studies course I require some activism, from writing a letter to a magazine complaining of sexist practices to boycotting a store with sexist window treatments to volunteering for a cleanup day at a women's shelter. Instead, in my composition classes, with coed classes of eighteen-year-old students who did not expect that this composition course would be women's studies, we edit a gender-exclusive text (a police officers' textbook from 1956) and call it a day—sort of. However, never underestimate enlightenment, that moment of "click," as a precursor to action. The enlightened person will eventually question the gendered aspects of media, marriage, athletics, and education and do something about it. Few women students can view *Still Killing Us Softly* and not question the cumulative effects of that mass of magazines stuck in the corner of their dorm room. More purple ribbons are seen during Domestic Violence Awareness Week after a study of *Trifles*. In fact, I was proud that my composition students, women and men, were fairly represented at a college ceremony to mark the year anniversary of the brutal murder of a woman student. Many others have come back from their fieldwork incensed about what their own research has revealed. For instance, the students who sit in college classrooms recording the number of times female and male students are called upon, acknowledged by name, interrupted, or praised will never attend another class without a consciousness of what they discovered in their fieldwork. Even the male students who pick sports or the Greek system as a topic find their sense of fair play assailed when they do equity research in these institutions on their own campus A heightened consciousness is a forerunner to activism.

DO'S & DON'TS

If you are going to teach a women's studies course in the guise of any other course, you can do so successfully, if you remember a few rules of feminist pedagogy. First, you *have* authority, but you are not *the* authority on the gendered existences of your students. Yes, most instructors have had more experience in the "real" world, but we must not rob the students of their own reality. That is why I insist on experiential learning—the students' experiential learning, not mine forced on them. For instance, I don't tell them that women are shortchanged in media presentations and drag out *my* evidence to prove it, thus building their resistance; instead, I give them a newspaper and let them analyze it. Trust me, students can count up the number of men and women and come to a logical conclusion. Which brings up another issue. Experiential learning is built on trust. If, for example, a student replicates Pollak and Gilligan's experiment in which students view a picture and write a story completion and the student gets results that contradict the original study, fine. If a student does a content analysis and finds a gender-equitable newspaper, fine. If they say *Still Killing Us Softly* is out-of-date, let them count all the liberated images of women and men in contemporary advertisements. If they make a case for the opposition, just make sure that the essay fulfills the requirements—but don't punish the student for an opposing view by grading down. When you teach women's studies/composition you have an advantage at these times—even if students fail to "get" the women's studies message, grade them on the composition side of it. Remember, most of our students in FreshMAN Composition are young. Teach as if you were planting a garden. Be patient as you wait for the results; some plants take years to bloom. While we may be the composition authority in the classroom, we are *not* the women's studies authorities merely by virtue of the name (women's). We shouldn't pretend to speak for all students—female or male!

The next rule is that "pushing" women's studies engenders resistance. It is fair to say in composition, for instance, "here is what you must learn in order to write clearly and effectively." But for the women's studies portion of the course, you can't push or insist on what students must learn. You can only make up exercises that will allow them to discover things for themselves. Again, use consciousness-raising exercises. Utilize the experiential or discovery model that puts students in charge of their own learning. Put them in charge of certain choices—and more choices and options are what women have historically wanted. For instance, when students do their collage, they can do magazine images of women *and/or* men. In the first essay, male students can choose to look at how the media shapes the perceptions of men—the choice is theirs. And if, after researching spousal abuse, they cannot see enough signs of it in *Trifles* to write a paper on it, or, as may be the case, the student has been a victim of abuse and cannot write on it, leave an opening; as an alternative I allow an essay on symbolism in *Trifles*. Even if you have a very detailed syllabus, leave plenty of room in your course for your students to be themselves—and find themselves. If you push your students into just looking at women's issues, you will probably encounter resistance from men and male-identified women. I have found that if you respect all your students and give them leeway, by the end of the course, they are *all* aware of and voicing outrage at gender inequity in our culture.

CONCLUSION

My colleagues—many of whom were having trouble teaching women's studies in women's studies classes—said it wouldn't work: students would never sit still for women's studies when they had *not* signed up for women's studies. So how did I manage such high evaluations from students, both women and men? How did I manage to get accolades like "I liked the way we talked about gender, applied it to real life, and learned to write papers from it" and "I learned more in your class than all mine combined, stuff worth remembering at least." My primary goal was to teach the students to write—and in many ways, that makes it easier to teach women's studies. Because, you see, even if they are not developmentally ready to become feminists, they can become better writers. And that was my job in the first place—not to turn out a class full of feminists—although I can dream!

Which leads me back to my first premise: first-year composition classes are ideal places to teach women's studies. There is no pressure to turn students into feminists; as a teacher of composition, I can settle for at least having given them a feminist-colored pair of glasses. They can choose to wear them now, or they may pick them up years from now, when they are ready to see things through the lens of gender. Another advantage is that first-year students don't know what college composition will be like. Perhaps all college composition courses all over America use the same text and teach gender. The students don't know. So they accept the women's studies content as normal—and they *are* learning to write, so that expectation is fulfilled. In addition, the course isn't called women's studies and there is plenty of room for men to study "guy" topics, such as the media images of men or gender in sports or the military. So men feel they belong in class. And the course stops short of requiring any activism, bra burning being one of their primary fears, although it is long on the types of consciousness-raising that transform students and produce the potential for social change.

I maintain that even if you only have the master's tools, you can go a long way to dismantling his house. While the master thinks I am teaching my students to read and write about *Moby Dick* like men, I am teaching my students, women and men, to read the world with an awareness of gender and a sensitivity to women's issues. I am turning out more carpenter's helpers who will help dismantle the master's house.

•   •   •

WORKS CITED

Glaspell, Susan. *Lifted Masks and Other Works*. Ann Arbor: University of Michigan Press, 1992.

Jaws. Dir. Steven Spielberg. Perf. Roy Schneider, Richard Dreyfuss, and Robert Shaw. Universal Pictures, 1975.

A Jury of Her Peers. Prod. Sally Heckel. Videocassette. Films Incorporated, 1981.

Lorde, Audre. "The Master's Tools Will Never Dismantle the Master's House." *Sister Outsider*. Freedom, CA: Crossing Press, 1984. 10–13.

Pollak, Susan, and Carol Gilligan. "Images of Violence in Thematic Apperception Test Stories." *Journal of Personality and Social Psychology* 42.1 (1982): 159–67.

Still Killing Us Softly. Dir. Margaret Lazarus. Videocassette. Cambridge Documentary Films, 1987.

12

GENDER STUDIES IN GOD'S COUNTRY
Feminist Pedagogy in a Catholic College

Susan Kuntz and Carey Kaplan

How can gender and women's studies thrive within the traditionally misogynist environment of a small Roman Catholic college? How, given limited resources and institutional pressure for reproduction of conventional knowledge, can instructors and students participate in authentically transformative feminist pedagogy? These questions, among others, confronted us as we strove during a decade or more to establish, first, women's and gender studies courses and, second, a gender and women's studies minor at Saint Michael's College.

Saint Michael's, a private, liberal arts college in northern Vermont, was founded in 1904 by a small French order of priests and monks, the Society of Saint Edmund. This order, historically committed to social justice issues, continued to guide the college's mission by means of Edmundite faculty, administrators, and a 50% presence on the board of trustees, including the chair of the board. After Vatican II, the Edmundites experienced the slow attrition common to many Roman Catholic clerical bodies during the 1970s and 1980s. Priests left the order—and the faculty of Saint Michael's—and few new ordinations occurred. The order aged. Concurrently, the college became for economic reasons a coed institution in 1972, and the college, like the rest of American society, was rocked by social, political, and cultural changes. By 1996, Saint Michael's had its fourth lay president; a non-Edmundite, non-Catholic chair of the board of trustees; and all lay administrators. The board of trustees was unable to maintain its quota of Edmundites and changed the requirement. By 1998 only 3% of the faculty were Edmundites; indeed the faculty was well over 50% non-Catholic. In addition, the college had gone from about 12 women students and 1,500 men in 1972 to a student population of 1,800 that was more than 50% women. The faculty, which in 1972 had two women professors and a few female assistant professors and adjunct instructors, by

1998 had six female full professors and 35% women in its permanent faculty (higher, of course, if adjunct instructors are included). In 1998 the college hired its first woman vice president for academic affairs/provost.

In the more than quarter century of our experience with Saint Michael's, we have watched the institution collectively and its members individually (though not unanimously) wrestle to reconcile or at least live with various tensions and contradictions. For example, the social justice commitment of the Edmundites has been juxtaposed both to the misogyny of the Church and to the all-male bastion that Saint Michael's was for so many years. New faculty in the past twenty-five years have been increasingly non-Catholic, even non-Christian, female, and secular in attitudes and educational goals—even within such traditionally conservative departments such as religious studies and philosophy. These faculty have had to embrace a mission statement that proclaims, "It is the mission of Saint Michael's College to contribute through higher education to the enhancement of the human person and to the advancement of human culture in the tradition of the Catholic faith." By the same token, those members of the college community who adhere most closely to the stated mission of the college have had to coexist with faculty and colleagues who appear to violate many of their most deeply held beliefs about education, theology, and culture. Catholic faculty have had to struggle with the ways in which transformative aspects of Vatican II have warred with less progressive understandings of the Church. Additionally and confusingly, Saint Michael's, like most Catholic schools, has always been devoted to the ideal of academic freedom. Thus it is our experience and that of our colleagues that, despite the college's mission, no Edmundite, administrator, or department head has ever questioned the content of a syllabus or interfered in a classroom.

Furthermore, one of the most deeply held and pervasive values of Saint Michael's is the concept of community. The ideal of community as it is adumbrated in faculty, trustee, administrative, and student bodies espouses inclusion, tolerance, difference, generosity, and charity in the most Christian sense. In practice, of course, the ideal suffers. The college community has its share of racism, homophobia, anti-Semitism, and regionalism and perhaps more than its share of misogyny.

When feminist author Tillie Olsen visited Saint Michael's in 1978 during a three-day symposium on women and the new scholarship, she observed that often innovation and change can happen at small Catholic schools because the issues are out in the open rather than obscured by hypocritical liberalism and compulsory political correctness and because the basic longing of an ethically and morally defined institution is toward ideals of decency and community. And, Olsen shrewdly continued, small Catholic schools often hire the most interesting and even radical faculty because fast-track, hegemony-oriented graduate students are not interested in what is perceived as the intellectual and professional backwater of a religiously connected academy. Schools like Saint Michael's are often, Olsen said, where change within the academy first occurs.

In our long struggle to see things change for what we see as the better at Saint Michael's, we have been upheld by perceptions like Tillie Olsen's and by what we believe to be the essential good will and moral and ethical honesty of the entity composed by the flawed and imperfect beings who are ourselves and our colleagues.

From the inception of our gender and women's studies program in 1990, we encountered pedagogical conflict. The gender studies minor mandated two courses specifically listed under gender studies, one introductory, one more advanced. Minors were also to take five other courses dealing with gender, no more than two in any one department. We knew that many courses, even those with explicit feminist or women's studies content, would be taught conventionally. We had no illusions that we could change the culture of the college merely by subsuming already existing courses under the rubric gender and women's studies. And we knew that feminist courses, like conventional courses, need careful, conscious, and thoughtful pedagogy if they are to avoid converting "what people experience in their everyday/everynight world into forms of knowledge in which people as subjects disappear and in which their perspectives on their own experiences are transformed and subdued" (Smith 35). We were, however, determined that those courses actually listed under gender and women's studies in the catalogue would incorporate our ideal of utopian, personally and socially transformative feminist pedagogy.

Unsurprisingly, at first we faced frustration: various well-intentioned faculty experimented with the introductory course for a couple of years. They were willing to teach the course but had trouble teaching outside the confines of their discipline and had little or no experience with or interest in innovative, participatory, empowering methodologies of feminist learning and pedagogy. Finally Dave Landers and Linda Hollingdale, both from the student counseling program and open to innovative pedagogies, especially group learning, agreed to design and teach this course. They were very successful but from the beginning had a waiting list of more than one hundred for the forty seats in the class. And, time taught us, the course they were teaching was most successful with students who were already thinking about and studying gender. We bumped this course up, making it the second-tier course and began to rethink the introductory course.

We wanted to have a large number of students, although almost all Saint Michael's courses, except for a few science lectures, are small (from fifteen to forty students). We knew that students can spend four years at Saint Michael's majoring in, say, business, mathematics, or biology, and never think for one minute that gender means anything other than a Saturday night date. If a chemistry major signed up for a gender studies course in order to fulfill her or his interdisciplinary studies requirement for no other reason than schedule fit, at least that student would have a chance to consider issues that might otherwise remain opaque or invisible (Middleton 35). We also wanted the course to reflect the breadth of the new scholarship, so that students would understand that the study of gender and its meanings had intellectually challenging relevance in all fields of study. Indeed, while we and those of our friends and colleagues who taught in this course consider that gender, race, and class issues are fundamental aspects of all disciplines and subjects of inquiry, we were well aware that this view is not widespread at Saint Michael's College or in the wider world.

Our large goal was to foster understanding and identification in relation to gender differences and inequalities. At the same time, we were well aware that transformative teaching arouses anxiety and fear. We wanted to acknowledge the threat implicit in our course, but we did not want an alienated group of students. This inherent contradiction, full of problems and challenges as it is, informed all our pedagogy.

We wanted a lively classroom, weekly reading and writing assignments, and weekly discussions. We wanted students to see that a wide variety of people, including priests and scientists, were studying, thinking, writing, reading, and teaching about gender. We hoped that an array of lecturers might undercut the traditional (and, at a Catholic school, ingrained) notion of a univocal authority and of the endless reproduction of traditional knowledge. We worked, moreover, to undermine codified authority by acknowledging our own doubts and confusion about material offered in presentations. For instance, one presenter, a biologist, lectured on making facile assumptions regarding the interrelation of gender, biochemistry, and genes, especially emphasizing that the jury is still out on the role of testosterone in male behavior. After the lecture, the class was confused and so were we, since the lecture material challenged conventional wisdom about gender and hormones. All our discussion leaders admitted to the same muddle the students felt. We went on from our shared confusion to examine what the presenter had said, why the conventional wisdom is at odds with her scientific understanding, and why we all experienced resistance to and anxiety about complicating and enriching our understanding of the biology of gender.

Most important: we wanted the pedagogy of the course to reflect the transformative and transgressive potential of gender and women's studies. We did *not* want yet another mandarin exercise in traditional classroom instruction. We wanted the class to create collaboratively an epistemology; we wanted empowered discussion; we wanted visible, measurable change in attitudes and behavior. Our goal has been to understand, and then to participate and intervene in, the construction of discourses through which a community of learners forms reality and ideology. We employed a variety of strategies to achieve these goals.

Most saliently perhaps, we used ourselves and the other discussion leaders relentlessly in order "to make visible to and explore with our students the aspects of our own life histories that impact on our teaching." We felt responsible to analyze "the relationship between our individual lives, historical events, and the broader power relations that have shaped and constrained our possibilities and perspectives as educators" (Middleton 115). Male discussion leaders, for instance, talked about their sexist assumptions and their personal experience of hegemonic privilege. Those discussion leaders who were lesbian or gay used that orientation and the life experiences that come with it to address gender and power issues at home and in the workplace. One discussion leader, for example, a lesbian, partnered a woman who had two children by alternative insemination; after she and her partner separated, she continued to be integrally involved in raising the children. She had also birthed five children and had grandchildren, some of whom were biologically related to her as well as others, equally loved and equally part of her familial life, who were not. "Stories" were a significant part of her teaching and helped her address easy assumptions about who and what families are "supposed" to be; what is right and wrong; what is natural and unnatural; and what constitutes intimacy.

Indeed, stories, narrative, and decentered, contingent, deferred, and partial meanings formed and framed our teaching. We assumed and urged our students to assume that "experience is at once already an interpretation and in need of interpretation" (Butler and Scott 37). On one occasion, a discussion leader entered a classroom on a warm evening and noted, aloud, that there were no cranks available with which to open the windows. Instantly, three class members generated three different narratives of why the cranks had been removed: the authorities' fear of suicide, homicide, and technological theft. The discussion leader, intuiting a teachable moment, mentioned that such narrativity and such hermeneutics were the essence of the investigation to which the course is committed. Why, she asked, do we tell this story now, who tells it, what form does it take, what class, race, gender generates it? She emphasized the impossibility of *know-*

ing the "answer" as well the energy and significance, the interest and knowledge generated by the attempt to interpret and understand. She also used the moment to comment on the centrality to this course of forming a community of learners working to find some common ground in their process of interpretation. Such freewheeling and inventive pedagogy is what we encouraged and applauded in the instructor meetings before each class. We found that often a group of students will meet us enthusiastically as we attempt such teaching/learning, with results that different instructors variously described as inventive, zany, lively, and athletic.

Fortunately, as we organized the course, our plans coincided with an administrative goal that gave us practical administrative support from the academic vice president (AVP) to whom we reported. We already had his ideological support, but we needed money (at Saint Michael's establishing a minor does not mean a budget) and clout. We received both when the AVP realized that we were willing to account for up to 150 students with two instructors and four teaching assistants, each being paid $1,000 for the semester. A course of this size was so cost-efficient and innovative that the AVP established bragging rights; the trustees and other administrators heard more about this course than they wanted.

With a $5,000 budget for teaching assistants, copying, paying outside lecturers, and providing dinner for faculty lecturers (who were unanimously generous about donating their time and energy gratis), we decided to take as many students as possible and to prove that there was sufficient interest in gender studies to make it a full and funded program.

During a fourteen-week semester, we scheduled a presentation by a different person for each week on as wide a variety of gender-related subjects as we could find. Each presenter provided a few questions designed to provoke ideas for the weekly written response. Lecturers also assigned reading material available in multiple copies on reserve in the library. We usually met in a large hall. On a few occasions we met in the cafeteria or a large video-equipped room. After each presentation, discussion groups met in classrooms that stayed the same from week to week. The alternation of presentation with discussion group and the wide variety of forms the presentations took (cultural simulations; performances; slide presentations; film presentations; lectures; lecture/discussions; single and multiple presenters; male, female, and transsexual presenters; gay, lesbian, and straight presenters) offered us many opportunities "to develop pedagogies [. . .] authentic to our personal and collective histories [. . . and] circumstances." We were able to find ways "of understanding how our own subjectivities have been constituted" and "of making visible the alienation that can result from interpretations of our own personal and collective histories purely through the eyes of theorists whose perspectives have arisen elsewhere" (Middleton 35).

As we invited lecturers, we attempted to balance male and female speakers, faculty and outside presenters, lectures and presentations involving hands-on activities, films, slides, and performances. We started with a broad lecture on the biology of gender, reasoning that the organism was a good place to start, and gradually moved on to lectures in specific areas of study: gender in the middle ages; gender in the trades. We wanted to involve as many speakers as possible to tell their stories about how gender has influenced their work and lives, on the principle that the stories we tell define the terms of our existence. Students, we hoped, might begin to understand that the history we engage, the science we investigate, the rules we follow, and the media we watch and read are all narrative representations that construct and relate our lives. Our pedagogical goal was to invoke new stories that might "inscribe into the picture of reality characters and events and resolutions that were previously invisible, untold, unspoken" (de Laurentis 11).

Although the course attracted a more diverse group of students than is typical of our residential, homogeneous population—students from all fields of study, lower- and upper-division students, and nontraditional students—our suspicion is that classes of this nature tend to draw a student enrollment sadly reflective of the larger society despite twenty-five years of social change. Our class was eerily similar to that described by Rosemarie Garland Thomson when she taught a course entitled, Women and Literature: Human Variation and the Politics of Appearance:

> Because the course fulfills a [. . .] humanities requirement, it draws from a range of ages and the students who enroll represent a wide variety of academic interests and experiences. The majority of students are women, some of whom are sympathetic to and familiar with feminism, some of whom are resistant to assertions of any cultural or historical gender differences, and most of whom are curious about investigating an academic subject that seems so close to lived experience. Men usually comprise ten to fifteen percent of the class. Some of the men are feminists themselves, or quite interested in women's issues, while often a handful of the men seem vociferously hostile to the course's persistent focus on the female position. (Thomson 16)

Although our class had about 25% men, this description captures the attitudes we encountered.

Student responses to this course varied broadly from complete resistance to all the material to heightened awareness of gender issues to a transformed view of the individual as she or he is socially constructed to various forms of activism. Most reactions were somewhere in the middle. For some students this class was the first opportunity they had had to think (broadly) about how gender influences lives and shapes the understanding they have of the world. For many, various class presentations affirmed their own heretofore inchoate notions about how the world is constructed differently for men and women. For still others, it changed the way they think about their daily interactions and the role gender plays in them. For a few, it meant working at the battered women's shelter or the rape crisis hotline or organizing diversity rallies.

The most severe pedagogical challenge, especially in the small groups and in responses to written material, was the feeling of many of the men and a substantial number of the women that men were being personally blamed for their participation in gender inequities. We knew the sense of threat was valid in the sense that we were communicating information that, if fully assimilated, could change power balances. At the same time that we acknowledged the appropriateness of student anxiety, we urged open-mindedness and generosity in an effort to avoid paralysis and hostility. Students named their anxiety with a fashionable neologism—"male bashing"—that seemed to go in tandem with another media-generated catchall fear phrase, "bra burning." We worked ceaselessly, but with mixed results, to emphasize that we have received the world as given; we are all participants in our own acculturation; and that to talk about existing inequalities is not to blame or define any individual male or female class member. We emphasized that the context in which learning happens is often a deciding factor in what is learned. We reiterated, like a mantra, that there are race, class, and gender components of epistemology and its utilization. We strove to envision the vociferous resistance we were encountering as healthy and potentially transformative. Influenced by Shoshanna Felman, we perceived rage and denial as the beginning of a breakdown of resistance to change:

> Ignorance [. . .] is not a passive state of absence—a simple lack of information: it is an active dynamic of negation, an active refusal of information [. . .]. Teaching [. . .] has to deal not so much with *lack* of knowledge as with *resistances* to knowledge. [. . . Ignorance] is not a simple lack of information but the incapacity—or the refusal—to acknowledge *one's own implication* in the information. (Felman 30)

Throughout the semester it became apparent that students engaged in discussions of gender by viewing it through different lenses—academic, personal, or political. While some discussed easily from an academic or theoretical base, they were less comfortable talking about their own gender-related experiences. Others moved quickly into the personal, dismissing the theoretical when it did not fit their way of viewing the world. Those who understood that the theoretical was part of the personal were most able to generalize from their experiences and act toward change. The format of the presentations and the opportunities for discussion, both oral and written, allowed students to enter the discourse where and when they felt comfortable. The goal of the course was for them honestly to engage the material presented, through whatever lens made sense for them. We particularly encouraged engagement that began with or included the personal, sure that a movement from the personal to the theoretical was likely to enhance and accelerate the process of examination, investigation, analysis, and self-positioning (Middleton 35).

We were, of course, eager as well to work with those students who began their understanding of gender issues less viscerally and more theoretically, those who typically wanted a coherent and familiar academic framework. In many cases, as the semester progressed, these two groups began to tread common ground, integrating the personal and the political in rich and productive ways, no matter from what positionality they began.

In response papers and group discussions, those students who were connecting life and the classroom were likely to write and talk about their recognition of the need for inclusive study of gender across the curriculum, the need to collapse the binarism male/female thus making stark contrasts impossible, and the need to recognize the complexity of social constructions of gender in relation to power, privilege, and potential. One young woman, typical of those we thought were "getting it," had to take stock of what she thought was intellectual sophistication about gender:

> I believed myself to be very knowledgeable in this area [. . .]. To my surprise, I found myself overwhelmed by the broad scope of information presented in this course. As the course progressed, I found myself in dismay and even upset because of the limited perspective I had acquired on gender issues. I immediately repositioned myself and decided to view this limitation as a positive experience that I could truly learn from [. . .]. I now understand that gender issues encompass my full existence and some of the issues directly involve the quality of my life [. . .]. However, I have not yet made reference to what I consider the most significant

topic covered in this course: global issues in gender. When I began this course, I only saw what was in front of me. I did not extend myself into the heart of the women's movement nor did I understand the power of what was being done or could be done. For me, the fight for gender equality began and ended with women in the work force and women's role in society.

While this young woman was ready to analyze and theorize gender issues, others, dealing with the material on a less theorized, less global, and more intimately personal level, also felt they learned. A male student explained:

In a couple of instances over the past few months it has seemed like my life has been guided by the material for this class. In one of the instances the coincidence was uncanny: we had a speaker on cross-dressing; I go home and find out a friend of mine is cross-dressing for money. The second instance was a bit more subtle, but still I found myself thinking about this class and the issues it raises. I found out the closest person to me on the entire planet is anorexic and was battling against this sickness during the semester [. . .]. These situations don't really fit together at all, and shouldn't be in the same paper. The only thing that brought them together in this light was class. I was lucky to be able to relate anything from the screwy melodrama that is my life to school. This class did it, I feel that somehow this is a testament to its worth.

This sense that gender studies has a direct connection to life is echoed in the following passage from the paper of a nontraditional student who had been homeless and on the streets of New York before circumstances conspired to enroll her in a adult degree program:

One of the most disheartening things I realized in this class is that a lot of people have a hard time acknowledging that sexism is a fact. I cannot help but think about the young woman in one of the discussion groups who suggested that perhaps one of the reasons women were discriminated against on the job was because they weren't trying hard enough to fit in. She actually said, "Maybe they're just not smiling enough." [. . .] To make the facts about how things are in the real world unavailable to students is irresponsible to say the least. Knowing the truth about how sexist our society is should be as important as any other class I'm required to take at this college.

While the connection between the course and life was valuable to some students on a personal or theoretical level (or both), others found the historical material particularly illuminating. These students embraced postmodern notions of definitional fluidity, of decentered subjectivity, of shifting narrativity and complex positionality. Students, for instance, who had learned history from a traditional perspective appreciated this study of gender as a "way of rediscovering and recovering the works and lives of historical women while bringing the current contribution and struggles of women into the spotlight." They obtained a new sense of history that allowed them to question both the "facts" and the processes by which they were obtained. A gendered view of the past asked them to look at the context in which events in history are presented and interrogate whether the traditional description represents a complete narrative. When discussing the gender studies program, one student pondered, "Regardless of whether or not the courses were in history, politics, theory, or literature, their objectives centered around recovering women's lives, accomplishments, and ideas [. . .]. Why would anyone object to recovering a more expansive and detailed view of our culture?"

Responses such as these were common enough to confirm our sense that student-centered learning directed at imbricating the personal, the theoretical, and the political was a valid pedagogy for this course. Student narratives also empowered us to remain cheerfully defiant of accusations of "unscholarliness" that we encountered on our own campus as well as in the literature (Middleton 115). A small cadre of our colleagues mounted an attack on gender studies courses as "propaganda," and as (horrors!) "nonobjective teaching" (unlike their own godlike and irrefragable utterances). Our pedagogical philosophy, coupled with student narratives, helped us to understand that our colleagues were reacting predictably when confronted with material and modes of learning that threatened their authority.

As students became more and more aware of cultural and social ambiguities inherent in constructions of gender and of the elaborate and obfuscated systems of power that organize our lives, we experienced a corresponding responsibility to acknowledge their new understandings and visibly to work to change to power balances whenever and wherever we could. Such reciprocity of learning and empowerment represents our pedagogical ideal; when it occurred, however partially, we sensed that we were fulfilling our goals for this course. Students wrote of "seeing things differently," not as clearly as before: "One of the most insightful things I learned during this course was that there are no black and white answers to the problem of gender; that in fact, the study of gender is plagued by many areas of gray." This blurring of views indicates, at the very least, initial engagement in a discourse that represents different ways of knowing and, at the most, recognition that multiple perspectives are legitimate.

Definitions of power in relation to gender were crucial in many of the presentations, in the discussions that followed, and in response papers. For example, one student, recognizing that the study of history must include women's lives and experiences, and that traditionally it has not, combined this new awareness with the understanding that knowledge gained from such study is power:

> Recovering the lives of women reveals the mistreatment we have received throughout history [. . .] it certainly does not benefit the majority (or powerful, represented segment of the population) to acknowledge the existing imbalance of power between men and women [. . .]. Although the woman's movement has furthered the awareness of women to their position, it has not yet succeeded in changing culturally dominant ideas and ideals. Examining this situation has helped me to understand why gender studies is sometimes considered an illegitimate field of academic study. What is legitimate about recovering insignificant or even negative lives?

This student understood, perhaps for the first time, how gender and power are interwoven and how implicit and unexamined significations of gender will be invoked in any attempt to realign power. In the process of writing the paper cited above, she found words for her new perception that hegemonic authority privileges a portion of society that justifies inequality and "blames women for gender discrimination." When numbers of students achieved analyses of gender/culture relations as sophisticated as these, we took the opportunity in the small groups and in our responses to papers to complicate their understandings. We urged them to become aware of and to examine the multiple positionings in their own lives that exist alongside their gender positionality (student, worker, daughter/son, race, class, religious identification). We encouraged as many as could to make the intellectual leap to "focus on simultaneous positionings in multiple power relations, and on the personal experiences of contradiction that such multiple positionings bring about" (Middleton 18). In those cases in which a student or a group of students collaboratively negotiated this perception, we noted that some of the easy simplifications, such as their combative concern about "male bashing," became less intellectually tenable.

Nonetheless, the issue of "male bashing" as an unexamined strategy for justifying the status quo haunted the course and will probably continue to do so. Several men, however, lived with their anxiety and theorized it in their final papers. One wrote:

> This class might very well be more difficult for a man to take than a woman for the simple fact that men often shut down their minds as soon as they hear the word feminism or are told that they oppress by virtue of the fact that they are rewarded by an oppressive system. However, I would say that this course *should* be more difficult, more uncomfortable for men, and that the discomfort that men feel while in the classroom is very necessary. Men have become too comfortable with their role in society, and women have been forced into discomfort and tremendous pain because the system kicks them in the head every time they try to stand up. Men need to become uncomfortable with their situation in society because that discomfort might lead to change.

Another wrote very personally about his experience as a male in this course:

> What we students hear may not be what we want to hear. [. . .] Perhaps we (men) fail to realize/open our minds to gender issues because we are afraid of facing the truth. [. . .] This course sometimes made me ashamed of being male. What I came to realize was, I could have chosen to continue feeling ashamed or I could learn from the emotion. To feel ashamed is to degrade your self worth, especially when you have no control over what gender you are. [. . .] I found the more I opened my mind to gender issues, the more I became aware. The people in our class who felt the class was about "male-bashing," were probably the people who [. . .] felt threatened by the material presented.

Although numbers of male and female students never grappled with these painful issues as profoundly as these two, the number who did was encouraging to us. We are well aware that it is easier to see oneself as a victim than as an oppressor; it is easier to think about righting wrongs when you yourself do not have to contemplate surrendering power. Additionally, the notion of multiple positioning allowed these and other men to move away from the counterintuitive sense of "I am the oppressor" to a more nuanced comprehension, something like: "Sometimes I am the oppressor, although usually not intentionally, and sometimes I am as much a victim as my female coworker, and sometimes I actually help deconstruct oppressive power."

Concurrent with expanded understandings of gender in relation to positionality and decentered subjectivity, students began to question the ways in which such significations have traditionally been represented (or more properly, not represented) *and*, movingly, they began to examine the potential to "right the wrong." Their responsiveness to utopian vision is one reason many of us enjoy interacting with students of this age. Their easily awakened idealism astounds and inspires us, even as we worry about the bruises life is likely to inflict on their naivety. We were moved by the words written by one student in the conclusion of her final paper in which she described the impact this class had on her:

> For me, the underlying idea of "potential" continued to grow more and more important throughout the semester. [. . .] We are a norm-obsessed culture, and what we consider to be correct is more powerful than any of us imagine—our prejudices can even be a distortion of a blatant, unarguable reality. [. . .] I feel that as a result of this class, I am much more aware of the injustices which women endure daily.
>
> Knowledge is power, and I know that because I am better able to recognize gender discrimination, I will be better able to fight it.

This hopeful and positive statement is typical of many. Scarred as we are by more than a half century of personal struggle with both external and deeply internalized issues related to gender, we wince at these words from a young woman who has yet to experience deeply the effects of discrimination due to gender in events she cannot change. On the other hand, we applaud her and others' willingness to recognize a struggle they would like to think is part of history, and to conceptualize the notion that they too will need to work toward and contribute to change. This utopian aspect of the gender studies course was one of the most important for us. Our professional and personal friendship thrives on our shared sense that education, even when it appears to be about the past, is profoundly about the future and about change and growth. We agree with Barbara Christian when she says that she "writes to save her life" (130). We would add that we read and write and teach in order to save our lives and the lives of our students.

Although most students talked about the issues presented in class in theoretical ways, many segued readily into personal experiences. One student suggested that this course was difficult to be a part of because the "interactions and perspectives we are studying about affect every area of life every day." The academic is personal because "gender issues are issues we can't escape." This awareness of the interrelationship between school and life—for many a surprising realization—gave structure to previously unexamined experiences and provided understanding of the "why" and "how" of their own lives. Their autobiographies provided them with insight into the personal significance of this course. As one young man explained:

> Coming from a heavily feminized upbringing, I thought I was missing something. [. . .] My mom divorced early, my aunt never married, and my grandfather passed away at a young age, leaving me with three women who continuously cared for me. [. . .] Understanding the woman's role has helped me define my role. Finding a way to apply the lectures to our own lives helps to define who we are, our opinions of women, and what we can do to make our world more gender equal.

Hearing the stories of others and through presentations in class, he was able to understand and appreciate his own circumstances in new ways; he could tell new stories about himself: "If this class has done anything, it has helped me to think more openly with a socially critical consciousness." This class gave him a structure within which to reflect on how others perceived him or treated him based on his upbringing, which he knew as "different" from and inferior to ("I was missing something") that which was normative. The gender studies course allowed him to rethink and restructure his understanding of his previously devalued "feminized" family.

This young man was not the only student to discuss gender theory in relation to family. While the undergraduate college years may be a time to form identity, throughout the semester it became evident how difficult it is for students to hold views different from those of their families. Often they noted that their parents held different views from their own; they did not, however, want to see their own opportunities as in any way affected by these views. When one young woman described her father, we learned that she was able to analyze critically his position through an academic lens but not through a personal one: "He is very much closed-minded and believes that men are the ones that should be educated and the superior race, that carry on the top ranking jobs of society." She described him in a detached manner, identifying his attitudes as characteristic of a gendered society. Nonetheless, she attempted to be tolerant and understanding when considering her personal relationship with her father as it applied to her life: "Although he believes this, I can't complain because he is educating me and obviously sees potential in me." As she developed her views in this infor-

mal paper, we were able to watch the process of her struggle to differentiate her intellectual perceptions from her emotions: "It aggravates me
though, that in dealing with the issue of academia and gender, he contra-
dicts himself." The intellectual and emotional complexity redacted here
are typical of the learning curve in this class and demonstrate one of the
reasons we feel committed to this course and to expanding this program. In
much of our teaching and advising we are all too aware of the depth of
alienation young people feel in the classroom. Any course or field or interdisciplinary study that collapses the artificial barriers between life and
learning, that makes college more than a means to a job or more than a
means of fulfilling middle-class expectations has our unequivocal support.

As we taught this course, we noted a transformative experience occurring as the "general" became "particular" and the "particular" "political,"
causing changes in ways of seeing and being. Perhaps facilitating and even
modeling this interconnectedness of the personal and the political were
some of the presentations that focused on experiences that altered the
speakers' lives. For instance, the two women who spoke on attending the
Beijing Conference on Women, interwove their experiences at the conference into a seamless and moving account of the experiential and intellectual significations of their deracination, affirmation, encounters, and
discoveries during their journey. As another example, a presentation on
gender in the trades encouraged many male students who worked in the
trades during the summers to reconsider and reevaluate their experiences.
As a result of this rending of the customary barrier between the intellectual
and the personal, a number of students wrote of new insights into old relationships or of experiences in which they found themselves behaving in
new ways. One student remembered a newspaper article given to him by
his father when he was fifteen:

> The premise for this piece was the breakdown of the father figure
> in our society. Could it be possible that my father was admitting
> his role in my life had been altered in a detrimental way? [. . .]
> This document, I suppose was intended for me to understand my
> relationship with my father, and understand the rigors and respon-
> sibilities of manhood; in addition to those insights, I came to real-
> ize, through this class, that manhood is relative to the society in
> which it is based.

His writing suggests that he gained a new understanding of his father and
his father's sense of himself that allowed the son to look at his own identity
and self-definition in a new, more conscious, and more complex way. His

insight allowed him to separate his own views from those of his father. He ended his paper by saying, "simply, he fits the stereotype quite well; he is the head of the household, and imposes his patriarchal views on his wife and sons. [. . .] Without intending to do so, my father shed light on my own search for manhood."

Personal growth that enabled new ways of knowing the world was expressed by one of the most challenging students in the class. Throughout the semester, he questioned, argued with, and negated the study of gender as a serious endeavor. Through many discussions both in and out of class, with and without instructors' input, he grappled with both theoretical and personal issues related to gender. In the conclusion of his final paper he expressed the effect that the course and his engagement with it had on his own life:

> I can honestly say that because of this class, my utopia has been blown apart. I was not aware that women who do the same work as men receive an average twenty cents less for each earned dollar. I was not aware of the incredible inequalities between men and women in developing countries like Pakistan. I did not take notice in how women were portrayed in movies or in television. I was not aware that Saint Michael's discriminates against women. All of these issues collectively proved to me the importance of gender differences. They all helped me realize that we have a serious problem and I was not very sensitive to it. The issues reinforce the value of this class and its ability to open new windows for me to look out and see the world from a whole different perspective. That perspective is not just from a white male's point of view but from the view of somebody who has seen the problems that result in our society from the social inequalities that have been derived from centuries of inequality between men and women. [. . .] After this semester, I realize that my notion of what was is far from being correct and that gender plays a very instrumental role in who we are and what we become.

This young man's understanding of the course, and other similar responses, reminded us of the enduring tension between utopian vision and daily experience:

> We cannot expect that students will readily appropriate a political stance that is truly counter-hegemonic, unless we also acknowledge the ways in which our feminist practice/politics creates,

rather than ameliorates, the threat of abandonment; the threat of having to struggle within unequal power relations; the threat of psychological/social/sexual as well as economic and political marginality. (Lewis 178)

The goal we set in designing this course was to introduce the broad study of gender in some of its academic and more popular formulations. While we wanted to structure the class to include collaborative learning, we also wanted to go beyond the classroom, hoping that the narratives of the class would provide bases for epistemological, personal, and political transformation. We think that the examination of gender and its meanings can enrich and make more personal and relevant any area of study and, indeed, any aspect of life. At the same time, we know and communicate that all of us are bound up in divisions based on race, class, and gender that empower "liberal capitalism and its knowledge industries" (Luke 37). Thus, our vision at the conclusion of this course and as we plan its continuance is based on cautious and tempered idealism. We want students who sit in classrooms at Saint Michael's to see many kinds of faces, postures, and expressions; we want them to begin to listen to voices and acknowledge differences; we want them to notice who is silent and who speaks; we want them to think about distribution of power and resources both in and out of the classroom; we want them to note that these distributions almost always contain a gender component.

•   •   •

WORKS CITED

Butler, Judith, and Joan Scott, eds. *Feminists Theorize the Political*. New York: Routledge, 1992.

Christian, Barbara. "The Race for Theory." *Cultural Critique*. Oxford: Oxford University Press, 1987. Rpt. in *Contemporary Literary Criticism: Literary and Cultural Studies*. Eds. Robert Con Davis and Ronald Schleifer. 3rd ed. New York: Longman, 1994. 123–31.

de Lauretis, Teresa, ed. *Feminist Studies/Critical Studies*. Bloomington: Indiana University Press, 1986.

Felman, Shoshana. "Psychoanalysis and Education: Teaching Terminable and Interminable." *Yale French Studies* 63 (1982): 21–44.

Lewis, Magda. *Without a Word: Teaching Beyond Women's Silence*. New York: Routledge, 1993.

Luke, Carmen, ed. *Feminisms and Pedagogies of Everyday Life*. Albany: State

University of New York Press, 1996.

Middleton, Sue. *Educating Feminists: Life Histories and Pedagogy*. New York: Teachers College Press, 1993.

Smith, Dorothy. *The Conceptual Practices of Power: A Feminist Sociology of Knowledge*. Toronto: University of Toronto Press, 1990.

Thomson, Rosemarie Garland. "Integrating Disability Studies into the Existing Curriculum: The Example of 'Women and Literature' at Howard University." *Radical Teacher* 47 (1997): 15–21.

13

EMBODIED LEARNING
The Body as an Epistemological Site[1]

Diana L. Gustafson

INTRODUCTION

The emphasis on social change recognizes feminist pedagogy as a form of feminist practice having its roots in the women's movement, and firmly situates feminist pedagogy in the traditions of critical and radical pedagogies that see education as a form of empowerment and a tool for social change. The intrinsic link between feminist pedagogy and organizing for social change reflects the connection between the classroom and the world outside it, and the feminist understanding that change is necessary and must be systemic. (Briskin 23)

Feminist pedagogy is a political standpoint that acknowledges the classroom as a site of inequalities and, at the same time, a site for interrogating and contesting power dynamics (Briskin 23; Manicom 365). "*Not* a handy set of instructional techniques" (Manicom 365, emphasis added), feminist pedagogy is a "pedagogy of liberation" (Manicom 367), a pedagogy concerned with politics, power, and transformation (Briskin and Coulter 262; Manicom 365). Unlike other progressive and critical pedagogies that are missing "an explicit gender analysis" (Brookes 27; Ellsworth 297), feminist pedagogy pays overt and primary attention to girls and women and the ways gender intersects with other institutional and systemic oppressions operating in and outside the classroom. Finally, feminist pedagogy is characterized by "embodied reflexivity" (Lather 48), a self-conscious, critical, and intense process of gazing inward and outward that results in questioning assumptions, identifying problems, and organizing for change. In a classroom informed by feminist research and analysis, teacher and student, as learners together, co-construct knowledge in their particular, local setting—new knowledge that challenges the normalized and naturalized view of women in the world.

Just as there are multiple and sometimes contradictory feminisms or feminist perspectives so too are there multiple feminist pedagogies (Briskin and Coulter 252). Embodied learning is one of these feminist pedagogies. Embodied learning is concerned with challenging *what* is learned and *how* it is learned (Mayberry 453). Embodied learning contests the primacy of androcentric, Eurocentric, institutionalized knowledges as a way of knowing our bodies, ourselves, and our world. Embodied learning blends two parallel and complementary ways of knowing: the knowing that is discoverable in and mediated by concretized text, and the knowing that is discoverable in our experiences as embodied beings. Together, teacher and student investigate critically their embodied knowledges and the ways that institutionalized knowledges are constructed to exclude embodied knowing. Because embodied learning recognizes and values embodied experiences, student and teacher can explore the social organization of knowledge and how their identities are "created by the dominant discourse of power and knowledge" while at the same time they can "create themselves in opposition to that discourse" (Ferguson 22–23). Embodied learning creates liberatory classroom space within a subjugated institutional space[2]—space where the learner recognizes her own power as a subject (Carty 22); space where women's "subjugated knowledges" are valued and validated (Foucault 81–82); space where new knowledge is co-constructed and legitimated. This paper explores the body as an epistemological site and embodied learning as a feminist pedagogy.

My formal introduction to the body as an epistemological site was in a graduate-studies course that blended an examination of contemporary writings about health and healing systems, notably traditional Chinese medicine, with training in a set of oriental breathing exercises called *qi gong* (pronounced "chee kung"). My professor called this process "*self-learning*." Tom Craig and Maureen Connolly refer to a similar process of implicating the body as "critical, performative pedagogy." After weeks of resistance and critical reflection I came to refer to this innovative pedagogy as "embodied learning" (Gustafson 54). Each of these ways of talking about embodied learning serves as an entry point into a discussion where educators value a way of knowing that is discoverable in our experiences as embodied subjects. At this moment in my theorizing I do not attach any definitive explanation or fixed meaning that serves to differentiate critically one from another. My preference for using embodied learning relates to the way this term centralizes the body as an epistemological site.

This chapter presents my current understanding of the body as an epistemological site. The discussion draws principally upon my experience of learning in a nonstandard classroom and is divided into two sections reflecting my dual positionality as a student and as an educator. The first section describes embodied learning from my student perspective and documents my experience of participating in a course where the body was implicated as content and pedagogy. I introduce the sociology course and the primary learning objective, and the format and its purpose as I have come to understand them. A brief overview of *qi gong* and the eastern cosmology of which it is a part contextualizes the discussion by outlining some of the course content about the body. Then I describe how combining textually mediated learning about this eastern cosmology with experiential learning in *qi gong* illuminates the invisible process of constructing knowledge of the body and the *self*. A discussion of the construction of my *self* includes some ways I had learned to conceive of my body and the power of hegemonic discourses to shape that construction. And finally, from my standpoint as a student, I describe my own experience of transformative learning.

The second section of this chapter describes embodied learning from my perspective as an educator. Like any other innovation, this pedagogical approach is a work in progress. Since Roxana Ng first introduced this course on *self*-learning processes it has undergone many changes. In this section, I argue that explicit in-class discussion about embodied learning as a way of knowing will make visible to students its attributes as a feminist pedagogy. Additionally, it may support five educational outcomes consistent with feminist pedagogy that move beyond the learning objective explicitly stated in the course syllabus. Discussing embodied learning as a way of knowing may (1) validate the body as an epistemological site; (2) create a forum for discovering commonalities and supporting diversity of women's embodied experiences; (3) unmask the androcentric, Eurocentric process of constructing and validating knowledge claims; (4) name the classroom as a safe, social location for women to reconstrue personal notions of the body and the *self*; and (5) politicize the learning event by identifying with/for students the tools and the language for reclaiming their/our bodies and legitimating embodied knowledge claims.

EMBODIED LEARNING: THE STUDENT PERSPECTIVE

Locating Myself in This Classroom

This course marked the beginning of my studies as a doctoral student and the beginning of my reconceptualization of the body and the *self*. That is not to say that prior to enrolling in this course I was unaware of the body. Quite the contrary, I found the body a thoroughly fascinating and magnificent creation. For years the body was the focus of my study and my work as a nurse and clinical educator. Or am I saying I was unaware of *my* body. Indeed I was. Those understandings were learned and reflected during a lifetime as daughter, mother, and lover, and as someone who loves to garden, golf, dance, and embrace friends. What I had not reflected upon was how these two ways of knowing about the body and the self were disconnected. That disconnection between textually mediated knowledge and embodied knowledge had not been visible to me. Engaging in this learning experience helped me recognize that disconnection and articulate some of the contradictions between those two ways of knowing my body and my self.

The Course

This section begins with a description of the course in which I enrolled, the primary learning objective, and the pedagogical approach as I have come to understand them. Entitled Health, Illness, and Knowledge of the Body: Education and Self-Learning Processes, this sociology course was offered for credit in the graduate studies department of a prominent Canadian university. Fifteen women met with the professor for three hours every week throughout a thirteen-week semester. *Qi gong* training was an integral component of this academic course and we spent the first half of each class learning and practicing *qi gong* while the second half of the class was spent discussing the assigned readings. The professor led both the *qi gong* exercises and the group discussion.

The primary objective of the course was to challenge students to explore two parallel ways of knowing about health and the body by looking at how health and the body are conceived and experienced in nonwestern societies. The first way of knowing is discoverable and mediated through systems of knowledge that are historically and culturally specific, and concretized in text (Smith 17). To investigate this way of knowing, students were assigned a weekly set of contemporary writings. Because the emphasis was on eastern cosmology and traditional Chinese medicine we read Harriet Beinfield and Efrem Korngold's *Between Heaven and Earth: A Guide to Chinese Medicine*, Giovanni Maciocia's *The Foundations of Chinese Medicine: A Comprehensive Text for Acupuncturists and Herbalists*, and Ted Kaptchuk's *The Web Has No Weaver*. The class viewed two videos on traditional Chinese medicine produced by western physicians and met with a westerner who practices traditional Chinese medicine. These primary resources were supplemented with others that introduced us to health and healing in other nonwestern cultures including Leslie Malloch's *Indian Medicine, Indian Health: Study between Red and White Medicine*. Two books in the popular press, *Quantum Healing: Exploring the Frontiers of Mind/Body Medicine* by Deepak Chopra and *Health and Healing* by Andrew Weil, were also on our reading list. Some texts challenged ways of knowing the body from western sociological, psychological, and phenomenological perspectives (Moore; Paget; Shilling; Stacey; Transken). Still other texts discussed the tension between "alternative"[3] health practices and the contemporary western biomedical model of health care (Church; Edelberg; Kaptchuk; Kaptchuk and Croucher; Weil).

Discussing our responses to these diverse materials constituted half of our learning time in the classroom. For a time my learning was not unlike that in any female-friendly classroom where a student might come to know about health and healing practices in other cultures. That is to say, what I learned about eastern cosmology was drawn primarily from these texts,[4] about half of which were written by women. Gradually, however, what and how I learned about eastern cosmology shifted as I began to attend to the experiences of my body. *Qi gong* training was presented as a complementary learning activity intended to help students assess the readings and explore a second and parallel way of knowing. Performing *qi gong* actively engaged me in the process of learning about my self. By "reading" the body as I would read a text, I confirmed embodied knowledge as a valid and valuable source of information. In other words, I used embodied text to assess the knowledge claims discovered during my reading of concretized texts. As Linda Carty (18) points out, the language, grammar, references, and concepts that constitute academic knowledges exclude embodied knowledge and the knowledges of women who experience the world from a different standpoint. Keeping a reading notebook helped me to articulate this central point.

All students in this course kept a reading notebook. The purpose of keeping the notebook was to record a regular weekly summary of and our reactions to the assigned readings. We also recorded our responses to the class discussions and the *qi gong* exercises. Twice during the semester we submitted our reading notebooks to the professor. She read the content of each student's journal and in the margins wrote brief comments or asked provocative questions as if engaging in a real-time conversation.

Students in the course also kept a health journal. The purpose of the health journal was to keep a regular log of health and body habits. While each student determined the content and focus of the data she recorded most of us wrote about how we felt about our bodies and our health. To encourage students to make maximum use of this journal the content of the journal was designated private. While each student provided evidence she was maintaining the journal, the health journal was not submitted to or read by the professor. Students received credit for maintaining both journals but neither journal was evaluated in the traditional sense of assigning a grade.

The reading notebook and the health journal were journaling activities intended to facilitate critical reflection on the course content and the self-learning process.[5] Journal writing can take many forms and is just one of many important tools Patricia Cranton (151–56) recommends for guiding critical reflection among adult learners. Journal writing helped me document my thoughts and feelings, identify and examine my assumptions, integrate new learning, and make connections. Many of the assumptions I unearthed and connections I made about health and the body arose from using these reflective learning strategies.

To summarize, this pedagogical approach employed two parallel ways of knowing to investigate how health, healing practices, and the body are imagined and experienced in nonwestern societies. Reading literary texts was a conventional way of learning while performing *qi gong* provided the experiential text. Reflecting upon and discussing nonwestern systems of knowledge allowed me to examine, at arm's length, the process of making meaning of experiences of health and the body. Reflecting upon the experience of performing *qi gong* allowed me to examine, in a novel and profoundly personal way, the process of constructing knowledge of the body. To explain how I arrived at this understanding I offer a brief introduction to *qi gong* and the eastern cosmology of which it is a part. This provides a context for the discussion on self-learning that follows.

Embodied Learning Using *Qi Gong*

Many of the readings and much of the discussion in the sociology course centered on a Chinese theoretical framework that combined Taoism, Yin-Yang, and the Five Phases. Tao is the "intrinsic order of all things" (Beinfield and Korngold 85) and is, by definition, undefinable. Yin-Yang is an irreducible premise of Chinese logic and refers to the interaction of bipolar forces present in all things (Maciocia 2–7). The Five Phases refer to the five interactive and fundamental powers that provide "the basis for describing the development of forms, systems, and events" (Beinfield and Korngold 86). Together, Taoism, Yin-Yang, and the Five Phases form a system of knowledge that orders the way one eastern culture conceptualizes and makes meaning of life, the forces of nature, and human existence.

In this schema, there is an interpenetration of the soma (the physical, sensory, and perceptual) and the psyche (the emotional, intellectual, and spiritual), and the person and the universe (Beinfield and Korngold 85–127; Maciocia 15–34).

This schema is operationalized onto body works. Blood and *qi* (which means "energy" or "essence") flow through the human body. *Qi* and other processes govern the functioning of the organ networks. The organ networks are a continuum of Yin-Yang protoplasm which, together with visceral structures and cavities, define inner and outer human shape. The organ networks are paired systems reflecting the opposition and interdependence of Yin and Yang (Maciocia 7–14). According to Taoist knowledge, the Yin organs maintain homeostasis while the Yang organs transform matter by governing digestive and elimination functions. There are ten meridians or acupuncture channels through which *qi* flows. These ten meridians correspond to each of the five paired organ networks. Performing *qi gong* is one way to stimulate the flow of *qi* and release any blockages that may develop along these meridians.

Qi gong are breathing exercises. Most of our *qi gong* training time was spent learning and practicing one set of five exercises. Each exercise corresponded to one of the five seasons of the year: spring, summer, late summer, fall/autumn, and winter.[6] The act of doing each exercise in the set focuses the mind, body, and the breath on the paired organ network that corresponds to that season. So, for example, the fall/autumn breathing exercise is directed at the lung organ network. The meridian which corresponds to the lung network runs along the vertical crease between the chest and the upper arm. The lung meridian is "massaged" during the fall/autumn breathing exercise. Performing the fall/autumn exercise stimulates the lung network to collect, mix, and disperse *qi* throughout the body.

Learning this set of breathing exercises required that I learn a set of physical movements and the rhythm of breathing that governs those movements. Because the rate of breathing dictates the rate at which the body moves through a set of repetitions I had to learn to control my breath at the same time I learned to control my body. Initially my full attention was required to coordinate mind, body, and breath. With practice, I found I could concentrate on my breathing and the work of the body continued in orderly cycles. Learning the physical and spiritual discipline for controlling and coordinating the breath and the body is essential to Taoist vitality and well-being (Beinfield and Korngold 117). By repeating the body movement I was replicating the cycle of breath which, in turn, echoed the rhythms of life and nature. Thus, learning *qi gong* allowed me to glimpse the internal logic of one eastern cosmology and to experience the body in a new conceptual context that challenged the dominant western discourse of the body.

This simplistic overview is the product of my brief engagement in textually mediated learning and experiential learning about a very complex knowledge system. This eastern cosmology is distinctly different from the western knowledge system in which I am steeped. It is in the western system of knowledge that I learned to make sense of my body, my health, and my relationship to the universe. While my construction of *self* was a product of both textually mediated and embodied learning experiences these two ways of knowing rendered different images of *self*—images that were disconnected and incongruent.

Women's embodied experiences have been reshaped (medicalized), misrepresented, or excluded entirely from the dominant images of the body and self. For example, in western culture women's embodied experiences of menstruation and menopause, intimacy and physical abuse, labor and sports have been "coordinated textually" by organizational and political processes (Smith 17). These normalized and naturalized images of body and self are disconnected from the embodied experiences of actual women in their particular, local settings.

The pedagogical approach in this course replicated and made visible the process of constructing knowledge by blending two parallel ways of knowing the body. The *qi gong* exercises focused my attention on the embodied knowledge I was creating in a particular local setting. The assigned readings represented the institutionalized knowledge about health and the body. With this pedagogical approach I was able to lay bare the process of constructing self-knowledge and to articulate the nature of my self as a social construction. What follows is an overview of what I learned about the construction of my self.

My Construction of *Self*

My *self* has a triune nature: body, mind, and spirit. My body is the physical part of my being, an organic vessel. It is a discrete, anatomical structure that houses the organs that maintain my physiological activities. My body is subject to heat, cold, pain, barometric pressure, and invasion by microorganisms. It is the vehicle that facilitates my movement in the world. My body is the machine which has reproduced another human life. The sex, shape, size, color, and mobility of my body represent my self to the world, and the world responds to me according to social, cultural, and political constructs and prescription. So, for example, my white skin, my able-bodiedness, my heterosexuality, and my average body size and shape generally afford me many unearned privileges at work, at school, and at play. My femaleness, however, results in varying degrees of disadvantage in these same social arenas.

My mind is the cognitive part of my being. It thinks, calculates, deciphers, and solves problems. My mind is housed in an organic vessel, the brain. In contrast, Chopra, who espouses a nonwestern conception of the body, argues that the mind (intelligence) is located in the brain and in every living cell. My mind is subject to control from many sources internal and external to my body, the physical part of my being. My mind is the part of my being that interacts and communicates with other human life. The speed, facility, aptitude, accuracy, and logic of my mind represent my self to the world, and the world responds to me according to social constructs about intelligence, aptitude, and so on. Because intelligence is constructed as the ability to be objective and creative, to think in linear and spatial ways, and to be ambitious in the pursuit of knowledge (Dworkin 43), and because women are variously regarded as emotional, intuitive, a/sexual, timid, passive, illogical, immoral, and generally lacking the characteristics associated with intelligence (Carty 20–21, Dworkin 52–53, Grimshaw 36–42) my femaleness is associated with varying degrees of disadvantage in some social arenas.

My spirit is the affective part of my self. It is my emotional and moral being. My spirit is shaped by the experiences of both my body and my mind. My spirit is my soul. As such it is the one essential part of my self that exists as part of my body and mind, and beyond and after them both. Even as I articulated this construction of a discrete spiritual self, I knew that I did not have a clearly articulated belief about a life hereafter where the spirit resides beyond the corporeal state.

If this triune representation of my self seems vaguely familiar that is because it is a classic western portrait of the self. The body-mind-spirit nexus illustrates the ways that I constructed self-knowledge that was rooted in three hegemonic western discourses about the body. First, I was struck by the similarity between my construction of a triune self and the Christian principles that construct God as a trinity. I cannot attribute this sense of a triune self directly to any internalized Christian values. I do not have any affiliation with organized religion. Still, as a white woman born and raised in small-town Canada, I am aware of the way Christian philosophy permeates the English language, art, the media, and social traditions. I believe this pervasive religious influence contributed, in part, to my triune construction of self. Exploring the contribution of Christianity to self-learning offers a myriad of paths worth traveling, all of which are beyond the scope of this paper.

The second contributor to my construction of a triune self was my schooling as a student of sociology. Chris Shilling traces the historical development in classical sociology of the mind-body separation from Plato to the days of Descartes who postulated the ultimate human location as "disembodied reason" to today's construction of the body as an "absent presence" (19). The separation of mind and body is an underlying premise of the sociological, psychological, and anthropological thought I studied as an undergraduate. Despite experiences in my personal and professional life that contradicted this separation of mind and body I had continued to cling to this dominant western construction of body and self. *Qi gong* training and the experience of mind-body integration it facilitated was an unsettling reminder of the way my embodied knowledge of self was disconnected from the self-knowledge I constructed within the hegemonic discourses of the body.

The third contributor to my triune construction of self was my history of growing up, living, being educated, and working in health care. Western biomedicine separates the body from the mind and from the spirit and decontextualizes the being from her particular location and universal connectedness.[7] Like Margaret Stacey, I assumed the universality of the human body and its biological base (18). Unlike Stacey, I assumed the universality of health and illness experiences. That is not to say that I did not believe in individual experiential differences. Rather, I assumed that health and illness had a physiological, pathological, and psychological basis that was universal.

As a student of western biomedical model, I also accepted unreflectively what Stacey might have referred to as a linear theory of medical development (15). I believed that western biomedicine was an advanced system of health care. To me, the western biomedical model was scientific, proven, and objective and, therefore, superior. It was the system against which I evaluated all other health practices. Learning about nonwestern health systems that melded mind, body, and spirit challenged me look at the contradictions between western institutionalized knowledges about the body and my embodied knowledge. In particular, I was reminded of previous experiences with the western medical model that revealed to me the partiality of the biomedical model and the value of "alternative" health practices.

In my personal search for ways to improve my health and well-being, I have, over the years, investigated other health practices. While the western health-care system offered me curative options for illness and disease, there was too little attention to health promotion and preventative medicine. Additionally, I preferred *being in* control of maintaining my wellness to *giving up* control to someone else to treat my illness. This led me to value the knowledge and skill of herbalists and massage therapists, for example. Not only am I committed to good nutrition and regular exercise but also my daily routine includes enjoying herbal teas and aromatherapy for their sensory appeal and restorative qualities.[8]

While I accepted "alternative" medicine for myself, I realized that I separated myself from others who choose "alternative" medicines. At the very least I considered their choices to be eccentric and illogical. Under more serious circumstances I regarded their decisions as a refusal to give up hope of a cure, or as a denial of the "reality," the inevitability, of illness, disability, or death. Additionally, I took a dim view of practitioners of "alternative" medicines whom I felt preyed on the fear, ignorance, and helplessness of the poor, uninformed, and ill people who sought out these cures. Even as I leveled these criticisms against other health practices and practitioners, I realized that I did not consistently apply the same critical framework to western biomedicine and its practitioners.

As a nurse caring for people with cancer and other diseases of the gastrointestinal tract, I knew the limitations of western diagnostics, surgery, and medication. I had been part of a system that encouraged ill people and their families to accept elaborate and invasive treatments that offered little hope of a cure and had devastating effects on the quality of their remaining life. Alternatively, I had witnessed the benefit of guided imagery, visualization, biofeedback, and therapeutic touch for the management of intractable pain associated with some cancers. Despite these experiences that called into question the biomedical model of health care, I carried with me a view of nonwestern health systems as Other, a potpourri of choices when the body and western medicine failed.

This way of seeing was a powerful indictment against nonwestern conceptions of health, healing, and the body. It ignored the culturally and historically specific internal logic of "alternative" health systems (Stacey 15). In North America, "alternative" noninvasive treatments enter into the individual plan of care only as adjunctive therapies (read: last-hope, last-chance therapies) after traditional western medical therapies have failed. As institutionally sanctioned plans of care, these noninvasive therapies entered as "pioneering" medical advances into hospitals known for their innovation (Kaptchuk and Croucher 115–37).[9] The use of such language to describe "alternative" healing practices speaks to the power of the dominant medical system to appropriate indigenous knowledges and refer to it as a discovery. This is reminiscent of the way that the colonization of North America is described in terms of pioneers who "discovered" and settled this continent. Use of such language also points to the ways that knowledge claims of other cultures, some of which are centuries old and derived from embodied knowledges, must be reconciled against the dominant western knowledge system before they are legitimated.

Embodied learning facilitated for me the process of articulating contradictions between the institutionalized knowledges that have guided my life and the subjugated knowledges I have created within and in opposition to those dominant discourses. The explicit recognition of the assumptions underpinning my conceptions of health and the body was a necessary first step in transformative learning.

Embodied Learning: Transformative Learning

As Ann Manicom (365) says, feminist pedagogy is about facilitating transformation. Patricia Cranton (151–52) lists several general steps involved in transformative learning. The process begins when the student recognizes the assumptions underlying a belief system that are guiding/constraining her behavior. Then she must participate in a safe and supportive environment with appropriate activities for questioning and making explicit those assumptions. Finally, the student must revise and integrate new assumptions into an overall perspective that replaces the old perspective.

In this academic course, and in negotiating the self-learning process, I needed to move through these three transformative steps to achieve the desired learning outcome. Embodied learning was a facilitated process of exploring knowledge about the self. The classroom became a site for interrogating and contesting the dominant discourse about the body. The reading notebook and health journal were two tools for critical reflection, and my critical gaze was maintained during class discussions. Still more work occurred when I met informally with other students outside class time to discuss our responses to this "nonstandard" classroom format. In these various ways I was able to identify and explore assumptions underlying the social construction of knowledge about health and the body. While engaging in critical reflective activities I also recognized my resistance to embodied learning.[10] To achieve the learning objectives as I understood them, I needed to identify the obstacles constraining my learning. I questioned the purpose of *qi gong* training and its impact on my learning about self.

With embodied learning I was able to achieve outcomes that might not have been possible with other feminist pedagogies. By engaging in a critical, self-reflective process I was able to question assumptions, identify problems, and make (modest) changes in my gaze and my actions. Embodied learning drew my attention to the social construction of what is valued as a health practice, who is valued as a healer, and the ways these values were made visible in my life. I also made explicit the contradictions between dominant institutionalized discourses and my lived experiences. In the months since I completed the course I have continued to integrate my revised assumptions into new understandings about health, the body, and the construction of self-knowledge. For example, at a recent academic conference[11] I invited the audience to join me in performing a breathing exercise. In this way I implicated our bodies as content and pedagogy in what would have otherwise been an abstract and disembodied discussion of the body as content alone.

Summary

Himani Bannerji writes, "knowledge comes in two types—a producer's knowledge and a consumer's knowledge. In the former we participate in our learning as creators and in the latter as mere functionaries and hoarders of information or 'facts'" (75). In the traditional academic setting, the student is presented a curriculum shaped by and constitutive of consumer knowledge. Textually mediated knowledge is often reified and uncritically absorbed by learners. Textually mediated knowledge is also dissociated from knowledge that is derived from our direct agency in the particular local experience of living (77). In a feminist classroom students are presented a curriculum and a pedagogy that allows them to become critical producers of knowledge.

Embodied learning, as a feminist pedagogy, affirmed for me women's subjectivity and validated my body as an epistemological site. I used knowledges made visible through embodied learning to evaluate critically the ways dominant androcentric discourses informed my knowledge of my body and self. I had the opportunity to identify those areas where embodied ways of knowing were excluded, marginalized, or misrepresented in textually mediated knowledges. Finally, when I made explicit my embodied knowledges I was able to begin the process of reintegrating them into a new more comprehensive way of seeing health, my body, and my self. Therefore, from my perspective as a student, embodied learning helped me challenge what I learn about the body and the self, and provided me with the tools and language to begin to construct new knowledges.

EMBODIED LEARNING: THE EDUCATOR PERSPECTIVE

From Another Standpoint

As an educator, I was intrigued by the way the professor introduced herself and the course on the first day of class. She was open about who she was, describing herself as a woman, a feminist, and a member of a racial minority. She also declared herself a learner in the classroom we shared. Any one of these identifiers made her exceptional in her position as a tenured professor in the creamy-white male-dominated halls of North American academia. When introducing herself she mentioned her childhood memories in China where her grandmother was a western-trained physician. She spoke about her present-day experiences as an adult in Canada where she incorporates *qi gong* and traditional Chinese medicine into her daily living.

The professor blended these images about her embodied learning with a discussion of the content that the course offered interested students. She spoke about the genesis of the course, its nonstandard format, and the learning objectives. At least three points were very clear. First, her practice as an educator was informed by a feminist research agenda and political stance. Second, she made it clear that she routinely modified course content and elements based on students' constructive feedback during and after the course. Third, she made it clear that this course might not be suitable for all students.

At this point she addressed the controversy swirling around her, the course, and her nonstandard approach to teaching the course. Speaking in nonspecific terms to protect the identity of the individuals involved she retold the story of a male student who had lodged a formal complaint against her with the administration. She admitted that this was not an isolated incident but rather one that exemplified her struggle to implement a feminist pedagogy. The student had accused her of using her class as a platform for feminism, of marginalizing him as a white male, and of using meditative and physical exercises that were inappropriate in a university setting (Ng 41). In her analysis of the gender, race, and class relations operating in the classroom and the larger institution at the time, Roxana Ng writes that "what I experienced has less to do with my competence as a teacher than with who I am" (41). Given the way that the controversy had played itself out in at different levels of the bureaucracy,[12] she secured the classroom by making explicit her feminist stance and her pedagogical approach.

She implemented four safeguards. She audiotaped her introduction of the course including the learning objectives and an explanation of the nonstandard format and its purpose.[13] She led the students in a set of breathing exercises, thereby clarifying the nature of the experiential component. The course syllabus included a warning to students who were "uncomfortable with a nonstandard classroom format." Finally, she invited only *interested* students to remain in the course.

While about thirty students attended the first class, only half that number returned to complete the course. While it is not uncommon for students at this institution to "shop" for courses during the first week of the semester, I was struck by the sharp drop in the number of interested students. The only two men who attended the first class did not return nor did the student who used a wheelchair. I was one of the few students to return who had declared a professional background or academic focus in health care. Of the students who remained about half were members of visible minorities.

While only speculative, I offer these explanations for the drop in enrollment in light of my own experience with, and resistance to, embodied learning. Perhaps those who initially expressed an interest in learning about health, illness, and knowledge of body were uncomfortable with challenging their familiar western paradigm in light of other systems of knowledge. I also wondered if challenging the dominance of white, Eurocentric, masculinist medical knowledge was particularly threatening in the company of an assertive, articulate, woman of color. Students may have been uncomfortable with exploring their interest in an unfamiliar and "nonacademic" learning environment. Finally, this feminist pedagogy may have been exclusionary, rather than inclusive, for students living with disabilities. The theme that runs through each of these possible explanations relates to creating a safe classroom. bell hooks, Reid-Walsh and Correa, Carty, and Bannerji have discussed whether a "safe space" for learning is possible when students and teachers engage in the uncomfortable and risky political work of unsettling hegemonic discourses. How to address this issue in the context of embodied pedagogy remains an issue for future exploration.

The distinguishing feature of this course, in other words, what made it nonstandard, was the experiential component. That incorporating an experiential component, *qi gong* training, into a graduate-level academic course is referred to as "nonstandard format" underscores one of the course's underlying assumptions, that is, the western separation of mind and body. Embodied learning was integral to achieving the primary learning objective. Embodied learning was a means to achieve the desired educational outcomes and an end (an educational outcome) in itself.[14] While this dual purpose of the format was stated in the course outline, it was not formally or explicitly explored in relation to individual or collective student learning during class time. To enhance the learning experience and reduce learner resistance I recommend regular discussion about the assumptions underlying embodied learning as a feminist pedagogy. Engaging in these discussions may support five educational outcomes consistent with feminist pedagogy that move beyond the learning objective explicitly stated in the course syllabus.

Outcome 1: The Body as an Epistemological Site

Since embodied learning is a novel pedagogical approach, it is important to discuss its underlying purpose and assumptions. Embodied learning implicates two parallel and complementary ways of constructing knowledge and therefore challenges the primacy and power of institutionalized knowledge. Without this information the experiential component may be understood by the student as a simple learning experience in and of itself rather than as a way of knowing about and understanding a learning experience. Initially, I believed that in learning *qi gong* I was developing an appreciation for an eastern health practice and another approach to exercise, meditation, and relaxation—another tool for healthful living. It was later that I realized that in learning *qi gong* I was reproducing the invisible experience of constructing self-knowledge. It was not clear to me that *qi gong* training also served as a pedagogical tool for achieving the primary course objective.

The primary objective was to challenge students to explore two parallel and complementary ways of knowing about health and the body. In a standard classroom I would likely have gained an intellectual appreciation of how health and the body are conceived in nonwestern cultures. In this classroom, I was able to experience the dis/connection between textually mediated and embodied ways of knowing that inform the construction of body and self-knowledges.

Making explicit the role and contribution of embodied learning may illuminate the connection between embodiment and knowledge production. The experience of living is mediated through the body. How one makes meaning of that experience is mediated by concretized systems of knowledge. So, for example, how one makes meaning of health and illness is related to having or being a body. However, the corporeal experience of health and illness is understood in the context of knowledge that is both accumulated and internalized by the individual, and externalized and objectified in social institutions, such as hospitals and the health-care system. Discussing the body as an epistemological site may assist students in exposing the process of constructing knowledge as well as the process of (de)legitimating knowledge claims. Some students may miss the chance for the much broader learning experience if the purpose of the experiential component is unclear. Facilitating that discussion in class may enhance the learning experience and increase the likelihood that a learner will explore and value both ways of knowing.

Outcome 2: Discovering Commonalities and Supporting Diversity

Valuing the embodied experience may have a second benefit, which extends beyond the specific learning objectives of this course. If the principles underlying the experiential component are articulated, the classroom can become the place for sharing insights about self-learning processes. This pedagogy offers a entry point into a gendered analysis of body politics. Engaging in activities such as the health journal and the reading notebook encourages a critical self-reflective gaze wherein students may develop personal insights about self and the construction of self-knowledge. Formal discussions about embodied learning may further encourage participants to share and critique these personal insights. Sharing may lead teacher and students to discover the commonalities and validate the diversity of women's experience.

Temporal and social location shape the stories each student can tell. Jane Gaskell says, "Concepts about how the world actually works are located in one's experience of the world" (137). Each woman's concepts about her body, health, and self is informed by her various life experiences and her multiple positionalities in the world. In sharing personal stories and insights a student may focus attention on how she comes to (not) know herself as an embodied being both in classroom and in life, or how she came to embrace and contest ways of knowing and systems of knowledge. This may lead her to consider her acceptance of, or resistance to, the naturalized and normalized view of woman that is coordinated and reproduced in the media, literature, research, and other texts. Or sharing personal insights may lead her to consider how knowledge of the body is used to assign unearned privilege to her while oppressing other women.

If students in the class are able to share insights about their embodied experiences and self-knowledge it creates a more complex fabric for collective examination. With a complex fabric, students and teacher can together reflect on the gendered, raced, and classed bodies that we inhabit and the ways those social constructions support the various collectivities to which we belong and the oppressive knowledges that shape our lives. Some women students may question the beauty myth. White students may be challenged to examine how our white skin affords us the option of "attending to or ignoring one's own whiteness" (Terry 119–20). Able-bodied students may be challenged to examine the ways our embodied experiences at a university are privileged when compared with students who experience the world from a wheelchair. Collecting and examining insights may allow students to consider, revise, and shape new assumptions about what is valued and why. Shared insights can also lead to shared power that can be translated into personal and collective political action. In this way embodied learning is about politics, power, and transformation.

Outcome 3: Making Explicit the Social Construction of Knowledge

Explicit discussions about the nonstandard format may have a third benefit for students by unmasking the social process of constructing knowledge about the body. Embodied learning may offer the tools, the opportunity, and the perceptual proximity to examine the system of knowledge in which we are enmeshed. Margaret Stacey argues that:

> Starting from different societies' own conceptions aids comparative study. Unmasking the social process of constructing knowledge demands that we expose our assumptions about health, healing, and the body. Such an approach helps us to see the fundamental assumptions that we make about our society, to recognize that, just as much as some people leave indeterminate things we are clear about, so we leave indeterminate some things which are clearly explained in other cosmologies. (16)

Before this course I had not considered the historical, structural, and ideological forces that shaped my ways of knowing the body. I had embraced western health practices and therefore the assumptions underlying these practices were hidden to me. I accepted institutional discourse and practices as given, natural, or scientific. My introduction to nonwestern health systems was the catalyst for more critical reflection on my lived experience with the biomedical model of health care. While there may be many routes to that awareness, embodied learning is a pedagogical approach that facilitated this critical moment for me.

To be critical of a knowledge system can mean to stand temporarily outside of it, or to stand in another location to view it. In a standard classroom the student would learn about other knowledge systems by reading about them, questioning, and critically reflecting upon these abstract concepts. But, in so doing, she would be able to keep that knowledge at arm's length as Other. Embodied learning enables students to also *experience* another system of knowledge by becoming subject *to* it and subject *in* it. Explicit discussion about the experience of learning in this classroom may help students grapple with embodied learning as another way of constructing knowledge. It may also encourage students to challenge the dominant knowledge systems which exclude and devalue this way of knowing.

Outcome 4: Reconstruing the *Self*

A fourth benefit of formal discussion of the nonstandard format is naming the classroom as a safe, social location for reconstruing personal notions of the self. The safe classroom, and the social networking that a safe classroom facilitates, may allow students to name those issues that constrain our potential as persons and residents of the planet. While Sheila Ruth talks about the political importance of "naming"[15] things, objects, and events Jacqueline Reid-Walsh and Elaine Correa point out that creating "safe space" and "equal voice" for such activities to occur are still "the ideal" for both faculty and students (78).

Family and community can be important components of and supports for individual health and well-being. In a large bureaucratic educational institution students can be separated from these ties. Students and professors can feel separated and alienated from others and from themselves. Sharing insights and experiences about self-learning may be one way to build a social network. Social networks can be tools for learning, for social support, and for planning political action. The classroom network would be distinguishable from other social networks as it would focus on the collective experience as a way to challenge assumptions and frameworks for construing the self and the body. As members of a group that shared and discussed experiencing the body in a classroom setting, women may feel they have support for challenging systemic knowledges that delegitimate embodied ways of knowing.

To create this social network would require changing the dynamics of in-class discussion. In this course, *qi gong* training and class discussions were led by the professor. While the professor tried on occasion to de-center control by saying she did not consider herself an expert in traditional Chinese medicine or *qi gong*, several factors maintained the traditional professor-student power differential. She shared personal stories about the body, health, and healing practices. While these narratives added greatly to our appreciation of the eastern culture of her birth, her stories together with her tenured status, her role as official marker, and her physical location at the head of the classroom, enhanced, rather than diminished, her expert status in the group.

Sharing responsibility for facilitating discussion may begin to address this issue and enhance in-class discussions. Rotating principal responsibility for initiating discussion to all class members may encourage students to contribute more often and more equitably. Changes to the format of discussions may facilitate sharing and the development of a social network.

Changing the physical location and configuration of the classroom may also facilitate in-class discussion.

Outcome 5: The Body as a Political Signifier[16]

Finally, discussing embodied learning may politicize the learning event by identifying with and for women the tools and the language to reclaim our bodies and legitimate embodied ways of knowing. Women are constrained to restrict content and use language so that it will not be trivialized or diminished as female, political, or offensive. In a patriarchal and racist society, the "right speech of womanhood," according to bell hooks, is either silence, soliloquy, or secret prose (6). Because of the ways bodies are inscribed and known by their differences as male or female, able-bodied or disabled, straight or gay, white or black, bodies are a politically significant cultural form (Bannerji 83). Sharing and storytelling are vehicles for communicating and making meaning. By choosing and renegotiating language, we, as learners, can reshape our own experiences by reshaping the ways we understand those experiences. We may not be victims of rape or assault. We may not be living with a disability like Susan Wendell (1993) or with a terminal illness such as Marianne Paget describes. But as women, we are victims of the fear that makes our bodies sexual objects, reproductive machines, the target of violence, and the focus of medicalization throughout our lives.

Education is political power. And where there is power there is an opportunity for resistance (Morgan 107). Education that combines textually mediated knowledge and embodied knowledge can be used for the purpose of sociopolitical liberation. Embodied learning combines theory with lived experience by implicating the body as content and pedagogy. Embodied learning provides the opportunity to question social practices and raise social consciousness. The educational outcomes achieved may be liberating. Challenging existing beliefs and assumptions means questioning established ways of acting and reacting. Having the opportunity to talk about other ways of knowing the body can provide women with the language and tools to act both for ourselves and for each other. Embodied learning does that by validating the body as an epistemological site and recognizing the power of the subject to create knowledge (Carty 22).

Language and tools are essential to promoting new knowledge and individual responsibility for developing new patterns of self-care, health, and well-being. Women need new language and tools for questioning the social, economic, and political forces that maintain the established system. Language and tools are needed to resist, to make change, and to reclaim our bodies. Embodied learning has the potential to provide women with the language and tools to revisit and contest hegemonic knowledges. So changed, they have the power and skill to transfer the learning beyond the learning event. Group or shared knowledge, tools, and language may empower a collective to political action that can chip away at the dominant knowledge systems by challenging what we know and how we come to know it.

•   •   •

NOTES

1. My thanks to Roxana Ng and Kathryn Morgan for their comments on this manuscript and for our ongoing conversations about feminist pedagogies.

2. My thanks to Sarah Todd for helping me articulate the political difference between "giving voice," a phrase often associated with empowerment, and creating a space for voices to be heard.

3. I use quotation marks around "alternative" to call attention to the way that traditional medicine and healing practices in other cultures are devalued when compared to the western biomedical model, which represents itself as a scientific, objective, advanced, and therefore superior health-care system.

4. Several of the assigned texts describing health and healing practices in nonwestern cultures were written by westerners with considerable experience in the culture about which they were writing. As a result, our introduction to these indigenous knowledges came from westerners whose representations of nonwestern cultural beliefs and practices were filtered through a western perspective. This raises questions about whose voices may represent indigenous knowledges. See Jacqueline Reid-Walsh and Elaine Correa for a thoughtful discussion of "authority of experience" and "authenticity of voice" (78–79). For a provocative discussion that questions the appropriation of indigenous knowledges for use by first-world peoples see also Teresa Macias's "Learning in the Occupied Territories: Third World Women, First World Classrooms and the Undertaking of Indigenous Knowledge."

5. "*Self*-learning" was not a term explicitly defined by the professor. As a result, the term was left open to interpretation by the student. I assumed (correctly) that this was intentional. By allowing the student to define the process for herself, the professor granted us the power and opportunity to create and engage in a learning process of our own design. This was appropriate to the advanced level of the students in this course. For students working at the secondary- and undergraduate-level educators may choose to define the process of *self*-learning with and for students.

6. The specific set of breathing exercises learned by students varies from year

to year depending on the negotiated decision between the professor and the student group.

7. While there are some western physicians devoted to a holistic approach to medical care, the biomedical model explicitly separates the body from the mind and the spirit, and from the socioeconomic factors, political forces, and environmental issues that impact on the individual and collective experience and interpretation of well-being in the world.

8. By restorative, I mean those qualities that help me feel relaxed and centered. I am distinguishing between those practices that are restorative and those that are healing. For me, restoration is that experience of integrating the body, mind, and spirit, of feeling whole, and calm in the universe. That is an experience I hold separate from the experience of healing. I have constructed healing as an experience of the body or the mind separate from restoration, which is an experience of the spirit. This distinction is consistent with my construction of body, mind, and spirit as separate entities. The "alternative" health practices I use are those that fit into my current understanding of health and self. That understanding is continually being revised within and in opposition to the dominant western health knowledge and healing practices.

9. Kaptchuk and Croucher used this language to describe a pain and stress relief clinic in a large American hospital. These and similar clinics in Canada and the United States incorporate health and healing practices from nonwestern cultures to fill the gaps in western biomedicine. The current North American fascination with "alternative" practices may arise from the ability to construct a racialized Other and to appropriate from other cultures those elements that the dominant culture lacks and needs (Haraway 390). My thanks to Teresa Macias for calling my attention to the moral and ethical dilemmas associated with appropriating indigenous body/health knowledges for use by the dominant health system.

10. I was resistant to both the content and the process in this nonstandard classroom environment. The course content threatened my reality as a woman and a nurse, and the pedagogical approach threatened my reality as a student and an educator. Refer to my "Embodied Learning about Health and Healing: Involving the Body as Content and Pedagogy" for a more detailed discussion of my resistance to learning.

11. Refer to my "Education & Self-Learning Processes: Learning about the Body in a Non-Standard Classroom Format" for a description of the content and the format of this address.

12. For the professor's description and analysis of the incident, see Roxana Ng's "Sexism and Racism in the University: Analyzing a Personal Experience" and Roxana Ng's "'A Woman Out of Control': Deconstructing Sexism and Racism in the University."

13. In and of itself, this was not an unusual practice in this department at this

institution. Students who missed the first day of a class could obtain a copy of the audiotape and review it prior to attending the next scheduled day of class.

14. Although *qi gong* was the experiential activity used in this course, other performative activities appropriate to the content have also been useful. See Craig and Connolly; and Levine.

15. The act of naming is a political act exercised by marginalized groups who challenge the dominant view by reorganizing, relabeling, and reclaiming normalized, universalized masculinist knowledge claims, concepts, objects, and practices (Ruth 45).

16. This title is borrowed from Himani Bannerji's (72) discussion of experience and agency in feminism.

WORKS CITED

Bannerji, Himani. "But Who Speaks for Us? Experience and Agency in Conventional Feminist Paradigms." *Unsettling Relations: The University as a Site of Feminist Struggles*. Eds. Himani Bannerji, Linda Carty, Kari Dehli, Susan Heald, and Kate McKenna. Toronto: Women's Press, 1991. 67–107.

Beinfield, Harriet, and Efrem Korngold. *Between Heaven and Earth: A Guide to Chinese Medicine*. New York: Ballantine, 1991.

Briskin, Linda. *Feminist Pedagogy: Teaching and Learning Liberation*. Ottawa: Canadian Research Institute for the Advancement of Women, 1990.

Briskin, Linda, and Rebecca Priegert Coulter. "Feminist Pedagogy: Challenging the Normative." *Canadian Journal of Education* 17.3 (1992): 247–63.

Brookes, Ann-Louise. "Teaching, Marginality and Voice: A Critical Pedagogy Not Critical Enough." *Canadian Perspectives on Critical Pedagogy*. Eds. Dick Henley and Jon Young. Winnipeg: University of Manitoba Press, 1990. 25–34.

Carty, Linda. "Black Women in Academia." *Unsettling Relations: The University as a Site of Feminist Struggles*. Eds. Himani Bannerji, Linda Carty, Kari Dehli, Susan Heald, and Kate McKenna. Toronto: Women's Press, 1991. 12–44.

Chopra, Deepak. *Quantum Healing: Exploring the Frontiers of Mind/Body Medicine*. Toronto: Bantam Books, 1989.

Church, Kathryn. "Case Story: Off the Beaten Path—Illness and 'Unproven' Treatments." *Making the Rounds* 1.18 (1996): 1–5.

Craig, Tom, and Maureen Connolly. "The Bible and the Body: An Experiment in Critical, Performative Pedagogy." Paper presented at the Meetings of the Canadian Women's Studies Association, St. John's, NFLD, June 1997.

Cranton, Patricia. *Working with Adult Learners*. Toronto: Wall and Emerson, 1992.

Dworkin, Andrea. "The Politics of Intelligence." *Right Wing Women*. Ed. Andrea Dworkin. New York: Putnam, 1983. 37–53.

Edelberg, David. "Commentary: Into the Heart of Healing." *Making the Rounds* 1.18 (1996): 6–7.

Ellsworth, Elizabeth Ann. "Why Doesn't This Feel Empowering? Working through the Repressive Myths of Critical Pedagogy." *Harvard Educational Review* 59.3 (1989): 297–324.

Ferguson, Kathy E. *The Feminist Case Against Bureaucracy*. Philadelphia: Temple University Press, 1984.

Foucault, Michel. *The Archeology of Knowledge and on the Discourse of Language*. Trans. A. M. Sheridan Smith. New York: Pantheon Books, 1972.

Gaskell, Jane S. *Gender Matters from School to Work*. Toronto: OISE Press, 1992.

Grimshaw, Jean. "The 'Maleness' of Philosophy." *Philosophy and Feminist Thinking*. Ed. Jean Grimshaw. Minneapolis: University of Minnesota Press, 1986. 36–47.

Gustafson, Diana L. "Embodied Learning about Health and Healing: Involving the Body as Content and Pedagogy." *Canadian Woman Studies* 17.4 (1998): 52–55.

_____. "Education & Self-Learning Processes: Learning about the Body in a Nonstandard Classroom Format." Paper presented at the Canadian Research Institute for the Advancement of Women Conference, Fredericton, NB, November 1997.

Haraway, Donna. *Primate Visions*. New York: Routledge, 1989.

hooks, bell. *Talking Back: Thinking Feminist, Thinking Black*. Boston: South End Press, 1989.

Kaptchuk, Ted. *The Web Has No Weaver*. New York: Congdon and Weed, 1983.

Kaptchuk, Ted, and Michael Croucher. *The Healing Arts: A Journal Through the Faces of Medicine*. London: British Broadcasting Corp., 1986.

Lather, Patti. *Getting Smart: Feminist Research and Pedagogy With/In the Postmodern*. New York: Routledge, 1991.

Levine, David N. "Martial Arts as a Resource for Liberal Education: The Case of Aikido." *The Body: Social Process and Cultural Theory*. Eds. Mike Featherstone, Mike Hepworth, and Bryan S. Turner. London: Sage, 1991.

Macias, Teresa. "Learning in the Occupied Territories: Third World Women, First World Classrooms and the Undertaking of Indigenous Knowledge." Paper presented at the Annual Graduate Students in Sociology Conference, Toronto, Feb. 1998.

Maciocia, Giovanni. *The Foundations of Chinese Medicine: A Comprehensive Text for Acupuncturists and Herbalists*. London: Churchill Livingstone, 1989.

Malloch, Lesley. "Indian Medicine, Indian Health: Study Between Red and White Medicine." *Canadian Woman Studies* 10.2/3 (1989): 105–12.

Manicom, Ann. "Feminist Pedagogy: Transformations, Standpoints, and Politics." *Canadian Journal of Education* 17.3 (1992): 365–89.

Mayberry, Maralee. "Reproductive and Resistant Pedagogies: The Comparative Roles of Collaborative Learning and Feminist Pedagogy in Science Education." *Journal of Research in Science Teaching* 35.4 (1998): 443–59.

Moore, Thomas. *Care of the Soul: A Guide for Cultivating Depth and Sacredness in Everyday Life*. New York: HarperCollins, 1992.

Morgan, Kathryn Pauly. "Describing the Emperor's New Clothes: Three Myths of Educational (In-)Equity." *The Gender Question in Education*. Eds. Barbara Houston, Kathryn Pauly Morgan, and Maryann Ayim. Boulder: Westview Press, 1996.

Ng, Roxana. "Sexism and Racism in the University: Analyzing a Personal Experience." *Canadian Woman Studies Journal* 14.2 (1994): 41–46.

_____. "'A Woman Out of Control': Deconstructing Sexism and Racism in the University." *Canadian Journal of Education* 8.3 (1993): 189–205.

Paget, Marianne A. "Life Mirrors Work Mirrors Text Mirrors Life . . . " *Social Problems* 37.2 (1990): 137–48.

Reid-Walsh, Jacqueline, and Elaine Correa. "Equity in the Women's Studies Classroom: The Politics of Voicing Difference." *Canadian Woman Studies* 17.4 (1998): 76–79.

Ruth, Sheila. "Methodocracy, Misogyny, and Bad Faith: The Response of Philosophy." *Mens' Studies Modified*. Ed. Dale Spender. Toronto: Pergamon Press, 1981. 43–53.

Shilling, Chris. *The Body and Social Theory*. London: Sage, 1993.

Smith, Dorothy E. *The Everyday World as Problematic: A Feminist Sociology*. Toronto: University of Toronto Press, 1987.

Stacey, Margaret. *The Sociology of Health and Healing*. London: Unwin Hyman, 1988.

Terry, Robert W. "The Negative Impact on White Values." *Impacts of Racism on White Americans*. Eds. Benjamin P. Bowser and Raymond G. Hunt. Beverly Hills, CA: Sage, 1981. 119–52.

Transken, Si. *Reclaiming Body Territory*. Feminist Perspectives Series, no. 25. Ottawa: CRIAW/ICREF, 1995.

Weil, Andrew. *Health and Healing*. Boston: Houghton Mifflin, 1995.

Wendell, Susan. "Feminism, Disability and Transcendence of the Body." *Canadian Woman Studies* 13.4 (1993): 116–22.

14

SOPHIA AND SOPHISTRY
Gender and Western Civilization

Prudence Ann Moylan

INTRODUCTION

The feminist scholar teacher's challenge to bring new research and practice to the attention of students has been particularly difficult in traditional required courses. This chapter demonstrates how one historian engaged students in the conversation among scholars about history as a study of separate spheres for men and women or a single sphere of human creativity in which gender signifies relations of power. Gender analysis provided the means to challenge the master narrative of western civilization. As Joan Wallach Scott stated in her well-known essay on gender as a useful category of analysis, "The point of the new historical investigation is to disrupt the notion of fixity, to discover the nature of the debate or repression that leads to the appearances of timeless permanence in binary gender representation" (43). Western civilization courses have become a touchstone of controversy for a political debate between a Eurocentric or a multicultural approach to history but this discussion rarely includes gender. Scott wrote on gender precisely because the excellent work of women's history was still marginalized and segregated within the discipline. The challenge I set for myself was to create a two-semester sequence of western civilization courses that used gender as a central category of analysis and that used feminist principles in the teaching and learning processes.

This chapter addresses both the theoretical and practical challenges of innovation in a core, required course in history that is based on a widely accepted canon of scholarship reproduced in multiple versions of standard textbooks. Topics covered include descriptions of the institutional context identifying the traditional academic structures and values that needed challenge as well as the institutional and disciplinary barriers circumvented. A step-by-step account of how the courses took shape includes defining central questions, selecting course materials, developing pedagogical strategies, and assessing both student work and the course design.

The traditional textbook portrayed the development of civilization in the West as a series of wars of conquest followed by periods of peace enforced by military power. Victory in war was seen as virtue and as essential to the achievements of civilization, especially the creation of political institutions. This presentation ignored the contributions of women to the development of civilization and ignored the cost of war in terms of the disruption and destruction of economic life, family life, and cultural resources. It was my view that as long as historians repeated this grand narrative without criticism they contributed to the contemporary reproduction of inequality among women and men and across cultures. How would a feminist perspective change the traditional narrative and which feminist perspective would be most useful?

In 1991, Gerda Lerner's *The Majority Finds Its Past* significantly influenced my thinking. Lerner summarized stages of the treatment of women in the field of history—from adding women, to critiquing traditional narratives, to developing new theories and methods, to achieving a new universal history that includes women's and men's contributions (145–59). Most textbooks only addressed gender by adding women, usually in sections dealing with family, without critique of the traditional narrative structure. The historical work critiquing the standard narrative was often perceived by students, even in women's studies classes, as excessively negative; this led them to defend against criticism what they had been taught as true. The new theories and methods of women's and gender history were difficult to incorporate into an introductory course and the new universal history seemed barely a glimmer of light on a distant horizon. Nevertheless, using Lerner's schema I was determined to design a course that not only added information on women but also critiqued current assumptions and introduced new approaches to historical analysis and interpretation.

Another schema in Birgit Brock-Utne's *Feminist Perspectives on Peace and Peace Education* distinguished among liberal, radical, and socialist feminisms (16–38). The radical feminist critique of patriarchy seemed central to an effective challenge of the master narrative of western civilization. Liberal feminism focused on the legal status of women and socialist feminism on women's work and economic status. I valued all three perspectives for their contributions to scholarship in women's and gender history. Nevertheless, the questions raised by radical femininists about the origins and reproduction of women's subordination as well as radical feminist interest in women's culture offered me the most useful strategies for transforming a course sequence on western civilization. The influence of these two feminist schemata will be demonstrated more fully in the sections of this essay dealing with selecting course materials and developing pedagogical strategies.

The western civilization challenge, as I named this endeavor, came late in my career. As a faculty member, from 1975 to 1991, at Mundelein College, a Catholic liberal arts college for women with an innovative weekend college program, I did not teach western civilization. When, in 1991, as a way of solving financial problems, Mundelein affiliated with Loyola University Chicago, I became a professor at a university with a core curriculum requirement in western civilization. Fortunately for me the College of Arts and Sciences at Loyola had a grant program to support innovation in the core curriculum. I applied for and received a Mellon grant that provided a one-course reduction in my teaching load in order to do research on gender and western civilization during the spring semester 1992. In my grant proposal I included a plan to hold conversations in fall 1992 with Loyola history faculty in order to share my ideas and learn from my colleagues. These conversations actually served to define some of the traditional academic structures and values my project would challenge. The first conversation with five graduate students and one faculty member raised many questions. The participants, all teaching western civilization, experienced some dissatisfaction with the current practice in teaching the course but no one really supported my effort to introduce gender balance. Changes in the direction of world history, multicultural perspectives, or science and ecology had more appeal. The most positive response was a mild interest in knowing the results of my experience. One of the strongest reasons participants gave for not including gender in their courses was that they had no knowledge of women's history. I learned a great deal from this conversation about the context for teaching western civilization at Loyola. The practice of giving each teacher autonomy in the design of her or his section of the course was valued. Young historians, new to teaching, were primarily concerned with presenting content not with teaching and learning processes. Students were perceived as empty vessels needing to be filled with information before they were able to participate in discussion. This was a dramatic confirmation of the fact that my project was a new approach. It made me decide to design a course that addressed all the traditional dimensions of the survey in new ways in order to maintain the possibility of influencing the teaching in other sections of the survey.

The second conversation on this project involved only two senior faculty members. Both were interested in my approach and raised practical questions. This conversation was helpful to me but what was perhaps most notable about the session was that only two of about fifty faculty and graduate students showed an interest in new approaches and/or gender issues and the history core curriculum. I learned the difficulty of starting a conversation on gender and teaching. I was also determined to look at ways to increase the awareness of gender issues and women's history in the graduate program so that graduate students in the future would feel competent to address these issues in teaching. Through the efforts of feminists in the department, by 1995 the history department had formalized a minor field of study in women's and gender history for both master's and Ph.D. students. History was the first department at Loyola to formalize the study of women and gender at the graduate level.

Administrators offered me more support than faculty. As I have noted, the College of Arts and Sciences approved my request for a one-course reduction in spring 1992 through a Mellon grant for core curriculum development. The history department chairperson supported this project by providing me with the help of a graduate student research/teaching assistant, John Sagone, in spring 1992 and 1993. His interest and commitment to the project grew into a real faculty-student partnership. I was especially grateful for this partnership because my original hope, as a feminist, to build a community of colleagues who would share in the design and implementation of a new approach to western civilization was effectively destroyed by my experience of the initial conversations with my colleagues. John told me that the project increased his interest in teaching and gave him more confidence to try innovative approaches. I concluded that history graduate students needed study and practice in teaching and in research as preparation for careers.

At Loyola most teaching assistants sit in on lectures, grade papers, and occasionally give a guest lecture. They do not teach courses or facilitate discussion sections. A program for teaching fellowships did provide a few students with teaching experience but this coincided with the year they began research on a doctoral dissertation. John and I made some progress in overcoming the general exclusion of graduate students from teaching in that we discussed the design of the course and he facilitated some class discussions as well as shared the marking of student reports. By 1996 I was sharing equally the planning and implementing of classroom learning activities and assessment with a teaching assistant but I still had sole responsibility for the course design, selection of materials, and design of course assignments. (Since teaching assistants were not assigned until the week classes began it was difficult to engage them in the design of the courses.) Writing this chapter has provided me with new insight and incentive to find ways to circumvent the disciplinary and institutional barriers to team teaching with graduate students.

Let me now return to the story of designing the first course in the western civilization sequence, HIS 101, the Evolution of Western Ideas and Experience to the Seventeenth Century. The feminist schema I discussed earlier influenced the organization of the course calendar, the choice of texts for the course, the design of individual learning projects, the design of small-group learning activities for class sessions, and the development of feedback and assessment processes for both learning and teaching.

DESIGNING AND IMPLEMENTING THE COURSES

Bibliographical research in women's and gender history was the first step in seeking material for the courses. The pleasure of exploring the rich literature on women in the western tradition was one of the benefits of this project. From interpretations of prehistoric cave paintings and goddess figures as evidence of a prepatriarchal perspective on the world, to studies of the diversity of women's status in the ancient mediterranean and the classical worlds, to depictions of the medieval peasant and the lady of chivalric legend, the vitality of women in history leaped off the pages. Joan Kelly's classic question, "Did women have a Renaissance?" opened a new critical perspective which could be applied to the study of the Scientific Revolution and the Enlightenment as well. In the modern period, women claimed their natural human rights as citizens, workers, and parents from the outset, but their claims were rarely recognized before the twentieth century. The information about women and the reinterpretation of historical patterns in light of women's experience not only allowed but also inspired the task of reframing western civilization. Despite the wealth of new scholarship I found only one essay, by Abby Wetan Kleinbaum, on integrating women into a western civilization course.

The next problem, of course, was how to introduce beginning students to this rich literature. What authors or topics were representative? What methodologies and documents provided a "truth" claim appropriate to students of the late-twentieth-century United States? Even a survey text dealing with women, *A History of Their Own*, by Bonnie Anderson and Judith Zinsser assumed some familiarity with the traditional western civilization narrative.

The solution to this problem in a traditional course structure would be the preparation of elegant lectures that combined the latest scholarship with traditional interpretations. This would be a daunting task for a historian even in her specialization but no historian claims western civilization as a specialty field. The absence of a professional hierarchy in this subject creates a disciplinary barrier to change rather than an opportunity. Innovation and excellence in teaching western civilization provide no path for advancement in the profession. As a full professor this was not a major problem for me; rather it was motivation for using my senior status to foster change.

Fortunately my knowledge of feminist pedagogy opened a way to circumvent this barrier. Rather than assuming it was my responsibility to create a new framework for western civilization I thought about how I could engage the students in such an enterprise. How could I design a course that would lead the students to ask the questions of the tradition that I had learned to ask and also teach them some methods for finding answers? Immediately, the necessity of covering all the scholarship was eliminated. Students needed to be introduced to the issues and taught how to explore the issues and the evidence. They did not need a premature synthesis. The goals of the core curriculum directed me "to assist [. . .] students: to be aware of their role in history and in the present condition of human society; to develop knowledge of and an active concern for the human community [. . .]" (Loyola University 26). Exploring the historical construction and maintenance of gender relations clearly would provide an important understanding of how history shaped contemporary life.

The solution to the problem of how to introduce students to the issues was to have them read two contrasting texts. Whose story was told and who told the story thus became central questions. The students were being introduced to a contemporary scholarly method, deconstruction of texts, as an aspect of critical reading.

SELECTING TEXTS

The first texts chosen were *A History of Their Own*, Vol. 1, by Bonnie Anderson and Judith Zinsser and *A Brief History of Western Civilization* by Thomas H. Greer. I chose this brief standard survey text to address common student complaints about too much reading. Women were almost totally omitted from the Greer text. This presented a problem I had not anticipated. The students had great difficulty "seeing" the omission of women. For students the Anderson/Zinsser text became the alternative or optional history compared to the "real" history in the Greer text. In subsequent years I used different western civilization texts by John McKay and others, by Lynn Hunt and others, and by Donald Kagan and others. These texts presented more fully developed considerations of social history including women and family as well as class distinctions, which enabled students to compare texts. The Anderson/Zinsser text was still considered a supplement rather than an equal text but the richness of information provided on women allowed students to question why women's participation in civilization was so briefly mentioned in the traditional text. The glossy production of new western civilization texts which include illustrations, documents, maps, and student study guides made a more dramatic impact on students regardless of the information presented. The very imperfection of the solution of comparing texts served to open up questions about historical interpretation and selectivity. Anderson and Zinsser organized their interpretation by distinguishing between urban and rural life, and between the Church and the nobility as institutions. They use broad chronological frameworks to show the continuity in people's lives. Standardized western civilization texts emphasized change and use normed chronological divisions for ancient, medieval, and modern history. In making comparisons students had to ask how historians developed chronological periods. Why did historians use political events and persons to define time periods for study?

Anderson and Zinsser clearly developed themes of patriarchy and misogyny in the western tradition but the massive amount of information they provided about women's work made it clear that women were contributors to civilization not victims. A few students preferred the Anderson/Zinsser book because it was not written in textbook language and because they liked reading about women. I was also aware in first choosing the Anderson/Zinsser book that it was as thick as the standard text and equal size was a consideration in representing equality to students. This material consideration was another reason for choosing not to develop a course pack of essays on women's history. Despite the excellence of selected readings, the fact that the collection did not have the status of a book would support the impression that women's history was diffuse and scattered, not an organized body of knowledge with formal recognition in book form. The fact that course packs were made up of published material was not immediately apparent to students in introductory courses. Course packs were also more likely to be seen as biased because created by the instructor to reflect a point of view rather than to give "both sides" of an issue.

COURSE ORGANIZATION

The choice of texts had a major effect on the course organization and calendar because reading assignments had to be distributed across a fifteen-week semester. Covering five thousand years of history necessitated a bird's eye view of the past. Students always have complained about the futility of learning the massive amount of information used in telling the story of the past. Often they have not developed analytical reading skills and so have a hard time selecting information even from carefully segmented textbooks. I decided to organize this imposing survey of the past around six themes which would be studied in six different time frames. Students studied only one theme in each time frame but they studied each theme at some point in the semester. Ideally students would learn to read more analytically by selecting information related to their theme. As they moved from one theme to the next every two weeks following the chronological framework I hoped they would build a sense of the interrelatedness of perspectives on historical interpretation. For example, if they had studied the theme of the natural environment and then the theme of the built environment, the link between resources and economic choices would be clearer. The organization of the course around six themes and six time frames produced several benefits. It provided a clear frame of reference for students. Movement across time and culture became a personal experience as students changed their theme of study.

A change in perspective every two weeks stimulated new interest and made everyone take a turn at the popular and the unpopular themes. The state, or politics, was probably the least interesting theme for students although it was the major theme in textbook coverage. The natural environment interested students but the texts provided the least information on this theme. Religion (the human and the divine), art and ideas, the built environment, and women and men were generally popular themes.

The texts were not organized around course themes, and coverage of each theme varied in different times and cultures. This difficulty provoked discussions on evidence and interpretation. Gender was not the only topic on which information was inadequate or hard to interpret, which helped students who were resistant to a feminist critique acknowledge its validity.

The structure of six themes by six time frames allowed for a two-week-per-theme semester plan, which provided the flexibility of a week for introductions and a week for summations. Week eight in the semester was a break from classes, and week sixteen was final exam week so classes actually met for fourteen weeks. This tight but slightly flexible calendar encouraged both teachers and students to stay focused on key ideas. At Loyola the course outline has become a contract as well as a plan for study since students have been identified as consumers/customers and have resorted to legal means to challenge grades. In this course, however, providing students with a detailed plan for the semester became part of the process of creating a feminist classroom climate of mutual respect. Students perceived the careful planning of the course as a measure of respect for their time and effort. Frequent assessment of the process (which will be explained later) also provided students with the opportunity to suggest changes or request explanations for why work was required. Following a well-designed plan was especially important for me when developing this new approach because I had a tendency to doubt the process and try to make changes whenever something didn't work as planned. Having shared the plan with the students I became part of the learning community and learned to make changes only after consultation with students.

After the first use of the six themes I made some revisions. The theme originally called "the built environment" was renamed "work." The concept of work had familiarity for students and expanded their ability to analyze human ingenuity and achievement. I changed the theme "women and men" to "family" since the texts dealt with gender relations primarily in the framework of family life. This proved a benefit because I had to rethink the place of gender analysis in the course. As a result I added the requirement that in each theme report students comment on how the experiences of women and men were similar or different. The original plan with a separate theme for gender only replicated the practice of isolating women's and gender history rather than seeing the gendered aspects of all facets of the historical narrative. One fascinating result of the change was that students noticed the historical discussion of families dealt almost exclusively with women; men were generally absent. It would be hard to find a better example of how historians have reflected and helped to reproduce societal assumptions of separate spheres for women and men. Perhaps as a consequence of this shift in the way gender analysis was developed in the course a small, but increasing number of young men chose a theme long popular with women and wrote their final essays on the need for changes in family life.

SMALL-GROUP PROCESS

The organization of the course facilitated the development of small-group process in class sessions. Requiring that each student voice a historical perspective seemed to me a basic element of feminist pedagogy. A group of five to eight students worked on a theme together. This student working group stayed the same for the semester but the theme studied changed every two weeks. Establishing permanent student work groups affirmed the relational aspects of learning in tangible ways. Students had a sense of permanence in working with the same people at every class. They got to know one another well enough to both accept and challenge individual eccentricities. Some groups interacted more constructively than others but this provided realistic learning situations. From previous teaching experience I knew that successful group work especially with eighteen or nineteen year olds required well-defined tasks. Each student brought an individual report to the first group discussion. The group then compiled a report designating the most important ideas on their theme in the time period. Individual reports and the group summary were turned in for evaluation. A second discussion group was made up of representatives from each theme group. In this group each member reported on a theme and listened to reports on the other themes. At the end of the discussion each student filled out a report form stating one idea they had learned about each theme. These forms were turned in at the end of the class. The use of two different group experiences gave students a chance to meet more of their classmates but it also caused some confusion. The course evaluation indicated that students liked group work but they wanted more evaluation from the teachers on the validity of their ideas. I was satisfied in reviewing student reports that they were in fact recognizing central ideas and issues, but they needed clearer affirmation of their understandings.

This was a salutary challenge. How could I provide more support for their work while maintaining the structure of student discussion as the primary learning strategy? The first effort to achieve this was to use a classroom activity called Take a Stand. The important ideas reported by the student discussion groups were written down as debatable statements. Half of the students were asked to take a stand on an issue by walking to the front of the room and standing at their chosen point on a continuum of numbers from 1, representing strong disagreement, to 10, representing strong agreement, written on the chalkboard at the front of the room. The other half of the students could ask for explanations from anyone on why he or she took a position but no arguments were allowed, only explanations. After the questions were asked and the students returned to their seats, the teacher summarized the way evidence could be used in the interpretation of debatable issues and why there could be more than one right answer in history. Another issue would be presented and the students would switch positions on taking a stand or asking questions. Although time never allowed us to consider every issue, the use of this technique gave students a clearer sense of how to deal with diversity of opinion, how to explain their own views with evidence, and how to evaluate the evidence used in opposing positions. Students reported that having to Take a Stand forced them to think about their views even when no one asked them for an explanation. Doing the exercise with a large group removed some of the fear of taking a position, especially for young women. The rules against debate or argument also provided a way to express personal views without fear of attack. Using the issues raised by students as a starting point, the teacher clarified and elaborated controversial issues and demonstrated how different interpretations could be based on the same evidence.

The summary report discussion groups were rated as less successful than the permanent working groups on theme study. In later versions of the course, rather than make individuals the representatives of their group's theme, the working group stayed together and planned a presentation on their theme for the class. The class members did evaluations of each group's presentation. This format created a public accountability for communicating major ideas and demanded some creativity from students to develop engaging performances. Adding performance and peer feedback to the western civilization classroom drew on many more aspects of intelligence than the traditional testing of knowledge. Reading and writing received emphasis as foundational skills in student presentations but were expanded in diverse forms of presentation including the quiz show, video mystery dramas, and news programs featuring weather reports on the Roman Empire sponsored by Roman cereals. The performance requirement fostered small-group learning skills. This task honored women's preference for relational learning strategies and collaborative projects, as reported in *Women's Ways of Knowing*, and provided men with a new or less familiar learning opportunity. The radical feminist commitment to recognizing women's cultural practices as equal to men's rather than the liberal feminist acceptance of men's experience as normative was my guide here. Students learned to organize their ideas for presentation, to explore their varied talents, to divide the labor among group members, and to complete the task within specified time requirements. At least some aspects of the work turned out to be fun—a truly revolutionary experience.

This change to group performance eliminated the reporting of statements on key ideas from each theme which had been the basis of Take a Stand. Performances were generally most effective in helping the working-group members to develop their understanding of the theme through the steps of reading, reporting, synthesizing, presenting, and getting evaluations. However, the audience of class members did not always grasp the main ideas and presentations rarely addressed the issue of diverse interpretations.

A new way to provide faculty guidance for student interpretations was needed. The solution was to provide debatable discussion questions for each of the working groups and ask them to develop contrasting interpretations within their group. The entire class was then divided into groups either for or against the debatable issue. One working group would start the class discussion by presenting their contrasting interpretations. Each side in the debate would then seek additional support from other students who had taken the same position in their own working groups. After all the interpretations had been stated the teacher explored the issues raised, the effective use of evidence, and the common assumptions shared by the conflicting positions. Students found debate and controversy stimulating but I found it even more satisfying to move them from polarized views on an issue to an exploration of common ground.

Feminist pedagogy in these western civilization courses has centered on fostering collaboration in small groups. Reading *Women's Ways of Knowing* clarified for me the importance of relationships in student learning and provided some suggestions for pedagogical practice. The importance of this approach has been reaffirmed by Deborah Tannen in her recent book *The Argument Culture*. She has challenged the growth of the "argument culture" and made the case for learning to talk to each other rather than argue. I found two books, *Collaborative Learning: A Sourcebook for Higher Education* and *Cooperative Learning: Increasing College Faculty Instructional Productivity*, helpful in planning small-group processes to foster thoughtful conversation. Reading newsletters and journals on cooperative learning and feminist pedagogy has become a welcome feature of my professional life.

INDEPENDENT STUDY PROJECTS

The original version of the course required students to complete three "further study projects" as well as the reading and writing of reports on themes. I provided thirteen study project options based on the six themes. Students could define their own projects with my approval; a few did this. Everyone was required to use a computerized map exercise which meant that each student had two elective projects. These projects aimed at getting students to see how the traditions of western civilization were present in the contemporary world. A project could be a photoessay on classical architecture in Chicago buildings or an essay comparing the information from *The New Jerome Biblical Commentary* and *The Women's Biblical Commentary* on the creation story in Genesis. In later versions of the course the computer map program was dropped because of technical problems. Emphasis on group work and students presentations led me to shift away from individual projects. Students in 1996 were required to do one independent study project. Suggestions for visits to Chicago cultural institutions or for campus events were provided. I encouraged students to do their project with a friend or a group even though each person wrote an individual report on the experience. This requirement now coincided with the goals of the freshmen experience program in the College of Arts and Sciences to acquaint students with city and campus resources. Faculty who teach first-year students were encouraged to include connections with the larger university and urban environment in their courses.

ASSESSMENT OF STUDENT WORK

When I originally designed the course I was worried about how to assess student work in groups. The requirement of individual reports on each theme in each chronological period meant that I received six short papers from each student. The three learning-project reports and the final essay made a total of ten items of written work as a basis for the course grade. The later versions of the course required six individual theme reports, one project, and one final essay as well as six performance ratings based on peer assessment. The course outline specified strict attendance require-ments. Three absences were allowed with no penalty but a fourth absence resulted in a cumulative assessment of penalty points lost for absence. At-tendance was the most tangible measure of participation though engage-ment in group discussion and presentation were specified as well. Poor attendance was often a predictor of poor performance on other learning tasks. Students who missed four or more classes were not likely to earn A grades. Since grades were crucial to students they were motivated to par-ticipate. The fact that their grade was primarily a result of their own choices eliminated much of the fear of grades and frustration that grades were arbitrarily determined by the professor. Assessment based on fre-quent, short papers allowed students to focus on the task and to improve their performance. Most students accustomed to the adrenalin rush of cramming for exams or "pulling all-nighters" for a paper found this slow, steady approach to learning a surprising change of pace which in the end they appreciated. One problem that I noticed was that the likelihood of ab-sences or late papers increased at midterms and in the last two weeks of the semester when exams and papers were due in other courses. The change of pace in my course allowed me to opt out of the unspoken compe-tition for time and attention with other instructors and courses. Students have had more control over planning their learning sequences when all their work was not demanded at one time.

I debated about whether or not to have a final exam in this course. Originally I included it because I thought first-year students needed to learn by experience the significance of exam week and I did not want a feminist course to be designated "easy" because no final was required. Over the years I have learned that the final essay was important for giving closure to the learning experience. From the outset the students were asked to consider the legacy of western civilization in light of their experience and the final essay asked them to discuss what they would preserve and what they would discard from their legacy. All essays were due at the scheduled exam period. Most students wrote essays in advance and brought them to me at the exam period but a few chose to use the exam period to write the essay. In either case the last meeting gave a positive sense of closure to the work of the semester. This use of the final exam also coincided perfectly with the core curriculum goal for historical study stated in the Loyola Undergraduate Catalog that students "become aware of their role in history and in the present condition of the human community" (26).

GRADES

Student grades were based 50% on participation and 50% on written reports. This combination signified the seriousness of participation and answered frequent student complaints that participation was not clearly defined. Here it was clear they were expected to come to class and coming to class would count in their grade. I simplified the calculation for myself by using a maximum of 100 points for attendance and 100 points for written assignments. I also thought students would be more likely to accept intuitively a marking system of 100 points rather than one of 50 points. There were twenty-eight class meetings so attendance at each class was worth 3.5 points. When a student missed four classes the points lost would be calculated at $3.5 \times 4 = 14$. Since attendance was half the final grade the number of points lost toward the final grade would be seven. Each of ten written assignments was worth ten points of the 100 points possible. If a student received an 8 on each paper, she would have lost a total of 20 points. Since written work was half the grade, a student would lose 10 points off the final grade. At the beginning of the each semester, we discussed what emphasis would be used for marking written reports. Students generally preferred to have 60% of their grade based on content and 40% based on grammar. We agreed that essays must contain three examples of the main idea for adequate content and must have a clear paragraph structure and correct sentences. Since requirements for written reports were precisely defined and the scoring of content and grammatical elements was discussed and agreed upon by students and teacher, the mystery of grading was uncovered. Most students found it possible to meet the standard established for written reports so they received high marks and were motivated to maintain their marks. As a teacher I preferred intrinsic motivation for learning but in a core, required course I was realistic and satisfied with this arrangement. Grades mattered to both students and administrators and I worked to establish clear assessment procedures as a support for learning rather than an obstacle to learning. The shared information and authority over grades was essential to developing a collaborative learning environment. Faculty authority in the classroom had to be based on a different foundation than the power to "give" grades. Sharing the power of deciding grades with students may have been the most dramatic revision of power relations in the classroom. I found reconceptualizing power as energy rather than control generated vitality in the learning process.

ASSESSMENT OF THE COURSE DESIGN

Another aspect of the collaborative classroom was the regular assessment of the course design, classroom activities, and teacher's performance. In the first course the midterm assessment required students to grade their own performance and to rate the learning activities of the course on the basis of their effectiveness in promoting learning. I reported the results of the course evaluation and we agreed to make some changes for improvement. Students requested more faculty direction and affirmation of their interpretations. This motivated the development of Take a Stand as a classroom exercise. Students also wanted to drop a requirement that they write feedback cards for each member of their working-group noting a strength and giving a suggestion for improvement. They felt writing the cards was too artificial and they could provide feedback in conversation. I agreed to drop this requirement but continued my search for effective methods of peer assessment in the course.

In later versions of the course the working-group members read and commented on one another's papers. This process allowed students having difficulty with written reports to see excellent work done by their peers. The skilled students were able to recognize their skill in comparison with peers but were also encouraged to see that in sharing their skill with others they did not lose it. The best students enjoyed recognition and the challenge of helping others. For me this practice resolved the problem of how to use examples of student work to demonstrate effectiveness. Rather than using a single student paper for the whole class, now every student read five or six responses to the same assignment. The requirement to comment on each paper helped students focus on how the papers differed rather than simply noting a repetition of information. This activity proved an egalitarian and inclusive method of peer review that students accepted as useful rather than artificial.

The course evaluations were also changed to be shorter and more frequent. Based on Stephen Brookfield's technique entitled critical learning incidents (CLI), every few weeks I asked students to answer six questions about their experience of the course. What surprised them? What troubled them? What worked best for them? What was a problem for them? What could they do to solve the problem? What could I do to solve the problem? These questions addressed their emotional responses as an integral part of their learning and required that they distinguish between their personal responsibility for learning and the ways in which changes in the course itself would help them. I always reported the results to the class, including the occasional very negative comments. This provided critical students with a knowledge that they were in the minority as well as identifying problems widely shared among the students. Too much reading came up as a common problem in my first use of this process. As a class we negotiated possible changes. I was not willing to reduce the reading requirement but I was willing to accept a student suggestion that they divide up the weekly reading and report summaries to one another. As a result the most dedicated students continued to read the entire assignment and the least dedicated dutifully read their section, reported on it, and listened to reports on the rest of the reading. Given the fact that students commonly report that in lecture courses evaluated by examination they choose to read or to attend class but usually not both, my agreement to this compromise on reading seemed realistic. I was surprised at how seriously the students took their responsibility to report to one another. They would insist on having time to finish their summaries before moving on to other tasks. I learned from the CLIs that students found even my short lectures too abstract and wanted some visual examples to help them follow my argument. Paradoxically, I found that the more successful I became at devising effective group processes the less willing the students were to allow me time to give my views even in a short-lecture format. Feminist pedagogy required that I redefine how I measured success as a teacher. The more independently students learned, the greater my success. The occasional student comment that "the teacher didn't do anything" I could take as a compliment. Student evaluations have consistently rated the course as very good to excellent on all criteria. Written comments indicated that students learned to think and observe more carefully, and they shared with me the credit for helping them learn.

I was fortunate to be able to present a report on this course in April 1993 at a national conference, the Inclusive Curriculum: Setting Our Own Agenda, sponsored by the New Jersey Project: Integrating the Scholarship on Gender. The creativity of course designs from faculty in all areas and disciplines was inspiring. My report was well received but questions about how I dealt with ethnicity, race, and social class as well as gender came up. The texts have included social history so issues of social class were addressed but very little was said about ethnicity and race. I have added some more discussion of the diversity of peoples in the Mediterranean and the importance of cultural exchange between Africa and Greece and Rome, but I am still working on how to address ethnicity and race in the introductory western civilization survey. The questions, however, inspired me in the creation of the second half on the survey Modern Western Civilization: The Social Sciences in Context.

MODERN WESTERN CIVILIZATION

Students at Loyola must take a two-semester western civilization sequence to fulfill their core curriculum requirements in history. The history department developed six variations for the second course in the sequence. Students may choose to continue with a general political survey or they may choose sections that emphasize the humanities, the social sciences, the natural sciences, the west in the world, or American pluralism respectively. I was asked to develop the second semester of the survey, modern western civilization since the seventeenth century, as a section emphasizing the social sciences. Once again I applied for and received support from the Mellon grant fund for curriculum development, this time as a summer grant, rather than a course reduction. My experience with the introductory course set me thinking about how to address the diversity of ethnicity, race, and social class as well as gender.

ORGANIZING THEMES

Even though the time frame of the second survey was far shorter, only three hundred years, the amount of detail in the story still overwhelmed students so the use of themes seemed a good idea. I asked myself what developments of the modern period had continuing influence in our time. Three themes emerged as having both clear historical roots and contemporary importance. These were nationalism, feminism, and industrial capitalism; all had roots in the eighteenth century and were concepts debated today. I linked these to the historical context for the development of the social science disciplines by connecting nationalism with political science, feminism with sociology and psychology, and capitalism with economics. This course had a tripartite structure.

Historical Theme	Documents	Social Science
Nationalism (ethnicity and race)	Political writings	Political Science
Feminism (gender)	Women's writings	Sociology/Psychology
Capitalism (social class)	Economic proposals	Economics

Each theme was studied in the time frame of 1750 to the present. The course began with nationalism because the theories of John Locke and Jean Jacques Rousseau and the American and French Revolutions provided a familiar starting point. The uses and abuses of nationalist theory and rhetoric throughout the nineteenth and twentieth centuries were traced and the work of the United Nations in the ongoing search for effective political institutions made a fitting conclusion to this segment. The transition to feminism was accomplished by returning to the American and French Revolutions and considering the founding declarations. The Declaration of the Rights of Man and Citizen was compared with Olympe de Gouges's Declaration of the Rights of Woman and Citizen; the Declaration of Independence was compared with the Declaration of Sentiments signed at the first Women's Rights Convention held at Seneca Falls, New York, in 1848. Documents showing women's struggle for political and economic equality, for control over their sexuality, and for parental rights revealed to students the fact that the struggle for equality of women and men began long before the 1960s. The transition to capitalism began by returning to the contrasting views of Adam Smith and Karl Marx on the sources of the wealth of nations. Justifications for economic theory and practice from the standpoints of owners and workers as well as government reports on the economic health of nations and individuals provided the information base for discussions of contemporary economic policies and issues.

In the first version of the course I asked students to choose a historical woman or man as a guide to the period in order to personalize the meaning of the course. Students read a biography of one person and wrote a book review that addressed how this historical person understood his or her ethnicity or race, gender, and social class. I provided a list of suggested persons as guides but allowed students to make an independent choice if they wished. The final essay in this course required students to reflect on what insights they had gained about the formation of their own sense of ethnicity, race, gender, and class identity. The first time I taught the course I worried that asking students to write identity essays would be seen as a challenge to their privacy. The students reported that they preferred to reflect on their own experience, rather than on a historical person. In later versions of the course each thematic segment concluded with the students writing an identity essay on that theme.

The task of "theorizing experience," as bell hooks names it in *Talking Back*, proved difficult for students (109–11). I provided guidelines for writing but these were not an adequate model so I began to think about how to add some examples of this kind of writing. I came across Caryl Phillips's *The European Tribe*, which provided the ideal example I was seeking for the course. Phillips uses his tour of European cities as a young man who has just graduated from Oxford to explore his experience of racism in Europe. This text worked on many levels: the students connect with a young man's travels; reflections on ethnicity and race in a European context provide a useful parallel to American experience; an excellent writer shows students how to theorize experience. *Talking Back* also provided a model for students that addressed issues of feminism and gender with ethnicity, race, and class. Although hooks theorizes her experience in the context of the United States, by this point in the semester the students clearly see the United States as part of western civilization. Both Phillips and hooks reflect on their culture from a young and black perspective that provided a welcome alternative to the predominantly middle-class, white perspective of students and teacher in the course.

Students discussed these essays in their small groups and shared their own essays with members of their group. The emphasis in the course on analysis of documents with conflicting perspectives created a climate in which exploring different viewpoints rather than seeking a single correct view became normative. This allowed students to accept and even value the variety of perspectives expressed by their group members. Although I believed in presenting contrasting viewpoints in course readings I found that the most effective appreciation of multiculturalism came from giving students the opportunity to share their diverse views with one another. After teaching this course several times I would now characterize it as western civilization with a human rights perspective that moved from initial claims and declarations of rights to the international human rights commitments as formally expressed in United Nations declarations. Perspectives with western roots have become the basis of international policies and actions.

DOCUMENT ANALYSIS

Unlike the first course in the western civilization sequence, which emphasized interpretive synthesis, the second course emphasized developing analytical skill through document analysis. All the texts for the course provide historical documents as well as historical interpretations of the themes. I relied on Hans Kohn and Dennis Sherman for documents on nationalism. Katarina Tomasevski and Dennis Sherman provide documents on feminism and Bruno Leone provided the collection of documents on capitalism. Six document analysis reports were required, two for each theme studied in the semester. The course outline included directions for document analysis. The first time I taught the course I divided students into groups and each group analyzed different documents. The group discussed members' individual reports and then presented a report to the class on the key points in their set of documents. Students liked the discussion of documents in groups but found the reports to the class boring. In later versions of the class students were expected to read all the documents but when they came to class I would give one document to each group for analysis. The group would write their answers to the seven analysis questions on newsprint, which would be posted when all the groups finished the task. I would review the four or five newsprint analyses, pointing out what made a good report and what had been omitted. I also reviewed the similarities and contrasts among the documents studied. My review replaced the student reports but engaged students in comparing the ideas they had been analyzing separately. This made a natural use of my expertise while affirming the initial work of the students.

Guidelines listing seven questions to be asked of every historical document were distributed with the course outline. Students answered the questions first in their group analysis of documents during class. After several weeks of experience, each student completed an individual document analysis of a document assigned to their group. Students read and commented on one another's analysis just as they had done with individual reports in the introductory course.

ASSESSMENT AND GRADES

The attendance policy and the assessment procedures were similar to the ones discussed earlier in relation to the first course in the sequence. Student grades were based about half on participation and half on individual written work. The Modern Western Civilization course required frequent critical learning assessments of the course and a midterm self-assessment of each student. Problems in this course focused primarily on the equality of participation in the groups. I reported the very strong positive affirmation of group work and then specified the criticisms. One student suggested having group members score one another on participation occasionally as part of the grade. I haven't tried this yet but it certainly could be included as a form of peer assessment. I found that specifically naming the behaviors that contribute to effectiveness in a group and encouraging students to do their part worked well. Over the course of the semester students got to know one another so this helped to improve group interaction. A guide to roles for group members in cooperative learning derived from David Johnson's *Cooperative Learning: Increasing College Faculty Instructional Productivity* was included in the course outline and when groups were formed students were asked to distribute the roles. I suggested that group members rotate roles periodically. The list of roles was both a useful reference and reminder of how groups work and a source of good humored banter among students.

Although I have had success in using small groups by defining individual and group responsibility and making group work a regular aspect of classroom sessions, it remains an area I want to improve. I would like to develop better strategies for affirming and developing student skills in group work and better ways to assess group participation. Nevertheless, for me one of the most enjoyable aspects of teaching with this format has been watching students engage in serious discussion without feeling the necessity to quantify what they are learning.

CLOSURE

Because the students wrote their personal essays in segments through the semester a final essay seemed repetitious and unnecessary. I felt, however, that simply ending the course with the official evaluations did not provide students with a sense of having completed their work. In 1997, I decided to develop a simple closing ritual to affirm our work together. It was a variation of what is often called a string ritual. We began in a circle, first thanking neighbors on either side for their contribution to the course; then we passed jute twine around the circle so that each person held the twine and we tied the two ends together. After a brief reflection on having spent a semester working together we passed a scissors around the circle and cut our connection to symbolize our departure onto separate paths. The students left class smiling and everyone has a piece of jute twine as a reminder of our work together. One young man, an anthropology major, complimented me on making the concluding experience in the course one of pleasure rather than of the pain of an exam. Of course, examinations have a place in academic work but in these core courses I think the joyous and shared affirmation of learning accomplished makes a fitting end.

CONCLUSION

I have found that the theater has provided me with the richest metaphor for teaching. The adage that teachers are frustrated actors has never applied to me but I do think of the repeated class sessions throughout the semester as a series of learning performances. These performances are like a repertory theater company where members take turns playing the various parts and through their understanding and their voices they bring the past to life. Students become the players who find in their own lives the resources to understand how the past shaped their experience. Once they have learned how to find the past in their lives they can choose to develop the traditions they find valuable and discard those they reject. By making feminist pedagogy as well as gender content central to core courses in history I believe I have enriched all students' understanding of the past as the creative achievement of women and men. By showing students that they have the power to decide what traditions to continue or to reject, I have challenged them to shape more egalitarian traditions for their own lives and for the lives of generations to come.

●   ●   ●

WORKS CITED

Anderson, Bonnie, and Judith Zinsser. *A History of Their Own: Women in Europe From Prehistory to the Present*. Vol. I. New York: Harper and Row, 1988.

Belenky, Mary Field, Blythe McVicker Clinchy, Nancy Rule Goldberger, and Jill Mattuck Tarule. *Women's Ways of Knowing: The Development of Self, Voice, and Mind*. New York: Basic Books, 1986.

Brookfield, Stephen. *The Skillful Teacher*. San Francisco: Jossey-Bass, 1990.

Brock-Utne, Birgit. *Feminist Perspectives on Peace and Peace Education*. New York: Pergamon Press, 1989.

Goodsell, Anne, Michelle Mahger, and Vincent Tinto, eds. *Collaborative Learning: A Sourcebook for Higher Education*. National Center on Postsecondary Teaching, Learning & Assessment, Pennsylvania State University, 1992.

Greer, Thomas H., and Gavin Lewis. *A Brief History of the Western World*, 6th ed. New York: Harcourt, Brace, Jovanovich, 1992.

Hunt, Lynn, Thomas R. Martin, Barbara H. Rosenwein, R. Po-chia Hsia, and Bonnie G. Smith. *The Challenge of the West*. Vol. I. Boston: D. C. Heath, 1995.

hooks, bell. *Talking Back: Thinking Feminist, Thinking Black*. Boston: South End Press, 1989

Johnson, David W., Roger T. Johnson, and Karl A. Smith. *Cooperative Learning: Increasing College Faculty Instructional Productivity*. ASHE-ERIC Higher Education Report no. 4, 1991.

Kagan, Donald, Stephen Ozment, and Frank M. Turner. *The Western Heritage*. Brief ed. Vol. 1: To 1715. Upper Saddle River, NJ: Prentice Hall, 1996

Kleinbaum, Abby Wettan. "Women's History and the Western Civilization Survey." *History Teacher* (Aug. 1979).

Kohn, Hans. *Nationalism: Its Meaning and History*. Rev. ed. Malabar, FL: Robert E. Krieger Publishing Company, 1982.

Leone, Bruno, ed. *Capitalism: Opposing Viewpoints*. Rev. ed. St. Paul, MN: Greenhaven Press, 1986.

Lerner, Gerda. *The Majority Finds Its Past: Placing Women in History*. New York: Oxford University Press, 1979

Loyola University Office of Registration. *Undergraduate Studies Catalog 1993–1995*. Chicago: Loyola University, 1993.

McKay, John, Bennet Hill, and John Buckler. *A History of Western Society*. 4th ed. Boston: Houghton Mifflin, 1991.

Phillips, Caryl. *The European Tribe*. Boston: Faber and Faber, 1987.

Scott, Joan Wallach. *Gender and the Politics of History*. New York: Columbia University Press, 1988.

Sherman, Dennis, ed. *Western Civilization: Sources, Images, and Interpretations*. 4th ed. Vol. II: Since 1660. New York: McGraw Hill, 1995.

Tannen, Deborah. *The Argument Culture: Moving From Debate to Diaglogue*. New York: Random House, 1998.

Tomasevski, Katarina. *Women and Human Rights*. Atlantic Highlands, NJ: Zed Books, 1993.

Zophy, Jonathon W. "On Learner-Centered Teaching." *History Teacher* (Feb. 1982).

15

FEMINIST TEACHING IN A LAW FACULTY IN NEW ZEALAND

Wendy Ball

All law professors were at one time students, but women law professors remain women. For them, the personal is the political.
—Carrie Menkel-Meadow

INTRODUCTION

Teaching law using feminist pedagogical theories and practices is a major difficulty for women lawyers and women academics in law faculties because the law is essentially gendered, essentially a male domain. As a feminist educator I am committed to transformative and practically based education that challenges the oppressive power relationships embedded in social institutions, such as the law. In undertaking such challenges, feminist legal academics are confronting the conservative nature of the law, which embodies race, gender, and class oppression. The challenge is to open students' eyes to these oppressions in the hope that they will develop a more inclusive and less biased approach to their practice of the law.

Traditional legal education has been described by a feminist critic as intentionally hierarchical:

First, the law school classroom is marked by a disparity of power (a "hierarchy") between teacher and students. The law professor uses ineffective and even needless mystifying educational techniques that, when combined with the professor's gratuitous aggression and didactic assaultiveness, produce an oppressive atmosphere. Second, the oppression and mystification in the classroom are not random, but are aimed at influencing or coercing students to accept their place in the real-world hierarchy and at teaching proper hierarchical behaviour. (Hantzis 157)

Feminist teaching comes from the other end of the pedagogical spectrum and deals with legal education in a more equal and interactive way:

> Feminist teaching methods and content have a totally different purpose from conventional legal education, which teaches analysis (breaking down), or even critical legal education, which teaches deconstruction or trashing (also breaking down). Feminist models which [sic] depend on teaching for empowerment (building up by conversations and sharing experiences, rather than by attack/ defense) and foster a more open and flexible understanding of the many ways problems can be solved. Building trust, collaboration, engagement, and empowerment would be the pedagogical goals, rather than reinforcing the competition, individual achievement, alienation, passivity, and lack of confidence that now so pervade the classroom. (Menkel-Meadow 81)

Thus a feminist teaching platform involves opening up discussion with students; challenging students and encouraging challenges by students; incorporating the personal; acknowledging emotions; and challenging preconceptions. The aim is not to clone "lawyers"; rather it is to develop strong individuals who will leave law school more confident in themselves and their ability to become effective advocates for their clients. But this pedagogy is difficult to enact within the rule-based nature of the law ("Women in the Courts," Task Force Report 11).

As a lesbian feminist legal academic teaching in a law school in New Zealand, I have faced many challenges to teaching within a feminist framework, particularly when teaching two courses, Crimes and Evidence. Both involve the study of traditional rule-based or "black letter" law and also case analysis of horrendous crimes. Additionally, in the Crimes course there are aspects of the law that touch on particularly sensitive issues, such as the law of sexual violation.

I view the law of sexual violation as a sensitive issue because it evokes an emotional or psychological response from some or all of the students and the teacher. (Subjects such as abortion rights, euthanasia, domestic violence, and children's rights are also sensitive issues.) However, my experience is that not all teachers recognize that sensitive issues require sensitive teaching. Some of the challenges involved in teaching sensitive issues include: (1) creating a learning and teaching environment that enables students not only to learn the subject matter presented but also to learn about their own responses; (2) challenging students' preconceptions; and (3) expanding their intellectual, conceptual, and emotional boundaries.

Catherine Hantzis observes that "[students] are happy not to be bored or scared; they like experimenting with new ideas in an atmosphere in which the price of failure is not too high" (157). This observation offers a challenge to all teachers: they must provide a secure environment and must lower the threshold of fear of failure. Without these "musts," effective teaching and learning cannot take place.

This article will focus on the challenge for a feminist academic of presenting a "sensitive" subject to a large class of students. The sensitive topic is the law relating to sexual violation (of adults and children). The class is composed of 150 to 170 third-year students of mixed gender, age, and culture. I have taught the law of sexual violation since 1995, as a component of the Crimes course, a compulsory subject for the degree of bachelor of laws in New Zealand. The following will detail my experiences in teaching an issue that (a) is not taught as a component in the Crimes course by other law schools, (b) is viewed with apprehension by the student body and faculty because of its potentially emotionally harrowing content, and (c) applies to one of the busiest areas of the criminal and family law courts:

> Law and legal education are important for what they may do to alleviate oppression and domination in our society. To the extent that even practice is molded in male terms, it too may be transformed or used in different ways. The goal, rooted in experience, of achieving a world without domination is what is most important, and in the efforts to accomplish these ends the practice may itself also change. (Menkel-Meadows, 84)

As a feminist who teaches in a law faculty, I will employ a feminist strategy in leading readers through this experience: personal narrative. Given the complexities of legal terms that confuse not only readers from other disciplines but also lawyers and students of law, I will attempt within this narrative to employ legal jargon as little as possible to keep the issue of teaching sensitive issues at the forefront of the article. However, I will necessarily refer to some points of law for clarification of subject matter.

WHY TEACH THE LAW OF SEXUAL VIOLATION?

As course convenor[1] for the Crimes course at Waikato University, I was faced with some nonnegotiable aspects of the curriculum that were prescribed by the New Zealand Council of Legal Education. But some areas of the curriculum could be negotiated. As a feminist academic doing research on child sexual victims and on battered women incarcerated for killing their abusive husbands, as well as having a practice background as a barrister prosecuting mainly sex offenders, I strongly felt it incumbent upon me to highlight the law of sexual violation. Furthermore, as teachers of those who will soon have significant power as lawyers to affect the safety of women and children, we have a responsibility to incorporate this topic into their required learning. The young legal practitioner will quickly face the law of sexual violation through custody or access disputes or defense or prosecution of rape or child sexual abuse. This is the area male partners in law firms traditionally use for these new lawyers to cut their teeth on, or as a male senior partner of a local law firm put it: "it is a good area to blood them on."

As some feminist legal scholars have observed, traditional law education sidelines what it regards as "women's issues":

> So, it may be that an institution decides it will not teach domestic assault in its compulsory criminal law course because it is taught in "women and the law" or "feminist legal theory": it is thereby placed outside the malestream curriculum. [. . .] Until the standard compulsory courses in the curriculum introduce material of particular concern to women they are conveying partial knowledge. (Graycar and Morgan 22; Finley 42)

Given that this viewpoint accords with my own experiences, and in the face of colleagues' resistance to the assertion that identifying and teaching such issues is necessary or sensitive, I decided to go ahead with this course. Nan Seuffert proposes a feminist pedagogy for law education in another sensitive area (domestic violence) on the grounds that "lawyers' understandings and analysis of domestic violence may affect their legal representations of targets of domestic violence" (64). In the same way, I saw the need to raise the consciousness of law students about issues relating to the law of sexual violation as a must, despite the many barriers that I faced. I believe societal myths and attitudes regarding rape, the question of consent, and the credibility of children need to be challenged and explored.

WHAT ARE THE BARRIERS IN TEACHING SENSITIVE ISSUES?

Institutional Attitudes

Janet Rifkin describes "law and the legal institutions it creates as both sources and perpetrators of patriarchy, a social system of male dominance legitimated by neutral rules of law, a system in which, until relatively recently in human history, 'neutral' principles of property treated women as chattels" (83). The law school ethos and environment remain masculinist, even while enrolling more and more women as students (Banks 138). Additionally, the teaching model for law is only now changing from the pure Socratic method to other more "student friendly" models. Thus, most of the predominantly male law faculty members are not quick to embrace the challenge of teaching sensitive issues. Hilary Astor highlighted "the resistance to covering violence in the law curriculum, identifying the risk (or fear) that recognising the prevalence of violence could overwhelm the curriculum, together with the widespread unwillingness (in academia and the wider community) to take responsibility for violence, embodied in the well-known public/private dichotomy" (124).

Class Size

In New Zealand, budget constraints have dictated that the compulsory courses in the School of Law are taught as large lecture classes, and this appears to be a situation that will continue for the foreseeable future. Thus, it seemed to me that there was no alternative but to devise a way to teach the law of sexual violation within a large group, despite the difficulty of teaching sensitive issues in a large group. Many men teaching Crimes have used these budgetary constraints as an excuse not to teach sensitive issues. Aware that emotional issues may arise in teaching the law of sexual violence, several male colleagues have told me it would be "too hard" to deal with these emotional issues in a large class, or indeed in any class.

Staffing Issues

Finding staff with the knowledge and background to assist in teaching the law of sexual violation presented further dilemmas to me as convenor of the course. Normally the Crimes course is serviced by two lecturers and one tutor. The main two-hour lecture on a topic is followed by a tutorial. To maximize the learning experience the tutorials have no more than twenty-five students and are normally convened by any one of the three staff involved in the course. As academics are not generally drawn from private practice, this barrier to teaching sensitive issues is likely to continue.[2]

To teach this topic effectively the teacher has to refer not only to the legislation that forms its base but also to case law. Both these use sexually explicit language. The legislation is the Crimes Act 1961 (NZ) that details the offenses of sexual violation against adults and children and uses necessarily definitive sexual terms to define the offense. Case law is the way the judges have interpreted the words of the legislation in the cases that come before them for decision. The facts of those cases are pertinent if students are to understand the resulting judgment and therefore it is necessary to give the details. Teachers' use of such sexually explicit language in a group of people of mixed gender, age, and social experience can block effective learning because students often feel threatened and at times embarrassed. Teachers are rendered vulnerable because such language may be misconstrued by some students as inappropriately sexual, offensive, and therefore potentially harassing.

Personal Histories of Both Students and Teachers

When teaching a sensitive issue, a teacher will need to anticipate that some members of the class will react from personal experiences or prejudices. Within any class there will be both abusers and victims of sexual abuse, and with 170 or more students per class, the number in either of those groups can be substantial. Feelings of hurt and anger can be triggered by the sexually explicit language, the case histories analyzed, and the views of fellow classmates. In addition, both teacher and students are exposed to the myriad of mixed feelings generated within the classroom—feelings of fear, anxiety, anger, and perhaps memories of sexual abuse.

MEETING THE CHALLENGES: STEPPING OVER THE BARRIERS

Despite these barriers I still felt, for all the reasons articulated earlier, that it was necessary to teach students the law of sexual violation. However, I still needed to overcome the barriers.

Overcoming the institutional attitude barrier

In real terms I have "headbutted" this barrier on many occasions, usually in the form of derisive comments about my focus on identifying sensitive issues and the manner in which I have addressed these issues in class. But after three years of teaching about these issues, and with three publications in this area plus two presentations to the University Teaching Symposium, not only have I gained personal confidence but also the derisive comments have diminished.

Overcoming the class size barrier

The institutional restraints have only tightened in recent years and one way to overcome this is by the teaching methodology I will describe later in this paper.

Overcoming the appropriate staffing barrier

Staff development training in the specific area of sensitive teaching has raised the confidence level of colleagues. In informal meetings, we thrash through new ideas, talk openly about our fears about classroom dynamics, and have begun to create a firm basis for acknowledging the very real need to teach sensitive issues sensitively. As readers may have suspected, many of these positive moves in peer group discussion have been like "preaching to the converted" because mostly women staff members attend. One can only hope that student appraisals and feedback will illuminate the positive aspects of staff development so that more staff members will participate.

Overcoming the personal histories of both students and teachers

My challenge as a feminist teacher is to make the classroom a safety zone to enable effective learning and put in place "safety nets" for myself and the students. To assist me in this task I elicited support from my colleagues, which enabled me to (1) canvass the necessary ideas relating to safety for both students and myself; (2) brainstorm discussion strategies; (3) structure the legal content of the lectures; and (4) provide personal support following classes through a debriefing session that normally ran over some hours.[3]

CREATING THE SAFETY ZONE

The first lecture involved setting up the safety zone. My aim was to create an environment that would allow for free expression and safety while at the same time enabling effective learning and challenging students' preconceptions.

This part of the Crimes course involved three weeks of two-hour lectures. The class was for enrolled students only, although normally I am open to having children, guest lecturers, and visitors attend my lectures. In teaching the law of sexual violation I checked attendance (an unusual move for this course) in order to ensure that no outsider would be present, thus creating safety by maintaining a clear group identity for the students.

The first class in which I taught the law of sexual violation had 165 students in attendance and I chose to begin by way of a conversation with the class as a whole. This conversation covered the following topics:

- the difficulty of raising a sensitive issue in such a forum;
- the risks involved for myself and the students in raising not only a sensitive issue but also one that involved sex;

- the probability that among the students I was addressing were survivors from both childhood and adult sexual abuse, as well as abusers;
- the fact that I was an abuse survivor (I took the risk of presenting this fact in order to indicate that I could be empathetic if students required referral and also to indicate why I was aware of the need for a safe environment in which to teach this subject.);
- the fact that emotional trauma, outrage, and indignation may be felt by both sets of people within the group;
- why I, as course convenor, viewed the law of sexual violation as a necessary topic to teach and discuss openly (the prevalence in society of such crimes; the need to challenge societal preconceptions; the need for informed legal practitioners to deal with such matters; the need to protect the women and children who are, in the main, targets of these crimes);
- why other law schools in New Zealand do not teach it; and
- the feelings that would likely arise as we traveled through harrowing cases: feelings from parents about children being abused; feelings from men that their gender was the main abuser; feelings of guilt from survivors who did not take charges through court, of anger about their powerlessness, and of vulnerability about their own feelings and the risk of exposing that vulnerability; feelings of denial, guilt, and outrage from abusers.

I moved away from the podium and closer to the class as I spoke and moved up and down the aisles to engage all the students. I was careful with my voice modulation to avoid a judgmental tone and was open to questions, including discussion points into the conversation.

As the next step in putting the safety zone in place, I placed the following information on overhead transparency. These transparencies were visible throughout all the lectures on this topic.

- the names and telephone numbers of organizations working in the area of sexual abuse, or student counseling; and
- the basic rules for safety:
  1. no guest lecturers, children, or persons not enrolled in Crimes allowed during these scheduled classes;
  2. "When the going gets too tough" strategies:
     (a) *safe hand signal* by centering palm out in the mid-torso region so that other students would not notice. I said that I would allow many class breaks during this topic and

> assured students that should they signal me, I would call a break shortly so that they could then either take a breather or leave;
>
> (b) *zone out*: de-focus eyes and psychologically disappear— an experience students agreed was familiar to them;[4] and
>
> (c) *leave* the lecture hall. This was a problematic strategy as it would signal their distress or, alternatively, make it difficult for those students who were leaving for other reasons (e.g., toilet break, child-care responsibilities); and
>
> 3. that students were to maintain as much as possible their role as "student."

Having set parameters that would assure safety and an open forum, I then spent a little time requesting other ground rules for safety in the presentation of this topic. Some of the familiar ground rules I requested were:

1. that we observe confidentiality in discussing issues that go beyond the law itself;
2. that students own their statements and start them with "I";
3. that the safety zone overhead transparency containing the referral numbers and the overhead containing the options for safety remain visible throughout the class as a focal point;
4. that the safety zone options, the referral list, and the ground rules be transcribed so that by the second class all students would have their own copy as well as keeping this information visible during future classes;
5. that students listen to the full comments made by classmates or teacher; and
6. that students respect differing views and refrain from defensive retorts.

TEACHING THE TOPIC

I then introduced the law relating to this topic by canvassing the history of the law from the concept of women's being the "property" of men to the 1982 autonomy clauses in the Crimes Act. This history is an important beginning to establish the basic premise of gender inequality and the need to open a forum to challenge this premise and to set the scene for the ensuing activity.

The first section of this series of lectures dealt with sexual violation of adults, with particular focus on women and their experiences, since they are in the main the victims of such abuse. This led to societal attitudes about women and rape, and I asked for class participation by brainstorming the current myths associated with these attitudes. Doing this exercise with such a large group has led to noisy debate and some humorous interludes. Although it would seem that this would be an ideal place for women to have the main say and men to remain quiet, in fact participation has been quite successful in that both men and women have freely provided examples of myths. I then moved to a discussion of the origins of attitudes or myths; the students agreed that these were family, media, church, and school.

The myths were called out by students, and I recorded them on the white board with a volunteer student scribe to ensure a hard copy, which was then given to students. Some of the myths identified were:

- "Women ask for it";
- "She deserved it";
- "The way she dresses means she wants it";
- "Women are cock teasers";
- "That's what women are for";
- "Wives must always give over"; and
- "Women mean yes, even if they say no."

All of these engendered discussion, for which I allowed at least 30 to 45 minutes. These were some of the discussion points raised in this section:

- Is marital rape a crime? On one occasion a male student in his forties challenged the class about whether it was legitimate for him to have sexual intercourse with his wife at his demand. Students much younger said no, on the basis of power and control issues, and further discussion ensued about where these attitudes come from;
- Definition of terms: As a lawyer who has worked in the area of sexual abuse for many years, I am always glad to be reminded by the youth of my class to reevaluate what I believe is common understanding. A young man (twenty years old) was confused about the term "digital rape" and asked for a definition in open class. He was obviously embarrassed but equally obviously "safe enough" to ask what this term meant. The discussion that followed made it safe to question all other terms used; and
- Issues of power and control: These are certainly the main discussion points of students in this class. Women students challenge men students to perceive rape as a violence issue rather than a

sexual issue and to see how our society uses power and control as weapons against women and children.

Facilitating such a discussion is always difficult. However, the fact that it was possible to conduct an open, frank, and potentially volatile discussion with such a large student body indicates that the safety zone was effective. Students took risks and exposed both vulnerability and naivete. I am sure the reader can imagine that in teaching such a subject, given the tension involved for both teacher and students, combined with the explicit language used, there are bound to be faux pas. I often stated at the outset of class that at some stage this can happen and that when it did, I would not minimize the issues.

For example, on one occasion I had pointed out that the definition of rape in New Zealand had been extended by the Crimes Amendment (No 3) Act 1985 that effected changes to the Crimes Act 1961 in four major areas: (1) rape was retained as an offense but new sections were added to the law to expand the concept/definition of rape to include other forms of sexual violation (digital, object, and anal penetration); (2) the language used in the statute is now gender neutral; (3) sexual violation within marriage is now an offense; (4) court hearings are now held in camera. In addition, the Evidence Act of 1908 (as amended in 1989) created further reform and protection in relation to sexual violation offenses, inter alia, in relation to the means by which child complainants can present their evidence (section 23D), and the process by which complainants' sexual history may be admitted into evidence. Then a student asked the question: "What was the definition of rape under the former law?"

The answer was that rape was constituted by nonconsensual penetration by a penis. On this occasion, I completely blanked the word "penis" from my mind and was left dangling a *pppp* with the result that the entire class called out in unison "penis," much to the dismay of passers-by.

To describe a classroom question-and-answer incident on paper destroys the emotions and fears that were displayed in the actual situation. The example given above where the young male put up his hand and asked in open forum, "Wendy, just what do you mean when you say digital penetration?" was an extremely tension-producing situation. Every student's eyes were turned alternatively toward this young man and me. No one laughed; the silence was palpable. As the teacher, I was filled with awe that he both felt safe in such an open forum to ask this question and was also aware of his fear in taking such a risk. I answered the question factually.

As part of the initial conversation with the class I assured students that I would be available to speak with them about their responses to this topic and told them when I would be available. During these times I have found that either students require referral to an appropriate counselor or merely want a sounding board for their feelings of frustration. In setting up a safe environment for students, it is important not to neglect the safety of the teacher. Ideally, when there are coteachers in a course there is good quality reciprocal peer support. This was not an option for me in the teaching of the law of sexual violation so I sought the peer support offered by a colleague with an interest in legal education and staff development. She provided support which included planning for teaching, dealing with the classroom dynamics, formulating the appraisal, and writing up the results of the project.

This support is extremely important because it enables teachers of sensitive issues to maintain an equilibrium so that personal feelings do not upset the balance of the safety zone for students.

THE FEMINIST TEACHING PROCESS

Writing about feminist teaching processes is in itself a major challenge because techniques and theories developed over the years as a platform for the practical aspects of teaching belie the difficulties in applying them. There are risks for the teacher in allowing open discussion, inviting conversations that exchange ideals and attitudes. In teaching law, rules give safe boundaries to topic discussion. When I empowered students, they transcended these boundaries and I often felt out of control or out of my depth in discussions which could become personal and political. But feminist pedagogical goals made this a worthwhile exercise, even though uncomfortable at times for the leader of such an enterprise. I feel that many teachers, particularly in the discipline of law, use the rules of law as protection, rather than viewing them as boundaries that inhibit the true potential of students:

> Dominant cultures are powerful forces, and those of us who have passed into the dominant culture must work hard to preserve our desire to express other forms and new ideas. Still, I think that the influence of the warmer and more nurturing classrooms (with mother images to counter the traditional patriarchs), experiential exercises and the use of personal experience, more participatory teaching and learning methods, greater contextual specificity in the discussion of cases, and more varied sources of material for legal study are all contributions that women have made to legal education. (Menkel-Meadows, 84–85)

ASSESSMENT OF THE TOPIC

Both the 1996 and 1997 Crimes examination papers contained an optional question on the law of sexual violation. If they wished to answer a question related to the law of sexual violation, students could choose to answer either an essay question or a problem-solving question. The essay topic was based on readings given to the students in preparation for class and required an understanding of the dynamics of the law of sexual violation. The problem-based question required a knowledge of legal rules and their application to a previously unseen factual situation. The Crimes examination contained seven questions in total, of which the students were required to answer only four. Thus it seems significant that in 1996 and 1997, on average 65% of students chose either the essay or the problem question on the law of sexual violation.[5] I took this high percentage to mean that students had achieved a level of safety in their understanding and application of this law. My interpretation is also supported by the fact that of the students answering this question, seven disclosed sexual abuse, further suggesting that the students' perceptions had been challenged and that the course had provided a "safe" way to begin dealing with the issues they were confronting.

APPRAISING THE EXPERIENCE

I applied to the University of Waikato School of Law Human Research Ethics Committee for consent to conduct a survey of students' perceptions of approaches to effective/protected learning in the area of the law of sexual violation and received consent to proceed. In conjunction with the Appraisals Officer of the university, my peer support team and I drafted an appraisal questionnaire that covered both course content and teaching methods. There were both open questions where students were invited to make comments and closed questions, where students indicated responses using a scale of 1 to 5.

In August 1996, at the first compulsory Crimes lecture after the law of sexual violation component, students who attended one or more of the three lectures on the law of sexual violation were invited to complete the anonymous appraisal. One hundred and fourteen students completed the appraisal. Analysis of the results revealed the following:

1. A high number of students attended all three lectures on the law of sexual violation, relative to other topics within the Crimes course, and there was no significant drop off as the lectures progressed. There was no gender difference in the attendance patterns.

2. Students gave diverse reasons for attending the lectures. Some reflected information given to students during the lectures, e.g., "It's a part of the law that practicing lawyers will be faced with" and "It gives another option when answering exam questions." Other responses reflected the importance of sexual violation as a social issue, e.g., "It is an issue that will not go away and one I have no doubt I will have to deal with in practice so it was a good introduction" and "Because I wanted to find out about this area of law as it is either becoming more prevalent in our society or has always been around but not spoken about."

3. Nearly all students who attended the lectures thought that the law of sexual violation should continue to be part of Crimes: two-thirds of the responses to this question indicated that attendance should be optional, one-third indicated that it should be compulsory. Those students who thought the law of sexual violation should be a compulsory part of the Crimes course stressed the importance of the topic for practicing lawyers; those who thought it should be optional stressed the impact that the topic might have on individuals. One student wrote, "I think the matter is hard to deal with emotionally especially if close to home, although I think an understanding of the complexities of sexual violation should be held by all practicing law it should be acknowledged that for some of the issues are so sensitive personally compulsory attendance should not be enforced." Another disagreed: "It is a reality and fact that these issues exist in the world and it is putting blinkers on students to give them opportunities to get out of attending them."

4. We asked a question about content to see what students expected to learn about of the legal aspect of this part of the course. Of the 114 students who responded to a question on students' expectations of the content of the law of sexual violation component, 44 stated that the content did not meet their expectations. Many of these students wanted more discussion of cases and greater factual detail in relation to cases. This had been the students' experience in other courses and in other Crimes topics, and my emphasis on exploring surrounding issues, rather than analyzing cases, seemed to make the topic, for these students, less valuable. The majority of students responded with positive comments about their understanding and appreciation of the content. Many students sought me out after class to comment informally on the course. These comments were all positive: "I found that so interesting and useful for me to work through my own abuse"; "I'm going home to discuss this with my family because it is an area we all need to know"; "Thank you for helping me to stay safe and still understand the law in this area." Students' written comments ranged from

the wholly positive to the qualified: "I enjoyed the content of these classes. They were free of the rules of law, and open to discussion that was more pertinent in raising the consciousness of the class to the real issues—the women and children who have been abused—and the need we have to offer good legal services to at least protect them from being twice abused in the legal system." "I thought the content was quite conservative and definitely safe. However, I felt too much of an issue was made at the beginning about safeness. If anything it made me uncomfortable and question my own life when it shouldn't have."

5. I was particularly interested in getting feedback on whether my presentation of the material was seen as balanced in two ways: (1) presentation of issues pertinent to law and gender equality; and (2) presentation of issues that had a direct impact on students who might have been either abused or abusers. Of the women who responded, a large majority (74.5%) felt the presentation was balanced: those who did not perceived an antimale bias. An overwhelming majority of men found the presentation balanced, but a significant minority (12%) referred to a bias toward the victims of sexual offenses rather than an antimale bias. One student wrote, "I think the content was balanced. I think it was good how the lecturer recognised that not just men are abusers. It can get a little demoralising being a male and being blamed for all the evils in the world." Others agreed in similar terms: "Balanced—it provided different views, it was not explained in a threatening manner." "As a woman I believe the lectures were given sensitively as with as much balance as possible in this topic." But others were more negative: "I thought it was well balanced, however I get sick of the PC thing—it is no good doing law if not prepared to learn about what really goes on." "Too much discussion on the moral angle. Not enough examination of the law—not academic enough, too sociological."

6. Asked whether the techniques used to create a safety zone were effective, 99 of the 105 students who responded concluded that they were. Some students referred to the effect the safety zone had on them, saying, for example, "At no time did I feel unsafe." Some students referred to the effectiveness of the safety zone for people who might need it, e.g., "if any one felt uncomfortable etc., they had every chance to leave. The lecturer was aware of possible areas affecting people and provided options for them to signal their wish to take a break, or leave." Other students observed that it is "difficult to protect everyone's feelings in such a large class" and that "regardless of how you address this, peer group pressure prevails." Others pointed out that the "going gets tough" options (zoning out, indicating that a break was needed, leaving) could call attention to people who did

not want to be identified ("Yes people were warned [. . .] but also no—I don't think anyone would leave as it would be too embarrassing." "Good effort was made to create a safety zone but unfortunately if things got too much then leaving lecture in public only makes things worse"). One student drew attention to the fact that students want to leave class for all sorts of reasons, including going to the toilet and collecting children from child care, and might be embarrassed if the class thought they were leaving in reaction to the subject matter.

7. Students were asked if their views and attitudes about the law of sexual violation had changed as a result of attending classes. Some responded that their understanding of the law had increased ("I understand it more, and the way the law treats different offenses"); others felt they were now more well informed about the wider context, including the relationship between victims and the legal system; still others felt they had become more objective and less emotional about the topic. Others reported that their attitudes had not changed ("No. I still regard sexual violation as a hideous crime that is often punished too lightly").

TEACHING THE LAW OF SEXUAL VIOLATION MOVES FROM THE MARGIN TO COMPULSORY

I made the topic of the law of sexual violation a compulsory part of the Crimes course in 1997. Since the appraisals suggested that the teaching techniques I had used in 1996 had in fact promoted effective/protected learning, I employed many of the same techniques and strategies in 1997. Since I still believed that the law of sexual violation was an important topic, that law students would benefit from learning about the law and about society's beliefs and attitudes, and that the benefit would flow on to society as a whole, it seemed sensible to ensure that as many students attended classes on this topic as attended classes on other topics in the Crimes course. Making this component of the course compulsory produced positive results. The course as a whole was appraised in 1997, and I took the fact that there were no specific references to the law of sexual violation part of the course as an indication that it was a noncontroversial component. Student attendance was high, and although there were more than twenty referrals to appropriate counseling, this was not an increase over the previous years when the law of sexual violation was not included in Crimes courses or when it was not compulsory. I felt that I had accomplished what I had set out to do despite the identified barriers. I was teaching soon-to-be lawyers about feminist issues and moving these issues from the margins to the center.

CONCLUSION

As I write this conclusion I pause and feel the fear of being condemned by academic peers. But then I remember that I am not only an academic lesbian feminist, I am also a lawyer, who recalls years of summing up to a jury.

So to the readers, a jury of my peers, I say this: our students are our future; our students will reflect our teaching as they progress in their careers and as we become either the "old, the enfeebled" or the people of the past. Therefore it is important that we treat them sensitively as people who have the potential to make a difference—a difference in how we perceive men and women; a difference in the methods they will employ as practicing lawyers when dealing with clients who have suffered trauma; a difference in their awareness of the reality of a male-dominated legal world. Our responsibility is huge—so huge that most teachers deny its existence. The challenge is to teach our convictions, to challenge the students of today so that they will be sensitive to the issues confronting women and men of tomorrow. If the verdict of my peers is guilty of caring for the future of our students, then I will indeed welcome no reprieve from the life sentence.

•   •   •

NOTES

1. A "course convener" is the Principal Lecturer in a course and coordinates the teaching by other lecturers, maintains quality control, and insures curriculum development and design.

2. I have a background in psychology and teaching practices, which my colleagues did not have, that added to my comfort in teaching in this area.

3. My acknowledgment to Jacquelin Mackinnon, Lecturer and Staff Developer of the School of Law for providing this support and encouragement.

4. Although this strategy was particular to this subject, the class was reminded that when they were in practice as lawyers, they would have to learn to disengage emotionally at times. We discussed the art of distancing oneself from the personal. However, this was contrary to what I perceived as feminist pedagogy, where the personal is important to the learning process. The class negotiated an agreement that when we discussed cases, the best way to find a midpoint between excessive involvement and emotional detachment would be to refer to victims and perpetrators rather than personalizing the parties by name.

5. This figure is based on informal notes that I kept at the time of examination marking.

WORKS CITED

Astor, Hilary. "The Teaching of Law." *Legal Education Review* 6 (1995): 117–27.

Banks, Taunya Lovell. "Gender Bias in the Classroom." *Journal of Legal Educa-tion* 38 (1988): 137–46.

Finley, Lucinda. "A Break in the Silence: Including Women's Issues in a Torts Course." *Yale Journal of Law and Feminism* 1 (1989): 39–49.

Graycar, Regina, and Jennifer Morgan, eds. *The Hidden Gender of the Law*. Syd-ney: Federation Press, 1992.

Hantzis, Catherine W. "Kingsfield and Kennedy: Reappraising the Male Models of Law School Teaching." *Journal of Legal Education* 38 (1988): 155–64.

Mack, Kathy, and Rosemary Hunter. "Exclusion and Silence." *Sexing the Subject of Law*. Ed. Ngaire Naffine. Sydney: Sweet and Maxwell, 1997. 170–91.

Menkel-Meadow, Carrie. "Feminist Legal Theory, Critical Legal Studies, and Le-gal Education or 'The Fem-Crits Go to Law School,'" *Journal of Legal Educa-tion* 38 (1988): 61–85.

Report, Task Force. "Women in the Courts." *Fordham Urban Law Journal* 15 (1986–1987): 11–25.

Rifkin, Janet. "Toward a Theory of Law and Patriarchy." *Harvard Women's Law Journal* 3 (1980): 83–95.

Seuffert, Nan. "Lawyering and Domestic Violence: Feminist Pedagogies Meet Feminist Theories." *Women's Studies Journal* 10.2 (1994): 63–96.

SUGGESTED READING

Ball, Wendy, and Jacquelin Mackinnon. "Teaching the Unthinkable: Approaches to Effective/Protected Learning in the Area of Sexual Offences." *Legal Educa-tion Review* 8 (1997): 99–111.

Field, Martha A. "The Differing Federalisms of Canada and the United States." *Law & Contemporary Problems* 55 (1991): 107–21.

Frug, Gerald E. "A Critical Theory of Law." *Legal Education Review* 1 (1989): 43–57.

Owens, Rosemary, and Ngaire Naffine. *Sexing the Subject of Law*. Sydney: Sweet and Maxwell, 1997.

Resnik, Judith. "Revising the Canon: Feminist Help in Teaching Procedure." *Uni-versity of Cincinnati Law Review* 61 (1993): 1181–99.

Feminist Pedagogy and the Community

16

LETTING FEMINIST KNOWLEDGE SERVE THE CITY

Melissa Kesler Gilbert, Carol Holdt,
and Kristin Christophersen

A Capstone is a chance to actually do something that has use in our academic career. It is a chance to get off our butts that are firmly planted in classrooms in academia and contribute something bigger than our own ruminations and contribute to something that will make it beyond our professor's recycling box. It is an opportunity (in our PUBLIC university) to give some much needed help to groups in our communities that need it.[1]

INTRODUCTION

There is a long-standing relationship between women's studies and community activism. When women's studies emerged in the early 1970s, it was as the academic arm of the Women's Liberation Movement. Yet as a discipline women's studies has become increasingly integrated into academia. In response, feminist scholars are calling for a "return to those earlier community ties because of their importance to theory building, the rendering of services to the community, and their potential for transforming the university" (Maher and Tetreault 51).

In the pages that follow we describe how we have taken up the challenge to bring our scholarship into the community by designing community-based courses for our women's studies program. We, the authors of this essay, have worked together as instructor and graduate mentors to revise traditional feminist pedagogy for application to community-based experiences for our undergraduates.[2] Our analysis is informed by dialogues with each other about our teaching practices and reflective journal entries contributed by students enrolled in our course.

The following is an account of the process we use in our course to not only serve a community of women in our city but also to encourage the future social responsibility and activism of our students. We examine our use of reflective journals as a space for students to question their individual personal location in relation to the feminist scholarship they are reading and the communities in which they function. We explore the different ways in which we build a supportive microcosm of a community within the classroom where students can learn from one another and begin to negotiate issues of diversity and inequality. And we describe the connections we create for our students with community activists that help them to discover their potential part in the work of social change.

We begin this pedagogical narrative with background on the development of community-based learning on our campus, the important role our women's studies program has played in organizing a network of community partnerships to sustain our coursework, and our specific project with a family-based social service agency that assists women with newborns.

LETTING KNOWLEDGE SERVE THE CITY

In 1994 our university established a new university studies program that required students in their final year of study to complete a senior capstone course. The hope was that students in these interdisciplinary community-based learning courses would take the knowledge and expertise they had learned within the academy and apply it out in the city to solve problems, address issues of concern to the regional community, and enhance urban life:

> The metropolitan region becomes an extended living laboratory and classroom where faculty, students, and the community combine their knowledge, skills, and talents in collaborative efforts. In this sense, the boundaries between teacher and students, university and community, learning and doing, become blurred. (Ramaley 1)

Departments across campus were encouraged to develop new partnerships with community businesses, nonprofits, and social service agencies that would put our university motto, "Let Knowledge Serve the City" to work.

WOMEN'S STUDIES: BUILDING WOMEN'S COMMUNITY PARTNERSHIPS

In spring 1996 our women's studies program began to organize a network of women's community partnerships that would encourage multiple capstone courses serving local women's agencies for years to come. The network grew out of the needs of women in our community, our faculty's teaching and research interests, and our students' learning goals. To develop our partnerships and capstone courses, we relied on a long history of interdisciplinary scholarship and networking by affiliated faculty already involved in feminist teaching and community-based service and the numerous internships and community-service practicums already in place within our program.

Our current network of community partnerships consists of a range of nonprofit public agencies that provide social, educational, literary, and health services to the city's women. The agencies address a myriad of women's needs in the community, including women's health, domestic violence, reproductive issues, welfare of women, women's history, cross-cultural relations, heterosexism, women's technological education, and the family. Together, our partnerships have reached out to a community of women that is diverse in race, age, ethnicity, social class, and sexuality.

OUR PROJECT: THE POLITICS OF MOTHERHOOD

Our community-based project was the second in a series of capstone courses working with one of our local partners, a family-based social-service agency. This series of capstones was designed to collect information about the clients, staff, policy makers, and local partners associated with our community partner. In the first course, students conducted client-satisfaction interviews with mothers served by the agency in order to determine why some clients were dropping out of the program.

In our course, the Politics of Motherhood, the focus shifted from the women served by the agency to the policy makers that were responsible for fiscally and politically supporting the efforts of the community partner. The agency was concerned with the lack of support they received from local officials and wanted to determine why women and children in the area were being overlooked by county-level policy.

Our students worked closely with the director of the agency to design an interview project that applied their feminist knowledge to questions posed by our community partner. The final goal of the project was to write a report to the agency that summarized city policy makers' views on family issues, the work of the agency, and future directions for their communities.

Each student began by choosing one of the major cities served by the county agency. These individual choices were based on the student's own social and political location, e.g., political affiliation, the neighborhood in which she lived, an interest in homeless families, teen pregnancy, or single motherhood. In order to prepare for their interviews, students researched the family-based demographics of the city on the Internet, in census reports, city budgets and action plans, and on other demographic databases. In small collaborative learning groups they constructed interview guides to encourage the policy makers to discuss their perceptions of local families, the agency, and the future of family policy. Each student then conducted two face-to-face interviews with a mayor and a city council member from the city they chose, transcribed the interviews, and authored a section of a report for the agency. In the final report students summarized their findings and wrote recommendations to assist the agency in their efforts to build coalitions with local policy makers.

On paper, the outcome of the project was a professionally crafted report that helped our community partner understand how the agency might raise awareness among policy makers about the problems faced by women and children in their community. In the life of our city, however, this project helped to create a new group of socially responsible students, many of whom plan on moving on to community activist work of their own.

The first step in making the transition from classroom student to community activist was for students to identify their own personal connections to the multiple social communities within which they operate.

IDENTIFYING PERSONAL AND POLITICAL CONNECTIONS

Early on in the course, students were asked to identify their personal perspectives on motherhood and the family and to describe their roles as members of their neighborhoods. They were encouraged to explore the relationships between their personal standpoints, their positions in their communities, the feminist scholarship they were reading, and family problems women face within our city.

Each week students read one chapter from each of the assigned texts: *Mothering: Ideology, Experience, and Agency*, edited by Evelyn Nakano Glenn, Grace Chang, and Linda Rennie Forcey and *Mothers in Law: Feminist Theory and the Legal Regulation of Motherhood*, edited by Martha Albertson Fineman and Isabel Karpin. These texts were chosen because they provided students with scholarship on the relationships among social location, policy, and ideology. We hoped the readings would enable students to make "links between one's individual actions and thoughts and the social, historical and cultural contexts within which one lives" (Goodman, in Scering 66).[3]

Students submitted weekly journal reflections on the feminist scholarship they were reading. The inclusion of journaling as a course requirement was intended not only to provide students an opportunity to dialogue with and about the feminist scholarship they were reading each week but also to establish a place to negotiate the relationships between theory and personal experience (Parry 48). We hoped that the readings and weekly journals would encourage students to see themselves as part of the community and aid in the "development of students' responsibilities to themselves, their peers, children, and adults" (Scering 64). The first step in this process was to get students thinking about their location and their standpoint.

MAKING CONNECTIONS: I HAVE TRUE LIFE EXPERIENCE

Students relied heavily on their own life experiences and experiences with their families and their communities as a context in which to consider the assigned readings. They were able to "use their own personal experiences and see them as valid elements in the learning process" (Parry 47). Explained one student, "In order to fully comprehend the argument the author was attempting to prove, I had to reflect on my own upbringing." Most of the students made connections with the readings. They found themselves, their families, their "true life experience" represented in the authors' words. Students' journals were filled with detailed accounts of how their lives were similar to the experiences they were reading about. One student wrote, "Within my own life, I can see how these kin-scripts have been in place. In caring for my elderly parents, I have taken on the role of the care provider." Another student noted, "My family responds to one another similarly to those mentioned in the article."

These connections made with the readings not only functioned as acknowledgment of the student's lived experiences but also they gave the students a voice of authority (Henkin 21, 23; Maher and Tetreault 18; Parry 46, 47). They had subjective knowledge of what they were reading about. One student wrote, "This is something I understand clearly." The journals provided students the initial forum in which they could assert this knowledge: "Having been single, non-married mother, student, worker, health-care professional, wife and mother, there are many small pieces that I can offer. Life experiences, understanding, empathy." Wrote another student, "I do feel after reading the articles for this week that I will be able to contribute my experience of having been a single/unwed mother."

Some of the students not only located themselves within the readings but also rediscovered these same lived experiences from a new or differing standpoint. Writing about this rediscovery in their journals, they were able to do what Roxanne Henkin refers to as "revis[ing] life stories and/or reinvent[ing] themselves in powerful, supportive, alternative ways" (27). These students spoke about the new knowledge they had about their lived experiences. One student wrote, "I have realized that I have led a very sheltered upper-middle class life." Another wrote, "It opened my eyes to how my own family has organized itself." The journals also revealed that students had mixed emotions about their new knowledge. For some of the students this new way of knowing was exciting and "eye-opening." Others wrote about anger or frustration: "I felt the article was very well written and contained a lot of data to support the theme. I will say though it made me very angry. I am a woman, who has been a single parent."

Not all of the students responded to the assigned readings and made journal entries with confidence. For a few students the push to think about their location and the context in which they lived their lives was very difficult. One student wrote, "I find that I feel so uncertain at times with myself, and where I fit into the whole picture. I try to reflect and ask myself, what do I want, and why am I doing this (being back in school that is)."

NEW DISCOVERIES: I AM VASTLY DIFFERENT

The journals also revealed that students had different levels of awareness about their personal and political location. Some of the students not only recognized and renegotiated their life experiences within the context of the readings but also, further, they came to be aware of how their location, their experiences, were different from others (Gilbert 258–59). Many of the students' journals revealed thoughts similar to the following:

> I had never really thought about mothering being defined from white, heterosexual, middle class woman. This is exactly what I am and I can see that my experiences and resources are far different from woman of color and woman of poverty.

Another wrote, "for sure I am vastly different than other races and classes. I would not want someone to understand me by using a perspective that did not have anything to do with what my life was like."

Students had strong emotional responses to these discoveries of difference. In their journals, students reported feeling "overwhelmed," "angered," "outraged," and "frustrated." A student wrote, "I could not believe my eyes. [. . .] Some of the things I read were appalling." As Janet Lee has noted, anger can motivate student learning, "fueling an interest to comprehend certain issues and encouraging them to work for personal and social changes" (15).

Guilt was another emotion revealed in students' journals, often expressed about their own participation in systems of oppression (Gilbert 259). One wrote, "Both the articles that I chose for this week had to do with black women, I was almost embarrassed to be a white woman."

Some students reported being surprised by the emotions that the readings evoked while others acknowledged the familiar emotional response associated with women's studies courses and feminist scholarship. Yet, one student went on to explain, even with this familiarity, "it's always good to remind myself that not all women are in the same situation as me."

A few students, however, found the negotiation of difference to be very difficult. For some of these students, these feelings were very complicated to navigate. In the end, the introduction of difference left them grappling with what they thought and felt about their own location. One journal entry revealed:

> When I go through my readings and respond, I am responding with how I feel. I hate segregation. Many of the writings are race specific. I try to look at how it applies to everyone. I feel that I do see the racial boundaries in these readings, and the differentiation for black women. But in these readings how can you be race specific when the issues may cover all nationalities. I am trying not to be specific to the white middle class, but trying to equate some fairness for all. Maybe what I am analyzing is my own point of view.

Following this process of introspection, we shifted the focus outward. Our task was to create a community within the classroom, where students could negotiate their perspectives in relation to one another.

BUILDING COMMUNITY IN THE CLASSROOM

In the process of building a classroom community we encouraged students to start thinking about diversity and their own potential roles in relation to their classmates. First, we asked students to reflect on their own life experiences, knowledge, and skills. Through this process, they were able to gain a sense of what they had to contribute to the class project. Second, through class discussions and working in small collaborative learning groups, they began understanding and appreciating what their classmates had to contribute; they began to recognize a diverse community within the classroom. Finally, we structured the project so that each student had access to support persons. We watched additional support networks emerge among various groups of students. This section describes in more detail the strategies we employed to immerse students in experience and dialogue about their location within the classroom community.

LOCATING SELVES: FINDING MYSELF IN A CLASSROOM COMMUNITY

One of the first steps in participating in a community is understanding the various roles to be filled and finding one that fits us, based on our needs as well as what we have to offer. We gave students their first written assignment to aid in this process.[4] The multiple purposes of the assignment were to assess their skills and make a plan to both share their expertise and to gain additional skills in the process of the course project.

Students were asked to consider all courses they had completed to this point, along with each course's objectives and the skills they had acquired as a result of each course. They assembled portfolios of completed papers and projects and analyzed their strengths and weaknesses. Based on the published objectives of their major disciplines, they measured their progress in attaining the desired skills of their disciplines. Based on the university's major education goals, they determined any experiences missing from their academic work.

Next, students summarized in writing what they could give as well as what they could gain from the course. They listed the skills they possessed which might benefit the course project and identified the tools of their disciplines that they were willing to teach their classmates to use. Finally, they created an action plan for building and improving upon their skills in the process of the course.

As a result of the portfolio assignment, several students gained confidence in their value to the classroom community.

> I felt very overwhelm[ed] initially. However, after I took everything home to read and took time to breathe, I felt excitement. I began to look at myself, and what I might have to contribute to the project. I don't think I came up with anything that I felt was earthshattering. I did, however, decide my interest and ideas in this project would probably begin to bloom [with] the project itself. I am excited to get a chance to participate and learn.

The portfolio work made for an interesting way for students to learn something about their classmates. As follow-up to the written assignment, an entire class period was devoted to discussing what they had learned about themselves, what they hoped to give to the project, and what they hoped to walk away with. After all verbal introductions were completed, students began to look forward to the chance to work together as a collaborative group. "I am a little overwhelmed by the strength of our group. Each individual in our group has so much to offer. [. . .] I am looking forward [to] participating in the complexity of this group."

Students grew increasingly confident that the project work would provide the opportunities they needed to meet the goals outlined in their plans. "I really feel that many of the areas that I have felt the least comfortable in will get some attention."

TWO HEADS ARE BETTER THAN ONE: LEARNING FROM EACH OTHER

Students now had a better sense of their location within the classroom community. The next step was what Scering calls "the development of a community of engaged learners who respect differences" (65). Using the readings in feminist scholarship as a building block, students began making connections between their own perspectives and the experiences of their classmates. In collaborative learning groups they came to depend on and care for each other in ways not possible in individual efforts. They negotiated the diversity within their small groups as well as the larger classroom community and gained a new respect for their differences. As Scering suggests, when students form caring and cooperative relationships, they move beyond negative attention to differences and develop a collective identity (66–67).

Interdisciplinary courses in which students from a variety of disciplines enroll can present some challenges. With students from a broad range of analytic orientations, we needed a shared foundation in order to communicate effectively. Discussing the knowledge students gained from the readings in feminist scholarship made this possible. It provided a common language with which students could discuss the issues affecting women in their communities. By midterm students were casually using feminist terms like "heterosexism," "kin-scripts," and "social constructions of motherhood" in discussions and in their journals.

Throughout the term, students completed the course readings in the order of their interest; however, the first few readings were assigned by chapter. Students wrote synopses of their assigned chapters and distributed copies to the group. They then presented their synopses to the rest of the class, generating discussions of the issues raised in the readings.

During a discussion of lesbian mothering one student disclosed her own lesbian identity, prompting another student to write in her journal:

Personally, I don't know a lot about this topic so it was helpful to get a point of view [. . .] in order for me to see another side, a human face to this controversy. Then, I can process what I read, my own knowledge, and a personal response from an individual. I can come up with my own idea and refine my own perspective on this issue.

Shirley Parry has described the importance of encouraging multiple perspectives in increasing students' "understanding of the dynamics of 'difference' and of self/other" (47). An exercise conducted by the university capstone coordinators aided us in this effort. Students were asked to pair up with one another and designate a speaker and a listener. They then chose a controversial topic of interest to them. After thinking about how they felt about the chosen topic, the speakers were instructed to argue the other side of the issue. In so doing, students explored and gained a better understanding of views much different than their own.

This exercise left students better prepared to join efforts with a very diverse group of classmates. They were well aware of the difficulties we all have at times, listening to "opinions that don't fit my own personal belief," as one student put it. Another student reflected in her journal, "This is a hard thing to do; it seems we all want to say what we have on our own minds and forget that to understand another person's perspective we must listen to them."

It was a relief for students to discover that with an interdisciplinary group there is a better chance that the diverse talents of other students can compensate for what they fear are their own shortcomings. One student wrote, "Developing questions is not an easy task and it's always helpful to work with others because they might know how to better articulate what you want to say."

The diversity of knowledge helped students to make connections they might otherwise have missed: "I am in awe when I listen to everyone. Sometimes I think we give ourselves so little credit for what we have to offer and yet in that little piece we can contribute, we may link many pieces together."

Students were able to broaden their horizons through the sharing of others' experiences, skills, and knowledge. They were showered with new insights, encouraged to process this new information and incorporate it into their own perspectives. Their learning ranged from very personal, real-life experiences to practical skills and gave students cause to think about issues they may face in their own futures. One student wrote in her journal, "I am amazed how many mothers we have in our class. I am not a mother. I don't think I will be anytime soon. [. . .] I hope the mothers can give me insight [into] what it is to be a mother."

Students also showed great respect for each others' backgrounds and opinions. One student expressed gratitude for the opportunity to work with a classmate who held very different political and social views from her own:

> While we are not bound to become life-long friends, I have enjoyed her input. I also have respect for her sticking it out with this class when she felt that her political and personal perspectives were much more conservative than my own. Through the process of working on this [project], she and I were able to have a fairly lengthy discussion around critical analysis of personal perspective. I believe it was productive for both of us, as we both know politically we are worlds apart.

Another student expressed her confidence in the class as a whole to respect one another's "biases and opinions." She wrote in her journal, "we may begin to feel friction in the final stages, but judging from the level of respect in the classroom, it should be more educational and interesting than hostile."

Near the end of the term, one student expressed her appreciation for all of the contributions from her classmates: "I am excited about the project coming together. I am beginning to see it all fall into place. We have had such a terrific group of people to work with. There are so diverse talents and skills."

CREATING SUPPORTIVE NETWORKS: WE ARE A TEAM

Building community means creating a network of support. We created two forms of support networks in the classroom. We assigned each student to a mentor with whom they could work through theoretically problematic issues in a one-on-one setting. Second, we created collaborative learning groups as a setting in which students could share the workload, communicate their accomplishments and frustrations, and critique each other's work. We also ensured that each student had access to the support of the entire class by giving them a list of phone numbers and e-mail addresses of all students, mentors, and the instructor.

Students had the opportunity, via e-mail with their mentor, to reflect on the week's events, both inside and outside the classroom. Together they worked at understanding and applying theory, writing skills, and progress in the class in general.

Most students developed a supportive relationship with their mentor.

One student wrote, "I appreciate your comments to me and do so appreciate all that I have learned from you and the other members of our class. It has been a treat to work with you and I have gained more from you than you know." Similarly, another student wrote, "I feel that with the [mentors] that we have, it makes a big difference. The support and advice that we are gaining will be a big asset to all of us."

In collaborative groups, classrooms are less individualistic and competitive, and students feel less intimidated and alienated (Parry 46). We organized collaborative learning groups of two or three students facilitated by mentors. A significant portion of class time was spent in these groups, discussing their assigned portion of the larger project. Students learned with and from each other at the same time. One student said of her group, "I really want to learn from this project. Working with others on a combined effort is making it much easier."

Each group was given responsibility for a portion of the project. It was up to them to define their piece of work and determine how they would address it. In this way, students were able to "gain power and control over knowledge and, as a consequence, to have authority in the classroom" (Parry 46; also see Brown 54). The mentors facilitated status meetings with the groups and each group presented regular updates to the rest of the class, stimulating discussions about their progress, any roadblocks they came across, and their solutions. Sometimes students were put at ease by these discussions through mere commiserating: "I was really glad to hear that I wasn't the only one that was frustrated with this project."

The group meetings were also a place for mentors to offer constructive criticism of students' project work. Most students found this input invaluable. Any criticism of their work was seen as a benefit to the entire group:

> I will make up samples for your critique, and please know that it does not offend me, or bother me, to make changes. We are a team, and the input to this project is a reflection of all of us. I only want to do the best I can to help support the group.

Another student said, "Being part of a team, I want to be able to support the other members and do my part."

A sense of mutual support within the collaborative groups was shared by most students, who came to depend upon each other a great deal. As in traditional classrooms, students also gravitated toward others outside their groups who were similar in age and interests. Several nontraditional, returning women students started sitting together; a couple of students who shared political interests began gathering in the hall before and after class.

The students' journals revealed that many did indeed come to feel a great sense of community at various points in the course. This came sooner and more easily for some students than for others. Very early in the term one student wrote in her journal, "We are all women, except for one, and that alone brings us together." After participating in a focus-group evaluation of the capstone courses, another student commented, "I like these people and it was good to hear their thoughts. One of the thoughts was that we had 'bonded' really well as a group." The sense of community gained by the students "makes the experience of college a far more positive, less isolating one" (Parry 46).

In their final journal entries, students wrote about their sense of loss at seeing the community they had built and come to depend upon disbanding. One student said simply, "I will miss everyone, I think that we have a great team." Other students reflected on the course in relation to others they had taken. They knew that, somehow, this had been a new experience for them:

> There haven't been many classes I've been in that, when they're over, I feel a sense of loss at having to have it end. I think after the presentation I will be happy but also a bit wistful. I will miss the class and the people because I think as a group, we have worked out very well.

MOVING BEYOND THE COMFORT ZONE: OPENING DOORS TO THE COMMUNITY

> One thing I like about this research project is it is making me think about my own perspective on things and what I know about my own community. I realize I don't really know anything outside my own comfort zone and look forward to finding out more about my community and the families in it. I have also realized that it is a very complex issue—making policies for a community—and that some people are served more than others.

Our students were already living in neighborhoods, many were negotiating family, work, and academics, and some were rolling up their sleeves for important political causes in their communities. Yet for the most part, they described the political work in this capstone as something new and groundbreaking, a form of "hands-on knowledge" that would take them beyond the comfort of their own experiences and into a community that they described as more "real" than what they had come to know as college,

"I am looking forward to working in a real life atmosphere. [. . .] This is not, after all, a little rinky-dink group presentation to my classmates, this is a real document that an agency will use, and a real presentation to a real agency."

The pedagogy of making feminist activism real for our students took many forms during the course of the quarter. From the onset, we were trying to teach toward a personal and political connection to the community for each student. Opening the doors to the "real" life community started by bringing community people into the classroom. We tried to provide students with personal connections to nonprofit activists and policy makers who could serve as their alliances to the surrounding city. Through these newly forged relationships students made unexpected kinds of connections that helped them to move between their roles in our classroom work and the ones they were playing in their own community. By the end of the term, our students were questioning the new roles they had taken on as activists and were thinking about a future where they might work for change in their own communities.

HELPING OUR COMMUNITY PARTNER

One of the most important connections that was formed early on in the class was the link to our community partner and, more importantly, to the individual woman who ran the program. We began by inviting the director of the family-based service agency to our regular class setting, introducing her to the students, brainstorming with her about the direction of the project, and then working closely with her in developing questions for community policy makers. Her visit during the second week of the course created a bridge to a community outside the four walls of our classroom—a community made up of children growing up in families where poverty, child abuse, and lack of access to medical care were putting them at risk. She represented to our students not only the problems facing the children and the women raising them but also the difficulties of doing her job and doing it well within a political and social climate that did not prioritize the needs of women and children. Our students' relationship with her became their first step out of the university and into a "real" community of people working for social change.

After her visit, many of our students started to recognize how the societal boundaries we had been reading about at the theoretical level might affect our partner: "Thinking about how all of this would impact an organization like [the agency] is frightening. Society does not seem to have much tolerance for people who need some type of assistance unless they fall into what they have considered worthy, and as we are seeing that is a very narrow window." Other students felt more connected to the project and excited about the potential impact of our work: "I feel so much better about our project since class this morning [. . .] after hearing [the director] speak about her organization, I think we will be doing some interesting work in terms of our class experience and also very beneficial work for the program."

Many students felt a new sense of the responsibility attached to their upcoming role in the project and started to take more seriously their community work. They became more concerned about "doing a good job" during their interviews, "asking the right questions," and not "spoiling the report" by making mistakes in their interpretations.

The most overwhelming response to the director's visit, however, was a strong connection to the individual woman whom they came to respect and, to a somewhat lesser extent, to the agency and community problems she represented. The students wanted to help *her* in any way that they could and in many cases put themselves on the line, going beyond what was expected of them during their interviews, to do so. Some students asked additional questions during the interview to gather more information for the director, or they used the interview setting to pave a way for her to speak at council meetings or meet with city mayors.

> She [a city mayor] was also very willing to learn more about [the agency] and I feel [the director] would find an open minded reception with at least two members of the city council if she presented [agency materials] to them. I tried to open the door for her after both of the interviews.

Another student wrote:

> After the interview was over he [a council member] asked me to tell him about [the agency]. I explained a little about it and told him about [the director]. [. . .] He was very receptive to hearing from her and I think it could be a positive experience. I hope I wasn't out of line to explain to him about [the agency]. But I felt that if she went soon to one of the meetings, it would be fresh on this council member's mind and she may make a stronger impression.
>
> I asked as many questions as were pertinent from our interview guide, but [. . .] I also asked questions hoping to find infor-

mation for [the agency director] that might help her in marketing her program.

When students returned to the classroom with interview transcripts in hand they brought with them new concerns about the best way to help the director. While they wanted to "get the stories straight" and provide "useful information," they also wanted be sure that they were meeting the director's needs:

> When I suggested that we be totally honest in our final report I did not mean that we should be argumentative or try and suggest that some cities or councilpeople are on the wrong track—not at all [. . .] my point was that if accurate information is something that [the director] is interested in receiving that we need to be totally honest for her, because that is who this project is really designed for.

As we reached the point where we were about to present the information to the director, it was clear that the relationship our students had to her was a primary connection for them to the community. She was our students' first contact with the community and by working with her, our students felt that they were working with the community she served. They hoped that their work would help her to create new relationships that in turn would benefit the women and children in the community: "I hope that the information will be helpful for [the director] and that she can use her creative skills to form some alliances with other organizations or churches that serve the population that they are trying to target."

> I know that each community could benefit from [the agency] and I would love to see us come up with recommendations that help [the agency] have more visibility and impact on the communities. [. . .] Something is missing in the connection between [the director] and the policy makers. Hopefully, our report will be able to address some of this.

PEOPLE WHO HAVE PERSONAL FACES TO ME: THIS IS MY NEIGHBORHOOD

All of the other research I have had the opportunity to do in my academic career has been around subjects that are of interest to me, but also so very disconnected from my immediate life. This [project] is especially interesting because it is my neighborhood and people who have personal faces to me (both the subjects of the research and the people being interviewed).

Midway through the quarter our students conducted interviews with the mayors and city council members of the cities that our community partner serves. Many of our students connected on a very personal level to the individuals that they interviewed, describing them not as interview subjects but as neighbors and kin. Students did not always agree with what the policy makers said and many times found their perspectives on the family to be outdated and filled with stereotypes. However, these policy makers became another important way of connecting to the community. Some of our students were searching for answers and others were looking for a kind of personal connection:

> I'm looking forward to hearing what these officials think about the very questions that we're wondering about: what is family, mom, community, child. I hope that they can give us some coherent answers, however, I'm afraid that these are things that the officials may have never really thought about.

> I conducted my first interview with the Mayor of [the city]. It was an interesting experience for me. He is effectively my neighbor— we only live a block apart. [. . .] One thing that struck me was how much I wanted to like him. Since I live in his district, I wanted to feel some sort of understanding.

It was not unusual for a student to be excited about the new connections they had made. For some students it was the first time they realized they had something in common with an authority in their community. Others had unexpectedly found a like-thinker in a city hall office. They came back to class ready to share their transcripts and to encourage other students to "get to know" the policy maker. When classmates began to criticize the comments of the policy makers or question their perspectives, some of the students became "protective" of their new community liaison:

> I noticed something funny today. Actually, I detected it in myself a while ago and then felt vindicated when I saw it in [another student] today. You see, I really liked the two people I interviewed. I thought they were very friendly and very nice and they were both Political Science majors (which I am) so they were obviously great!

And even though they said some things that made my eyebrows raise, I still like them. And so, I was feeling a little possessive, or maybe protective is a better word, when people criticized or commented in a not totally positive way to the things they said. I thought I was just overly possessive/protective, until I noticed [another student] doing the same thing today when we were looking over her transcript. She tried to explain why he might have said certain things, almost making excuses, and so I felt better. I'm not the only one who wants to defend "their" interviewees.

Our students described their desire to defend the policy makers' words as trying to ensure that the appropriate meaning of the comments would be represented in the report. However, it was clear in the classroom that our students were not only protecting the voices of their interviewees but also they were protecting the relationship they had formed. They were looking out for their neighbor and being protective of a bond that felt, for some, like kin: "It's kinda like me and my little brother. I can be mean to him all I want, but if someone else tries to pick on him, they had best look out for big sister because I will GET them."

This feeling of possessiveness went beyond the policy makers themselves. Several of the students described the cities that the policy makers served not as subjects of their project but as their own neighborhood—"the place where I live." While some students did live down the street from the people they interviewed, others broadened their sense of their neighborhood beyond city and county boundaries. Students were concerned about their community if the policy makers' remarks were prejudiced or showed a lack of responsibility for the problems facing women and children:

I was surprised at his description of families. He didn't really have one. I realized that [the city] does a lot for seniors, but for families, in general, not much is done. I was disappointed because I am a resident of [this city] and was hoping we did more for needy families.

Some students looked back to the director of the project and the agency to provide help for a community that now felt like "their own": "I really think if [the director] returned once again, soon, she may have a good chance of influencing my community. I would like to see [the agency] be a part of [the city]."

For some students the conversations with policy makers helped them to realize that they might be able to play some part in changing the community themselves:

I hope that when this class is over my perspective will have broadened enough so as to be able to help my community encircle all the different types of families that exist there. I now know, after talking to the mayor and city council member, that there is still a lot of work to be done, but that it can be done. That is refreshing!

CONCLUSION: ON MY OWN—BECOMING AN ACTIVIST

I know that I have a long way to go. But each day as I learn more, through my education, I find such a need to help fight against some of the inadequacies that face women in general.

Our community project helped to move our students' knowledge of the inequities of society from inside the boundaries of our feminist classroom outside to a community where they lived, worked, and went to school. As teachers and mentors, we asked them to question their personal location within the scholarship they were reading. We encouraged them to work through tough issues about diversity and injustice within our microcosm of a community in the classroom. And we introduced them to community people who could help them to uncover different paths to and perspectives on community work. By the end of the term, some students were going back to questioning their own perspectives: "In light of the questions that we formulated on the policy makers' definition of a family, I started to wonder what my definition is." Many of our students were trying to find ways to move beyond the comfort of their own experience, and out of the classroom limitations, to make a difference of their own.

In order to find their own activist voice they grappled with their role in the community project. When they first became involved in the capstone they questioned their new role in relationship to the agency and the policy makers. They wanted to be taken "seriously" and hoped that they would be more than "some kids doing a school project." They questioned how they really could do anything "new" or "important" for the agency given what others with years of experience had already done. But some of them worked out roles that felt comfortable, for example, as an outsider looking in: "I do know that when you are standing in the middle of something you really do not have a clear picture, maybe that is our role."

As the project continued some of the students felt a need to disassociate themselves with the classroom project and the agency in order to find their own voice. One student explained that when the interview questions made her policy maker "twitch," she felt "it was as if I needed to separate myself from the formation of the questions so she would not think I was an utter moron while I was trapped in her home." Other students wanted to go beyond the interview setting and continue to talk with the policy makers on their own time:

> I was speaking with a classmate the other day about how we wished we could go back and just talk with our interviewees. Ask them whatever we wanted, what interested us in what they said before, and see if they really were as narrow in their thoughts as they might appear. As [my policy maker] said, he's glad I brought this up, cuz [sic] it's something they'll need to think about.

This student recognized after the interview that she had made a difference by asking a question that raised the policy maker's awareness of an issue in the community, and she decided that she could further educate others by asking more questions and having similar conversations with others. Another student decided that her next step was taking her new knowledge about a particular policy maker in her community to the polls, "When I drive home sometimes I see him in his garage. Not too exciting for me— I don't think I like him. Next local election I am going to check out his opposition."

Our students worked through many ways in which they could incorporate this new hands-on knowledge into their lives. Whether it was through traditional political means like voting, or by volunteering at social agencies, or doing grassroots activist work, they proposed numerous ways to bring their feminism out into their community. At the same time, they still felt that they needed more help and were not unrealistic about the challenges to social change: "There needs to be a social revolution but again I don't know how it would start. I think the frustrating part is knowing that the contempt exists but not having any answers on how to change things."

Despite their realizations of the difficulties they would face, students continued to push for change and came to see their role as more of an activist. One of our students had clearly come full circle:

> It's important to look at mothering for many reasons. Personally, it is something that I think about a lot because I plan to be doing it eventually, within five years maybe. But it is always a struggle because as I sit in my classes, trying to develop my mind to go out and change the world, I also am considered taking years out of my life, to spend at home and be with and raise my children. So, which is more important? Can I even make that call? It's tough. And, being who I am, I think that we need to make decisions less

difficult. Try to change society's opinions about how we work this parent thing. And of course in this culture we have set up the personal is political. And as much as I don't like that, I need to understand it so that maybe I can fight it. Or use it to my advantage.

*   *   *

NOTES

1. Throughout this essay we incorporate the voices of students taken from 126 e-mailed journal entries written during our 1996 capstone course. We have made minor grammatical and spelling corrections to students' contributions, but have otherwise retained their original language.

2. We would like to take this opportunity to thank the other two graduate mentors for this course, Debra Bufton and Cheryl Creel, for their insight and expertise.

3. Although Goodman's focus is on K–12, it has application in the university setting.

4. Information regarding self-assessment and portfolio assignments comes from assignment handouts developed by the course instructor Melissa Kesler Gilbert.

WORKS CITED

Brown, Julie. "Theory or Practice—What Exactly Is Feminist Pedagogy?" *Journal of General Education* 41 (1992): 51–63.

Fineman, Martha Albertson, and Isabel Karpin, eds. *Mothers in Law: Feminist Theory and the Legal Regulation of Motherhood*. New York: Columbia University Press, 1995.

Gilbert, Melissa Kesler. "Transforming the Classroom: Teaching Subtle Sexism Through Experiential Role-Playing." *Subtle Sexism: Current Practice and Prospects for Change*. Ed. Nijole Benokraitis. Thousand Oaks, CA: Sage, 1997. 245–63.

Glenn, Evelyn Nakano, Grace Chang, and Linda Rennie Forcey, eds. *Mothering: Ideology, Experience, and Agency*. New York: Routledge, 1994.

Henkin, Roxanne. "Emerging Feminist Themes Found in Graduate Students' Portfolios Written by Women Elementary School Teachers." *Action in Teacher Education* 15.4 (1993–94): 20–28.

Lee, Janet. "Teaching Feminism: Anger, Despair, and Self Growth." *Feminist Teacher* 7.2 (1993): 15–19.

Maher, Frances, and Mary Kay Thompson Tetreault. *The Feminist Classroom: An Inside Look at How Professors and Students Are Transforming Higher Educa-*

tion for a Diverse Society. New York: Basic Books, 1994.

Parry, Shirley C. "Feminist Pedagogy and Techniques for the Changing Classroom." *Women's Studies Quarterly* 24.3/4 (1996): 45–54.

Ramaley, Judith A. "From the Past President of Portland State University." *Community-University Partnerships at Portland State University: 1995–1997*. Portland State University, 1997.

Scering, Grace E. "Themes of a Critical/Feminist Pedagogy: Teacher Education for Democracy." *Journal of Teacher Education* 48.1 (1997): 62–68.

CONTRIBUTORS

Jonathan Alexander is Director of the University Honors Program at the University of Southern Colorado. His primary scholarly interests are in queer theory, and he has lectured and published widely in les-bi-gay studies, media studies, and literary theory and criticism.

Wendy Ball is a Senior Lecturer at the University of Waikato Law School in New Zealand. Her research interests include child abuse and neglect issues in the law; legal recognition of children's rights; and domestic violence and battered women who kill. She has been responsible for the implementation of a staff development process within the School of Law and has a general interest in good teaching practice and a particular interest in the teaching of sensitive issues.

Margaret M. Barber is an Assistant Professor of English at the University of Southern Colorado, where she has coordinated the Women's Studies Program and taught courses on early women writers, Shakespeare, and composition. Her recent work has focused on the use of networked computers in the teaching of composition and development of technological resources for students of literature.

Sandra Bell is an Associate Professor in the Department of Sociology/Criminology at Saint Mary's University in Halifax, Nova Scotia, Canada. She is the author of *Young Offenders and Juvenile Justice: A Century after the Fact* (Nelson Canada, 1998) and numerous articles on Family Court and youth justice issues. Her current research involves an examination of the impact of social/correctional programs on women and girls in conflict with the law and how these programs contribute to the cycle of dependency and violence against women. She is a member of the Department of Justice Working Group on Restorative Justice mandated to implement a restorative justice model in the Province of Nova Scotia.

Kathleen A. Boardman is an Associate Professor of English and Director of the Core Writing Program at the University of Nevada, Reno. She teaches courses in writing, composition pedagogy, autobiography, and Native American literature. Recently she has written on western American memoir and on the history of feminism in composition theory and practice.

Cheyenne Marilyn Bonnell is a visiting Assistant Professor of English at Northwest College in Powell, Wyoming. Her research interests are in women's studies, American Indian literature, and distance learning.

Kristin Christophersen is a doctoral candidate in the School of Urban Studies at Portland State University. She is currently teaching a course on the sociology of gender. Her teaching and research interests include social problems and community activism.

Maryanne Dever coordinates the Undergraduate Teaching Program in the Centre for Women's Studies and Gender Research at Monash University in Melbourne, Australia. Her research interests include feminist pedagogy, cross-cultural feminism, postcolonialism, and women's writing. She has published in the *Asian Journal of Women's Studies*, *Feminist Teacher*, and *Tulsa Studies in Women's Literature*. Together with colleagues at Monash University she is currently researching women's studies' vocational outcomes.

Melissa Kesler Gilbert is currently on the faculty in the Women's Studies Program at Portland State University. She has published articles and book chapters on such topics as feminist pedagogy and computer-assisted learning, women and retirement, experiential role-playing in the feminist classroom, discrimination against women in federal employment, and family-leave policies. Her oral history project on the women who founded the Boston Women's Health Book Collective was the basis for her video documentary, *"Something From Inside Me: Esther Rome."* She has received numerous grants for her community-based learning projects, which have promoted the use of feminist oral narratives in service to Portland's women's health clinics, teen-advocacy programs, feminist bookstores, YWCA, and family-based social-service agencies.

Diana L. Gustafson is a doctoral candidate in the Faculty of Sociology and Equity Studies in Education and in the Collaborative Program for Women's Studies at the University of Toronto. Her current research involves advancing the agenda of inclusive education in nursing. Employed in the health-care sector for twenty-five years, she is a longtime member of the continuing education faculty in health sciences at Mohawk College of

Applied Arts and Technology, Hamilton, Canada. She is currently working on a book on health-care reform and its impact on Canadian women and families.

Carol Holdt is an M.S. candidate and a graduate teaching assistant at Portland State University, where she teaches introductory sociology courses. Her thesis focuses on the ongoing nature of women's childbearing decisions, in particular repeated decisions to remain voluntarily childless. Her teaching and research interests include gender and family issues and the intersection of race, class, and gender.

Annis H. Hopkins is the Women's Studies Program Instructional Specialist at Arizona State University where she teaches a women's studies survey course on live cable television—the first ongoing class of its kind in the United States. She is responsible for academic advisement and integration of technology into the women's studies curriculum; she created and maintains the program's Website and assists faculty and students in developing skills with technology. Her research and teaching interests also include lesbian culture, lesbian literature, and basic writing.

Carey Kaplan is a Professor of English and founder and Director of Gender Studies at Saint Michael's College. With Ellen Cronan Rose she wrote a feminist consideration of the canon, *The Canon and the Common Reader*, and has published work on Doris Lessing and Margaret Drabble. Saint Michael's faculty and students have recognized her pedagogy with four awards for excellence in teaching. She has also received a college award for outstanding scholarly work, and this year was given the Jackie M. Gribbons Award for Leadership by the Vermont Council of Women in Higher Education.

Susan Kuntz is currently Dean of the Prevel School at St. Michael's College and Professor in the Department of Psychology. Her writing research interests are in the areas of cognitive development, assessment, and critical pedagogy. She has chaired the statewide Standards Board for Professional Educators and has served on numerous regional and national boards for teaching and curriculum.

Maralee Mayberry is an Associate Professor of Sociology and Women's Studies at the University of Nevada, Las Vegas. Her most recent work focuses on feminist science studies and feminist pedagogy, although she has written about unique educational environments during the last decade. She is a cofounder of PROMISE (Projects for Multicultural and Interdisciplinary Studies in Education) a nationally recognized feminist knowledge project housed on the UNLV campus. Based on the contention that feminist theory and pedagogy have been marginalized in science and science education and that science has been marginalized in feminist education, PROMISE designs and implements transdisciplinary curricular materials and courses. She has authored and coauthored a series of papers on the applications of feminist science studies to science curriculum.

Marina Morrow currently teaches in the Women's Studies Programme at the University of British Columbia in Vancouver, Canada. During the past ten years, Marina has worked as a teacher, social policy analyst, and feminist activist in both the community and the university. Her research and writing interests include violence against women, critical feminist and anti-racist pedagogy, the women's movement, social policy analysis, and social change.

Prudence Ann Moylan is a Professor in the Department of History at Loyola University of Chicago. Her research and writing interests include gender and peace, feminist pedagogy, and the history of women's education. She is currently coediting a collection of essays on Mundelein College Chicago 1930–1991, the last women's college in Illinois.

Peter Pinney is Associate Professor of English in the College of Rural Alaska at the University of Alaska, Fairbanks. His teaching and service interests are in composition and grant writing. He is actively working to stop political religious extremists in their attempt to deny basic civil rights for several groups of Alaskan citizens. He is also addicted to e-mail.

Margaret (Peg) N. Rees is a Professor of Geology at the University of Nevada, Las Vegas. Her geological research interests are in sedimentology and stratigraphy, and she specializes in Cambrian age rocks (545–490 million years ago). Peg is recognized internationally for her research on rocks of this age in Antarctica. During the past several years she has become interested in feminist science studies and feminist pedagogy, particularly as it applies to the teaching of geoscience. As a result, she is cofounder, with Maralee Mayberry, of PROMISE (Projects for Multicultural and Interdisciplinary Study and Education) at UNLV and has coauthored and copresented papers on feminist science teaching experiences and curriculum developed by PROMISE members.

Jane A. Rinehart helped to found and direct the Women's Studies Program at Gonzaga University where she is an Associate Professor of Sociology and

Women's Studies. She teaches introductory courses in women's studies and a course on feminist theory. Jane coedited an anthology on leadership and contributed a feminist critique to a collection of essays exploring the "McDonaldization" thesis. She has also published articles on a positive characterization of marginality, feminist pedagogy, and the creation of a mentoring community, the usefulness of collaborative learning strategies in computer science courses, and teaching feminist theory as a form of political action.

Ellen Cronan Rose is Director of Women's Studies at the University of Nevada, Las Vegas. Her most recent book, written with Carey Kaplan, is *The Canon and the Common Reader*, and she has also published articles on feminist collaboration (with Kaplan) and feminist pedagogy. In a former incarnation, she published books and articles on contemporary women writers—principally Doris Lessing and Margaret Drabble. Now she practices feminist pedagogy in subject areas ranging from introduction to women's studies course work to gay and lesbian history and knows more about academic administration than she did in her former professorial years that she had ever hoped to know.

Evangelia Tastsoglou is Associate Professor in the Department of Sociology at Saint Mary's University, Halifax, Nova Scotia, Canada. She also teaches in the International Development Studies and Women's Studies Programs. Her research and writing interests include gender and migration, ethnicity and race, cultural studies, and feminist and antiracist pedagogies.

Jodi Wetzel holds a Ph.D. in American Studies from the University of Minnesota and began her career in campus-based women's programs in 1973. She has worked in women's centers, women's studies, and inclusive curriculum projects in New England, the Midwest, and the Rocky Mountains. Currently, she is a Professor of History and Director of the Institute for Women's Studies and Services at Metropolitan State College of Denver. She is coauthor/editor of an introductory women's studies text, and her research interests include the backlash against feminism and the culture wars. She has received several awards for educational leadership.

INDEX